THE GROWTH OF VICTORIAN LONDON

Frontispiece. Camberwell Grove in the 1870s.
Edward Walford, *Old and New London*, VI, 283.

The Growth of Victorian London

DONALD J. OLSEN

HOLMES & MEIER PUBLISHERS
NEW YORK

[c1976]

307.76

to Mildred Campbell

First published in the United States of America 1976 by
    Holmes & Meier Publishers, Inc.
    101 Fifth Avenue
    New York, New York 10003

Library of Congress Cataloging in Publication Data
    Olsen, Donald J.
        The growth of Victorian London.

        Bibliography: p.
        Includes index.
    1. Cities and towns – Planning – London – History.
    2. Architecture – London – History. 3. London – History –
        1800–1950. I. Title.
    HT169.G72L6474   301.36'3'09421   76-25164
        ISBN 0-8419-0284-4

    PRINTED IN GREAT BRITAIN

Contents

List of Illustrations

List of Maps

Acknowledgments

I wish to thank the John Simon Guggenheim Memorial Foundation for the grant which, in 1967–8, enabled me to do the research on the Chalcots estate in the Eton College Records; and P.L. Strong, Keeper of the College Library and Collections, for his help in enabling me to make use of those archives. My work in printed sources was much facilitated by the assistance of the staffs of the Engineering Societies Library in New York, the Boston Public Library, the Seattle Public Library, the London Library, the British Library, the RIBA Library, the New York Public Library, and the Vassar College Library. My student assistant Robert Edwin Renaud has done a great deal to speed the process of preparing the manuscript for press and, along with Anna Rubino and Mary Knox – also Vassar students – and my friends John A. Dierdorff and Alonzo H. Smith, Jr., has helped in reading the proofs. Valerie Jobling has been of enormous help with checking footnotes, quotations, and proof. My colleague Hsi-Huey Liang was good enough to read and criticize the manuscript and my friend Martin Stanford has been of great assistance in matters of style. My mother, Mrs. Anna M. Olsen, did much of the work involved in preparing the index. Finally, I should like to thank Michael Stephenson, Alan Hamp, Douglas Sellick, and Peter Kemmis Betty at Batsford's for their advice, encouragement, and patience, and Annette Brown for valuable help with picture research.

For permission to use illustrations from their collections I would like to thank the following: London Museum map I, figs. 47, 96; Bromley Public Library 78; Greater London Council 1, 8, 84; Hammersmith Public Libraries 58; Hendon Public Library 72; B.T. Batsford Frontispiece, 2, 3, 4, 9, 11, 15, 17, 21, 22, 25, 27, 30, 32, 33, 34, 39, 51, 53, 57, 63, 64, 65, 69, 70, 71, 73, 74, 80, 81, 82, 86, 87, 89, 90, 93, 94, 95, 98; City of Westminster Public Library 5; Kensington & Chelsea Public Library 49, 52, 54, 56, map III; Guildhall Library maps II, IV; Stanford's Library map of London, figs. 6 and 92; The Mansell Collection 48, 75; Brent Public Libraries 60; London Transport Board 7, 97; A.F. Kersting 45, 50; Routledge and Kegan Paul, map V (from Dyos and Wolff, *The Victorian City*, I, 336); National Buildings Record 10, 12, 59, 62; Victoria & Albert Museum 13, 16, 46, 55, 76; Peabody Trust 44, 85; Richmond Public Library 77; National Monuments Record 14, 22, 26, 38; Peter Jackson Collection 18, 31, 41, 42; RIBA 19; British Railways Board 23, 24; Radio Times Hulton Picture Library 28, 29, 61, 66, 67, 68, 83, 88, 91; Trustees of the Bedford Estate 35, 36, 37, 40; Grosvenor Estate Office 43.

Preface

Practically no one has anything good to say about what the Victorians did to London, and no one at all about the impact of the twentieth century on the metropolis; yet practically everybody agrees that London today is the most civilized and agreeable of the world's great cities. To have brought into existence the London we know today someone, sometime, must have done something right. This book will try to discover what the Victorians did to London and what, in so doing, they revealed about themselves.

The first chapter sets out some of the aesthetic, social, and moral ends that Victorian London was designed to embody and promote. The chapters that follow examine in detail the ambivalent love-hate relationship the Victorians sustained with the London their Georgian parents had bequeathed them. They will show how they transformed the inner structure and outward appearance of central London, while on the outskirts they developed, in villa suburbia, their most extreme repudiation of earlier patterns of urbanity. Subsequent chapters deal with attempts to create a better environment for the working classes, and to improve communications throughout the expanding metropolis, in the context of Victorian social values.

For the past quarter-century I have been trying to find out what makes London unmistakably itself, what has given it that special mixture of qualities so much easier to enjoy than to define. At first I sought the answer in the policies of its great landed proprietors, exercising a wise and personal guidance over the operations of their leasehold estates. Being fortunate enough to gain access to the archives of two of the best-managed estates – those of the Duke of Bedford and the Foundling Hospital – I did indeed find proof of intelligent and enlightened planning, although more from the initiative and perseverance of the agents of the respective landlords than from the landlords themselves.[1]

By 1964, after further research and reflection, the significance of my earlier findings seemed to point towards a more discouraging interpretation. 'For all its minor triumphs,' I then concluded, 'the history of the great London estates remains one of partial victories and strategic retreats.' The ground landlord, I found, was only one element in a complex pattern of varied and conflicting actions that made the metropolis what it is.[2] If the great aristocratic landlords, with their unmatched legal and economic powers, and their determination to exercise them, were unable to achieve more than very moderate success in their attempts to impose considered town plans on their portions of London; why, I argued, was there any ground to hope realistically that the far weaker political agencies of modern town planning might succeed? To the rhetorical question – 'Are the goals of town planners attainable in a more than temporary or superficial sense in our society?' – I strongly suggested a negative answer.[3]

My chapter in *The Victorian City* (1973) was based on a study of two far less well-managed leasehold estates, those of Eton College in South Hampstead and the Duke of Norfolk in Sheffield. There I found not so much planning that had failed to achieve its object, as situations in which planning would have been either irrelevant or harmful. In Sheffield, the Duke of Norfolk's office 'did nothing', I concluded, 'because there was nothing to be done'.[4] Both it and Eton College co-operated with 'social and economic realities . . .'.[5] I have since been trying to determine just what those 'realities' were that seemed so much more powerful than either private or public planning agencies.

The present volume is the result. It is essentially an extended interpretative essay, based almost entirely on qualitative evidence, which I hope will stimulate debate. Apart from the latter part of chapter five, which is based on archival research in the Eton College Records, my evidence is drawn mostly from Victorian printed sources, in particular the three major professional architectural journals: the *Builder*, the *Building News*, and the *Architect*. Together they form the most extensive body of information as to how London looked to the Victorians, and how they were trying to change it.

The infrequency of footnote references to secondary works may give a misleading impression as to my degree of indebtedness to the current generation of nineteenth-century London historians. Not only their publications, which have in the last few years vastly extended and deepened our knowledge of the Victorian metropolis, but their conversation and their friendship have given me immeasurable instruction and delight. It is impossible not to begin with Sir John Summerson who, with Steen Eiler Rasmussen, first asked all the right questions and gave most of the right answers. Beyond, in alphabetical order: William Ashworth, C.W. Chalklin, H.J. Dyos, Hermione Hobhouse, Priscilla Metcalf, M.H. Port, Francis Sheppard, F.M.L. Thompson, Gordon Toplis, Anthony S. Wohl.

Donald J. Olsen
London
August 1975

CHAPTER ONE

A Topography of Values

... Architecture has a noble and lofty office to perform ... Besides minister-
ing to our comforts and satisfying our material wants – besides pleasing the eye
and embellishing our cities – architecture has to raise up monuments which
may tell to future ages of our habits of thought, of our governing or prompting
ideas, and of our state of civilisation. ... It is the duty of our architecture to
translate our character into stone.

Building News, IV (1858), 617

SPECIALIZATION, SEGREGATION AND PRIVACY[1]

The key to an understanding of London's virtues lies in the nineteenth century. We can
dismiss the hypothesis that the twentieth century found a Great Wen and transformed it into
everybody's favourite city. The vandals of postwar London have only pursued with greater
ruthlessness the destruction that preceded 1939, when real estate developers worked with
equal zeal and architects and planners with equal incompetence. Only the toughness of an
earlier London has enabled it to remain even today a bower of delight despite the ravages of
public and private redevelopers.

A more attractive hypothesis would be that it is to the eighteenth century that we owe
most of what is admirable in London. Too little remains of Georgian London to make such
a theory plausible, as it might be for, say, Dublin. Most of the London we enjoy is Victorian
either in its fabric or its layout, or at least its inspiration. Whatever its shortcomings Victorian
London ought to be approached not as a sin to be expiated, nor even as a blunder to be
explained, but as an achievement to be celebrated.

It has been customary to stress the unregulated growth and the squalid environment of
Victorian London, at least until the enlightened controls and beneficial services of the
London County Council at the end of the century entered to restrain the operations of
unrestricted laissez-faire. Jephson's description of the state of London before 1855 confirms
the impression given by Dickens or Mayhew or the minutes of evidence of the Health of
Towns Commission:

> Of that period it is to be said that there is none in the history of London in which less
> regard was shown for the condition of the great mass of the inhabitants of the metropolis;
> no period when the spirit of commercialism recked so little of the physical condition and
> circumstances of those upon whom ... it depended; no period when the rights of

property were so untrammelled by any consideration for the welfare of human flesh and blood. . . . Never a time in which land-owners, house-owners, and builders did as freely as they liked with their own, regardless of the injury or damage inflicted upon others . . .[2]

To Sir John Summerson the London that developed after 1830 was an anti-climax, a running-down of themes established in a more vigorous century. Street improvements such as New Oxford Street, 'unworthily executed under third-rate architects, show how utterly the sense of urban responsibility, so strong under George IV . . . had broken down'. The handling of later projects by the Metropolitan Board of Works was 'beneath contempt – a morass of irresponsibility, ignorance and peculation'. Private building developments show a 'decline of taste and competence . . . After 1850 it is rare to find an architect of any reputation meddling with estate development. Exceptions are curious rather than edifying . . .' The Victorians brought about a 'revolution against taste itself'.[3]

It could be argued that such criticisms, while true, do not go far enough. For beyond producing its own peculiarly Victorian products of ugliness, over-crowding, and disease, London in the nineteenth century foreshadowed and anticipated all that we find most deplorable in our cities today: the artificial separation of home and work, the proliferation of commercialized amusements, the destruction of an older sense of community as suburb-anization produced dull, anonymous, socially irresponsible single-class neighbourhoods. This last set of charges is the most serious for, after all, the Victorians did solve the problems of inadequate drainage and unsafe water supply, while the twentieth century can at least pride itself on doing away with the worst of Victorian over-crowding and poverty, and even the London fog. And if we insist, as we do, on putting up buildings and planning neighbourhoods that make even mediocre Victorian townscapes – such as Covent Garden and Piccadilly Circus – seem as worthy of preservation as Colonial Williamsburg, that is our fault, not theirs. But the underlying structure of Victorian London, physical and social, remains the structure of the London of the 1970's, and embodies all that we have been taught to deplore in the contemporary city. It is that structure that I hope to account for and, in some measure, justify.

The Victorians were, in part consciously, transforming the metropolis into an environment designed to reinforce certain specific values, notably privacy for the individual and his family; specialization and segregation were important means to that end. They gave London order and system, not – like the Paris of Baron Haussmann – essentially visual and spatial in nature; but rather functional, moral, and social.* The virtues of today's London exist not in spite of, but because of their approach.

The nineteenth century saw the systematic sorting-out of London into single-purpose, homogeneous, specialized neighbourhoods. The process dates from the seventeenth century, when Covent Garden, St James's, and Bloomsbury were first developed, and the distinction between the City and the West End began to be made. By later standards the

---

* The visual and spatial reshaping of Paris had functional, moral, and social ends of its own, markedly different from those pursued by Victorian London. See Anthony Sutcliffe, *The Autumn of Central Paris. The Defeat of Town Planning 1850–1970*, Edward Arnold, 1970.

degree of social and functional differentiation was at best moderate. Even the new districts of the eighteenth century had within them wide variations in population, with the wealthy occupying the squares and the principal streets, the middle classes the adjacent smaller streets, and the poor the back courts and mews: one could speak of fashionable or unfashionable streets, but not fashionable or unfashionable neighbourhoods. Pockets of extreme poverty in immediate juxtaposition to the residences of the very rich persisted well into the Victorian period. Similarly each new district had its market and its street of shops, and was to a certain extent a self-contained, balanced little town.

All this changed in the nineteenth century. The omnibus, genteel yet economical, enabled newer districts to be formed without stables or mews, and thus without the kind of back courts that in the older quarters often deteriorated into miniature slums. Strict social segregation became a prerequisite for success in any new development. The underground, the tramway, and the cheap workmen's train enabled more and more of the artisan classes to live in their own socially homogeneous neighbourhoods at some distance from their work. Older neighbourhoods that had been socially mixed became less so, as public and private improvement schemes swept away rookeries and rebuilt back streets for commercial or middle-class occupation.

The shift from multi-purpose to single-purpose neighbourhoods reflected the pervasive move towards professionalization and specialization in all aspects of nineteenth-century thought and activity. Mr Wingfield, prescribing embrocations for the putrid throats of Mrs John Knightley's children, was succeeded by the modern general practitioner; Mrs Gamp by nurses trained under Florence Nightingale; historians like Macaulay by historians like Maitland. Industry put into practice Adam Smith's teachings as to the advantages of the division of labour. Cities, too, and London most of all, transformed themselves in order to provide more and more specialized services. 'The city is the spectroscope of society,' wrote Adna F. Weber in 1899; 'it analyzes and sifts the population, separating and classifying the diverse elements. The entire progress of civilization is a process of differentiation, and the city is the greatest differentiator.'[4]

'. . . In a very short time it seems certain, that all England will be a London,' predicted the *Builder* in 1844, by which it meant that 'all the advantages possessed at one time exclusively by the latter will become universal . . .'[5] One might go further and argue that the railway and the telegraph made all England into one extended city, or at least one urbanized region. They permitted the kind of specialization of function that had not been possible for the ancient, mediaeval, or Renaissance town. What admirers of the kinds of satisfactions offered by the mediaeval city as opposed to those of the modern industrialized city sometimes neglect to consider is that the ordinary mediaeval burgher spent the whole of his life in his own city, whereas if anyone spends the whole of his life today in, say, Rotherham or Wolverhampton, it is his own fault. Culturally deprived towns need not have culturally deprived citizens so long as they have access to the extended city that is England (or today, Europe).

The Victorian era was not far advanced before the *Times* could be read the morning of publication throughout England. For the prosperous businessman Brighton became a functional suburb of London, just as Windermere was for Manchester and Scarborough for

Leeds. The residential train opened opportunities beyond one's city, narrowly defined, for the upper middle classes; the excursion train did the same for the working classes.

A capital city attracts to itself a disproportionate amount of the talent, wealth, taste, and power of the realm, achieving by such unnatural concentration disproportionately great results in the arts, politics, economics, and all those aspects of civilization whose ends are better achieved by concentration than dispersion, gregariousness than solitude. 'City life may not have produced genius,' admitted Weber, 'but it has brought thinkers into touch with one another, and has stimulated the divine impulse to originate by sympathy or antagonism.'[6] The justification for great cities is that they both encourage and embody excellence. It is their function to be better than other cities and to attract individuals and institutions that are similarly 'better'. This has not always made capital cities loved in the hinterlands. By 'creaming off' the talent of the country they are envied and hated, just as the direct-grant schools are by the comprehensives. Doubtless Shakespeare and Dr Johnson would have raised the cultural standards of Stratford and Litchfield had they not been tempted to the metropolis, whatever the cost to their own inner development.

Much, and not the least valuable sort of culture flourishes better in smaller communities. It would be perverse to argue that the genius of Emily Brontë would have been improved by prolonged residence in the capital. Much that is healthiest in popular culture succumbs to the competition of the meretricious glitter of metropolitan society. Yet for the individual working-class man or woman city life is more often a prerequisite for personal fulfillment or creative activity than for someone of the middle or upper classes. The library and society to be found in a country house or even a rural rectory might well be fully as stimulating as anything a town could offer; but a farm labourer's cottage could have no equivalent to the educational and cultural resources of a great city. '. . . The concentration of population is particularly favorable to the working-men,' Weber argued. 'It gives every man the chance to show "what is in him". Moreover . . . a dense population is the most favorable to strong organization. The trade union movement . . . [in England] would have been impossible without the association of large numbers in the cities.'[7] It was London that enabled Beatie Bryant in Arnold Wesker's *Roots* to break free from the comfortable, unquestioning acceptance of things as they were of her farm-labouring family.

It is of course an undue simplification to think of London as one crowded *salon*. The possibilities of solitude and dispersion exist there at least as much as in the provinces. 'Every man of the world,' as Weber was not the first to point out, 'knows that isolation and solitude are found in a much higher degree in the crowded city than in a country village, where one individual's concerns are the concern of all.'[8] The difference is that both solitude and gregariousness are in London more likely to be chosen by the individual than imposed on him by the nature of the community. The loneliness, the anonymous individualism of the city can be one of its advantages; particularly since it can be combined with its opposite with comparative ease. The daily alternation of the Stock Exchange with the secluded suburban villa, the British Museum with the bed-sitting-room in Earl's Court, permits the businessman and the scholar alike to combine the advantages of the two extremes. Toynbee's 'withdrawal and return' are provided by the rhythm of a single urban day.

This is not to say that most Londoners begin or ever began to take advantage of their city's life-enhancing possibilities, any more than Sheffield or Leicester people take advantage of the possibilities accessible by Inter-City express. But then one wonders how deeply involved the ordinary fifteenth-century Florentine artisan was in the High Renaissance. Let us not exaggerate the degree of participation of the average man in the higher aspects of the civilization of any period. What matters is that in a metropolis the possibility is there, and the nature and extent of the opportunities offered the individual in any environment will affect the kinds of responses he makes.

The city with its subordinate parts was only one of the areas in which the Victorians pursued differentiation as an end in itself. 'Subdivision, classification, and elaboration, are certainly distinguishing characteristics of the present aera of civilisation,' wrote George Augustus Sala in 1859.[9] The specialized neighbourhood and the specialized institution were paralleled by the specialized room, the specialized meal, the specialized fork. 'It is characteristic that for each of the many English sports there is a special costume which is the only thing possible,' Steen Eiler Rasmussen has remarked.[10] The ritualization of life reached a high degree of expression in Victorian times, and much of it survives to lend flavour and emphasis to our more homogeneous and egalitarian lives today. There is no inherent reason why cold toast and marmalade should appear *only* at breakfast, warm toast and jam *only* at tea, yet it would be a pity if either meal were to lose any of its distinctiveness. Foreigners are always being astonished to discover that tea itself can only be had at restricted hours of the day, as if it were subject to licensing laws; yet were it always and everywhere available, half the pleasure would be gone.

The Victorians acted on the principle that certain types of architecture, certain types of furniture were alone suitable for certain types of buildings or rooms with particular functions. Thus Sir Osbert Lancaster has pointed out the necessity of crimson wallpaper and paintings of storms at sea to the proper Victorian dining room. Not only the room and its furniture, but the china, silver, food, and the dress of the participants were designed to remind them that they were at lunch rather than at dinner, at elevenses rather than at afternoon tea. The novel practice of dining *à la russe* broke the meal itself into separate courses, each with its characteristic type of food, dish, implement, and drink. The principle underlying the Benedictine Rule – predictable order enlivened by festive variety – governed not merely eating but all aspects of the daily life of the well-conducted Victorian.

Much of the ritual can be accounted for as conspicuous consumption, a way of filling up the time of a bored leisure class, and of keeping an inordinate number of servants busy. 'In London there are thousands of heads of families who have no profession whatever,' Rasmussen wrote as recently as 1937. 'Idleness is so thoroughly systemetized, that in order to comply with all the rules of convention a man is kept busy from morning till night according to a fixed scheme.'[11] The proliferation of unnecessarily differentiated objects also has economic justification: the prosperity of Staffordshire and Sheffield would have been considerably less had middle-class families not been made to feel the necessity of separate sets of china and cutlery not only for each meal but for each course of each meal. Increasing the number of meals to the present seven – early-morning tea, breakfast, elevenses, lunch, afternoon tea, dinner, supper – did even more to fill time, make work, and maximize expenditure.

Yet Victorian over-consumption differs in kind from both eighteenth-century and twentieth-century conspicuous waste. To deal only with the latter: today the emphasis is not on the acquisition of a vast number of differentiated durable items at one time but on the successive acquisition of rapidly obsolescent items. One of the reasons for the late marriages of middle-class Victorians was the enormous capital investment necessary to set up a proper household: but once one had acquired the proper complement of china, utensils, sheets, blankets, furniture, carpets, draperies, and the like one could relax in the knowledge that they were there to stay. 'The house in Inverness Terrace, which provided so perfect a setting for the endlessly repeated cycle of Cousin Jenny's daily life,' Sir Osbert Lancaster recalls, 'had been presented to her completely furnished by her father as a present on her wedding in the late 'seventies or early 'eighties and not the smallest alteration nor addition had since been made.'[12] Today quite the opposite practice holds, suggesting that we derive the satisfaction from transience and novelty that the Victorians got from permanence and variety.

The nineteenth century excelled in the mass production of specialized pleasures. The department store, the luxury hotel, and the monster restaurant enabled the middle classes to participate, at low cost, in experiences hitherto reserved to the wealthy few. The gin palace, the music hall, and the excursion train enabled the working classes to do the same. Nowhere on earth was there a greater concentration of such pleasures and possibilities than in London.

Most of such pleasures and possibilities took place in buildings erected specifically for that purpose. Perhaps the most significant architectural development of the nineteenth century was the creation and proliferation of what might be called the professional as opposed to the amateur building – what is today called 'purpose-built'. Prior to that period most urban buildings were amateur, adaptable for a variety of purposes. Eighteenth-century London, apart from its churches and an occasional public building, consisted of a collection of one standard pattern of house, in one of four sizes determined by the Building Acts. It could be converted into a hotel or lodging house by putting a brass plate on the front door and letting the rooms separately. Different furniture and a different plate on the door turned it into an office building. A display window in the front, ground-floor parlour transformed it into a shop.

After Waterloo there appeared one after another new type of building designed from the outset for a specialized function. The office block in the modern sense did not become common until the 1840's, a decade that saw the first development of model dwellings designed consciously for working-class occupation.

Blocks of flats, at first for the artisan classes and only much later for middle-class occupancy, were greeted with hostility and suspicion as to their compatibility with English ideas of propriety and family life. The debate over the importation of French flats to London reveals a great deal about Victorian values and how architecture and the structure of the town were expected to support such values. It was the common staircase, used by tenants of varying social classes, depending on which floor they occupied, that disturbed the English most about the prospect of flat life. It seemed to undermine both privacy and social segregation.

'Dr. Weyden . . . often remarks on the sharpness of social distinctions amongst us, and on what he calls our mania for isolation,' Charles B.P. Bosanquet observed of a series of letters which describe, in the *Kölnishe Zeitung* for 1853, a visit to London. 'The Englishman is a non-gregarious animal . . . and even in his coffee-house, and eating-room, he boxes himself up between high partitions.'[13] W.M. Ackworth defended in 1889 the English traveller's hostility not only to American-type railway coaches but even corridor trains as threats to individual privacy:

> . . . We maintain in England our 'lonesome stuffy compartments', simply because we like them. . . . I would rather be 'boxed up' in a Midland third-class than have 'the privilege of enjoying the conversation of the general public' in the most luxurious car that Pullman ever fashioned. . . . [In an English compartment] one is 'safely locked in and pro-tected . . .'[14]

What the Victorians desired was privacy for the middle classes, publicity for the working classes, and segregation for both. The ideal environment for individual and familial privacy was the single-class villa suburb. There bourgeois respectability could best flourish. 'Upper Norwood,' wrote the author of *The Suburban Homes of London* in 1881, 'affords to the citizens a delicious retreat from the care, the hurry, the tumult, and the smoke of the busy day.'[15] The suburbs that proved most successful were the ones that were most suburban, that is to say the most dull, the most uniform, with the fewest cultural or social institutions, since they thereby offered the fewest counter-attractions to those of the home and the hearth. 'Railways and omnibuses are plentiful,' wrote a correspondent to the *Builder* in 1856, 'and it is better, morally and physically, for the Londoner . . . when he has done his day's work, to go to the country or the suburbs, where he escapes the noise and crowds and impure air of the town; and it is no small advantage to a man to have his family removed from the immediate neighbourhood of casinos, dancing saloons, and hells upon earth which I will not name.'[16]

The suburb allowed one freedom from metropolitan pressures to do as one wished: for Mr Pooter, Holloway provided the perfect environment for being absurdly conventional; for Jolyon Forsyte, St John's Wood was the ideal place in which to defy conventionality. In the 1840's one escaped into a villa miraculously transported from the Lago di Como to Surrey; in the 1870's into a seventeenth-century Dutch farmhouse; by the nineties into an overgrown Tudor country cottage: each of them individual yet standardized, one's own yet inconspicuous. Boredom was the price willingly paid for a respite from urban tensions. Social segregation simplified problems of behaviour, expenditure, and beliefs: one simply did what the neighbours were doing.

Thackeray in his *Book of Snobs* includes a cautionary tale to point the moral that the dom-estic virtues were more secure in the suburbs than in central London. The story begins with the coal-merchant Mr Sackville Maine happily married, living 'at his pretty little cottage' at Kennington Oval. His home was

> a picture of elegance and comfort; his table and cellar were excellently and neatly supplied. There was every enjoyment, but no ostentation. The omnibus took him to business of a morning; the boat brought him back to the happiest of homes, where he would while away the long evenings by reading out the fashionable novels to the ladies as they worked; or accompany his wife on the flute (which he played elegantly); or in any one of the hundred pleasing and innocent amusements of the domestic circle.

Unfortunately prosperity and membership in the Sarcophagus Club tempted him to move from Kennington to Pimlico, where his wife and children languished in the unaccustomed splendours of the Belgravian squares, while Sackville Maine could be found, 'tippling Sillery champagne and gorging himself with French viands', at his club.

> Where's his wife . . . Where's poor, good, kind little Laura? At this very moment – it's about the nursery bed-time, and while yonder good-for-nothing is swilling his wine – the little ones are at Laura's knees lisping their prayers; and she is teaching them to say – 'Pray God bless Papa.'
>
> When she has put them to bed, her day's occupation is gone; and she is utterly lonely all night, and sad, and waiting for him.
>
> Oh, for shame! Oh, for shame! Go home, thou idle tippler.[17]

And, more to the point, leave the house in Belgravia and move, if not back to plebeian Kennington, to Streatham or Upper Norwood or some other proper suburban retreat that offers no urban competition to the gentle pleasures of the fireside.

The segregation of the middle classes had as its counterpart the even more systematic segregation of the working classes, both into model dwellings and into homogeneous districts of cottage housing. Even the respectable working classes could exercise no more than limited freedom of choice as to their neighbourhood: they lived where their employment, or a low level of rents, or the provision of cheap workmen's trains permitted. Philanthropy in the nineteenth century and council housing in the twentieth encouraged their movement out of the back streets and mews of the older mixed neighbourhoods into segregated block dwellings or suburban estates, model or otherwise.

Rasmussen has argued that what makes London 'unique' is its scattered low-density development, the single-family house with its own garden, and the controls made possible by the long-leasehold system and the concentration of landownership. All these circumstances must be taken into consideration in any assessment of London, but the same causes exist in Birmingham and Sheffield without producing there anything like the same results. What makes London special is its variety, the number of possibilities it offers both to the resident and the visitor. The abundance of specialized neighbourhoods is as important an ingredient in determining London's character as the abundance of specialized institutions; its shops, theatres, pubs, libraries, and parks derive much of their peculiar enchantment from their location, whether concentrated with their fellows or juxtaposed with contrasting or complementary phenomena.

The pleasures of London are not scattered indiscriminately, but concentrated in certain districts. Sometimes the result is mind-boggling uniformity, like those interminable stretches of Oxford Street that seem devoted to nothing but the sale of women's shoes. Other times what makes a district special is its peculiar mixture of functions, like the one that until recently brought about a nightly encounter between opera-goers and market porters.*

The physicists' concept of 'critical mass' may be applicable to cities, to the extent that a certain number of particular kinds of individuals have to be concentrated in one area to make possible a creative explosion. Suburbs at their most dull and monotonous contribute negatively to such a situation: by drawing off the commonplace and the conventional, they leave the central areas to be enjoyed by the lively and original few, undiluted by the mediocrity of the majority. Social mixture is not necessarily and always desirable. 'Ghettos', whether social or cultural, can be the forcing-grounds for creative activity impossible in a more mixed environment. Concentrate intellectuals and you get Hampstead, trendy journalists and you get N.W.1, vice and gastronomy and you get Soho, golf-playing stockbrokers and you get Sunningdale: mix them all together and you get the cultural insipidity of the New Towns.

Dr Johnson's London was small enough in population and area to do without specialized neighbourhoods or more than a handful of specialized institutions, such as its coffee houses and pleasure gardens and Mrs Montagu's and Mrs Thrale's salons; only through the proliferation of specialized neighbourhoods was London able to retain something of its old cultural intimacy through the population explosion of the nineteenth and twentieth centuries. Golders Green may be the price we have to pay for Hampstead, Wimbledon for Chelsea, Clapham for Soho, the anonymous suburbs of the North-West for Lady Metroland.†

We find cities satisfying in inverse proportion to their degree of social and functional homogeneity, and in direct proportion to their degree of differentiation and diversification. It is the comparative absence of specialized neighbourhoods and institutions that makes the capital cities of Australia, for all their beaches, such bland alternatives to the cities of Europe. (King's Cross, the one significant specialized neighbourhood in all Australia, may arguably be a less important centre of Australian culture than Earl's Court.) By carrying the process of specialization and segregation to the extremes they did, the Victorians created a London that promoted not only individual privacy and the life of the family, but all of the qualities that the ideal city ought to possess.

THE WHIG INTERPRETATION OF VICTORIAN LONDON

A remarkably gloomy view of Victorian London dominates the literature on the subject.

---

* 'The criterion of homogeneity is not that all people inhabiting a given area should be the same, but that the probability of their being of a particular characteristic should be alike in all parts of the area.' Duncan Timms, *The Urban Mosaic*, Cambridge University Press, 1971, p. 42.

† I wrote the above sentence before viewing Sir John Betjeman's evocative tribute to Metroland on television, which almost convinced me that Harrow, Pinner, and Rickmansworth need no justification beyond themselves.

Blue books and journalists' accounts concentrated on the evils of London – which were abundant enough – while the popular press focused its attention on the titillating activities of the criminal and aristocratic extremes of society rather than on the prosaic doings of those in between. However much contemporaries stressed the contrasts between wealth and poverty, most Londoners lived neither in hovels nor palaces but in something much more ordinary. Gertrude Himmelfarb has shown that Mayhew's poor represented but a tiny proportion of the London working class of the 1850's.[18] And however deplorable Booth's discovery that 30 per cent of the population of London in the nineties – even after the great general rise in the standard of living in the late Victorian period – lived in conditions of poverty, that left 70 per cent who did not.[19] Very few of that 70 per cent lived in conditions of luxury; most ranged from Booth's category of 'working-class comfort' through the various gradations of middle-class gentility. It is this group, the urban equivalent of the Howard Martin family that was, to Emma Woodhouse, both above and below her notice, that we know least about. They did not form the subject of parliamentary investigations; they were rarely written about in novels: although they provided the reformers and writers in many instances these did not, by and large, write about the class to which they belonged, except to castigate it for its bad taste, or its mistaken political and social beliefs.

Too many historians are still treating the Victorian period as Voltaire treated the thirteenth century, or, less culpably but equally mistakenly, as Macaulay treated the seventeenth. For Voltaire, what we have later come to regard as the 'High' Middle Ages was the embodiment of error, a real and present danger to his own age, whose values and institutions were to be combatted and ridiculed, not approached sympathetically with the aim of understanding. No serious mediaevalist emulates Voltaire's approach today, but it is harder for the Victorian specialist to disregard the similarities and connections between his contemporary concerns and the subjects of his historical research: he too often bewares of too much understanding for fear of too much forgiving.

A more insidious danger than railing against the nineteenth century for being less enlightened than the twentieth is the Whiggish one of regarding it as achieving its justification not in itself but in the later developments of movements to which it gave birth. F.M.L. Thompson has pointed out the 'teleological structure' of recent studies of working-class housing, 'in which Victorian failures, however understandable and explicable, point on inexorably to the only conceivable answer to the housing of the working classes, twentieth-century council housing'.[20]

Architectural historians are often guilty of the unhistorical use of historical evidence. Just as Victorian architects reacted against the Georgian aesthetic, so have the architectural leaders of the present century striven to produce buildings that would be as unlike those of the Victorians as possible. Even sympathetic historians like Henry-Russell Hitchcock and Sir Nikolaus Pevsner have sought to rehabilitate Victorian architecture by tracing in it the beginnings of twentieth-century functionalism – much as literary historians once tried to confer respectability on eighteenth-century writers by labelling them pre-Romantics. Such selective approaches have the virtue of discerning meaning and purpose in a seemingly chaotic field, but they consign to oblivion the great majority of buildings actually put up, and assume that neither Victorian architects nor their contemporary critics understood what they were doing.

Cornices, string-courses, reveals, architraves, and the rest of the architect's vocabulary provoke different emotional responses from succeeding generations, and call forth different intellectual interpretations. When we enjoy a Victorian building, we usually do so for reasons that would strike a Victorian critic as irrelevant. Just so did the Victorians: when they admired Georgian buildings, they did so in a patronizing way, and for extra-architectural reasons: for being old-fashioned, spacious, homely, or venerable, and for their historical and literary associations. They loved Richardson and Goldsmith and Johnson for more nearly the 'right' reasons than they admired the architectural environment in which such writers had worked. Similarly we can respond directly to George Eliot, but only by contortions and through an effort of the will to Butterfield.

No special knowledge or set of conceptual tools is necessary to see what Trollope or J.S. Mill or Macaulay is getting at; even the semi-literate can read Dickens with pleasure and some degree of understanding. Modern audiences at Covent Garden can derive quite the same innocent pleasure from *Lucia di Lammermoor* or *Faust* that their great-grandparents did. But the immediate aesthetic response possible to the architecture of any period up to the Regency fails us when we approach a Victorian building. Victorian architecture frustrates our best intentions, and defies our attempts to enjoy, much less understand. Like Etruscan texts, Victorian buildings are obviously trying to tell us something, but what that is we do not know.

'Were the rows of square brown brick boxes which Keats and Shelley had to look on, or the stuccoed villa which enshrined Tennyson's genius, to be the perpetual concomitants of such masters of verbal beauty,' asked William Morris in 1888; 'was no beauty but the beauty of words to be produced by man in our times; was the intelligence of the age to be for ever so preposterously lop-sided?'[21] That an age of astounding literary achievement grew progressively blind and perverse in its response to the visual arts is a received opinion too inherently improbable to remain unquestioned. A more satisfactory explanation would be that the Victorians developed a visual aesthetic so different from what preceded or followed it that it defies analysis by conventional criteria.

LONDON AND VICTORIAN CIVILIZATION

How Victorian was Victorian London? How far, that is to say, can it be used as evidence for the inner nature of Victorian civilization, for the real as distinct from the professed aspirations of the age? I would argue very much indeed, from a conviction that the Victorians got, in London, the sort of metropolis they really wanted. The 'they', of course, excludes the working classes, who rarely were able to impose their wishes on their environment, and most of the articulate intellectuals and aesthetes, whose values in any event tended to be neither urban nor suburban but rather rural and reactionary. Not but that such intellectuals did not profoundly influence the way in which London grew and changed, but through the operation of a 30- to 40-year time-lag, by the time the builders and developers responded to the suggestions and demands of the intellectuals, the intellectuals had changed their minds as to what they wanted.

The city in general and London in particular provide a fruitful way of getting at the *zeitgeist* of any period. The customary approach of the intellectual historian to that elusive phenomenon is to read the writings of contemporary intellectuals: scholastics in the thirteenth century, humanists in the Renaissance, Puritans in the seventeenth century, *philosophes* in the eighteenth, socialists and reformers in the nineteenth, radicals in the twentieth. The advantage of such an approach is that one gets explicit, coherent, self-conscious views on society, nature, man, institutions, morality, science, and all the rest; the disadvantage is that intellectuals by their very nature are unrepresentative. The thirteenth century was not, outside a few rarified circles, a particularly rationalistic or coherent age; the eighteenth century was not profoundly anti-Christian. Yet the written evidence from the leaders of thought of the two periods respectively supports such mistaken conclusions. Any history of thought that is restricted to the ideas of the articulate minority will produce equally suspect results. One way to broaden the scope of an investigation of the ideas and values of a people is to turn from an examination of what they said to one of what they made. London as one of the most conspicuous artifacts of the Victorians is here before our very eyes and can, I think, be made to yield up significant information about the people who made it.

But who, in fact, *made* Victorian London? Essentially the speculative builder, responding with some sensitivity to the desires of that – quite substantial – segment of society with enough money to exercise choice. He was also, to be sure, responding to the desire of the same segment of society to invest its savings in a safe and reasonably profitable industry; this latter fact was a constant, however, and simply assured an abundant supply of capital for building at any period, whether one of depression or boom. London, like most of England, remained a buyer's market down to the Second World War, and always left the middle and upper classes at least with sufficient choice of residence or business location so that their wishes really could be reflected in the buildings that went up, the districts that rose or fell in standing: in both the architectural appearance and social geography of the metropolis.

London was not just any artifact. As the greatest city in the world, the capital of the Empire, the highest expression of the most urbanized society of the nineteenth century, it represented both what the Victorians wanted to do and were able to do. The nature of British society kept it from reflecting – like Berlin or Versailles, Turin or Vienna – no more than the wishes of an absolute monarch or even a small dominant elite. Nash's developments were the closest thing to a London *created* by a single governing intelligence; the rest of the nineteenth century was a repudiation of everything that Regent Street stood for. The great landed proprietors theoretically had vast powers for shaping and reshaping their estates, but in practice were able to achieve what ends they did only by co-operating with the realities of the market. And that market did reflect with considerable accuracy the ideals and aspirations of a large segment of Victorian society. Beyond that the actions of Parliament and of the vestries and the Metropolitan Board of Works reflected the opinions of the electorate and ratepayers as to what was appropriate for public bodies to do to the metropolis. The results of the combined actions of public and private bodies and individuals were in no sense brought about by 'absence of mind', but instead represented with fair accuracy the kind of London middle-class Londoners desired. If it failed to satisfy the demands of successive aesthetic and social orthodoxies the fault lay partly in the intractable nature of the pre-Victorian inheritance, partly in the fact that such orthodoxies failed to incorporate the legitimate wishes of the large public that elected representatives, provided capital, commissioned architects, and bought or rented buildings.

Whatever may be said about Victorian England, it was not poor, it was not lethargic, and it was not unaware of what was going on. It did not have to produce the kind of urban environment that it did. It had technological resources that no earlier age had had, and when it decided to make use of them, as it did with the creation of a railway network or a vast and expensive system of sewers, it did so. It is sometimes said in extenuation of the inadequacies of the Victorian city that the challenge of unprecedented population growth, industrialization, and technological change was simply too great for the Victorians adequately to respond to, and that they, in effect, made the best of a bad job. There is something to be said for such an argument, yet much of what we, from our later vantage point, regard as inadequacies, was deliberate.

To posit a monolithic 'Victorian mind', or even a set of 'Victorian middle-class values', is hazardous. The complexity and diversity of Victorian civilization have led many historians to question the appropriateness of dealing with it as a whole. They prefer to break it up into its component periods, movements, schools of thought, styles, or social classes, as more amenable to critical analysis. But, paradoxically, the very complexity and diversity of Victorianism gives it its unity. Certainly this is true of the architecture and planning of Victorian London.

We are justified in applying the label 'Victorian' to a porticoed town house in the Cromwell Road, a red-brick villa in Fitzjohn's Avenue, a Gothic office block in Queen Victoria Street, a French Renaissance terrace in Grosvenor Place, and a terracotta hotel in Knightsbridge because they all share certain characteristics which they do not share with representative buildings of either eighteenth- or twentieth-century origin. Such characteristics are related to central non-architectural and even non-visual aspects of Victorian life and culture. The architecture of Victorian London was an integral part of the civilization that produced it.

However long the period of Victoria's reign, and however diverse and changing the aims and convictions of her subjects, the history of London at least has enough unifying features common to the early, middle, and late segments of that reign; enough assumptions shared by a wide social, ideological, and political spectrum to suggest that 'Victorian England', as distinct from 'Georgian England' and 'Edwardian England', really existed.

The decade preceding 1837 contained enough events and novel phenomena, both symbolic and practical, to convince the most rigorous upholder of the gradualist, seamless-web interpretation, that it saw London moving from one distinct period into another: the creation of the Metropolitan Police, the introduction of the omnibus, the Great Reform Bill, the democratization of the close vestries, the coming of the railway, the invention of the Hansom cab, the retirement and death of John Nash, the burning of the Houses of Parliament, the publication of Pugin's *Contrasts*. Within the decade 1901–1911 the motor car, the motor bus, and the electric tram appeared on the streets of London; underneath London electric trains ran both on the old underground and the new tubes; Norman Shaw's Piccadilly Hotel signalled the death of the old Regent Street, and the Russell Hotel announced the same for Bloomsbury; the London County Council was building suburban housing estates; Selfridge's and the first of the Lyons Corner Houses had opened. Edwardian London was already very much our own London; late Victorian London was something quite different.

The chapters that follow will examine some of the unifying qualities that characterized London and its suburbs in the years between 1837 and 1901: an obsession with classification and subdivision, a longing for contrast and variety, a fascination with height, and with verticality of all sorts; the facilitation of movement, the glorification of home and family, an emphasis on the symbolic and visible manifestations of a hierarchical social structure at a time when its real constraints were being removed; a rejection of urban values; a tendency to view problems from an historical point of view – to see, for instance, architectural forms not as purely aesthetic manifestations, but as expressions of the total culture that produced them – and in particular a preoccupation with the eighteenth century. Future historians may decide that the key to an understanding of the twentieth century lies in our attempts to come to terms with the Victorians. Certainly one key to Victorian civilization is its uneasy, love-hate relationship with Georgian England.

CHAPTER TWO

London in 1837: the Georgian Legacy

Victorian London was, to a very great physical extent, Georgian London.[1]
Sir John Summerson

BRICK AND THE RULE OF TASTE

At the start of the nineteenth century a dense, overwhelmingly brick, and stylistically uniform metropolis – from Hyde Park to the eastern outskirts of the City, from the New Road to the Thames and beyond – housed nearly a million inhabitants. Most of that earlier city was still there at the start of the twentieth. The main difference between Georgian and Victorian London was not what it was but how it was regarded.

The Great Fire and the suburban developments of the eighteenth century had made the London of 1837 a comparatively new city. Unlike most European capitals, it contained few monuments of any considerable antiquity. While a handful of mediaeval and Tudor structures survived beyond the area of the Fire, most of what passed for 'old' London was at best early Stuart. Numerous examples of the architecture of Charles I – in such streets as Holborn, Chancery Lane, Drury Lane, Fetter Lane, the Strand, Cheapside, Bishopsgate, Aldgate, and Smithfield – could be seen as late as the 1870's.[2]

The Victorians looked on such survivals with affectionate condescension, as contributing to the picturesqueness of some of London's older quarters. The more regular architecture that succeeded the Fire and its consequent Building Acts evoked for the most part only disgust. Even the conventional admiration for Christopher Wren was insufficient to save large numbers of his City churches from destruction. The *Building News* was condoning, and even encouraging their selective demolition in 1875:

> We have lately had occasion to notice the almost useless existence of some of our old London City churches which have survived, or have been rebuilt, since the Great Fire of 1666. Their scant congregations, their enclosed position, locked in between buildings on at least three sides, their imperfect lighting and worse ventilation, are sufficient reasons for abolishing them, even if only to provide funds for building new edifices in more desirable districts.[3]

If late Stuart architecture was inadequately appreciated, Georgian architecture, particularly that dating from 1760 and after, seemed the very negation of beauty. In 1898 Sir George Laurence Gomme deplored the replacement of the picturesque houses of Tudor and early

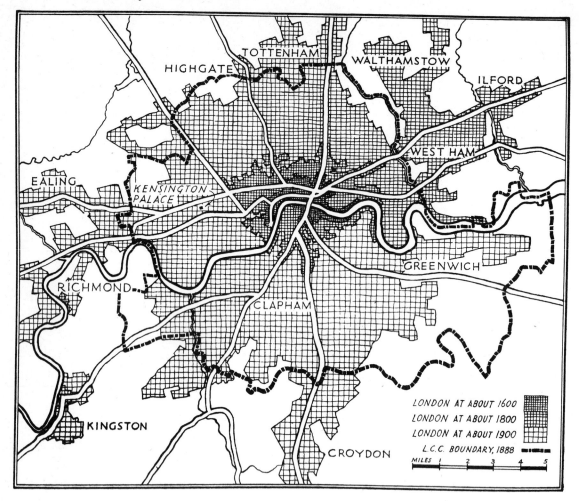

Map I   Extent of built-up area in 1600, 1800,
and 1900.

Stuart London by 'the hideous monstrosities of Harley Street, Gower Street, and so on . . . The Georgian spirit of architecture was against art, and declared for so-called utilitarianism, as if utility could exist without the element of art.'[4] Practicing architects and critics were as insensitive to the beauties of the Georgian style as laymen. 'I believe,' Walter Emden told the Society of Architects in his presidential address in 1899, 'that at no period of architecture was style and design so debased as in the latter part of the 18th and the beginning of the 19th century. The squares of London and the rows of houses in many districts which date from that period speak strongly in this direction . . .'[5] Few Victorians would have disagreed with the judgment. At the start of the reign Sir John Soane had attacked the uniformity of late Georgian estate planning in London for its 'disgusting insipidity and tiresome mono-tony'. He blamed both the leasehold system and 'the rapacity of the Builders' for a situation whereby 'our buildings are limited to mere heaps of bricks, with perforations for light and the purposes of ingress and egress, without the least regard to elegance of Composition'.[6]

The Victorians wasted little emotion in nostalgia for their Georgian past. Thackeray might feel more affection for his wicked eighteenth-century predecessors than he publicly professed, and the age of Queen Anne by the 1870's came to acquire a certain aura of glamour, but her Hanoverian successors and their subjects, while they might be objects of curiosity, evoked little admiration until the very end of the century. Georgian London, everywhere physically present, served as a constant reminder of the shortcomings of eighteenth-century civilization. 'The Adelphi,' wrote 'Ralph Redivivus' in 1838 of Adam's masterpiece, 'possesses merely largeness, unaccompanied by magnitude of forms and proportions, and is equally devoid of richness.' Robert Adam, he admitted, 'was certainly a man of some talent . . . but, unfortunately, he was not gifted with the most refined or delicate taste . . .'. The Adelphi stood as a reminder of the great rise in architectural standards that had taken place between the 1770's and the 1830's:

> . . . Now, alas! nobody thinks it worth while to turn down from the Strand even to take a peep at Adam's magnificent pile; or if any one does, he returns filled with astonishment . . . that such a paltry gingerbread piece of architecture should ever have been admired, for now-a-days many of the gin-palaces about town exhibit quite as much grandeur, and far more consistency of design.[7]

However much the London of 1864 left to be desired, the *Builder* of that year reminded its readers that the London of Waterloo was even worse:

> At that epoch (1815), scarcely more than fifty years ago, the vast dingy mass of old brick-and-mortar London, with its mean, low houses, crushed with their cumbrous tiled roofs, and unenlivened by their small, badly glazed, and insufficient windows . . . was still intact.
>
> . . . The metropolitan agglomeration of crowded and dismal buildings, and narrow streets and alleys, which formed the main portions even of the aristocratic parishes of St. James and St. George, still enjoyed all their ancient prestige of density, dirt, and dinginess.[8]

Earlier, the *Building News* (1857) could find 'nothing answering to the name of street "architecture"... in the capital of the world'. Until the last 25 or 30 years,

> dowdiness, blankness, and sulkiness seemed ... to have been considered quite *comme il faut*, and the order of the day. Portland-place itself shows very little more attempt at design than does Bedford row, of which it may be termed a second edition, enlarged, and, it must be confessed ... if nearly as homely and unpretending in style, several degrees less *triste*. A century ago the taste for display manifested itself chiefly in dress. While they decked out themselves with lace and embroidery, even people of fortune were content to let their houses be seen in the *dishabille* of bare brick walls, with holes in them for windows.... We dress out ourselves less, and our buildings ... far more. Formerly – that is, within the present century – a street house, with a cornice to it, was something to be stared at; and as to window dressings, they were scarcely so much as dreamt of for dwelling-houses ...[9]

That such dismal streets and gloomy squares continued to be the residences of the great and powerful of the land was a paradox much relished by Victorian novelists, who were able to give their villains appropriately deplorable houses without sacrificing verisimilitude. Harley Street was much used to epitomize Georgian London: if perhaps marginally less dreary than Gower or Baker Streets, its residents were of higher rank. The Merdles in *Little Dorrit* lived in Harley Street:

> Upon that establishment of state, the Merdle establishment in Harley Street, Cavendish Square, there was the shadow of no more common wall than the fronts of other establishments of state on the opposite side of the street. Like unexceptionable Society, the opposing rows of houses in Harley Street were very grim with one another. Indeed, the mansions and their inhabitants were so much alike in that respect, that the people were often to be found drawn up on opposite sides of dinner-tables, in the shade of their own loftiness, staring at the other side of the way with the dulness of the houses.
>
> Everybody knows how like the street the two dinner-rows of people who take their stand by the street will be. The expressionless uniform twenty houses, all to be knocked at and rung at in the same form, all approachable by the same dull steps, all fended off by the same pattern of railing, all with the same impracticable fire-escapes, the same inconvenient fixtures in their heads, and everything without exception to be taken at a high valuation – who has not dined with these?[10]

Dickens found little more to admire in the Grosvenor estate and in Mayfair:

> They rode to the top of Oxford Street, and there alighting, dived in among the great streets of melancholy stateliness, and the little streets that try to be as stately and succeed in being more melancholy, of which there is a labyrinth near Park Lane. Wildernesses of corner houses, with barbarous old porticoes and appurtenances; horrors that came into existence under some wrong-headed person in some wrong-headed time, still demanding the blind admiration of all ensuing generations, and determined to do so until they

1 '''. . . Bedford row . . . homely and unpretending in style . . .''' Bedford Row, east side, 1908.

tumbled down; frowned upon the twilight. Parasite little tenements, with the cramp in their whole frame, from the dwarf hall-door on the giant model of His Grace's in the Square to the squeezed window of the boudoir commanding the dunghills in the Mews, made the evening doleful. Rickety dwellings of undoubted fashion, but of a capacity to hold nothing comfortably except a dismal smell, looked like the last result of the great mansions' breeding in-and-in; and, where their little supplementary bows and balconies were supported on thin iron columns, seemed to be scrofulously resting upon crutches. Here and there a Hatchment, with the whole science of Heraldry in it, loomed down upon the street, like an Archbishop discoursing on Vanity. The shops, few in number, made no show; for popular opinion was as nothing to them.[11]

If in retrospect Georgian London looked insufferably tame and placid, an expression of mindless architectural conservatism, to the Georgians themselves it had been a wonderful spectacle of activity and growth. Expressions of shock and admiration at the rapidity of the expansion of London long antedated the Victorian era. Henry Kett was not the first to exclaim over the speed with which London was devouring the surrounding countryside in 1787:

The contagion of the building influenza . . . has extended its virulence to this country, where it rages with unabating violence. . . . The metropolis is manifestly the centre of the disease. In other places, the accumulation is made by occasionally adding house to house; but in London, street is suddenly added to street, and square to square. The adjacent villages in a short time undergo a complete transformation, and bear no more resemblance to their original state, than Phyllis the milk-maid does to a lady mayoress. The citizen who, twenty years ago, enjoyed at his country seat pure air, undisturbed retirement, and an extensive prospect, is now surrounded by a populous neighbourhood. The purity of the air is sullied with smoke, and the prospect is cut off by the opposite houses. . . . In the vicinity of the capital every situation is propitious to the mason and the carpenter. Mansions daily arise upon the marshes of Lambeth, the roads of Kensington, and the hills of Hampstead. The chain of buildings so closely unites the country with the town, that the distinction is lost between Cheapside and St. George's Fields. This idea struck the mind of a child, who lives at Clapham, with so much force, that he observed, 'If they go on building at such a rate, London will soon be next door to us.'[12]

Eighteenth-century London grew increasingly orderly, regular, and tasteful, particularly on the great aristocratic leasehold estates: it astonished visitors from the provinces and abroad by its wealth, cleanliness, and extent. But its virtues reflected private rather than public patronage, while the restrictions of the London Building Acts and prevailing architectural fashions kept external ornament to a bare minimum. The absence of local building stone and the abundance of local clay led to its being overwhelmingly built of brick, quickly blackened by the smoke of coal fires. Wide, uniform streets, and spacious squares gave dignity to the newer portions of the town. A few great private mansions existed, but for the most part the aristocracy concentrated their building zeal on country houses, and were content to inhabit no more than larger versions of the standard London town house in terraces shared with others. London had no royal palace fit to be mentioned in the same breath with those of any number of minor German princes: St James's Palace was an object of embarrassed amusement, and only Inigo Jones's Banqueting Hall remained of old Whitehall, to remind Londoners that in overthrowing Stuart despotism they had deprived themselves of unimaginable architectural delights.

The Revolutionary and Napoleonic Wars, by raising the cost of building materials, labour, and credit, slowed the rate of expansion and the process of embellishment of the metropolis. Russell and Brunswick Squares and the network of streets that grew up in the 1790's and early 1800's on the adjacent Bedford and Foundling Hospital estates were exceptional. Public building in particular languished. Yet within a decade a revolution in taste, combined with an unprecedented spurt in building activity promised, under the patronage of the Prince Regent, to turn London once and for all into a visually magnificent city.

STUCCO AND THE QUEST FOR SPLENDOUR

'Once, and only once, has a great plan for London, affecting the development of the capital as a whole, been projected and carried to completion,' Sir John Summerson has pointed out.[13] The formation of Regent's Park, the cutting through of Regent Street, the creation of Trafalgar Square, and the replanning of St James's Park seemed to point the way to a systematic rebuilding of the whole of the metropolis along similar lines of stuccoed, neo-classical theatricality. The decade that ended in 1825 was one in which builders and architects, landowners and investors, leaders of taste and the general public were agreed both as to the feasibility of a more magnificent London and the form that magnificence ought to take.

One of the curiosities of English history is the persistent anti-urban bias that has, with rare intervals, pervaded it. During the centuries in which England was supported by a largely agricultural economy, one might expect cities in general, and London in particular, to be regarded as non-productive and parasitic burdens: the Elizabethan and early Stuart proclamations prohibiting new building in London, however misguided, were understandable reactions to the view of London as a hotbed of riot, idleness, and sedition. But persistence of the fear – or at best dislike – of London into the time that England became the most industrialized and urbanized society on earth remains a paradox. Modern reformers find it as hard to assimilate London into their notion of the good life as did mediaeval theorists. The eighteenth-century country house, the nineteenth-century suburban villa, and the twentieth-century New Town reflect the conscious decisions of their builders to create an environment as different as possible from the metropolis. The distrust of London, or what London was thought to represent, is not confined to the Cobbetts and Ruskins and Howards and their immediate followers, but is shared by the inarticulate multitudes as well.

Some persons, of course, have always resisted the bucolic tide and openly proclaimed their delight in London – Defoe and Dr Johnson and Lamb, for instance. Compilers of guide books and tourist literature have managed to work up a degree of enthusiasm for their subject. But for the most part writers have spoken of London to condemn rather than to praise, to promote reforms rather than to revel in its existing qualities. Even today, only when some building or neighbourhood is scheduled for demolition are its virtues belatedly recognized.

The period of the regency and reign of George IV is exceptional in that it produced concerted voices not only in defence of but in glorification of London: and London not merely for its historical associations, or as capital of the realm, but for its specifically urban qualities. Chadwick and Shaftesbury and Mayhew had yet to point out that London was unhealthy, over-crowded, and miserable. In the euphoria of the years between Waterloo and the Great Reform Bill there were those – by no means blind, callous, or Philistine – who dared proclaim it healthy, happy, and beautiful. (Cobbett, to be sure, maintained the older tradition of suspicion and loathing.) Regent Street and Regent's Park meant not merely a new thoroughfare for north-south traffic and fine new buildings, but demolition of slum property, formation of a network of drains and sewers, creation of a new waterworks, and building a great canal. Combining as they did sanitary, social, and economic with aesthetic improvements, street and park seemed to point the way for the positive transformation of London into a city that would stir the pride and command the affection of the whole British people, and represent to the world the taste and humanity as well as the wealth and power of the British nation.

The decade of the twenties saw a surge of enthusiasm for the idea of London as a great imperial capital, along with a flood of projects to make her more worthy of that role. '. . . Now, when the spirit of improvement is so much awakened,' wrote the author of one such set of projects in 1825, 'why should not such fair occasions of embellishing it with specimens of architecture, that might at once be evidence of our victories, and our taste be made use of?'[14] Two years earlier J.C. Robertson and T. Byerley had exulted:

> If during a war, unexampled in its duration, and in the expense at which it was sustained, the British metropolis continued not merely to add house to house, but street to street, and to increase in magnificence, it was to be expected that, 'the piping time of peace' would give a new impulse to improvement.

Regent Street, 'a noble street', and Regent's Park, 'one of the greatest ornaments of the metropolis . . . around which noble terraces are springing up as if by magic', were demonstrations of the way London was making itself worthy of its political and economic pre-eminence.[15]

In another book published in 1823 a mythical visitor from France exclaimed over

> the vast and magnificent improvements which the British metropolis now offers to the observation of an admiring world. . . . the progress made since the signature of the last treaty of peace, in extending and beautifying London, is almost miraculous. Most extraordinary does it . . . appear to strangers, that after having maintained, almost exclusively at your own expense, the burden of one of the longest and most expensive wars which Europe ever witnessed, you should at its termination find the means of erecting such numerous and costly piles of elegant architecture; nor can we, in beholding them, fail to reflect how incalculable are the resources of a free, enlightened, and united people.[16]

The *Quarterly Journal* in 1827 hailed Regent's Park as 'the dawning of a new and better taste, and . . . a just subject of national exultation'. The writer predicted that it and its surrounding terraces would, when completed, 'present a union of rural and architectural beauty on a scale of greater magnificence than can be found in any other place'.[17] Regent Street, wrote John Britton in 1828, 'exhibits a succession and variety of architectural elevations which cannot fail to amuse the eye and astonish the mind. This street may be said to constitute the greatest improvement ever made in London . . .'[18]

In *Metropolitan Improvements; or London in the Nineteenth Century*, published between 1827 and 1831, James Elmes and Thomas H. Shepherd captured the heady optimism and the aesthetic conviction with which cultivated Londoners then approached the future of their metropolis. 'Behind the book,' writes Sir John Summerson, 'is the apprehension that London, within a matter of 15 or 20 years, had taken on a new character. And so it had.'[19] The 'rule of taste', so soon to be broken, still held. Greater archaeological knowledge led to disputes between admirers respectively of the Greek and Italian schools, an increasing proportion of new churches adopted some variant of Gothic, and the Egyptian Hall in Piccadilly was an ominous portent: still the vast majority of buildings actually going up and the predominant critical consensus remained within the classical tradition. But greater variation was now possible within that tradition. Flamboyance, spectacle, and drama were now more easily achieved: the wonders of stucco permitted, at little expense, architectural effects that would have been impossible in the earlier brick-surfaced London. The sheer size of Nash's endeavours – Regent's Park with its 543 acres, Regent Street a mile long – offered him opportunities for extended compositions such as none of his predecessors had achieved.

Elmes was troubled by none of the doubts that were to disturb the Victorians as they contemplated the demolitions necessary for their street improvements:

> Among the glories of this age, the historian will have to record the conversion of dirty alleys, dingy courts and squalid dens of misery and crime . . . into 'stately streets,' to 'squares that court the breeze,' to palaces and mansions, to elegant private dwellings, to rich and costly shops, filled with the productions of every clime, to magnificent ware-rooms, stowed with the ingenious and valuable manufactures of our artisans and mechanics, giving activity to commerce with all the enviable results of national prosperity.

Nor did he regret the destruction of a portion of the countryside: 'rich and varied architecture and park-like scenery' were self-evidently to be preferred to 'paltry cabins and monotonous cowlairs . . .' Romanticism had not succeeded in shaking his distaste for untamed nature: 'Fields, that were in our times appropriated to pasturage, are now become the gay and tasteful abodes of splendid opulence, and of the triumphs of the peaceful arts.' Splendid public buildings helped the tourist trade, attracting 'opulent and ingenious foreigners . . .' They not only provided employment for 'the labourer, the artisan and the artist . . .' but they stimulated patriotism, 'a passion that is the parent of all great actions that conduce to the public wealth'.[20]

While generally approving of Nash's designs, Elmes avoided what he called 'nauseating sycophancy . . .'[21] Thus, Chester Terrace, 'like most of that gentleman's works, combines genius and carelessness. Genius, and powerful conception, in the composition, and a grasp of mind equalled by no artist of the day in the design: and carelessness, sometimes degenerating to littleness, with a deficiency of elegance in the details.'[22]

Any possible deficiencies in correct taste were compensated for by its contribution of variety and surprise to the urban scene. So Elmes found the compositions of Regent Street 'a great and manifest improvement upon the plain dingy brick elevations of our ancestors',[23] a judgment with which even its Victorian critics would grudgingly agree. The variety of treatment contrasted delightfully with 'the eternal *two windows iron railing and a door, – two windows iron railing and a door,* – of the (then) new streets and squares of St Mary-le-bone'.[24]

Nash's grand design was only the most conspicuous of the new improvements: Elmes and Shepherd were able to examine and illustrate an impressive assortment of recently-completed public buildings that were for the most part architecturally consistent with the Regent Street development. All seemed to point the way to a reconstructed London that would display throughout uniformity of design, grand architectural compositions, and theatrical splendour.

Such expectations were not to be fulfilled. In comparing the 'galaxy of talent in poetry, in the sublimest works of imagination, such as no nation has hitherto surpassed, in legislation, in the art of war, and in the more peaceful arts and sciences . . .' of his own age with that of Pericles, of Augustus, and of Louis XIV, Elmes remarked, prophetically, 'that the duration of these brilliant epochs or times of perfection, have generally been brief in proportion to their splendour'.[25] For by the time his book was completed, the impulse to make London another Imperial Rome had died.

In the realm of private speculation the sudden collapse of the building boom in 1825 had already left many ambitious schemes uncompleted: it would take years, in some instances decades, merely to finish programmes for which commitments had already been made. Cubitt's building agreements in Belgravia and Bloomsbury, to take the most dramatic examples, had all been signed by 1825, but would not be carried out in full until after his death in 1857.[26] Under such circumstances it would have been folly for a speculator to embark on any but small-scale ventures. The death of George IV meant the end of knowledgeable and determined royal patronage.

More important causes were the Great Reform Bill and related measures that were to impose a greater degree of middle-class control over the operations and expenditures of both national and local government. To taxpayer and ratepayer alike, economy was to be the guiding principle. Where money was to be spent on new projects, they were to be practical rather than aesthetic in purpose: sewers, perhaps; new roads and bridges where necessary to reduce traffic congestion; but nothing that was intended simply to be beautiful.

In 1836 the historian Sir Archibald Alison argued that fine architecture was impossible in a democracy:

A genuine democracy is at once shortsighted . . . and selfish, stingy and rapacious; parsimonious to all other parties or objects, avaricious and rapacious for its own advantages, or the fortunes of its favourite leaders; and such a spirit is the precise reverse of the

2 'Regent Street, wrote John Britton in 1828, "exhibits a succession and variety of architectural elevations which cannot fail to amuse the eye and astonish the mind".' Regent Street, east side, from Thomas Shepherd and James Elmes, *Metropolitan Improvements*, 1828.

3 'Chester Terrace ... "combines genius and carelessness".' Chester Terrace, from Shepherd and Elmes, *Metropolitan Improvements*.

disposition required for architectural greatness, which of all other things requires most the elevated views, grandeur of conception, and durability of design, which belong to bodies whose interests and habits are detached from the shifting quicksands of popular administration, and fixed on the permanent character of aristocratic government.[27]

More cautiously, the *Builder* in 1893 suggested:

. . . There seems in general to be the more chance of getting architectural improvement carried out in proportion to the independent or despotic character of the Government. The great improvements in Paris were mostly carried out under the First or Second Empire, and the immense scheme at Vienna was also carried out under a comparatively despotic rule. . . . The more we verge towards Republicanism, in modern life at least, the more the general tendency seems to be towards merely practical improvements, leaving beauty to take care of itself.[28]

The Victorian electorate came to regard the projects of the Prince Regent not as examples to be emulated or surpassed, but as extravagant frivolities. If urban splendour was to be sought, it reasoned, let private rather than public wealth be used.

Urban splendour came to seem not merely extravagant but wrong-headed. The Victorians grew disenchanted with the city as such, and sought fulfilment in other environments, rural or, more practically, suburban. The failures of the Victorians with their cities can perhaps be understood and even forgiven if it is borne in mind that their hearts were really not in city-building. Cities were at best necessary evils whose deplorable features might, by judicious measures, be lessened; they were not even potentially a positive good. What the intelligent Victorian sought was not so much a better city as an alternative to the city. The new technology of the time made one such alternative, in the shape of villa suburbia, for the first time a feasible one.

Doubts as to the inherent value of the city as such were reinforced by an aesthetic revolution that produced 'a sudden and universal revulsion against all that had been achieved. . . . The whole rule of taste was in process of being dethroned; and the last and not least effective phase in that long dominion, was irrationally condemned.'[29] By their newness, pretensions, and visibility, Nash's improvements came to represent all that the proponents of the new aesthetic detested in the last phase of classicism; in attacking them they implicitly defined their own, opposing values.

Already in 1838 the *Civil Engineer and Architect's Journal* was finding many of the façades in Regent Street 'vile enough in point of design . . . All have the appearance of having been erected from hasty unrevised sketches.' They displayed 'tawdriness and show, and very little richness; a great deal of poverty and meanness, without any approach to simplicity . . .'[30] In the same year W.H. Leeds found both Regent Street and Regent's Park 'marked by paltry pomposity and parade', in which 'meanness is mixed up with would-be grandeur, and what is intended to convey an idea of splendour only calls attention all the more forcibly to the miserable taste, and even shabbiness of its Brummagem finery'. He endorsed Pugin's denunciation of them as 'nests of monstrosities'.[31]

Two years later the *Dublin Evening Post* called the design of the whole 'childish and ridiculous . . .' and described the taste of the Prince Regent as 'tawdry and glaring'.[32] The *Builder* in 1844 wrote that the houses surrounding Regent's Park presented 'the maximum of ornament . . . but the minimum of convenience. They are . . . violent digressions from true taste . . .' It recorded with approval that some of the villas in the park itself had been 'remodelled so as to preserve no resemblance to their original form and architectural character . . .'[33]

One writer in 1851 specifically used *Metropolitan Improvements* to point out the revolution in taste that separated its principles from those dominating London architecture in mid-century. After quoting Elmes's comparison of George IV to Augustus, he remarked:

> Could the Augustus of England indeed return with the full recollection of all he had done to embellish the metropolis, how might his eyes wander in search of those most 'important and tasteful improvements;' – Carlton Terrace [i.e., the original Carlton House itself] erased and wasted from the page of memory; the Marble Arch . . . gone, no one knows where, to make room for a screen to hide the former beauties of Buckingham Palace; the much-vaunted Colonnade in Regent-street altogether demolished and put away . . . So great a revolution it is hardly possible to credit. The architecture of the period [of *Metropolitan Improvements*] was essentially Classical . . . All attempt at Gothic then was voted barbarity, and laughed to scorn. Now it is just the reverse: we have Gothic Houses of Parliament, libraries, halls, churches, aye, even the very Methodist body have been vaccinated into a *furor* for Gothic. . . . The almshouses, hospitals, workhouses, schools, villas, houses, cottages – everything now is Gothic . . .[34]

Gothic and its popular derivatives never in fact achieved anything like the universal acceptance the passage suggests, but it is nevertheless correct in asserting that the kind of classicism represented by *Metropolitan Improvements* was both dead and damned by 1851.

THE DECAY OF NASH'S LONDON

Aesthetic fashion does not necessarily determine the social prestige of a neighbourhood, but in the case of the Regent's Park terraces the two went hand-in-hand. The Vicomte d'Arlincourt was mistaken in describing Regent's Park as 'the perfumed abode of the aristocracy'.[35] The inhabitants of the terraces never equalled the architecture in splendour: even at the start they represented, at best, the mercantile aristocracy. Social decay was evident as early as the 1840's. Thackeray in the *Book of Snobs* observed that 'the plaster is patching off the house walls . . .'[36] The *Builder* in 1849 referred to the neighbourhood around Park Square and Park Crescent as 'this region of stately drear, now languishing in the dinge and gloom of bygone importance . . .'[37] In 1870 the *Building News* reported that Nash's façades, 'with all the regulation whitewashing and colouring, have become dingy, and the statuary dilapidated . . .'[38] The terraces were 'quite outside the fashionable world'.[39]

Their very unfashionableness may, paradoxically, have preserved them more or less in their original appearance; for it was to the interest neither of the Crown estates nor of the tenants to invest in the physical alteration or the replacement of property of such moderate

4 'It quickly became the most important shopping street in the West End . . .' Regent Street, *c.* 1880.

value. Not, that is, until the 1950's, by which time public taste had altered sufficiently to produce a campaign vigorous enough to induce the Crown Commissioners to abandon their scheme for total demolition.[40]

Regent Street, by contrast, fell a victim to its own success.[41] It quickly became the most important shopping street in the West End, and the changing fashions of the retail trade induced the tenants as early as the 1830's to alter the shopfronts in ways out of keeping with the total architectural appearance of the street.[42] The growing scale of merchandizing and the varying needs of individual shops produced structural alterations that further destroyed its original coherence.[43]

The most dramatic early alteration was the removal of Nash's colonnades from the Quadrant in 1848. '. . . It was argued,' recalled the *Builder* a half century later, 'that it was a refuge for bad characters, and so the colonnade was destroyed, without, it is to be feared, the beneficial effect on public morals which was supposed to justify its destruction.'* Even at the time the *Builder* deplored the change: 'One of the most striking features of modern London has been cut off its face, and a great public injury committed . . .'[44] Less and less of Nash's original conception survived as the century progressed. The *Architect* commented in 1873:

> The melancholy fate of NASH's sky-lines in Regent Street, in spite of all that the control of the Crown itself could do as universal landlord, is sufficiently indicative of the invincible determination of the individual London tradesman to act for his own private interests and disregard altogether any mere considerations of combined appearance. His real motive, in fact, is rather a desire to disclaim his neighbour than to co-operate with him . . .[45]

For the most part such acts of aesthetic vandalism struck the Victorians as praiseworthy attacks on the despotism of an outmoded academic taste. Thus the *Building News* spoke favourably of a new shopfront at Howell and James's, drapers and mercers in Lower Regent Street, 'in which red brick and terra-cotta of a light salmon colour have been very tastefully combined', regretting only that more buildings had not similarly 'broken away from the Classical trammels'.[46]

One of the results of the Georgian revival at the end of the century was a tendency to look somewhat more leniently even on Regency design. The *Builder* in 1897 bemoaned 'the various "uglifications"' along the line of Regent Street, whereby 'the whole continuity of the great scheme of our grandfathers' day is ruined'. This was particularly true south of Oxford Circus:

> . . . All kinds of additions have been made to the houses; here a Mansard roof . . . next door a row of dormers, over the way a wretched iron-cresting, further on a whole new story has been added on to two houses, whereas the one between them is left in its original condition, suggesting a pleasant comparison to a mouth with a tooth knocked out. Where are poor Nash's Classical outlines?[47]

* B, LXXII (1897), p. 288. A correspondent of the *Building News* denied in 1858 that its destruction had 'purified Regent-street from the French harlots and foreign sharpers, except on rainy days, when there is no one to be annoyed.' BN, IV (1858), p. 906.

5 *below* '. . . the changing fashions of the retail trade induced the tenants . . . to alter the shopfronts in ways out of keeping with the total architectural appearance of the street.' 163–5, Regent Street, *c.* 1900.

6 *right* 'Less and less of Nash's original conception survived as the century progressed.' Piccadilly Circus, looking east down Coventry Street, before the destruction of its eastern side by Shaftesbury Avenue.

7 'The most dramatic early alteration was the
removal of Nash's colonnades from the Quadrant
in 1848.' The Quadrant, 1884.

Meanwhile the original 99-year leases were running out, and any attempt to use their expiration as an occasion for restoring the street to its original appearance – or even maintaining it as it was – would have been economic folly. Robert Kerr described the situation to the Royal Institute of British Architects in 1894:

> The little shops, once so ample, have had to take in not only the back parlours, but every inch of the back gardens; what had been kitchen-offices were now warehouse basements; and as for the residential accommodation above, not only had it been abandoned in that capacity, but a new tenant would give as much for the shop alone as for the entire house, so that the upper stories, with their miserable staircases, were either utilised for workrooms and storage, or let off contemptuously for what they would fetch. The shops, when enlarged to the utmost, were grouped together in twos and threes, adjoining houses in back streets were absorbed, and the cry was for more space. All this time the structural stability of the houses, never good, had been so tried by alterations, that public attention was now and then called to the appearance of danger; and as for sanitary questions, the less said the better. The failure of a street was a familiar phenomenon; but here was prosperity with a vengeance.[48]

Professor Kerr's account might almost serve to describe the experience of the Victorians with the whole of the London they inherited. However fondly we may look back on Georgian London, the Victorians who had actually to live in it found it cramped, inconvenient, and ugly. For the most part they had to put up with its functional and aesthetic inadequacies, but by degrees they were able to impose their own stamp on it. If in improving the sanitation and enlarging the premises they blurred its original qualities, whether of decorum or magnificence, coherence or elegance, it would be wrong to assume that they did not know what they were doing. The additions and alterations that the Victorians imposed on their metropolis constitute important evidence as to their conception of the good life, and how London could be made to support and enhance it.

CHAPTER THREE

The Rejection and Destruction of Georgian London

Commercial public works, of a magnitude unrivalled since the days of imperial Rome, if not since those of the proudest Egyptian dynasty, are educating our workmen, from the lowest to the highest, to a style of craftsmanship entirely unknown in this country at the commencement of the present century. Private wealth, under the stimulus already given to good taste, is replacing the dead walls and unmeaning windows of the Georgian style of street building, the poorest and least picturesque that was ever common in any civilised nation, by not altogether unsuccessful efforts to create a *Victorian* London.
Builder, XXVI (1868), p. 582

GEORGIAN CIVILIZATION AND URBAN VALUES

The Victorians rejected Georgian London just as they rejected the rest of eighteenth-century civilization. The alterations they made in its appearance – the new buildings they erected, the new streets they pushed through the existing fabric, the new structural types they evolved, the new specialized neighbourhoods they formed, the new styles in which they built – reflected their determination to make the metropolis express their own transformed values.

A building or a street, a neighbourhood or a town is unmistakably altered and modified by the extent to which, and the way in which it is loved. Georgian London was hated by most Victorians most of the time. Certain house plants, we are told, respond to human affection, and wither in its absence. Georgian London was too solid and sturdy to wither, but its spirit withdrew and slept, to be awakened by the kiss from the Prince in the shape of the late-Victorian eighteenth-century revival.

Late Georgian London, and what is imprecisely known as 'Regency' architecture were hated most of all. From the standpoint of the 1970's, the vehemence with which the Victorians attacked Regent Street seems excessive. Having grown up in the plastic age, and living in one in which shadows are, if anything, preferred to substance, we find it difficult to appreciate the moral objections to stucco facing. Having abandoned classical studies to a handful of specialists, we do not feel personally affronted by the inaccuracies of Nash's handling of Roman details. Whatever reservations the serious architectural critic still may have about the Regent's Park terraces, they strike the ordinary person as being among the most imaginative and exhilarating features of modern London. The peeling and flaking façades of the postwar years demonstrated the crucial role of fresh paint to maintain the illusion of grandeur, but they are painted and well maintained now, and contribute immensely to the delight of being in London.

But of course we do not see them, as Elmes did, as a promise of a new millenium, but merely as pretty aspects of the varied London townscape. Conversely they do not represent a threat, as they clearly did to the Victorians. We do not take them seriously enough to hate them; the Victorians took them very seriously indeed.

It was not just constructional dishonesty that the Victorians disliked in Nash's terraces, but also the conviction implicit in the project that cities in general and London in particular were worthy of pride and even worship. The Victorians rejected the idolatrous cult of the city. For them London was no longer the expression of national glory, to be embellished with concrete representations of national prosperity, power, and taste; but instead a shameful display of all the evils of the age. The minutes of evidence of the Royal Commission on the Health of Towns, the novels of Dickens, the revelations of Mayhew, the inescapable fact of the cholera epidemic of 1848, and the increasing stench of the Thames made earlier rhapsodies about the splendour and happiness of London look like wilful refusals to admit the existence of the evils of modern urban life. To devote one's efforts to providing London with triumphal ways and studied Neoclassical façades was to compound vice with hypocrisy, to perpetuate a falsehood, to deck the harlot with silks and jewels.

After 1830 'Metropolitan Improvements' ceased to mean schemes for beautifying London, but came to be limited to ones that dealt with specific evils – traffic congestion, insanitary dwellings, inefficient sewage disposal – in which aesthetic considerations would be secondary, if, indeed, they entered at all.[1] London became an object of concern, sometimes for systematic enquiry or fascinated examination, but rarely for pride or self-congratulation. At a time when every other aspect of national life strengthened the Englishman's sense of his superiority to less fortunate peoples, the failure of London to occupy the place in popular sentiment that Paris, Copenhagen, and Vienna did for their respective countries is significant.

Much of the literary evidence that the Victorians hated London means in fact that they hated the London that their Regency parents and eighteenth-century grandparents had bequeathed them; their rejection of London and, by extension, of urban values as a whole, can be understood as a rejection of their parents, yet another symptom of generational conflict.

What seem – even to the Victorian Society's most ardent members – to be the excesses of the Victorian planners and builders of London were in fact conscious efforts to create an environment that would be as unlike the one they had inherited from the despised eighteenth century and morally repellent Regency as they could contrive. If the Regency prized smooth stucco, the Victorians produced the roughest stone surfaces possible; if the Georgians preferred unobtrusive grey bricks, the Victorians produced the brightest red bricks they could manage; if the Georgians sought restrained, uniform, monochrome façades, the Victorians revelled in glazed, polychrome tiles; if the Georgians admired flat cornices topping their buildings, the Victorians sought jagged skylines; if the Georgians desired uniformity, the Victorians demanded variety; for symmetry they substituted assymetry; for regularity, irregularity; for the two-dimensional, the three-dimensional; for the unadorned, the 'enriched'; for the horizontal, the vertical; for the low, the tall . . . Nothing can have been more conscious and deliberate than the Victorian reaction against all that it thought the eighteenth century stood for.

The Victorian city displayed its rejection of and contempt for the Georgian city not merely in its architecture but in its total layout. It abandoned the pattern of terraces designed as total architectural compositions, of garden squares, of mews, for the looser form of detached and semi-detached villas; with curving, irregular streets replacing the older gridiron pattern. Its suburbs took the form of tongues of development – including ribbon development – sticking into open countryside or totally surrounded by green fields: suburban peninsulas or islands. Sometimes they were expansions of existing villages, other times they were completely new settlements, often centred on railway stations. Subsequent filling-in, particularly from the 1860's onward, has obliterated much of the novelty of such developments, with their striking confrontations of the natural by the artificial.

But try as they did to introduce statements of their own advanced taste into the older streets of central London and to create suburbs different in kind from their predecessors, Georgian and Regency London remained obstinately there. The continued, unmistakable physical presence of Georgian London is the most important feature of the Victorian metropolis, a ubiquitous reminder that once men had thought differently about cities, life, and beauty.

THE EXAMPLE OF PARIS

The makers of Victorian London were pursuing negative rather than positive goals: they had clearer notions of what they did not want London to be than what they did. Victorian London is best defined by what it was trying to avoid. Londoners had constantly before their eyes two symbols of what they did not want: Gower Street and Regent Street. Cheap and rapid rail travel provided the middle-class Londoner with the opportunity to inspect a third: contemporary Paris.

The Paris of the Second Empire could be seen as continuing the Georgian tradition of uniformity and classicism and the Regency pattern of urban display that London had abandoned. Nineteenth-century French literature – for all its cautious experiments with Romanticism and its attempts at 'Shakespearian' effects – remained firmly in the classical tradition, while contemporary English writers reacted sharply against their eighteenth-century predecessors. So Paris became the visual and formal embodiment of the Enlightenment a century after Voltaire.

If London rejected the model presented by the Paris of Napoleon III, it did so more reluctantly than it did the model of the London of George III and George IV. The vast alterations that Baron Haussmann was making in the French capital were achieving results too attractive to be summarily dismissed as 'un-English', and called forth a great deal of thoughtful comment and soul-searching. Paris, a city comparable in wealth, culture, and importance to London, was taking a course of development precisely opposite, and doing so with great apparent success. Critics of London architecture, the London leasehold system, the London building industry, and even London's system of government could cite Paris as everything London ought to be but wasn't.[2] If London lived vertically in houses, Paris lived horizontally in flats; if London dispersed itself in encircling suburbs, Paris concentrated itself within slowly expanding boundaries; if London classified itself into functionally and socially segregated neighbourhoods, Paris maintained a mixture of both classes and uses in its different quarters; if London built cheaply in brick and stucco, Paris built for the ages in stone; if London was chiefly leasehold, Paris was wholly freehold; if London was governed by a bewildering variety of local authorities, Paris lay under centralized imperial control; if London expressed its wealth and its aspirations towards beauty in streets of architecturally contrasting buildings, each proclaiming its individuality, Paris imposed, in its new streets, rigorous uniformity of design; if London experimented uneasily with the Gothic, Paris remained firmly classical.

At the beginning of the Victorian period what seemed most remarkable about Paris was its antiquity, permanence, and solidity. 'To build a house in Paris is a very serious thing,' observed the *Dublin Evening Post* in 1840:

> You go to the stone quarry . . . and not to the brick-field. You must employ oak instead of Canada pine. . . . for the private houses of the first class . . . you must proceed in Paris as you would in London or Dublin if you are about to design a public edifice. . . . Hence it is that, notwithstanding the vast number and beauty of the buildings made by Napoleon, and the great addition that has been made during the present improving reign, the *air* of Paris is that of an old city; while London looks . . . neither new nor old, a sort of *Provisional City*, a multitudinous congregation of houses, that are constantly . . . in a state of transition of being run up or run down . . . Houses are built, in London, to answer temporary purposes, or for the accommodation of two, or three, or four generations.[3]

London was then more spaciously laid out. 'Travellers to Paris so late as thirty or five and thirty years ago,' recalled William Haywood in 1861, 'will . . . remember it as a city of narrow irregular streets, closely packed, and mean houses and shops . . . With the exception of two or three new works – the Rue de Rivoli, the Pantheon, and a bridge or two – Paris of 1820 was almost identical with Paris of the time of Louis XIV.'[4] The ruthless demolitions and comprehensive rebuilding under Napoleon III completely transformed its outer appearance. The cosmetic nature of the improvements, whereby the new streets hid more than they replaced an older Paris, was not lost on English critics. 'Paris will soon be a network of boulevards lined with stone buildings, which will mask a group of narrow, dirty streets, and hide the objectionable dwellings of the poor,' observed the *Building News* drily in 1861.[5] But the new thoroughfares were undeniably impressive, and gave Paris – except for a few earlier monuments deemed worthy of isolation and emphasis – the appearance of a wholly new city. Poverty and antiquity alike were decently screened from view.

Few thought that London either could or ought to try to duplicate Paris. The call was less to imitate Paris in her means than to rival her in the achievement of urban splendour, using a more appropriately English and individualistic approach. The *Builder* in 1868 urged a programme of metropolitan embellishment on nationalistic grounds: 'The stately magnificence of a capital city is one of the elements of national *prestige*, and therefore of national power and influence,' it argued, in a partial return to the mood of the 1820's. 'The architectural beauty of Paris is not the least of the claims of the French nation to rank their capital as the metropolis of civilisation.' It asked that London follow her example and set about making its 'architectural aspect . . . worthy of the capital of the richest nation in the world . . .'[6]

London imitated Paris in its street improvements which, while narrower than the new thoroughfares in Paris and more varied in their architecture, were as destructive of what lay in their path. Even by the standards of Imperial Paris in what was to be its last year London did not feel hopelessly inferior. '. . . London is becoming quite as thoroughly transformed . . . as Paris . . .' boasted the *Building News*:

> Even now, to a spectator standing on either of the West End bridges, nearly all the more prominent structures which meet his eye are such as he may have seen in course of erection; . . . upon many of them individually, and certainly upon them collectively, is impressed a character of boldness not altogether unworthy of the age. If he seek for unity of style, he will indeed be woefully disappointed. At the same time there is an entire absence of that monotony which so painfully characterises the contemporary French works, which are perhaps more equally and academically correct.[7]

To the *Building News* in 1873, the rebuilding of London demonstrated the superiority of British pragmatic individualism and the picturesque over the tame classicism and conformity that state direction had imposed on Paris: 'No Imperial edict has decreed in our case the demolition of the city which existed in order to rebuild one of theoretical perfection, either political or architectural. . . . All that has been done here has been done by private enterprise and in a prudent spirit.' In London rebuilding was piecemeal and individualistic: 'each building is independent, and neither leans upon its neighbours for support as to architectural effect, nor contributes in any way to their support . . .' The rebuilt Paris had 'unity and comparative monotony . . . conducive to a certain general low standard of excellence, but wholly destructive of a higher grade of individual merit'. The writer preferred the London method: '. . . we . . . would rather stand the risk of being occasionally shocked, than lose the chance of being sometimes, though less frequently, charmed'.[8]

THE METROPOLITAN IMAGE

To mid-Victorian Londoners Paris stood for absolutism, uniformity, classicism, and centralization: the antithesis of what their own metropolis ought to be. Yet it would be wrong to suggest that London was wholly unaffected by the Parisian example, any more than it had entirely abandoned its earlier quest for magnificence. 'Foreign cities vie in presenting to our gaze palatial buildings . . .' remarked the *Builder* in 1881, 'and we . . . emulate them . . . "Haussmannising" has now come to be a word well understood in reference to the improvement of our cities.'[9]

'London is working out a monumental character in her streets,' declared the *Building News* in 1858, 'by isolated and unsystematic efforts, but slowly . . .'[10] The monumentality was not something that Napoleon III would have recognized as such. Those who called for a more magnificent London held a different conception of beauty, one that derived more from Blaise Hamlet and the Brighton Pavilion than from Regent Street, but that would in the final analysis have dismayed both Nash and George IV. Instead of grand uniform designs they demanded picturesque variety. Instead of refinement of form they longed for richness of material. Following Ruskin, they desired hard, durable materials that would be difficult to work but that would endure as monuments to Victorian taste and morality. What strikes us as wilfully ugly in their architecture was meant to be rugged and honest. An article in the *Builder* in 1864, which envisaged the London of 20 years hence, when the Strand and Fleet Street would be widened and their existing buildings replaced, revealed the new aspirations of the age:

> Thus will this great ancient artery . . . regain its former importance and dignity, and form a grand central thoroughfare consisting of a long avenue of important buildings, each realizing in a greater or less degree the interesting individuality of character . . . The dingy old monotonous brick is, indeed, already fast disappearing, to be replaced by hand-somer structures, not of the sham stucco, like Regent-street, but buildings of real stone, enriched with inlays or columns of polished granite, marble, or terra-cotta, and decorated with real sculpture of great artistic merit, and of suitable character, as to its symbols, foliated decorations, or statuary.[11]

It is all there: the concern for importance – meaning size and conspicuousness – the fascination with wide, impressive thoroughfares on the Parisian model, the hatred both of Georgian brick and Regency stucco, the love of hard, polished stone in contrasting colours and textures, the stress on the separate identity of each building, and the insistence that ornament have *meaning*.

Victorian criticisms of London fluctuate between complaints that it was not magnificent in the way that Paris was, and assertions that it was, in its own very different way, achieving something equally grand. 'What a wonderful place is this London of ours!' the *Builder* exclaimed in 1844:

> Its appetite of increase is insatiable – fields, villages, towns, disappear in rapid succession, as they are absorbed in the forest of houses. And yet it is not the size of London which excites the admiration and astonishment of foreigners; it is the ten thousand indications of wealth, afforded by the endless succession of private streets and squares, the splendour of the shops, the illuminations of a city which knows not darkness, the numerous con-trivances for obliterating time and space, for making money and spending it. . . . not Rome in the Augustan age, enriched by the pillage of all nations, could boast of a tithe of the riches, or moral wealth and spread of intelligence, so pre-eminently manifest in our own modern Babylon.[12]

'. . . Since London is . . . the largest of any city, it follows it should show an equally unexcelled array of public buildings,' F. Chambers, Jr., told the Architectural Association in April 1849: 'It is notoriously otherwise. Rome, Paris, Naples, very far exceed us even now, and how many of our noblest buildings date no farther back than the last ten or twenty years!'[13] As the century progressed the new Houses of Parliament, the complex of museums and institutions at South Kensington, and the government offices in Whitehall would somewhat answer the criticism; but for the most part what the Victorians liked to call 'architectural London' consisted of private rather than public buildings, individual structures rather than grand assemblages.

The Great Exhibition might be expected to be one occasion that would bring out expressions of unbounded pride in London, and the author of one anonymous guidebook does not disappoint:

London, 'Busy, Clamorous, Crowded, Imperial, London,' may be considered not merely as the capital of England, or of the British Empire, but as the metropolis of the civilised world – not merely as the seat of Government, which extends its connections and exercises its influence to the remotest point of the earth's surface – not merely as containing the wealth and the machinery by which the freedom and the slavery of nations are bought and sold – not merely as possessing a freedom of opinion, and a hardihood in the expression of that opinion, unknown to every other city – not merely in taking the lead in every informing science, and in every useful and embellishing art – but as being foremost, and without a rival, in every means of aggrandisement, and enjoyment of everything that can render life sweet and man happy. . . . It is alike the abode of intelligence and industry, the centre of trade and commerce, the resort of the learned and inquiring, the spot that has given birth to and where have flourished the greatest kings, statesmen, orators, divines, lawyers, warriors, poets, painters, and musicians; besides historians who have immortalised them. It is the refuge of the oppressed, the poor, and the neglected; the asylum of the unfortunate or the afflicted; and the abiding-place of him who wishes to advance his fortune, or further his progress in the arts, sciences, literature, or any pursuit that ennobles man and dignifies his nature. . . .

Indeed London is now not merely the largest city in the known world, but it exceeds in opulence, splendour, and luxury (perhaps in misery), all that ever was recorded of any city.[14]

Yet in the whole outburst there is not one reference to architectural beauty. Another contemporary panegyric, one worthy of Mr Podsnap, goes so far as to dismiss aesthetic considerations as unworthy of so great a city:

With what proud and exciting feelings . . . an Englishman ought to enter London after a prolonged absence in other countries! The public buildings are few, and for the most part, mean, – the monuments of antiquity, not comparable to those which the pettiest town in Italy can boast, – the palaces are sad rubbish! – the houses of our peers and princes are shabby and shapeless heaps of brick. But what of all this? The spirit of London is in her thoroughfares, – her population! What wealth – what cleanliness – what order – what animation! How majestic, yet how vivid is the life that runs through her myriad veins! How as the lamps blaze upon you at night, and street after street glides by your wheels, each so regular in its symmetry, so equal in its civilization, – how impressively do you feel, that you are in the metropolis of a *free people*, with healthful institutions, and exulting still in the undecayed energies of national youth and vigour.[15]

In later decades it became less necessary to affect indifference to questions of external appearance. A succession of metropolitan improvements cut great gashes through the existing fabric and provided sites for extended rows of new buildings: wholly Victorian streets, representing the spirit of the new age, undiluted by remnants of the older metropolis. By the eighties the Victorians could feel that they had made their stamp on London: that it was no longer the inheritance they were forced to inhabit for want of any other, but something they could call their own. The *Builder* paused in its usual scolding of London and her makers in 1881 to admit that it really had been and was being 'improved':

Day by day and year by year the rebuilding of London goes on apace; here one street and there another street presents new architectural features, and so it is in almost every direction that we turn; and London, if the truth be told, is fast becoming a handsome city. . . . we may sigh as improvement knocks down the old gabled shops and tenements, the quaint inns and galleried court-yards, the churches and the curious streets that were the existing records of the life of another century; still it would be ungracious to withhold praises from the general aspect of much of the London of to-day. Old buildings, large and handsome, secular and ecclesiastical land-marks . . . are swept away to make room for something more pretentious and more adaptable for the requirements of the present generation.

This was the period of the wholesale destruction of Wren's and others' City churches, now emptied of their former resident congregations and occupying land of immense sale value.

The church has to give way to commerce, vested interests in narrow streets are bought out, and wide thoroughfares flanked by new structures take their place. Limestone and plate-glass lend brilliancy to perspective, while here and there picturesque ruddy brick gives emphasis, and gives a much-wanted colour to the otherwise monotonous group.

The 'Queen Anne' style was by then very much in the ascendancy.

. . . Gradually we look upon new London, its parks, monuments, embankments, trees, public and private buildings, with some sort of pride. Such a result is satisfactory to those who believe that the comfort, the virtue, and the moral welfare of a great city are enhanced by the contemplation of order and elegance . . .[16]

The West End was being transformed as drastically as the City, with the creation of Northumberland Avenue, linking the Embankment with Trafalgar Square; Charing Cross Road, proceeding from there north to Oxford Street; and Shaftesbury Avenue, running from Holborn to Piccadilly, especially notable. 'The lines and backgrounds of our streets are changing rapidly . . .' observed the *Building News* in 1888. 'Old . . . landmarks have been changed . . . That once centre of fashion, Piccadilly-circus, is . . . scarcely recognisable. . . . Private owners have vied with each other in putting up costly fronts with elevations of imposing height . . .'[17]

Perhaps the most remarkable quality about the new London was the increasing height of buildings. 'Year after year the London houses are assuming a more important appearance, – a circumstance which may be readily proved by an examination of a few of the streets . . . built thirty or forty years ago,' boasted the *Builder* in 1857. 'The warehouses in the City, the banks and other offices, are in many instances towering above their former height . . . Our public structures are in like manner increasing in substance and extent . . .'[18] Deadened as our sensibilities are by the still more monstrous erections of our own time, it is hard to recapture the sense of awe and wonder that the new office buildings, blocks of flats, and hotels evoked when they first appeared, towering above their Georgian neighbours. Their greater height was likely to be emphasized by vertical features in their design, and by soaring towers and spires, or at least by an arresting roof-line.

'The roofs of London are rising with portentous celerity,' exclaimed the *Builder* in 1871. No longer did London houses seem low by comparison with those in Paris, as rising land-values and the fashion for higher ceilings pushed new buildings ever upward:

City houses which, when first built, were considered almost too lofty and too aristocratic in their air for the abodes of business, – such as the buildings in Moorgate-street [*c.* 1840], for example, – are now looked down upon as but little removed from 'poking'. A lofty office is felt to be a requisite for a man who would be thought to drive a first-class business. . . . Health is greatly promoted by the increased size, especially by the increased height, of rooms.

New tall buildings dominated the view from any hill in or around London. Notable among these were the Langham and Grosvenor hotels, 'rearing great castellated structures to an unusual height'. Pennethorne's Public Record Office (1851–66) 'displayed a very picturesque outline'. The new Houses of Parliament, with the clock and Victoria towers, and 'the spires and pinnacles that adorn the same noble pile, cast the twin towers of the Abbey into shade, and have done more to improve the architectural *ensemble* of London, when viewed from a distance, than it was possible to anticipate'. The new train sheds at Charing Cross and Cannon Streets, although 'frightful mistakes . . . lose much of their shapeless deformity in a distant view'. The Albert Hall and other buildings in South Kensington also exemplified 'the tendency of the present rebuilders of London to mount . . .'[19] The *Builder* was still exulting in 1876:

. . . Whenever we see new buildings going on in London, we find floor rising above floor. We have not yet arrived at the stage of rearing that multitude of towers which characterised the Mediaeval cities of Italy, but we are certainly tending that way. . . . Spires and towers of churches no longer rise in solitary beauty towards heaven. Their most aspiring companion . . . is the great hotel at the Victoria Station, which shows a lofty castellated outline almost recalling . . . that of the old palace of the Popes at Avignon.[20]

8 *below* '"City houses which, when first built, were considered almost too lofty and too aristocratic in their air for the abodes of business, – such as the buildings in Moorgate-street [*c.* 1840], for example – are now looked down upon as but little removed from 'poking'."' Moorgate Street, 1895/6.

9 *right* 'The new train sheds at Charing Cross and Cannon Streets, although "frightful mistakes . . . lose much of their shapeless deformity in a distant view".' Cannon Street Station, 1866.

10 *right, below* '". . . the great hotel at the Victoria Station, which shows a lofty castellated outline almost recalling . . . that of the old palace of the Popes at Avignon."' Grosvenor Hotel, *c.* 1865/6.

The end of the century brought doubts as to the desirability of London growing taller and taller. The 14 storeys of Queen Anne's Mansions (1876–88) produced by-laws setting maximum heights, but the average height of new buildings nevertheless increased. 'On returning to London after many years' absence, the most striking feature is undoubtedly the enormously increased height of the buildings,' the *Builder* observed in 1881; '. . . in this respect the old feeling of the comparatively meagre look of our own city after a return from the Continent no longer exists.'[21] By the nineties, the American skyscraper came to seem a frightening portent:

> Look at New York, with its teeming population and gigantic tenement houses and hotels, or Philadelphia, or Minneapolis, vying with one another in the erection of lofty buildings. . . . The same mania has seized London builders and promoters of gigantic hotels and residential flats . . . can promoters expect people to dwell in 10th and 13th stories at the peril of their lives under flaming gas jets?[22]

'The big-building mania which has been so long popular in the United States seems at last to have found its way into this country,' wrote the *Building News* in 1896:

> The large 'office buildings' of New York and Chicago have been introduced into our City and West-end streets – happily restricted as to height, but colossal in other dimensions. Monster hotels are not yet 'played out.' . . . in London . . . in the same street may be seen . . . the old remaining houses which appear diminutive and low, and the new buildings of often double their height. . . . Take, as an example, the houses facing the Strand and the monster buildings of the new Cecil Hotel, or go down Surrey or Arundel street and notice the sudden jump-up of the roof or skyline from the old to the new buildings. . . . if this kind of increase goes on, a future generation, when it comes to look on the few old streets and houses remaining, might believe the 18th-century citizens were a race of Liliputians . . .[23]

If late Victorian London could evoke no more than qualified enthusiasm from cultivated observers, the fault may lie as much in their altered expectations as in its own inadequacies. The classical revival of the nineties was making it harder for architects and critics to appreciate the very unclassical merits of contemporary London. They now saw as blemishes what were its greatest virtues: its variety and diversity both in outer appearance and inner nature.

VARIETY, ORIGINALITY AND CONTRAST

Nineteenth-century Europe was characterized by increasing diversity, enabling a larger proportion of society and a greater number of minorities to find verbal, aesthetic, and material expression. Cultural nationalism, romantic individualism, and the proliferation of styles as against the earlier dominance of a single standard of taste must be set against other forces promoting standardization and uniformity. The city by its very nature encourages diversity, just as the village imposes conformity. (Cultural patterns may vary widely from village to village, but within any village the possibilities open to an individual are more severely constricted than in any town.)

Just as the Enlightenment stressed what men had in common – their humanity, their rationality, their perception of universal laws of conduct, standards of judgment, and rules of taste – so post-Romantic thought stressed the distinctiveness of things: people, nations, buildings, historical periods, styles, the hours of the day, the fragments of life. The tendency towards subdivision and specialization further emphasized the distinctiveness of one man from another, one building from another, one human activity from another. Demographic and economic growth resulted in a sufficient abundance of people and things to permit unprecedented differentiation of skills, objects, and styles. The architecture of individual buildings and the structure and appearance of the whole of London both expressed and promoted variety, originality, and contrast.

Victorian London denied the values of its Georgian past and rejected the practices of its Parisian contemporaries most dramatically in its pursuit of aesthetic individualism. 'Like government and legislation, the tendency of modern architecture is towards what has been called the disintegrating policy, that of promoting individual interests at the cost of the State,' explained the *Building News* in 1889; 'the idea of Unity and State control permeated municipal architecture – a *regime* we find carried to an excess in Paris and many German cities. The assertion of the individual in the rebuilding of our streets is apparent to all who notice what has been done of late years.'[24] However diverse London became, the cry was always for even greater variety. This was partly because of the extent and persistence of an older Georgian uniformity, partly the result of the insatiable appetite of the Victorians for novelty.

The revolt was not merely one against classicism, but against the domination of any orthodox aesthetic. As early as 1834 a correspondent of the *Architectural Magazine* who proposed that controls be imposed to insure uniformity of elevation in new streets in London, citing the New Town of Edinburgh as an example, was rebuked by the editor for his reactionary views. He feared that 'restraining the taste of individuals' would produce monotony; the New Town he thought 'one of the tamest congregations of buildings in Europe', making Edinburgh almost 'as dull as Berlin . . .'.[25]

Economic individualism encouraged visual diversity. Private investment did far more to embellish London than governmental patronage or public policy. 'Its proudest edifices are the results of individual enterprise, unaided by the government,' boasted the *Builder* in 1845; 'for though the latter affects rivalry, it cannot hope to surpass the numerous monuments of individual enterprise with which this great metropolis is adorned: its docks, bridges, canals, the colleges and hospitals, theatres, clubs, palaces, picture-galleries, breweries, distilleries, and other public works.'[26] The juxtaposition of examples was what contemporaries found particularly remarkable about London. For while the great capitals of the continent, and some of the lesser ones, could boast of the benefits of royal patronage in the form of triumphal ways, grand public buildings, and vast open spaces, London was unsurpassed in its expressions of private wealth. Even in the 1820's the 'Marquis de Vermont', after agreeing with Canova that Waterloo Bridge was worth the trip from Rome to see, expressed surprise that that 'stupendous work', like the London and West India Docks and the new network of canals, 'were all the unprotected efforts of private speculators'. So, too, he found, were the new Drury Lane and Covent Garden theatres, and the houses in Regent Street and around Regent's Park. The spectacle exemplified 'the mighty powers of accumulated capital, of capital created by industry and trade, under the guardian banners of law and liberty', and, of course, 'the happy effects of your admirable constitution . . .'[27]

The Regency buildings that the Marquis admired were functionally diverse but shared a common stylistic dress. The new Victorian aesthetic sought variety as an end in itself: in form, colour, texture, size, and in intellectual and emotional content. Visual contrasts were valued not only as between adjacent buildings but within any given building and upon any given façade. Ornament, which later puritanical critics have regarded as at best a forgiveable aberration, was central to their notion of architectural beauty. Abundance of detail and prodigality of incident are as characteristic of St Pancras Station as of *Bleak House*. The identity and separateness of every building from every other, and every subordinate part of every building were jealously preserved and vehemently emphasized. The portico to stress the doorness of the door, the heavy dressing to show the windowness of the window, the scalloped gable to express the roofness of the roof were structural assertions of the absolute value of the individual. The freedom of each architect, each householder to express himself as he saw fit had moral and political as well as aesthetic significance. The façade was to represent the special creative vision of its designer, just as the house represented the independence and identity of the family it contained.

Such an approach has often been mistaken for anarchy, just as Victorian individualism has been caricatured as a pretext for the powerful to exploit the weak. In fact, just as the power of the state expanded along with the growth of individual liberty in nineteenth-century Britain, so did architectural controls – imposed by the architects themselves – multiply to keep the new visual liberty from producing chaos. Jack Hexter has pointed out that the sixteenth century saw the intensity of *both* secular and religious life increase: the one need not and did not expand at the expense of the other. Just so the rule of law and the power of political institutions manifestly strengthened during the Victorian period at the same time that the real freedom of the individual to pursue his own life increased. The dismantling of the older, only partially effective mercantilistic and paternalistic powers of the state was more than counterbalanced by new social and sanitary legislation and, most important of all, by the establishment of effective machinery for enforcement. But to point out the inadequacy of an older view of Victorian England as ever having been a *laissez-faire* society does nothing to deny the importance in it of individual initiative and vigorous competition. State controls *had* to expand to cope with the simultaneous expansion of individual and corporate activity.

Similarly the increased ornamental content of Victorian architecture required stronger formal and structural devices to keep it under control. And if the architect often failed, if in many buildings the whole is less than the sum of the parts, the magnitude of the challenge is in no way diminished. For an age that is finally discovering that, with rare exceptions, less really is less, even the vices of an architecture that gloried in excess are appealing.

With new building materials, natural and artificial, and the possibility of transporting others from all parts of the world, the potentialities for novel decorative effects were multiplied. Widening opportunities of cheap foreign travel, the developing science of architectural history, and the dissemination of architectural knowledge through new, specialized periodicals increased the possibilities for stylistic variation.

Much of the appeal of distant and exotic forms has been stigmatized as escapism. The *Building News* in 1895 accounted for the fascination of the architecture of distant periods and places as a psychological counterpart to the urge for holiday travel:

> . . . It is not merely in a physical sense that our age wants to get away from itself; it is still more the case in art, and especially in architecture. The great Romantic reaction, which began a century ago and is not over yet, has only been a convulsive attempt of the modern world to escape from its modernness. . . .
>
> When a man of business makes a fortune in the City . . . he commonly builds himself a house, and though he wants all modern conveniences in it for practical use, he seldom wishes it to appear as modern. . . . he is a 19th-century man who wishes he had belonged to the 18th, or 17th, or 16th century. He cannot get there, but he loves to have suggestions of the olden time constantly round him. He is like an Englishman in the Tropics, who has been known to grow buttercups and daisies under almost inconceivable difficulties, not because they are fairer than Tropical flowers, but because daisies and buttercups remind him of the home where he would be.[28]

For William Morris 'the historical sense . . . may be said to be a special gift of the nineteenth century, and a kind of compensation for the ugliness which surrounds our lives at present . . .'[29] It gave, among other things, a new dimension of pleasure to the contemplation of buildings of other centuries. And the discovery that the architecture of any period embodied its total culture meant that a building could set in train thoughts and feelings far richer than its formal qualities alone could ever have evoked.

There were, to be sure, frequent complaints that too great a knowledge of other styles inhibited originality. '. . . Our intimate acquaintance at the present day with examples of all styles, has no small share in hindering us from working out one that would be decidedly our own,' argued the *Building News* in 1858.[30] Yet no return to primal innocence was possible. And the rewards were considerable: for giving up the possibility of a genuinely original style, the Victorians gained the freedom to move with pleasure and assurance among all styles that human ingenuity had ever devised. Aesthetically the Victorian became not merely a citizen of the world but a citizen of all times past.

London, thought the *Architect* in 1869, 'if the architect were allowed to work by no rules but those of his own art . . . would become, in a few years, one of the most imposing capitals of Europe'.[31] The structures that were then going up, particularly in the City, were in fact varied, assertive, and individualistic. 'Substantial and handsome buildings adorn many a City lane or narrow street,' T. Chatfeild Clarke told the Architectural Association in 1877. '. . . Each edifice presents as much unlikeness to its neighbours as possible . . .'[32] Walter Emden, in his presidential address to the Society of Architects in 1899, argued that one of the causes of London's beauty was 'the fact that the architect being free, and not hampered by the necessity of erecting great boulevards of similar elevation, produces buildings which, from the broken appearance they give when grouped together, produce a pleasing and picturesque effect . . . far more . . . than a more regular style could be'.[33]

Sir George Laurence Gomme gloried in the diversity of the London scene in 1898:

A ride on the top of an omnibus through any of the great routes . . . reveals to those who have the feeling for the picturesque beauties in London streets which are wholly local in character. The variety of architecture, the change of scene from shops brilliantly fitted up and at night brilliantly lighted, to private houses bright with flowers, and very often bright with the lights of some festive gathering, then to patches of green which mark a square-garden, or the grounds of an old-fashioned house still preserved in the midst of newer surroundings . . . combine to make up the peculiar charm of London scenery.[34]

Whether praised for its picturesque variety or condemned for its aesthetic anarchy, London impressed all critics by its stylistic mixtures and juxtapositions. 'Architecturally, London may be said to represent chaos itself,' Percy Hunter told the Architectural Association in 1885:

The law and order which we boast of in our civil life is absolutely wanting in the architecture of our metropolis. There is nothing expressive about it, except that of intense selfishness and utter disregard of subordination to general convenience; a reign of anarchy where every man does what is right in his own eyes, and what is wrong in the eyes of all his neighbours. . . . There is an incongruous diversity in the architectural fronts resulting from an anomalous collection of different styles; there is irregularity of outline without picturesque effect . . .[35]

It was only towards the end of the century that the quantity of Victorian buildings was great enough for their diversity to alarm. Architectural periodicals understandably concentrated on reporting the appearance of new buildings rather than confirming the persistence of old ones. But it is well to remember that 'the buildings of the Georgian age survived in enormous bulk and in full use, to the extent that little of Georgian London was actually destroyed before the eighties.'[36] Only by bearing that fact in mind can we visualize the new Victorian buildings, intruding into what contemporaries regarded as a desert of Georgian brick. Today we see surviving examples of Victorian architecture surrounded mostly by other buildings of Victorian date or later. They were not, ordinarily, designed to be seen in such a context, nor were they when new. The Gothic revival church or office block, the Queen Anne block of mansion flats, the Italianate club-house, the red-brick public baths that to later generations seem so grim, so wilfully ugly, when new struck the observer, cultivated and Philistine alike, as a welcome relief from the surrounding ubiquity of Georgian brick or Regency stucco. Similarly the suburban villa often, in its early days, stood alone in the green fields, or at least stood with a handful of its fellows as one of a few suburban intruders in a basically rural environment.

Many in America can recall the delight with which they greeted the first few examples of functionalist architecture, how happily they contrasted with the ubiquitous *beaux arts* buildings of the central cities or the mock-Tudor or Cape Cod of the suburbs. Yet gradually delight turned to dismay as the functional became the universal style. The Lever Building on Park Avenue still elicits a favourable aesthetic response, but how much less now than it did when it was not yet surrounded by vulgar imitations! So at first did Victorian architect-designed buildings charm by novelty and contrast. Set against a background of drab Georgian brick they seemed neither over-decorated nor over-emphatic, their splashes of strident colours, their varied and rough-textured exteriors, their irregular sky-lines made sense when they were individual exclamations of exuberance set in a background of restraint and understatement. To the Victorians Georgian architecture was not so much understated as mute.

The rise of the architectural profession, hostile to the old, self-trained speculative builder, meant that the architect, in order to justify himself and his fees to a sceptical public, had to produce something recognizably different from the non-professional builder. Hence the emphasis on the overstated, the individual, the idiosyncratic, on originality at all costs.

New styles were welcomed for their novelty as much as for their intrinsic merits. The *Building News* in 1883 saw Queen Anne less as a possible new universal style than as a means of lending needed variety to the streets of London:

> In passing through the Strand, Fleet-street, Cheapside, or any of the streets in which new buildings have taken the place of the old ones, we shall find almost every style has been tried, to introduce a little diversity, or as a 'set-off' to others. . . . of late years, the revival of 'Queen Anne' has given architects a new faith in red-brick and coloured fronts. . . . much may be done to render the brick front presentable, and to avoid the monotony of the flat window-pierced wall, if the architect could be prevailed upon to . . . use moulded terra-cotta or concrete as dressings.[37]

The idea came to be expressed that the style ought to be chosen less with regard to the surroundings of the building than to the use to which it was to be put. The *Building News* defended the erection of the Royal Courts of Justice Chambers in a Renaissance style directly across the Strand from the new Gothic Law Courts:

> . . . The new chambers are designed in bold antagonism to the great structure opposite . . . Nothing could have been a greater contrast in style. On one side we have the most severe type of Gothic of which London can boast, and on the other a building of French Renaissance of rather florid features. Yet there is something appropriate in the selection of styles for two buildings of rather opposite uses. In one, the administration of the laws demanded a building of rather stern, if not sullen features; in the other, the more animated convivialities of a festive board enjoined a lighter style.[38]

The argument here is not that form ought to follow function, but rather a recognition of the symbolic and psychological uses of architecture. More than that, the passage expresses the heady pleasure that Londoners were experiencing from the sharp, even brutal visual contrasts that their streets now provided. The subtle variations on a common theme that delighted the Georgian pedestrian had long since ceased to satisfy the heartier and more exotic appetites of the Victorian connoisseur, for whom an architectural façade was more

11 'So at first did Victorian architect-designed buildings charm by novelty and contrast. Set against a background of drab Georgian brick they seemed neither over-decorated nor over-emphatic . . .' British and Irish Magnetic Telegraph Company offices, Threadneedle Street, 1859.

than an arrangement of light and shade: at best, an evocation of a past civilization, a distant culture, a state of mind, a set of principles, or a fundamental human emotion.

After such highly-spiced and varied dishes as the thoroughfares of central London, the ordinary residential street was as bland and soothing as a blancmange. The contrast between the uniform, Italianate stucco of respectable suburbia and the prodigy buildings of the City reflected the contrasting intensities of thought and activity of the two: '. . . that which is denied to town houses is often freely permitted, nay, is desired, in public buildings and in places of business, and accordingly in the heart of our great commercial cities structures full of individuality are beginning to spring up in all the great thoroughfares . . .'[39] For the adult male at least, *both* architectural environments would ordinarily be experienced daily, as he moved from home to office or club and back again:

> In passing from the crowded streets and lanes of the City to the western suburbs a remarkable contrast is to be found, indicating . . . different social habits. It is the contrast of busy competition, life, and energy, with the calm of relaxation and repose. Architecturally the aspects of Cheapside or the Strand present a significant antagonism to the aristocratic localities of Belgravia and Mayfair. They manifest, indeed, a strange difference in style and sentiment – the streets and traffic of the one being heterogeneous, multiform, and cosmopolitan, while those of the other are homogeneous and destitute of all variety; an almost sickening similarity reigns, and the architectural alliteration and repetition of features are so perfect that to become a denizen of the neighbourhood would be to lose one's individuality and almost identity of abode.[40]

In fact the inevitable mobility of the middle-class Londoner kept his individuality from being submerged in the uniformity of suburbia or over-stimulated by the variety of the City.

History and accidental survivals gave the Strand its dramatic qualities. Northumberland Avenue, created all at once, delighted contemporary critics by providing a comparable collection of visual contrasts:

> . . . What we now see in the buildings of Northumberland Avenue is a striking example of true English indiscipline in . . . its best form. The edifices are large, costly, and stately, but no adventitious aid to effect is sought for in the adoption of the partnership principle. Each building is a separate composition, and . . . the appearance of grandeur, instead of being lessened, is much enhanced. Dragooning is notably and positively absent. Independent individualism reigns. Spontaneity is the spirit of the whole. The many works are not in any way one, but in every way many . . .[41]

Georgian London was becoming Victorian London not by frontal assault but by infiltration and subversion. 'In whatever direction we now turn our eyes . . . we see vast changes have taken place within the last few years,' the *Building News* reported in 1873; 'and old London, that is the London of our youth, is becoming obliterated by another city which seems rising up through it, as mushrooms do in a sward.'[42] The new buildings differed from their predecessors in size as well as in style. They made their early Victorian and Georgian neighbours look tiny and insignificant by comparison. 'The older buildings in our streets are rapidly falling out of proportion by the erection of these lofty structures,' complained the *Building News* in 1891:

> . . . We have to submit to the inevitable craze for monster hotels and residential chambers, such as those which now overpower the few small and quiet-looking houses in Arundel-street, Surrey-street, and Cecil-street. Here we find the old brick fronts of four stories not reaching more than half way up the adjoining warehouse or hotel, appearing, in fact, crushed. One of the ground stories of these large structures extends to the third story window of the house adjoining. [43]

The disproportion in height and the sharp discontinuities of style that had seemed so piquant in the seventies shocked the more classically-minded critics of the nineties. It was not simply the rediscovery of the eighteenth century that was by then taking place, but that follies lose their attraction when they are multiplied and placed side by side. The massive Renaissance blocks of Edwardian Kingsway and the postwar reconstruction of Regent Street that today seem so ponderous and dull, represented a belated attempt to reimpose order and coherence on the streets of an otherwise anarchic London.

THE BATTLE OF THE STYLES

'If a stranger were to ask himself what style the architects of London were working in, he would be sorely puzzled for an answer,' the *Building News* remarked in 1875. 'His attention would be divided pretty equally between Gothic, Classic, Italianesque, and Nondescript attempts.' [44] The historian is even more puzzled. Despite frequent calls for a genuinely *Victorian* architecture that would be as universally employed as the styles of any earlier period, and despite the multitude of candidates for what was to be the new vernacular, the Battle of the Styles was still in progress in 1901.

'During the last forty years there have been many experiments in architecture and many fallacies propounded, and our streets and buildings bear witness to them,' the *Building News* decided in 1900, with the air of a reformed rake:

> Every new style that has been introduced has been an experiment, and we can now look back to certain buildings with a sense of amazement as well as relief that we could ever have tolerated such a stupid departure from our normal modes of construction for the sake of a few faddists in a particular style, or have permitted our streets to be disfigured by buildings that have no redeeming quality in them.

The end of the Victorian period, like the beginning, accepted more-or-less classical or Renaissance as the aesthetic norm. And while it was still putting up red-brick and terracotta structures like Claridge's, the Russell, the (old) Imperial, and the Great Central Hotels, the sombre monumentality of Norman Shaw's Piccadilly Hotel seemed to represent the path that twentieth-century architecture was going to take. It felt it had some cause to look back on the stylistic experiments of the mid and late Victorians with detached amusement:

> Nearly every part of London records incongruities of style, mainly in some extreme phase

12 '"The older buildings in our streets are rapidly falling out of proportion by the erection of these lofty structures."' Discontinuities of style, material, and scale at Piccadilly Circus. The Criterion Restaurant and Theatre between Georgian brick and Regency stucco.

of Late Gothic or Modern Renaissance. Here we had an Elizabethan almshouse, or hospital; there a Venetian Gothic restaurant or warehouse, or some Chinese vagary. A few of these incongruities still exist, and we look upon them as curiosities.[45]

BEAUTY AND EXPRESSION

'The greatest change, perhaps, that has passed over English architecture within the last dozen years is this,' observed the *Building News* in 1881: 'that it has given up, in great part, the search for beauty, and has entered, instead, on a search for expression.'[46] In attempting to account for the weakening of both the Gothic Revival and the highly modified Renaissance of the earlier Victorian period in favour of the 'ugly' but potentially more expressive variants of sixteenth and seventeenth-century models, the writer may have stated a far more generally applicable explanation of what happened to architecture in Victorian England. For Nicholas Taylor, it is precisely the earlier styles that the 'Queen Anne' superseded that were characterized by '. . . bold, even brutal . . . expressiveness . . . *l'architecture parlante* . . . the architecture of rhetoric . . . built into bricks and mortar . . . rich, glowing materials encrusted with symbolic statuary as a permanent harangue to the public'.[47] All architecture has something to say, but the Victorians wanted their buildings to say more and say it louder.

The rhetoric of architecture is inevitably harder to grasp than that of poetry or painting, and whatever ability one generation may have to understand and respond to its message may be lost completely by the next. Such linguistic discontinuities do not merely cut our age off from the Victorian, but separate and make mutually incomprehensible the architecture of one Victorian generation – and sometimes one Victorian school – from another. If it is possible today to perceive an underlying unity in an ostensibly disparate array of stylistic productions, it is only in the unspoken assumptions that underlay them, not in their external shape, form, or texture. If the language differed radically, the 'messages' the buildings delivered were often remarkably similar.

'In the Early Victorian period the British upper middle classes were working out for themselves a set of new architectural symbols,' Henry-Russell Hitchcock tells us, suggestively.[48] That art had a moral function was axiomatic. What particular morals it ought to represent and how it might best go about doing so were matters of controversy, but a building or a picture or a statue that simply existed in formal perfection without meaningful content was regarded as a failure. Taking for granted that a building ought to set in train certain ideas and feelings, they debated what those ideas and feelings ought to be, and how to express them architecturally.

One negative feature common to all architectural thinking and most architectural practice throughout the Victorian period was the inability or refusal to 'read' what Georgian buildings were trying to say. The standard 'plain brick walls with holes in them' were regarded as having no architecture whatsoever and consequently no meaning. The monumental Regency compositions, on the other hand, had a great deal to say, but what they said were lies. By pretending that stucco was stone, by pretending that a row of private houses was a single vast palace, by their improper use of classical decorative motifs, they published falsehoods and encouraged dishonesty.

13 '. . . the rediscovery of the eighteenth
century that was by then taking place . . .'
54, Mount Street, Grosvenor estate, *c.* 1897.

Yet despite the universal condemnation of architectural critics, increasingly coarse versions of stucco Regency terraces remained the norm for new high-class residential districts – Belgravia and Pimlico, Brompton and Kensington, Tyburnia and Bayswater – into the seventies; when first white brick and then red-brick 'Queen Anne' superseded them. New churches in these neighbourhoods would, from 1837 on, invariably be Gothic, but apart from an occasional eccentricity, what Sir Osbert Lancaster has called 'Kensington Italianate' reigned throughout the fashionable western suburbs. Detached and semi-detached versions of the same style mingled with a few examples of the picturesque *cottage orné* in the villa suburbs to the north and south.

The City showed greater architectural variety, and more use of stone, but apart from a few attempts to adapt the Gothic to commercial ends, 'remained predominantly Renaissance in inspiration', Nicholas Taylor assures us. 'The Renaissance symbolized efficiency, clarity, economy, civic administration, and secular probity – the "confidence" which in a quiet way was the basis of London's mercantile pre-eminence.'[49] The Renaissance *Palazzo*, especially as interpreted by Barry in the Reform and Travellers' Clubs, proved well adapted to commercial purposes, 'one of the prime Early Victorian stylistic symbols of functional expression . . .' according to Henry-Russell Hitchcock.[50] The *Builder* in 1846 regarded the Travellers', Junior University, and Reform Clubs as 'forming an epoch in modern practice . . . The necessity of studying and understanding something more than the orders had, even before that late date, not been completely felt . . .' As a result, 'windows and cornices received their appropriate decoration, proportion was more regarded, and ornament employed with a less sparing hand'.[51]

Contemporary critics, with varying degrees of caution, saw progress and aesthetic advance in the façades of the new streets and in the new buildings going up. Whatever lapses of taste they displayed, they were preferable to the drabness and insipidity of an earlier London that encompassed them. The *Building News* in 1857 was convinced that London's architecture was '"looking up." . . . whereas formerly no attention was paid to external appearance, except in the case of public edifices, regard is now had to . . . "politeness" in building . . . The taste . . . may sometimes be very questionable; nevertheless it is, upon the whole, indicative of advance in the right direction.' The 'partial alterations' of existing streets, 'as far as they go . . . manifest a decided improvement, not only as regards style, but general architectural expression, and better execution likewise.' Although there was 'more of variety and freedom . . . in the treatment of detail than used to be . . .' architects did not strike out on their own with sufficient audacity: '. . . we get more of imitation than of invention – of clever copyism than of artistic originality . . .' There was greater innovation in constructional technique than in style. There was less use of deceitful stucco: 'What in Nash's time would have been mere plaster, and of the most slipslop quality as to taste and design, is now not infrequently of genuine Portland stone, if not for the entire structure, for all its dressings and decorative details.'[52] But even better executed, more decorative, and more expressive architecture that remained within the classical tradition failed to satisfy the more serious aspirations of the age.

The prospect of the City and the principal thoroughfares of the West End being rebuilt

14 'The *Builder* in 1846 regarded the Travellers'
Junior University, and Reform Clubs as
"forming an epoch in modern practice . . .".'
Travellers' Club, *c.* 1900.

in the style, however modified, of the Renaissance did not please the increasing number of architects who were demanding the picturesque. 'There is something so oppressive to the imagination,' wrote James Edmeston in 1862, 'if one pictures sites like these as being rebuilt in the studied, carefully cut up, divided, and subdivided styles of Italian architecture, as practised in this day, that one would almost rather they remained as now, with little or nothing to boast of architecturally, as a whole . . .'[53] By 1868, though, variety had triumphed over uniformity, and the *Building News* found, 'in the City, buildings worthy of notice . . . at almost every step. There is the graceful Grecian style, the palatial Palladian, and the gimcrack Gothic. . . . the student may be fitted with his favourite style of architecture anywhere between St. Paul's and the Aldgate pump . . .'[54]

RED BRICK AND TERRACOTTA

One distinguishing feature of Victorian architectural thought was its preoccupation with the question of the appropriateness of different building materials. In earlier periods the question had rarely arisen: one built with local stone if it was to be had, or local brick if brick earth existed nearby; if one had the money, stone might be imported for more pretentious building. The invention in the latter years of the eighteenth century of different varieties of artificial or imitation stone, and in particular the development of stucco made it possible to cover the local material used in construction with a more attractive or impressive outer coating. Cheap transportation by canal and rail gave a greater choice of material both for structural purposes and for superficial ornament.

Modern architectural historians stress the structural innovations of the Victorians, particularly their use of iron in building, as prefiguring twentieth-century developments in engineering and architecture.[55] The Victorians, too, debated the appropriateness and morality of new constructional materials and techniques, and were rarely as happy about the increased use of glass as later critics have been. But they were even more preoccupied with the question of architectural surfaces, and in particular with which were best suited for the smoke and fog of London.

The Victorians found the weather at least as fascinating a subject as we do; perhaps, as a result of their passion for ventilation and the widely-accepted airborne theory of disease, even more so: certainly their discussions of the relative merits of the climates of South Kensington and St John's Wood, and of the different quality of the winds in Croydon and Denmark Hill show a remarkable sensitivity to minor variations. They never forgot that London had a predominantly damp, overcast climate, and that the smoke from its coal fires dimmed the sun, darkened and corroded everything it touched, and contributed to frequent, yellow, impenetrable fogs.

To Henry James, 'the smoke and fog and the weather in general, the strangely undefined hour of the day and season of the year, the emanations of industries and the reflection of furnaces, the red gleams and blurs that may or may not be of sunset . . .' gave London much of its peculiar fascination. '. . . The atmosphere, with its magnificent mystifications, which flatters and superfuses, makes everything brown, rich, dim, vague, magnifies distances and minimises details, confirms the inference of vastness by suggesting that, as the great city makes everything, it makes its own system of weather and its own optical laws.'[56]

Such a special kind of atmosphere required a special kind of architecture. Much of what seems to us harshness of outline, overstatement of detail, and brutality of surface in Victorian buildings stems from the determination of their designers to make them both withstand and be visible in a dark, sulphurous atmosphere which is today no more than an unhappy memory. With clean-air legislation and the systematic washing of façades, we see the buildings of the past as their contemporaries never did, or did only on an occasional bright day when they were very new.

Regency architecture was meant to be seen in brilliant sunshine. One of the rhetorical tricks employed by Elmes in his lyrical descriptions of Regent's Park in *Metropolitan Improvements* is his repeated references to the play of sunlight on the buildings and their surroundings. Regent's Park in the 1820's was comfortably away from the smoke of central London and it probably did enjoy a comparatively clear atmosphere, but even then it cannot have enjoyed constant summer sunshine. By later decades, when it was hemmed in on all sides by smoking chimneys, even repeated painting could not keep it looking fresh and attractive. In general painted stucco seemed better suited to the ambiguous moral tone and transparent atmosphere of Brighton than to earnest, foggy London.

Real stone, while morally unexceptionable, proved equally susceptible to the darkening, corrosive chemicals in the London air. The reaction that began in the seventies away from stucco in domestic buildings, and stone in commercial and public buildings, in favour of red brick and terracotta was not entirely a matter of the whims of fashion, but represented in part an attempt to create building surfaces that would both withstand and look good in the London atmosphere. The *Building News* discussed in 1881 what was happening to building stones in London:

> . . . Stone has never been employed with any amount of success in London; all our stone buildings have been more or less failures. The smoky atmosphere has done its best to clothe our most costly buildings in a thin drapery of soot, or has accelerated the work of natural decay; they soon become dark and sombre masses, their architectural beauty and details become less and less distinguishable, and people pass them with a scant acknowledgment of their architectural pretensions. . . . how many architectural masterpieces in the City . . . are ever looked at? – the chief reason being that their stone façades have assumed such a sombre monotony of grey or black that all play of light and shade is lost.

Even recent buildings in stone – the new hotel at Holborn Viaduct Station, new façades in Snow Hill, Cheapside, and Queen Victoria Street, and along the Embankment – were showing discolouration. The St Stephen's Club, the War and Foreign Office, the Grand Hotel in Northumberland Avenue, had all 'lost their freshness'. The new Law Courts in the Strand were 'putting on a grey tint of carbon . . .'[57] Brick might physically resist corrosion more successfully, but found it at least as hard to make an architectural statement through the filmy grime.

Two solutions were tried: glazed, washable bricks that would retain their original colour and freshness indefinitely; and deep red brick façades that would absorb and blend with, while withstanding the chemicals in the atmosphere. The former was frequently suggested and put into practice less often, usually with startling results. 'If we could build our façades with glazed materials, face them with stone-wear, or coloured tiles, much of the deposit of smoke and dust might be avoided,' admitted the *Building News* in 1878, 'but the glare would be intolerable . . .'[58] The latter seemed the more satisfactory approach and contributed to the general triumph by the eighties of 'Queen Anne' in its various forms. 'To judge from a few instances of recent taste . . . the stately stone front, with its colourless Classic details, has been set aside for the rival claims of a less dignified but more picturesque modification of a vernacular brick style,' the *Building News* reported in 1881.[59]

The seventies saw the end of serious attempts to establish Gothic as a new universal style, although it continued to be almost universally employed for churches. 'Pure Gothicism was the presiding taste a few years ago,' pronounced the *Building News* in 1875, 'but it certainly is not paramount at present.'[60] The completion of the Law Courts in the Strand in 1882 was seen more as the culmination of a Gothic revival that was coming to an end than as a harbinger of future development. The *Building News* regarded their formal opening as 'an event of itself sufficient to make 1882 an epoch in the architectural history of the century . . . In no other building . . . has so vigorous and austere a form of Gothic architecture been carried out in its integrity, and if the last, it will probably remain the boldest and most uncompromising work of the Gothic revival we possess.'[61]

The eighties saw the triumph of red brick; the nineties were the decade of terracotta. It was by 1888 already transforming the appearance of Oxford Street, until recently 'bald . . . ugly, and . . . mean', according to the *Daily News:*

> At the rate at which improvements have been effected there during the last two or three years, Oxford Street will certainly become, in another twelve or fifteen, one of the most handsome of European streets.

It saw a parallel with the suburban Queen Anne style of Bedford Park, Pont Street, and Cadogan Square; and thought that the new buildings in Oxford Street could 'foreshadow the rise of a new kind of architecture . . .'[62]

The *Building News* celebrated the triumph of red brick and Queen Anne as a reflection of individualism and liberalism:

> The public . . . have gained in variety what they have lost in formality. Red brick, once abhorred, has its day of retribution . . . the proportion of solid to void, once a matter of rule . . . is ignored altogether . . . regular features and horizontal lines which produced a stately breadth in our public squares and streets during the Hanoverian era, are no longer allowed to interfere with private rights and the individual fancies of builders.[63]

The same journal in 1891 found terracotta 'superseding not only the softer kinds of stone for exterior work, but in some instances iron and marble . . .' and cited among other buildings the Natural History Museum, Butterfield's St Paul's Schools in Hammersmith, the new Royal English Opera (now the Palace Theatre) in Cambridge Circus, and the Cafe Monico. It denied that terracotta was 'a sham . . . like cement or stucco . . .' and urged its use in

15 '"At the rate at which improvements have been effected there during the last two or three years, Oxford Street will certainly become, in another twelve or fifteen, one of the most handsome of European streets."' Oxford Street.

preference to stone which, however 'truthful', was liable to 'rapid decay in the acid-laden atmospheres of our large cities . . .'[64]

Not only was the mixture of styles in the same street viewed complacently, but the mixture of materials in the same façade called forth praise. The *Architect* thought that combinations of stone, terracotta, and brick were 'more effective, sometimes particularly in regard to general harmony of colour, than the use of only one material'. In predicting that English architecture would 'gravitate towards . . . the vernacular, emerge from the foreign influences, and develop into something of an Elizabethan character', the writer reflected the increasingly assertive nationalism of the period, and recognized its aesthetic affinities with another that prized invention over judgment, richness over restraint, and took delight in mixing shades, textures, and colours that more sober periods would have thought incompatible.[65]

The passion for cleaning façades has in recent years restored more and more late Victorian house fronts to their original rich hues, and on one of the rare days when the low-lying winter sun emerges to light them, it is possible to recapture some of the affectionate delight with which they were viewed when new. Red brick, the *Building News* announced in 1895, 'has almost entirely taken the place of stone, not as being cheaper . . . but as being more decorative and capable of greater artistic effect'. Along with terracotta it dominated new commercial and residential building alike: in Oxford Street, the Strand, and the City as well as in Sloane Street, Cadogan Square, and Knightsbridge.[66]

'We are passing through a crisis of change and reconstruction,' wrote the *Building News* in 1894. 'Demolition and rebuilding are in the air.' It was struck by the variety of styles in the new buildings:

> The English Metropolis is . . . the gathering place of all nations, and, therefore, the various styles of the world have had here their fair opportunities for either development or decay. . . .
>
> It would be difficult to say which of these several varieties of European architecture have taken the firmest root. . . . Flemish appears to have contested very strongly with our vernacular styles, such as our English Renaissance of the 17th century. Late Gothic and French Renaissance have also reasserted themselves . . . The choice seems to lie between English and foreign Renaissance, and . . . the Italian element is less strong in it than it was a few years ago. . . . We have a marked reappearance of Late Gothic and Early Renaissance forms . . .

From a later perspective perhaps the most remarkable aspect of the nineties was the appearance of many buildings – and not just those designed by Voysey – that succeeded in recapturing the spirit of high Georgian architecture. The *Building News* bowed in their direction by refering to 'an English version of Roman or Palladian which has been largely used of late . . . which generally passes under the name of "Georgian", and which was practised in the 18th century'.[67]

By now the eighteenth century as a whole, not merely a romanticized vision of an age of Queen Anne that looked back into an equally fuzzy seventeenth century, exercised a positive appeal to modern sensibilities. 'Old 18th-century associations have thrown a sort of spell or charm over the flat brick-gauged arch . . .' the *Building News* observed in 1900. 'In the neighbourhood round Kensington Gardens-court, Cadogan-square, and other western suburbs, where the "Queen Anne" style flourishes, there the "gauged brick" revival abounds . . .'[68] By the end of the century Queen Anne herself might have viewed without a gasp some of the buildings put up in her name.

It is a commonplace that the reaction to Victorianism began long before the death of the Queen. It is too easy to assume that it took the form of rejecting nineteenth-century values in favour of twentieth-century ones – sexual permissiveness, equality for women, social justice, an increasingly omnipotent state; and in the Arts a rejection of representation, ornament, and didacticism; a retreat from reason and a fascination with force and action – too easy because the anti-Victorian late Victorians could not know (however much they might hope) what the new century was to bring. What seemed at the time to characterize that reaction was a revival of the values and attitudes of the eighteenth century. Just as Victorianism can be defined as a conscious rejection of whatever Georgian England stood for, so anti-Victorianism frequently took the form of a rediscovery and re-evaluation of Georgian civilization.

Neoclassical principles of street-planning re-emerged in the nineties, along with the revival of interest in Georgian architecture and culture as a whole. Unfortunately this was just when the builders themselves had at long last taken to heart decades of pleas from critics that they emancipate themselves from the old pattern books. In 1896 the *Builder* was once more suggesting that under certain circumstances a street be 'regarded as an architectural whole, and the separate building-owners compelled to keep their fronts subordinate to a general design . . .' Nash's Quadrant and his Regent's Park terraces were accorded praise for their general conception, if not for their details.[69] 'Let us just walk through that handsome line of thoroughfare with which London was adorned in our grandfathers' days,' it wrote of Regent Street. 'Now we say advisedly that no greater improvement was ever effected in this city . . .'[70] Such a change in sentiment was insufficient to save Nash's masterpiece from the vandals of the twentieth century, yet it suggests that a few Londoners were beginning to perceive their good fortune in living in a still reasonably intact Georgian city.

One practical result of the change in attitude was the beginning of organized efforts to preserve from destruction, or at least record the remaining architectural monuments of eighteenth-century – as well as earlier – London. The Georgian revival, the stirrings of preservationism, and the growing conviction of the desirability of architectural controls to impose visual order were portents that indicated the direction advanced opinion was taking in the nineties. But cities and their builders in the nature of things lag behind advanced architectural thinking: with rare exceptions, the new buildings going up at the close of the century were as varied, as fragmented, and as subdivided as the skill of the designer could make them. Six decades of architectural experiment and stylistic innovation had at last succeeded in making Georgian London Victorian. Just as Georgian London had been rejected as soon as it was completed, so Victorian London at its most perfect state seemed to contemporaries an object of shame rather than of pride.

The *Building News* did admit in 1898 that the long-condemned monotony of Georgian London had been broken:

> Our streets and squares proclaim a variety of resource in design. That now worn-out platitude which distinguished our dull architecture as that of 'Gower or Baker Streets' only serves to indicate the advances we have made in the design and building of our houses and shops. We can no longer complain of their dulness or gloomy character. Wherever we go we find the once dominating dingy brick front, with its neat pointing and gauged flat arches, is gradually disappearing, or its solid complacency, so characteristic of the 18th-century English character, broken through by the stirring activities of commercial competition. Everywhere we find a restless desire to introduce something new, occasionally very excrescent and erratic; not only a variety of material, but a diversity of feature.

The whole range of historical and national styles was now available to the architect:

> Foreign importation has not been without its influence in this reaction from dull monotony. . . . the Strand and Oxford-street. . . . are full of experiments in the way of bay-windowed fronts, arcaded and recessed loggias, features borrowed from foreign lands, visions of cities like Bruges, or Ghent, or Amsterdam, or Venice, pleasing breaks in the monotonous line of shop-fronts, though some of them strangely exotic to English usage.

Economic individualism and free competition both stimulated and provided a model for visual confrontations between deliberately contrasting shapes, colours, and textures: 'Then we have the rivalries of competing trades; effusive displays of metal-work, lead-glazing, mahogany, and electric light – all bewildering manifestations of the aggressive attitude of industrial progress . . .' Subdivision and fragmentation operated even in shop-windows: 'There is a decided attempt to retrieve the vulgar obtrusiveness of plate glass by making the framework more ornamental, by dividing the glass into smaller panes, by shaping them ornamentally. A further attempt is to recess the window or make it bay-like, so as to introduce outside recesses or lobbies.'[71]

'. . . We very seldom pass a new building now which does not obtrude itself upon our notice by a display of ornament, by an affectation of style, or peculiarity more or less pronounced,' complained the *Building News* in 1893. Such qualities were 'rampant and vulgarly obtrusive' in Oxford Street, Charing Cross Road, Shaftesbury Avenue, Rosebery Avenue, and even Northumberland Avenue:

> Showiness is one of the elements; elaboration of detail, amounting to a crowded effect upon the eye, startling contrasts of materials – generally bright red brick with dazzling white stone dressings – producing a very spotty effect when one gets near, are present. The façade must be flashy; it need not be in accordance with any architectural canons of taste or of style, much less be correct in its proportions and details, all which things are looked on as puristical and flat.

The new exuberance characterized both domestic and commercial architecture:

> We see it in the jerry-builder's house, the smart front with its bayed windows and lintels, and doorway carved in inferior stone, its stained-glass panels, and tesselated tile lobbies. We notice it also in the modern shop, with its bizarre front of plate and stained glass; the imitation Queen Anne gables and parapets of commercial buildings, hotels, and blocks of residences and offices . . .[72]

Though purists and advanced critics might disapprove, Victorian London was coming into its own.

SPECIALIZED BUILDINGS

'Since the end of the eighteenth century London has undergone a marvellous change,' wrote Charles Eyre Pascoe in 1888:

> . . . This monster London is really a new city. . . . new as to its life, its streets, and the social condition of the millions who dwell in them, whose very manners, habits, occupations, and even amusements have undergone as complete change within the past half-century as the great city itself . . .[73]

The increasing stylistic and structural differentiation of Victorian London was accompanied by an equally remarkable degree of functional differentiation. The London labour force had always been characterized by extreme specialization and subdivision into particular skills, both within and without the traditional regulated crafts. Charles Booth showed how complex and intricate were the operations of both the manufacturing and service industries at the end of the century, and how little affected by the standardization and simplification of tasks associated with the Industrial Revolution. In the middle of the century Mayhew had shown how varied and ingenious were the efforts of those at the bottom of the labour scale to maintain themselves by providing specialized services. Whatever the agonies and frustrations involved in surviving the challenges posed by Victorian London, the struggle for existence favoured a complex pattern of individual adaptations: extreme degrees of variation were the result.

The architectural response was equally varied and resourceful. Not only did the external appearance of buildings strive to announce their separateness and their purpose, and to make as many additional statements – moral, intellectual, and emotional – as they could; but their structure and internal arrangements reflected the ever-increasing specialization, subdivision, and urge towards complexity of Victorian life and civilization. Such tendencies frequently went beyond a rational response to economic and practical demands and became ends in themselves. Most of the specialized architectural forms performing new urban functions had parallels in other cities at home and abroad, but again and again London either invented, or more often carried to extremes of brilliance or absurdity or idiosyncracy building types or building plans originated elsewhere. Notable among such new or transformed types were the railway station, the office block, the hotel, the block of flats, the restaurant, the theatre, the gin palace, and the department store.

London came to resemble a nest of Chinese boxes, each containing a smaller, if distorted, version of itself; or perhaps a physical representation of the correspondences, macrocosm and microcosms of Tillyard's *Elizabethan World Picture*. There had always been the complementary but partly duplicating division between City and Westminster; now Westminster's division into independent villages became a common observation; the outward growth of the metropolis engulfed and transformed but rarely destroyed many more pre-existing villages and created others. Each village or neighbourhood contained within it buildings or institutions that operated in turn as small-scale versions of the larger city, much as the modern ocean liner became a miniature city: mimicking, and often parodying the activities, rituals, and operations, as well as the social structure of the greater world.

THE SPECIALIZED NEIGHBOURHOOD

The most important specialized neighbourhood, or rather cluster of such, was the City itself. Beginning in the seventeenth century, first its aristocratic and later its more prosperous commercial residents moved either to the new streets and squares of the West End or to suburban villages like Hackney or Hampstead. The rising value of City land and consequent soaring rents by the nineteenth century were forcing its poorer inhabitants to do likewise, leaving the City free to concentrate on mercantile functions. '. . . The City of London . . . is becoming more and more the *office* of the world,' explained the *Builder* in 1868. 'Stately buildings replace the ugly and cramped houses of the Georgian era, and these buildings are almost entirely parcelled out in offices. The City lives out of town.'[74]

With a sizeable proportion of its buildings dating from the late seventeenth century, and an essentially mediaeval street pattern, the City in 1837 was ill-equipped for its new function as the financial centre of the world. The dramatic rise in land values made extensive programmes of rebuilding both desirable and feasible. The City Corporation was wealthy enough to engage in ambitious schemes, creating new streets and widening old ones, while private investment adorned both new streets and old with structures remarkable for their size, expense, and appearance. 'The City of London is being rebuilt, and the causes for such rebuilding are clear,' T. Chatfeild Clarke told the Architectural Association in 1877:

> . . . Not only have the houses existing been found unfit by their arrangements for the wants of commercial life as now carried on, but the mode in which the space has been covered is inconsistent with the economical use of valuable areas . . .
>
> Looking back over a space of a quarter of a century or thereabouts, what a difference do we find in the City of London! Improved streets, new thoroughfares – such as Cannon and Queen Victoria Streets – formed; new and extensive markets; gigantic railway stations with hotel accommodation; new City Halls; enormous stacks of offices and warehouses taking the place of many an open and almost unused garden or yard; and a Viaduct formed to span Farringdon Street with all its approaches; making a series of works, independently of new bridges, which would do credit to any city in the world.[75]

The West End, always sharply differentiated from the City, became a second focus of business, and lost its exclusively residential character. London, the *Architect* pointed out in

1873, had two 'perfectly dissimilar' centres: '. . . there has . . . been created, in the shape of the great "West-End", not merely a vast expanse of residential town, but a field of special west-end business, wholly distinct, and indeed different from that of the City . . .'[76] The development of fashionable residential quarters north and south of Hyde Park, not to speak of more distant villa-suburbs, together with the increasing demands of retail trade and the service industries, had already transformed many parts of the older West End into business quarters. Externally most of the area still looked residential, but in fact the gentleman's private residence was becoming confined to narrower and narrower boundaries. The *Architect* and the *Builder* in 1876 both published a map showing in black 'those portions which are so laid out and composed as not to be available for high-class occupation', and in cross-hatching those that were:

> . . . The residential part forms but a fraction of the whole, and . . . there is . . . likelihood of the black encroaching still further on the grey . . . The clubs, the joint-stock banks, the hotels, the private lodging-houses, and the professional chambers, are gradually, but surely, ousting peers, both spiritual and temporal, millionaires, and others . . . Shops and lodging-houses are creeping up to the very portals of Grosvenor and Berkeley Squares. Mayfair is already shaken by more than one unwelcome intrusion. . . . the Portland and Bedford estates have been long besieged upon their eastern sides with a pertinacity of mischance which has left many of their symmetrical streets in the 'parlous' condition of lodgings, and the upper part of this house to be let.[77]

The transformation of the older residential portions of the West End was more a matter of putting existing houses to different uses, with or without structural adaptations. Shop-fronts along the Strand, Regent Street, and Oxford Street reflected shifting fashions in retailing; but in the quieter streets behind them architectural changes – which ordinarily took place, if at all, at the expiration and renewal of leases – involved at the most the addition of a bedroom storey, the plastering over of a brick façade, or the installation of plate-glass windows. The streets on the spaciously-planned eighteenth-century estates were more than wide enough for the needs of traffic, and the street-improvement projects of the Metropolitan Board of Works rarely penetrated such districts. Down to the end of the century on the Bedford, Portland, and Portman estates, and down to the eighties on the Grosvenor estate, the reflective pedestrian could feel that, if time had not stood still, it was at least moving very slowly.

By the nineties it was clear that the days of Mayfair and St James's as residential districts were numbered. Already hotels and the better class of lodging houses had invaded some of the streets, while other streets where private town houses still predominated were ripe for intensive redevelopment. 'The great piles of offices and residential blocks erected at Kensington, Knightsbridge, and other parts of the West End are threatening to destroy the private houses in their neighbourhood by raising rents and creating a desire to rebuild to greater height,' predicted the *Building News* in 1899:

> If we take the neighbourhood bounded by Piccadilly on the north to King-street and St.

James'-square on the south, the Green Park and Regent-street on the west and east respectively, we shall find several large blocks of buildings, in progress or already finished, of this class. . . . In a few years we may see other old houses in St. James's-square rebuilt as many-storied blocks, and the quiet air and aristocratic appearance of the old square will gradually disappear. . . . We can imagine the effect of a few 'skyscrapers' in squares like those of St. James's, Berkeley, and Grosvenor. We have monster hotels already near some of them, and this cosmopolitan taste in building is gradually extending amongst us by the yearly arrivals of wealthy American families. . . . Sudden jumps in the skylines of all our main thoroughfares are ominous of what we are to expect . . .[78]

Prophecies ordinarily turn out to be laughably wide of the mark, but here we have the twentieth-century fate of the West End succinctly foretold.

THE CLUB

The first issue of the *Civil Engineer and Architect's Journal*, which appeared in 1837, pointed out the number of new kinds of buildings that the age had invented:

. . . We must allow that architectural talent has a much more extensive field opened to it than formerly, since our Club-houses, Literary Institutions, Insurance Offices, and other buildings of that description, constitute almost entirely new classes of public edifices . . . 'Arcades,' as they are termed, and Bazaars, form likewise another new feature in the London of the nineteenth century . . .[79]

The first-mentioned example, the special building to house the club, was already a prominent feature of the London architectural scene, just as the club itself was occupying a growing role in the social, political, and intellectual life of the metropolis. The *Builder* commented in 1844 on the novelty of the special club-house:

Prior to 1800, we had no building of any magnitude in the form of a club-house . . . In the new order of things . . . clubs are no longer associations of good fellows, but associations of men united according to caste, political or other feeling, and governed by certain rules and regulations. The first and most important object of all . . . is to unite the economy of a chop-house with the superior accommodation of a first-rate hotel . . .[80]

'The development of the West End Social Club has been a very remarkable sign of the times during the last fifty years,' remarked Sir Walter Besant at the end of the century. '. . . It marks . . . an ever-increasing desire for separation and exclusion.'[81] The club not only provided London – particularly the neighbourhood of St James's – with some of its most impressive architecture, but discouraged the development of hotels, cafés, and restaurants by anticipating their services so well and so cheaply for the leisured and professional classes. '. . . The improvement and multiplication of Clubs is the grand feature of metropolitan progress,' wrote A. Hayward in 1853:

There are between twenty and thirty of these admirable establishments, at which a man of moderate habits can dine more comfortably for three or four shillings (including half a

16 'By the end of the century, Queen Anne herself might have viewed without a gasp some of the buildings put up in her name.' 170, Queen's Gate, R. Norman Shaw, 1888.

17 *below* '"... the improvement and multiplication of Clubs is the grand feature of metropolitan progress ...."' Clubs in Pall Mall; from right to left: Carlton, Reform, Travellers', Athenaeum. T.S. Boys, 1842.

pint of wine) than he could have dined for four or five times that amount at the coffee-houses and hotels, which were the habitual resort of the bachelor class in the corresponding rank of life during the first quarter of the century.[82]

The club also served as a model for such later specialized institutions as did develop, by providing within its walls a varied and seemingly self-sufficient world of pleasure in miniature.

In plan and in architecture the club-house had a venerable model – the palace – and so did not constitute a completely unprecedented building type. Far otherwise was the railway station, of all the new building types probably the most original, and certainly the one most fraught with drama and emotion.

THE RAILWAY STATION

It used to be said that one could live a completely useful and satisfying life never leaving New York's Grand Central Station or the buildings reached from it by direct underground passageway: today the complex of tunnels that serve as an extension of Montreal's Central Station would be a more attractive example. It would be cruel to subject anyone to a life confined to one of London's termini, either in the Victorian period or today, even if one included the customary associated hotel; yet they did offer far more services and pleasures than simply enabling people to get on and off trains.

The railway terminus was not just a way of supplementing any deficiencies central London might have by adding to it the residential capabilities of the suburb, the recreational possibilities of the seaside, and the economic resources of the whole of the national hinterland; but an inescapable architectural presence in itself. Carroll Meeks found it the most useful approach to an understanding of nineteenth-century architecture because it forced designers to cope with wholly unprecedented demands, with no earlier models to turn to for guidance.[83] The Victorians themselves were vividly conscious of the architectural significance of the railway station, and of the degree to which the great metropolitan termini were transforming both the face and the nature of London. 'As our whole railway system is essentially a characteristic of nineteenth century life, and one which has had no precedent or foreshadow in any previous age of the world,' wrote the *Architect* in 1873, 'so the constructive and artistic work which it has called into existence must be regarded as forming an area unique in the history of science and art.'[84] The *Building News* two years later placed the railway station at the very centre of contemporary architecture:

Railway termini and hotels are to the nineteenth what monasteries and cathedrals were to the thirteenth century. They are truly the only real representative kind of building we possess. Our churches, scholastic establishments, and domestic structures are more or less copies of mediaeval buildings. If we want to see our representative buildings we must turn to our railway stations, our banks, and our warehouses.[85]

Competition among the different railway companies and the disinclination of the government to permit the erection of what would have had to be an immense single central station gave London more termini than any other city in the world. The late thirties produced the Doric 'Arch' and the forties Philip Hardwick's elegant Great Hall behind it at Euston, the destruction of both of which ranks high even among the architectural crimes of the 1960's. Most Victorians would have seen both go without a murmur. For the *Architect* in 1873 the 'stone portico of Brobdignagian proportions' was 'not an entrance at all, but a huge mass of useless masonry fit neither for pedestrian nor vehicle'. The hall was 'another display of grandiose style, and lavish, if not utterly wasteful expenditure', and seemed 'more fitted for the performance of an oratorio on a gigantic scale than as the receptacle for the box and portmanteau items of personal luggage, or for the wanderings of bewildered travellers . . .'[86]

The *Building News* was equally contemptuous of other early attempts to meet the challenge of the Railway Age:

> The kind of termini and stations erected, when first the railway system was introduced . . . is an example of our thorough inability to meet the requirements of a new class of structure. Engineers blundered, though persistently following up the new problem. Now brick and stone and timber roofs – now light iron cobweb-looking erections, became the starting point of that great network of arteries which soon covered the land. Here and there an architect's hand was apparent. Greek temples of the prostyle order, or Italian palazzi-looking buildings, became the most glaring anachronisms of the period . . . beyond which huge sheds of timber or iron spanned the metals.

It singled out Lewis Cubitt's King's Cross (1851–2) as 'one of the first and noteworthy attempts to break through this tasteless travesty . . .' It praised both its originality and 'the massive boldness of its front, and the noble span of its circular timber ribs. . . . A glance at the boldly-arched façade is enough to convince anyone of its purpose – it is expressive, if not beautiful.'[87] The fifties also saw Brunel's vast new trainshed at Paddington.

The other early termini – London Bridge, Bishopsgate, Fenchurch Street, and the original Waterloo – had less that was astonishing. It was the sixties that saw the greatest surge of construction, producing, one after the other, Broad Street, Cannon Street, Holborn Viaduct, Charing Cross, Victoria, and St Pancras; with only Liverpool Street to come in the seventies, St Paul's (today's Blackfriars) in the eighties, and diminutive Marylebone in the nineties. The alterations they and their approaching lines and bridges made to the appearance of the metropolis called forth grudging admiration for the engineering skill involved, but dismay at the aesthetic results. 'The most careless observer of the streets of London cannot fail to be struck with the great changes of outline which the prospect has everywhere undergone within the last three or four years,' reported the *Building News* in 1866. 'These changes are mainly due to the new railway termini and the gigantic hotels connected with them. North, south, east, and west, the eye lights on some enormous pile, whose roofs and turrets rise sharply above the skyline of its humbler neighbours.' The huge trainshed, today the most admired feature of the surviving Victorian stations, elicited the severest criticism:

> It was not enough that the Paddington Terminus was elegant as well as commodious; it was not noticed that Waterloo answered its purpose without marring the prospect; that

18 *below* 'For the *Architect* in 1873 the "stone portico of Brobdignagian proportions" was "not an entrance at all, but a huge mass of useless masonry fit neither for pedestrian nor vehicle".' The Great Arch at Euston Station, 1890's.

19 *right* '"... more fitted for the performance of an oratorio on a gigantic scale than ... for the wanderings of bewildered travellers ..."' The Great Hall, Euston Station, 1849. Philip Charles Hardwick.

London Bridge Station, though repeatedly altered, had accommodated its traffic without emulating the pyramid of Cheops or the Tower of Babel. All these examples, proving that on strictly utilitarian grounds these enormous roofs are not required, have been ignored; the result is seen at the Charing Cross and Cannon-street Termini.[88]

Ruskin had led the way in attacking the presumption of the railways in daring to introduce ornamental features into their stations. The London termini strike architectural critics today as admirably functional expressions of their various purposes, but when new seemed designed only to irritate the aesthetic sensibilities of their users. The *Building News* surveyed them all in 1868. It found Paddington the 'most elegant' of the stations. Victoria was 'the most comfortless . . . certainly . . . intended only for temporary use . . . A goods shed, a barn, or a brickfield are scarcely subject for architectural criticism.' Charing Cross was 'very long, very wide, very high, and very hideous'. Waterloo had 'no pretension to elegance or ornament, but it accommodates its traffic, is well ventilated, and does not offend the eye . . .' The exterior of London Bridge 'does not display any architectural talent, though it betrays some considerable effort'. The effect of the interior was 'certainly bad . . .' That of Broad Street, by contrast, displayed 'extreme lightness . . . The exterior is superior to that of any other London station, and exhibits considerable taste.'[89]

The new railway stations, bridges, cuttings, viaducts, goods yards, locomotive shops, with all their associated machinery, stationary and moving, added immensely to the richness of texture of the townscape, contributing wonder and beauty to the metropolis. Yet to most critics railway architecture and engineering debased London, with the viaduct carrying the London, Chatham and Dover across Ludgate Circus, blocking the view of St Paul's, best exemplifying the brutalizing presence of the railway on the metropolitan scene.[90]

The *Building News*, while attacking particular railway stations, never wavered in its conviction of their importance as a general architectural phenomenon. 'Railway-station architecture is constantly making spasmodic efforts to force itself upon public notice,' it observed in 1875:

One monster station or hotel after another has risen in the metropolis, each vieing, it would seem, to eclipse the others either in point of size or in architectural pretensions. Every style has been tried to captivate and draw the attention of the travelling public, from Egyptian and Greek to Gothic. Architects and engineers have combined to produce structures worthy of this age of commerce and locomotive travelling, in which their respective arts shall have the fullest scope. . . . Our metropolitan termini have been the leaders of the art-spirit of our times, however loath we may be to admit it, and despite our declaring them to be the works of engineers without artistic merit except of the lowest order.

It found the newer stations – the Gothic St Pancras and Liverpool Street as well as the Italianate Paddington, Victoria, Charing Cross, Cannon Street, and Ludgate Hill – worthy of as much admiration as blame:

Their external scale and design are appropriate, but they all lack unity of parts and

20 *top* '"... The exterior is superior to that of any other London station, and exhibits considerable taste."' Broad Street Station, 1868.

21 *above* '"... Charing-cross Hotel becomes a mere palatial mask to the vast shed behind it ..."' Charing Cross Station and Hotel, 1864.

thoroughness. Thus Charing-cross Hotel becomes a mere palatial mask to the vast shed behind it, and Cannon-street and the other stations are similar combinations of structural design. There is a glaring discord directly we pass through the hotel and booking-offices.

Even Sir Gilbert Scott's St Pancras, 'a remarkable application of Gothic of an Italian type to the wants of railway structures', while 'the first vigorous attempt to blend the style of the building with the station proper', failed to solve the problem: '. . . We have two essentially separable architectural portions – the hotel and the station – the one a mask to the other.' The still-uncompleted Liverpool Street – today threatened with redevelopment – called for the most extended discussion:

> Here we have Gothic of a severer type than at St. Pancras – Continental in feature. It is plainer and simpler in its treatment than its great rival . . . Architecturally, there is an expressiveness about the long, broken façade, with its dormered and broken roof, its square, slate-roofed tower, and its regular windows, that bespeaks somewhat of its purpose, though we might have mistaken it, but for its approaches and surroundings, for a college or an asylum. It is, at any rate, a station designed in the last approved mediaeval fashion, and stations must follow suit as well as other buildings.[91]

By the late 1870's the railway geography of London had achieved substantially its present form, with St Paul's and Marylebone the only completely new termini to come. Liverpool Street would be extended in the nineties, and the two stations at Victoria would be rebuilt, while the makeshift accumulations at Waterloo would be replaced by the present terminus in the twentieth century. Charing Cross and Cannon Street would both lose their hated trainsheds, the first by unexpectedly collapsing in 1905, the second more deliberately in 1956. Euston was wholly rebuilt in connection with the mainline electrification of the 1960's. Yet any traveller from the 1870's would, with occasional surprises, be able to find his way about most of the major London stations today.

Once he had boarded a standardized Inter-City express, the increasingly uniform environment that British Rail has worked to impose on the railway network would insensibly take over, but in the termini themselves it is still possible to perceive some of the individuality of each pre-Grouping company. No longer do the different sources of coal impart a distinctive smell to the stations of each company, but enough remains to recall the day when each system was a self-contained universe, with its London terminus the proudest monument to its wealth, power, and extent. The 14 major termini (counting Victoria as one, and excluding through stations like Ludgate Hill) that served London at the end of the century – and still do today – may stand for the folly of unrestricted competition, but also exemplify the prodigality with which Victorian capitalists, architects, and engineers showered their gifts on London, adding to the bewildering variety of experiences that made it what it was. Though such experiences included congestion, pollution, and overcrowding, they were not confined to them. The delicacy of the Paddington trainshed, the massive power of the Euston arch, the richness of the St Pancras façade, the intricacy of plan of the old Waterloo, the assertiveness of Cannon Street and Charing Cross, the irrational audacity of Marylebone's very existence, Blackfriars' self-identification as the gateway to St Petersburg, Leipsic, and Baden Baden, stood as monuments to the self-confidence, determination, and pugnacity of their builders. Nowhere does Victorian London survive today more vigorously than in its railway termini.

THE HOTEL

The railway first destroyed the traditional coaching inn by depriving it of its reason for existence, and then both made possible and helped create the modern hotel. With the possible exception of Canada, Britain has seen a closer relationship between railways and hotels than any other country. Starting in the fifties, each of the major companies built and operated a chain of hotels, usually located at or near its principal stations, as an integral part of its services and operations. The inherent convenience of having a hotel either adjacent to or part of the station and, in recent decades, the scarcity of capital for rebuilding, has kept the network of railway hotels remarkably intact into our own times, survivals of a past age's conception of luxury, comfort, and splendour. Most of the hotels that cosseted the affluent visitors to Victorian London have gone or remain, like the Langham, Metropole, and Westminster Palace, used for other purposes. But the Great Western Royal and the Great Northern still provide for modern travellers as they did for Trollope's characters; the Great Eastern survives as the only first-class hotel remaining in the City; while the main dining room of the Charing Cross Hotel is now sought by both culinary and architectural pilgrims. The Grosvenor Hotel (not operated by British Rail) still dominates Victoria Station, while the buildings of the Midland and Great Central guard the entrances to St Pancras and Marylebone. Those at Cannon Street, Holborn Viaduct, and Euston are no more.

If the railway hotels were the first, others soon surpassed them in elaborateness and luxury. They served the needs not only of provincial visitors and foreign tourists, but provided the middle-class London resident with an inexpensive alternative to the club, and the lady with a place where she might dine in public without scandal. To the architect they gave opportunities for experiments in plan and for enormous façades where his invention could take forms impossible in the narrow confines of most building sites. The interiors opened possibilities of decorative variety earlier found only in the largest country houses, and permitted division and subdivision into specialized rooms and areas to an extent hitherto undreamed of.[92]

'Until within the last few years we have no hotels worthy of the name in London,' explained the *Building News* in 1862. Americans, 'accustomed to the princely accommodation in such hotels as that in the Fifth-avenue, at New York', were shocked by 'the scanty means and confined space of ordinary London hotels. Continental visitors found them costly and comfortless.' Provincial visitors satisfied themselves with 'dingy coffee-houses and taverns . . .'[93] 'There is no capital in Europe, always saving Constantinople, which, until recently, was not better provided with good average comfortable upper and middle-class Hotels than London,' according to John Timbs. 'A few private houses knocked somehow into one have been thought a large and grand hotel, for it is only within the last few years that the obvious necessity which existed for constructing a building specially for Hotel

22 'If the railway hotels were the first, others soon surpassed them in elaborateness and luxury.' Grand staircase, Hotel Cecil.

purposes has been slowly recognised in this country.'[94]

While antedated by the hotels at Euston, the Great Western Royal at Paddington (1851), by Philip Hardwick, father and son, really established both the railway hotel and the grand hotel in general as a metropolitan phenomenon. It contained 'about 130 bed-rooms, and about 20 sitting-rooms, many of which will be arranged together, with dressing-rooms attached, and other conveniences, so as to form several complete *suites of rooms*', according to the *Civil Engineer*. The aim of the proprietors was 'to provide the public with every comfort and luxury at moderate charges',[95] and this set the tone for most of its successors: they were simply too big to rely on the patronage of the wealthy and the few, who in any event would be likely to have other, better facilities for their accommodation and entertainment.

The Great Western Hotel proved highly profitable, and brought forth many successors, also catering for 'the great social want of the middle and travelling classes . . .' The *Building News* by 1862 was convinced that 'the day for the stuffy, little, ill-ventilated, ill-arranged hotels is closed or fast closing'.[96] The first really large hotel unconnected with a railway company was the Westminster Palace in Victoria Street (1859), 'in a scraggy French style'.[97] Timbs' *Curiosities of London* described it as realizing 'the expectations even of the luxurious of the commercial classes. . . . It has thirteen sitting-rooms, gentlemen's and ladies' coffee-rooms (the latter an exceedingly fine apartment), several committee and dining-rooms, with one hundred and thirty bedrooms, besides servants' apartments.'[98] It was the first London hotel provided with lifts.[99] The *Building News* predicted that its catering facilities would benefit Londoners, particularly those residing in the new blocks of flats in Victoria Street: '. . . Although many of those are the members of clubs, still there are evenings when a walk across the park takes up too much time or is disagreeable.'[100]

'One of the greatest changes in London during the last score or so of years is in the matter of hotels,' reported *Dickens's Dictionary of London* for 1880. 'In proportion to its size, London is still far worse provided in this respect than most of the great Continental or American towns.'[101] But speculators and developers were working to close the gap. The creation of Northumberland Avenue as a link between Trafalgar Square and the Thames Embankment provided the occasion for the erection of three of Victorian London's most pretentious hotels, the Grand, the Metropole, and the Victoria. The first, by F. and H. Francis and J.E. Saunders, and whose curved façade still stands at the corner of Charing Cross, was saved from the threat of demolition in 1975. In 1881 the *Building News* thought that 'for size and internal completeness', it surpassed 'any similar building in the metropolis, and combines the peculiarities of the Continental and American systems . . .'[102] Francis and Saunders also designed the Metropole, 'one of the largest in Europe', and whose opening in the spring of 1885 called forth an extended and admiring description from the *Building News*. Its interior provided both the multiplicity of services and the contrasting visual experiences demanded by the discriminating traveller:

Passing through a spacious and handsomely decorated vestibule . . . adorned by mosaic pavement and grand antique marble Corinthian columns, resting upon pedestals with gilded capitals and cantilevers, the visitor enters . . . the grand *salle à manger* . . . which is

23 'The interiors opened possibilities of decorative variety . . .' Hotel Cecil. Smoking Room.

24 *below* '"One of the greatest changes in London during the last score or so of years is in the matter of hotels."' Ladies' drawing room, St Pancras Hotel, June 1876.

lighted by lofty semicircular-headed windows, with mahogany casements. . . . On the left . . . is a large hall, from which the grand staircase ascends, the centre well-hole of which is occupied by two lifts for passengers and luggage. The reception room on this side is . . . decorated in an Italian style with panels of tapestry made at the Royal Windsor Works, chiefly representing the Royal palaces, and surmounted by pediments. The pilasters are ornamented by painted arabesques, and a deep frieze over the wall linings is enriched by painted decorations of *amorini* and festoons on a blue ground, with clouds . . . The ceiling represents the blue sky, in which are introduced Cupids and flowers, the decoration being light and chaste in effect, and said to be taken from those in the Gallery of Apollo in the Louvre. A corridor at the side of this room, pleasingly varied by an alcove, with seats screened off by panels of Mesharebeyeh woodwork, and treated in an Arabic manner, gives access to the library and drawing room. The library is panelled in oak to a considerable height, with pilasters in the Elizabethan style. . . . The drawing-room . . . is a splendid *salon* in the Louis Seize style, decorated to imitate one of the Empress's apartments of the Tuileries . . .

Next in the rear to the *salle-à-manger* is the 'Oak room,' or secondary *salle*, an apartment surrounded with an oak dado and tapestry panels . . . Adjoining this is a private dining room in the Jacobean style . . . The portraits which are introduced in the oak lining comprise James I, and the great men of the period, Sir Walter Raleigh, Ben Johnson, Lord Bacon, &c. These rooms and the Whitehall entrance form a suite of apartments decorated in oak in the Renaissance style . . . Arriving on the first floor, spacious corridors afford access to the suites of sitting and bed rooms, which are decorated and furnished through-out in a most costly manner with wall-hangings of silk damask, with plush dadoes and other richly-printed textiles. The Royal suite of rooms, including the Marie Antoinette chamber, which is an exact copy of the Marie Antoinette boudoir at Fontainebleau, are as chastely elegant as they are costly. . . . The upper floors are chiefly occupied by bedrooms, with sitting-rooms *en suite*, each having its own bath room and w.c. There are in all about six hundred bedrooms. . . . There is a small semaphore which is raised outside each room whenever the visitor touches the electric bell, thereby saving a great deal of unnecessary labour.[103]

In 1905 a room at the Metropole could be had for five shillings.[104]

'London has become a pleasure lounge for the idlers of the globe,' wrote Charles Eyre Pascoe in 1888:

Americans, French, Germans, Indians, Colonials, and persons of leisure and wealth from all parts of the world flock to the capital city during the season. . . . This increasing influx of the world's citizens has led to the monster hotel which once belonged solely to New York and Paris. 'Travelled Americans' fifteen years ago invariably criticised our London hotels adversely. Their one grand point scored in smoking-room debate was – 'You have no iced [sic] water and cocktails.' Now they may freeze in the one and burn themselves with the other.[105]

25 'The creation of Northumberland Avenue . . .
provided the occasion for the erection of three
of Victorian London's most pretentious
hotels . . .' The Grand Hotel, 1880.

26 '"This increasing influx of the world's citizens has led to the monster hotel which once belong solely to New York and Paris."' Hotel Cecil from the Embankment.

THE RESTAURANT

At least as significant as the proliferation of luxury hotels was the coming of the restaurant, and in particular of that special London phenomenon, the monster restaurant: the multi-storeyed complex of carefully graded and segregated eating-rooms – each with its own menu, price-range, and decorative scheme – of which the Lyons Corner Houses are (or were) the most familiar twentieth-century examples.

What we would recognize as restaurants seem to have been common in Paris before the Revolution, but not in London until after the mid-nineteenth century.* Henry Lennox wrote a grisly account of a typical London eating-establishment for the *Building News* in 1857:

> You enter these . . . 'Dining Houses,' if they merit such an appellation, for assuredly they always appear to me fitter places for an unclean beast than for a Christian. One *coup d'oeil* enables you to take in . . . the wretchedness that pervades the entire place. You enter a narrow doorway, say two feet wide, and you stand in the 'dining-house,' a room some 20 by 15 feet, with a low dirty ceiling, which seems to emulate the opaqueness that pervades the whole room. Six small, narrow 'boxes' on either side of the room, fitted up for the accommodation of the visitors, are the places that the customers take their meals in; and the darkness 'that is almost felt,' perhaps prevents them from witnessing the coarse food of which they are partaking . . . What a contrast is here presented to the lively *cafés* fitted up in France and other places – the light, airy room, wherein the gay inhabitants partake of the meal set before them in evident relish, glancing, meanwhile, at the news of the day, or talking with their companions over the same.[106]

'Till within late years', Thomas Verity told the RIBA in 1879, 'a common reproach to London was the general insufficiency of the accommodation provided for those who, either from necessity or choice, were in the habit of seeking their dinners elsewhere than in their own homes.' Thackeray's *Book of Snobs* pictures such a world, in which the middle classes dined out only – if frequently – at pretentious dinner parties in the homes of their friends and associates. 'There were indeed the clubs,' Verity continued, 'the best probably in the world, but they supplied the wants of a comparatively small section of the community, and that too a section owning in most cases houses and establishments of its own.' For those not belonging to a club London could offer, from the fifties onward, hotels, 'often of vast proportions, where the prices were generally on a scale of equal grandeur, and where splendour rather than comfort seemed often to be the aim and object of the management.' More practically, 'in the city and around the law courts were taverns . . .' Soho seems already to have had what we today would recognize as very good restaurants indeed, but the universal testimony is that they were patronized exclusively by foreigners: 'Lower down again in the scale come

* A. Hayward, writing in 1853, goes into considerable detail about the various delights of contemporary Parisian restaurants, but refers only to clubs and private establishments in his treatment of the gastronomic possibilities of London. He reports that the first restaurant in Paris opened in 1770 and that there were 100 by 1789. A. Hayward, *The Art of Dining*, 2nd ed., 1883, pp. 23, 37–44.

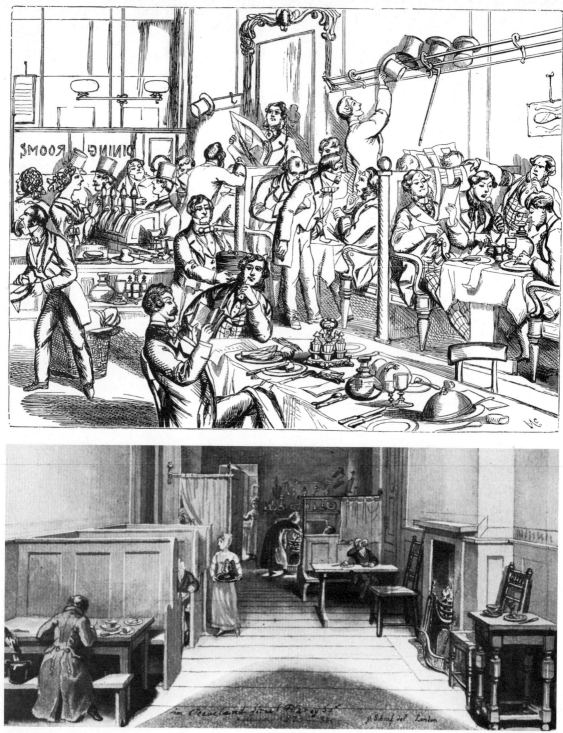

27 *top* "'. . . these . . . 'Dining Houses' . . . appear to me fitter places for an unclean beast than for a Christian.'" Dining rooms in Bucklersbury, 1857.

28 *above* "'Six small, narrow 'boxes' on either side of the room . . . are the places that the customers take their meals in . . .'" Coffee house in Cleveland Street, Fitzroy Square, by George Scharf the elder, d. 1824.

the foreign establishments, which dispensed their hospitalities mostly in the neighbourhood of Leicester Square.' Finally there came 'the little dining rooms or eating houses, where the surroundings were generally of a nature to destroy the appetite even of the least fastidious . . .' Food of sorts could be had from public houses, but none were resorted to for the sheer pleasure of the experience. '. . . There were few places,' Verity concluded, 'where people could lunch or dine at a moderate cost and in a cleanly, comfortable manner, with the advantage of a ménu consisting of something beyond a chop or steak'. It is surprising to the modern reader to learn of the central role of railway refreshment rooms, in particular those operated by Spiers and Pond, in bringing about the Victorian gastronomic revolution:

> It was soon found that dirt and discomfort were not absolutely indispensable to economy, and . . . certain establishments, principally in connection with railway stations, at first in small refreshment rooms, but lately in handsomely appointed saloons, such as those at the Midland and Holborn Viaduct Stations [came into existence].[107]

St Pancras and Holborn Viaduct, with or without refreshment rooms, were not even projected when, in 1857, the *Building News* launched a small campaign for the establishment of one or more decent restaurants in London. It cited the inadequacies of the London Tavern and the Albion for special banquets, where diners sat 'before a narrow table on skimping chairs, without room for the legs . . .' Less formal diners-out were even more in need of a new kind of eating establishment:

> . . . Even in those houses where the meat is good and the dinner quickly served, the rooms are, with few exceptions, low and straitened, and the guests crammed together on inconvenient benches or equally uncomfortable chairs, the American ordonnance of quick eating or gobbling being a matter of necessity.[108]

Shortly thereafter it was able to report that its recommendations had been, 'in one instance at least, all but completely realised'. A new and admirable establishment had recently been opened at the corner of Chancery Lane and Fleet Street:

> Although not originally planned for such purpose, the upper floors of the building . . . are now appropriated as the locale of a dining-room establishment of the kind which has been long wanted. . . . There is an air of quiet taste as well as comfortableness in the place, which contrasts not a little forcibly with the disregard to appearance, the dowdiness, and even squalor, of many well-reputed and largely frequented taverns. . . . the well-appointed costume of the tables [is] almost appetite-provoking. Compared with . . . other Fleet-street dining places . . . [including the Cheshire Cheese] this one is as winningly attractive as they are repulsively *triste* . . . There is an air of sober, refined comfortableness that puts the modest visitor at his ease: there are no splendours to abash him, or to terrify him with disagreeable forebodings as to the amount of the bill . . .
>
> Now that the example has been set it will, perhaps, be followed by similar establishments, under the name of dining-halls, being started . . . where the stranger in London could get a dinner, without having no other alternative of choice than between the cook-

shop eating-house, the mere chop and steak tavern, or such places as the Old and New Hummums in Covent Garden.

To be successful such 'dining-halls' would require a large turnover: 'Greater choice of dishes, and better cookery and serving up, can be afforded . . . when a whole joint is sure to disappear almost within ten minutes after it has been taken off the spit. The larger the number of persons to be provided for the greater the economy . . .' They could serve almost as clubs for the middling classes:

> . . . It occurs to us to ask if it would not in some instances very well answer to ingraft the club-house system upon a public dining establishment; one floor being appropriated exclusively to subscribers, who would have their own coffee-room, reading-room, &c., to which strangers would not be admitted . . .[109]

The suggestion, involving ever-greater subdivision and social segregation, was so wholly in accord with the prevailing tendencies of Victorian life that it is surprising it was not widely acted upon. The argument as to the economies of scale was, indeed, heeded, and it is typical of the Victorian way of doing things that the first restaurants quickly expanded from single dining rooms attached to single kitchens to gastronomic department stores, and as parts of even more complex buildings. If the restaurant began as a part of a railway station it continued its evolution, as often as not, connected with a theatre or a music hall.

The association of eating and drinking with attendance at theatrical performances is not the least amiable feature of English life. The English digestive system requires some sustenance, however small, at at least two-hourly intervals. Perhaps an unbroken line connects the orange-sellers in Elizabethan playhouses with the smiling girls bearing trays of synthetic ice-cream up cinema aisles. More remarkable are the provisions for full-course meals in English theatres, cinemas, and concert halls. Twenty years ago the only place in Hull outside the railway hotel where one could have an evening meal – and then it was high tea – was a cinema restaurant.

St James's Hall, the concert rooms between Regent Street and Piccadilly, already had a restaurant in the same building when the Gaiety Theatre in the Strand opened its associated restaurant in 1869:

> On a recent visit we discovered the Gaiety Restaurant to consist of a luncheon bar on the ground floor (with a *café* beneath), a principal dining-room on the first floor (with private rooms in the entresol), a second-class dining-room on the second floor, and a billiard-room above. . . . There is a certain ostentation of design apparent everywhere . . . which seems to suggest the architect, the stained glass designer, or even the scene painter . . .[110]

A decade later it was rebuilt.[111] The new decorations were designed to make a meal at the Gaiety an integrated aesthetic and educational experience:

> Entering by a spacious vestibule from the Strand, laid with mosaic, we first examine . . . the great luncheon buffet . . . the upper portion of the walls being adorned with a series of tile paintings, emblematical of the progress of agriculture from the first clearing of the

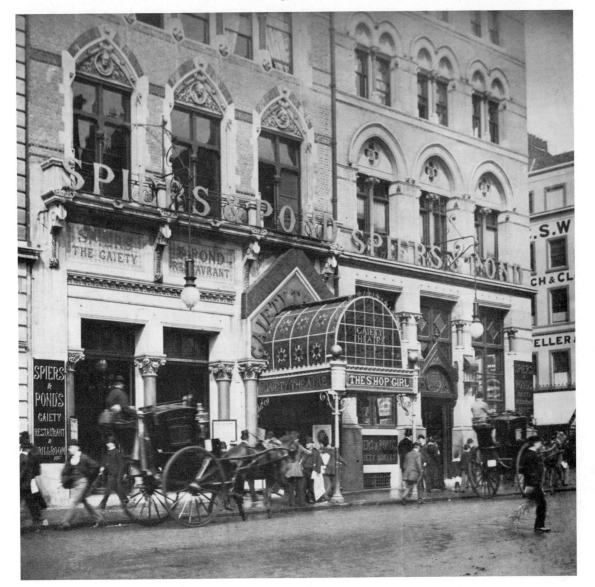

29 '"There is a certain ostentation of design apparent everywhere . . ."' The Gaiety Restaurant and Theatre as rebuilt, 1894.

primeval forest to the harvest gathering; another series represent the progress of wine making. The windows on the Catherine-street side . . . are filled with stained-glass representative of Shakespearian subjects . . . The ceiling is panelled and decorated in Kalsomine painting . . . the subjects are figures with scrolls and mottoes from dramatic authors, together with animal representations. . . . The grill and supper-rooms are in the basement . . .

The table d'hôte occupies the first floor, and is a spacious apartment, with all necessary cloak-rooms, and there are set out a number of tables to be served every day at 5 o'clock. . . . We have little space left to notice other rooms, the smoking-room, culinary department, &c. . . . We may especially remark upon the very complete system of lifts . . .[112]

The even more famous Café Royal in Regent Street, which dates from 1865, was not attached to a theatre, but its complexity of internal arrangement was fully equal to that of the Gaiety.[113] It consciously imitated the cafés of the Parisian boulevards, and by subdivision and segregation made itself acceptable to the tastes and requirements of Londoners.[114]

Meanwhile Soho was beginning to be discovered by the English as a place where they themselves might conceivably, with some trepidation, dine. The *Builder* described it as 'still a sort of petty France', and treated it as if it were at least a thousand miles away from the West End:

Most of the shops are thoroughly French, and they have evidently been established solely for the supply of the foreign colony. Here are French schools for the education of the young, and wine-shops and restaurants where an Englishman who entered would be looked upon with surprise. . . . There are few tables-d'hôte at these hotels and restaurants, and dinners are mostly served *à la carte*. In consequence, the various occupations of eating, drinking, smoking, card-playing, and animated talking are all carried on at the same time.

The orderly division of life's activities into their appropriate times and places was, that is to say, not the rule in Soho that it was in the more genteel parts of London.

The natives of different countries vociferate and gesticulate in their respective tongues . . . Four years ago . . . a correspondent of the *Times*, being in search of a good dinner, thought he had found what he sought at one of these restaurants, and, in consequence, wrote a very appreciative account of a dinner, which, he said, was better than he could have obtained at a West-end club, and which cost him a considerably less amount . . . It is doubtful whether the concomitants of smoke and noise would be agreeable to many Englishmen, but, at all events, Mr. Kettner, of Church-street, has had the letter reprinted in large letters, and has placed two copies of it in his window.[115]

From such small beginnings did Soho's present pre-eminence in London's restaurant world develop. Kettner's is happily still with us, and one suspects that Soho remains much as it did a century ago: the revolution is what has occurred in the eating habits and life styles of the rest of London. Until the twentieth century the authenticity of Soho was more than any but the most adventuresome and bohemian Englishman could face. What the majority could and did face in increasing numbers and with growing pleasure were the carefully institutionalized adaptations of the Parisian restaurant that established themselves along the principal thoroughfares of the West End, offering reassuringly English meals in surroundings of great splendour at moderate prices, where the decencies of social segregation would be observed, and the proprieties of dress, manner, and behaviour enforced.

One thing was certain: the English restaurant was designed for eating, not for dawdling away the afternoon or for an evening's desultory conversation. The Parisian café was viewed as the inevitable consequence of the inadequate Parisian flat. '. . . What exists in Paris to a degree which seems to English people astonishing is . . . café life with *appartements* which frequently extend but little beyond the solitary sleeping rooms,' explained the *Architect* in 1873. 'It is obviously not this that requires to be provided for in London . . .'[116] It had once been suggested 'that the Thames Embankment itself should be converted into a boulevard – that it should be lined with cafés, restaurants, little paradises and pavilions, white marble tables, coffee-stalls, and pretty paraphernalia of the kind', the *Building News* recalled in 1876; 'but every one remembers how the proposal was received. It was denounced, as if there had been suggested another burning of St. Paul's.'[117]

Perhaps the most successful and best known of the new monster restaurants was Spiers and Pond's Criterion at Piccadilly Circus, long disused except for the theatre, and now threatened with partial demolition. The *Building News* in 1875 described it as 'one of the best specimens that have recently been produced of architecture of this festive class . . .'[118] Its architect, Thomas Verity – who had also been responsible for the rebuilding of the Gaiety Restaurant – discussed it with some pride in the context of a paper, 'The Modern Restaurant', which he read to the RIBA in 1879:

> . . . The present building, being the most important of its kind yet erected, may be taken as a type of the modern house of public entertainment. . . . as after a trial of seven years the proprietors tell me they can suggest no material alterations, the Criterion may be considered to fairly meet the requirements of this particular business.
>
> . . . The public portion includes dining rooms of various capacity, restaurant, grill room, buffet, smoking room, a grand hall (now used as a table d'hôte, but originally intended for a ball room), lavatories, retiring and cloak rooms, and lastly a theatre.
>
> The service departments . . . are arranged in a central block one over the other, corresponding, in level with the different dining rooms, and in communication with one another by means of lifts and staircases, and comprising kitchens, sculleries, larders, pantries, cleaning rooms, wine, beer, and ice cellars, and store rooms for plate, glass, linen, groceries, and all kinds of provisions. . . .
>
> There is . . . a side entrance to the buffet from Piccadilly, having on the right a small bar, (where those with strong palates or with none at all may indulge in the fearful concoctions with comical names, so much in vogue on the other side of the Atlantic), and on the left is a cigar shop. There is another entrance to the buffet from Jermyn Street . . . Advantage has been taken of the difference of level in the two streets, to obtain in a half-basement a second class dining or grill room . . .
>
> On the first floor . . . is a room . . . devoted to the 'diner Parisien,' and on the east is a

room of similar dimensions for banquets, &c., and ranged along the corridor, leading to Jermyn Street, are private rooms of different sizes for parties from ten to fifty persons . . .

. . . The average number of dinners and luncheons is 2,000, and on several occasions the enormous number of 4,500 has been reached.[119]

Dickens's Dictionary of London for 1880 regarded restaurants as among the great attractions of the metropolis:

A very few years ago the expectant diner, who required, in the public rooms of London, something better than a cut off the joint, or a chop or steak, would have had but a limited number of tables at his command. A really good dinner was almost entirely confined to the regions of club-land, and, with one or two exceptions, respectable restaurants, to which a lady could be taken, may be said hardly to have existed at all. Artful seekers after surreptitious good dinners, who knew their London well, certainly had some foreign houses in the back settlements of Soho or of Leicester-square, to which they pinned their faith, but the restaurant, as it has been for many years understood in Paris, practically had no place in London. Time . . . has altered all this. It is probably true that, even now, it is impossible to dine in public in London as well as that important ceremony can be performed in Paris. . . . one thing is certain; that if you know where to go, and how to arrange your campaign, you can dine as well in London . . . as any reasonable *gourmet* can wish.[120]

Other notable late Victorian restaurants included Gatti's Adelaide Gallery, at Charing Cross; the Tivoli and Romano's, both in the Strand; the St James's Restaurant, Piccadilly, rebuilt in 1875 in Venetian Gothic; the Café Monico in Shaftesbury Avenue (1888–9); and most notably, the Holborn Restaurant, whose fifteen public and private dining rooms survived until 1955.[121] Scott's, whose sadly deteriorated building still stands in Coventry Street, opened in 1893.[122]

The *Building News* in 1894 thought that the restaurant had by then taken over many of the functions of the club:

Public dining-rooms and restaurant facilities continue to develop in London in a very sumptuous and attractive style, much to the detriment of the West-End clubs, whose members no longer entertain their friends therein so hospitably as heretofore, or even dine themselves at their clubs so frequently as they used to do. The new hotels built of late years now afford facilities for the dining public at more moderate prices, and furnish their tables so well as to attract an increasing amount of custom.[123]

'Another cause of the desertion of the club is the increased popularity of the restaurants,' wrote Sir Walter Besant later in the decade:

They are more expensive than the club; but they are bright and lively. Ladies can, and do, go to these restaurants without reproach:* their presence has made a great alteration:

---

* 'Ladies Shopping without male escort, and requiring luncheon, can safely visit any of the great restaurants – care being always taken to avoid passing through a drinking bar. In some cases a separate room is set apart for ladies, but there is practically no reason why the public room should be avoided.' *Dickens's Dictionary of London, 1879*, reprinted Howard Baker, 1972, p. 127.

there is always an atmosphere of cheerfulness, if not of exhilaration; one is always welcome; the waiters are all obliging; and the dinner is often a great deal better than that provided at the club. All the year round the higher class restaurants are crowded . . .[124]

In 1899 there opened what must have been one of the most startling attractions of the theatre district:

The Grand Hotel and Brasserie de l'Europe, on the north side of Leicester-square . . . will offer to the public a combination of the café-restaurant and the beer-hall . . . with that type of brasserie which the experienced Parisian has found preferable to its many predecessors. In the basement is a large lager-beer hall, where, together with the finest brews from Munich, a number of German dishes and 'delicatessen' will be served. Such dainties as caviare, Berliner rollmops (rolled herrings), Brunswick cervelat, Wiener and Frankfurter sauerkraut . . . may here be asked for and obtained; and for the preparation of these and all other German dishes a German cook will be responsible. . . . On the ground floor is the Grand Café, which, both in appearance and in style, will be found quite Continental, while above is the 'Italian Room,' which it is intended to use as an *à la carte* restaurant.

The proprietors had not forgotten that Leicester Square was, after all, in London:

Messrs. Baker and Co., in their desire to reproduce certain features of the French and German cafés, have by no means neglected the wants of those customers whose tastes are uncompromisingly English. Both in the Lager Beer Hall, and in the Grand Café, there will be an ample menu in the English style, so that the attractions of the 'grill-room' will in no sense be absent from the new 'Brasserie.'

Mr. Walter Emden . . . is the architect . . . The lager-beer hall in the basement is decorated in the Alhambra style . . . The grand café on the ground floor is elaborately decorated in the style of the German Renaissance, the panels of the walls being filled in both with mirrors and with pictures representing events famous in German history. In this room a striking effect is obtained by hanging from the beams and columns festoons of leaves and flowers in repoussé copper, and the fruit on these imposing garlands being represented by electric lamps.[125]

Finally, at the very end of the century, came the ingenious Lyons, on this occasion with an entirely underground restaurant in Throgmorton Street:

Here we find a restaurant for providing first-class refreshments, dinners, &c., on a very complete scale, built, lighted, ventilated, and drained entirely below the level of the street. . . . for completeness in the arrangement of the cuisine, lavish expenditure in costly fittings, in marbles and mosaics, decorations, and sanitary appliances, these new premises leave little to be desired. Entering from Throgmorton-street through a spacious lobby, we descend by a marble staircase, lined with gold mosaic, semicircular in shape, or by a lift, to the level of a large and handsome restaurant adorned with oak panelling, marbles, a decorative frieze and ceiling, and paved with mosaic . . . The coloured modelled frieze in low relief depicts an old German story – the Legend of the Magic Ring . . . Beyond this

30 '". . . there is always an atmosphere of
cheerfulness, if not of exhilaration; one is always
welcome; the waiters are all obliging . . .'"
Interior of a London restaurant. Pascoe, *London
of To-day*, 1893, p. 81.

31 *below*   '"The grand café on the ground floor
is elaborately decorated in the style of the
German Renaissance . . ."' Grand Hotel and
Brasserie de l'Europe, Leicester Square.

apartment we enter the dining-room . . . its marble-lined walls of Devonshire spar with coupled pilasters of verde antique, with bronze Ionic capitals and frieze and rich red marble dado. Bevelled mirrors, inclosed in the marble background . . . adorn each bay of this long room, and give it a brilliant appearance. The saloon between restaurant and dining-room, intended for private dinners, &c., is an oak-panelled and handsome apartment . . . the grill-room is 40ft. below ground-level.[126]

PUBS AND THEATRES

'. . . Theatres, restaurants and gin palaces all rise in response to the popular call . . . in these instances there is, broadly speaking, a general agreement and codification of our desires . . .' Halsey Ricardo complained to the Congress of the RIBA in 1900.[127] Restaurants were largely patronized by the respectable middle classes, and the Victorians took food seriously; the burgeoning of theatres, and, still worse, gin palaces provided less occasion for rejoicing. Yet they both gave unrivalled opportunities for architectural and decorative expression, and survive as some of the most characteristic products of Victorian ingenuity and genius. While they cannot be regarded as wholly new building types, they both achieved heights of elaboration and complexity in the nineteenth century never approached before or since. Together they gave birth to that extraordinary hybrid, the music hall, which partook of the character of each.

The gin palace and the music hall were focal points of working-class neighbourhoods, oases of colour, excitement, and luxury elsewhere lacking. In reporting on the 'spirit of architectural improvement in the metropolis,' the *Architectural Magazine* in December 1837 condescended to notice 'the general rage for ornamenting the fronts of gin-shops and public-houses'.[128] The decade saw a notable surge of expenditure on both the exterior and interior of pubs, virtually creating the modern type, with its 'plate-glass windows, richly ornamented façade, gilded lettering and brilliant lamps . . .'[129] Temperance reformers contrasted the luxuries of the public house with the squalor of the homes from which most of its inmates came. 'A few years since the trade of the publican was carried on in a quiet unassuming manner,' a writer for the *Building News* recalled in 1857:

> Their houses and taps were, for the most part, antiquated, retired, and gloomy. . . .
>
> How changed is the whole system! . . . The corner public is radiant of gas, redolent of mahogany, and glittering in mirrors! . . . the old and dun-colored taps and parlors are all transformed into gorgeous saloons or refulgent halls; or else the drawing-room is arranged as a theatre for music, song, and scenic performances. . . .
>
> All parts of the metropolis discover, at every turning, large buildings of splendid elevation, fitted up in a style of grandeur, not to say elegance, quite unsuited to the rational demands of the humbler classes who throng them daily.[130]

By the fifties, the middle and upper classes had abandoned the pub to the working classes, their clubs providing a more satisfactory and certainly more private substitute. Not that the pubs encouraged the mingling of classes. Their several entrances led into carefully segregated parlours, where elaborately carved screens would protect each group of drinkers from observation by the others. Such 'internal divisions promoted privacy, reduced opportunities for disorder, and preserved class distinctions'.[131]

The middle classes abandoned theatres as well as pubs to a working-class clientele. Even the amusements of the Victorians were rigorously segregated along class lines.[132] The theatres, like the pubs, went to considerable pains to protect the several types of spectators from embarrassing encounters with others. 'There is scarcely a theatre in London the approaches to which are not superior to those of the theatres in Paris,' boasted the *Building News* in 1862, 'for here the visitors to pit, boxes, and galleries are separated, and have distinct ways for entering and leaving; whereas across the channel the same doorway serves for all, in most cases, and even, in the French Theatre, the visitors to boxes and galleries descend the same staircases.'[133]

To see the new and transformed building types merely as architectural phenomena, or even as reflections of changing patterns of public behaviour is to regard them through twentieth-century spectacles. To see them as the Victorians did we must ask how they affected the central institutions: the home and the family. To the extent that it helped isolate them in the outer suburbs and thereby preserve them from urban contamination and competition, the railway probably strengthened the home and the family. By offering powerful attractions to the male members of the family, the pub, the music hall, and the theatre probably weakened them. 'A poor mechanic who toils twelve hours needs comfort and repose rather than splendour . . .' the *Building News* observed in the course of an article condemning the moral effects of the gin palace in 1857:

> The allurement of classic and faultless decorations, set off by jets of gas, multiplied by mirrors to thousands . . . the luxury of show, what is that to the poor occupant of a third floor back, of a single room, in which he is domesticated with, perhaps, a wife and children? Alas! the contrast would sicken any but the depraved imagination of him whose orgies, oft repeated, render him insensate to the endearing ties of children or connubial repose. The weak man, desperate in indulgence, attracted by the too seductive allurements of the gin palace in the new style, repelled by the discomfort of chill and filthy chambers . . . flies towards the tempting evil, and avoids that squalid home which might, even in adversity, be made a source of comparative comfort to himself and of security to his family.[134]

Restaurants and hotels, while less blatant threats to the sanctity of the hearth, insofar as they made evenings in town pleasanter, could be regarded as potentially anti-domestic forces. Certainly the dark allusions to the iniquities of the 'hotel-life' that was supposed to prevail in America suggest that the Victorians regarded hotels with some suspicion. The discreet private dining rooms which the new restaurants provided clearly were not intended for family use.

Yet none of the new building types so far examined did more than provide plausible excuses to postpone the journey home: the home itself, whether a terrace house facing a garden square or a villa within protecting walls, remained, ready to accept the erring father

32 'Even the amusements of the Victorians were rigorously segregated along class lines.' Royal Victorian Coffee Palace and Music Hall (the Old Vic), 1881.

or the wayward son when he tore himself away from the delusive joys of the central city. One new building type, though, seemed to threaten the physical basis of family life by altering the very nature of the home, although to its defenders it promised to reinforce the very separateness that protected the family from the outside world. That portent for good or evil was the block of flats.[135]

THE BLOCK OF FLATS

Victoria Street, laid out in 1849, saw in the 1850's the first tentative experiments in flatted living for the middle classes, experiments that ended in both aesthetic and economic failure.[136] Yet the street, and a few others, continued to attract new speculations in one or another variety of blocks of luxury flats, although during the fifties and sixties flats were more talked about than actually built or lived in. One of the difficulties was their association with the experiments in blocks of model dwellings for the artisan classes. 'The fact of its being a philanthropic movement . . . created such prejudice against it in the minds of the classes just above them,' according to the *Building News* in 1868, 'and we are aware of only one building in London divided into flats, and let to tolerably well-to-do occupants of the middle classes,' as opposed to the very rich.[137] The architectural journals consistently favoured the building of flats for the middle classes as more solid, cheaper, and more susceptible to architectural treatment than the standard terrace house or suburban villa.

Despite such arguments the speculative builder and the majority of the English population of all classes have down to the present day resisted attempts to induce them to live horizontally in flats rather than vertically in houses. The unpopularity of high-rise council flats is notorious; while the privately-owned block of flats has flourished only in the more fashionable districts of central and west London. It was possible to dismiss all this as unreasoning prejudice in the 1850's and 60's, when few Englishmen had even had the chance to see a self-contained flat, much less live in one. But more than a century later, the unmistakable rejection of the idea of flat-living, most emphatically by a large proportion of those who do actually live in flats, suggests that the prejudice is deep-seated.

Francophobia entered into the distaste of the Victorians for flats, although they were often rejecting their distorted image of French life and the Parisian dwelling rather than the things themselves. The living habits of the Parisians proved an inexhaustible source of fascination for Londoners. 'The French have been accustomed to be satisfied with a much smaller quantity of everything than we are,' R. Phené Spiers explained to the Royal Institute of Architects in 1871:

> They use very little water, and believing that they can wash themselves with the corner of a wet towel, they do not see the necessity for a bath; and the same with regard to food and everything. The rooms are only just as large as is necessary. They have not large families, or it would be difficult to understand how they could manage with such small accommodation. As a rule, these flats contain not more than a quarter the space which there is in our English houses.[138]

'We need not be reminded that French ideas of comfort differ from English ones,' the *Building News* told its readers in 1857:

> A French family may not care at all for privacy – may see nothing objectionable in thoroughfare rooms – in having bed-chambers not only adjoining to and immediately communicating with sitting-rooms, but inaccessible except by passing through the latter. Of course, they do not feel incommoded, or they would not put up with such highly objectionable arrangement of plan. Put up with it, however, they do; and their doing so does not say much for their refinement.

It admitted that 'in the fitting up of a boudoir they may be unrivalled . . .' but found their other domestic arrangements as improper as they were destructive to individual privacy. Their cooking arrangements were wholly condemned, in particular their unaccountable practice of placing the kitchen next to the dining room, whereby the latter would 'be exposed to the intrusion of both sounds and scents from the culinary laboratory that may be by no means very agreeable'. Admittedly, meals when they appeared would be more likely to be hot, and theft by the servants was made more difficult, but these were minor considerations compared to the offensive disregard of the principle of domestic segregation. The kitchen itself was likely to be a single room, instead of the subdivided cluster of 'offices' of a well-regulated English house:

> According to English notions a kitchen requires to have several dependencies connected with it, such as larder, pantry, store-closet, scullery, &c.; yet it appears from the plans of French houses that there is frequently nothing whatever of the kind provided, which is all the more strange because the kitchen itself is, in some instances, upon such a miniature scale as to be no longer than a rather roomy closet, therefore anything but a particularly good neighbour when in immediate proximity to a sitting-room, or, indeed, at all fitted for carrying out any more ambitious culinary operations than the dressing a salad or poaching an egg.

It could only account for the cramped, inconvenient, and ill-arranged nature of the modern Parisian flat, with its shocking social and functional juxtapositions, by the reflection that the French cared less for the family and the home than the English:

> A Frenchman cares less for comfort at home than for amusement abroad: he is content to dine even with his wife, and perhaps family also, at a restaurant's, and his idea of a house scarcely extends beyond a *salon* and *salle à manger*, and, provided they be showily fitted up, he himself puts up with much that to an Englishman would be intolerably annoying.

Even more serious than the improper arrangement of rooms within a flat was the threat to the privacy and separateness of the family from the other residents of the block:

> . . . Nothing can overcome the decided objectionableness attending the congregating a number of families beneath the same roof, with only a 'common stair.' In the case of 'chambers,' that are used only as offices or places of business, a common stair does not

occasion any particular inconvenience, but it becomes a rather serious one where families, who are strangers to each other, actually reside; and where, besides, the inmates and their visitors, those who bring things sent home by tradespeople must pass up and down.[139]

What was worse, the occupants were likely to be of different social classes: 'Where houses are laid out in "flats", as domiciles for separate families, they surely ought to be with the view of their being occupied by persons of the same class – at least, not wholly dissimilar in their social position . . .'[140] Yet such mixture of classes was notoriously prevalent in Parisian houses. The *Architect* described the promiscuity of Parisian domestic life in grisly detail:

> . . . It would be difficult to quote any custom of the French which English people might less readily fall in with than that which assigns the tenancy of the half dozen successive storeys of the same house to just as many utterly dissociated and indeed discordant people, ranging from a jaunty viscount on the *premier étage* – not merely to a very small *rentier* on the *troisième,* but to a little nest of the humblest work-people on the *cinquième,* all meeting on the common stair . . .

If the block of flats was to be successfully imported to London such social mixture would have to be rigorously prevented:

> The English idea of a house of flats presupposes something very different . . . The lower floors must of course be comparatively expensive, and the upper ones comparatively cheap; but 'gentlemen' would certainly expect to meet 'gentlemen' on the stair; and as for their ladies, it is difficult to assign a limit to the distress and shame that would be occasioned by an habitual encounter on mutual steps and risers between one caste and another.[141]

The problem was to reconcile the flat with family life, something which of course did not really exist in Paris:

> It must be borne in mind . . . that Paris possesses a very small middle-class population, and comparatively few married men. London, on the contrary, contains from one year's end to another an enormous majority of middle-class families. The Londoners are eminently prolific; the Parisians, in their accepted worship of Malthus, carry economy to the extreme limits of prudence. As a rule Paris lives in a flat, London in a house of its own.[142]

The 'family' of course both did and did not include the servants. One of the aims of house-plans was to ensure the maximum of surveillance of the servants by the family, while preventing the servants from doing the same. Although never completely satisfactory from either point of view, the arrangements worked tolerably well in the standard design of house; there was great fear that conditions might be far otherwise in a flat:

> . . . There are objections to the working of the flat system on the Paris plan which would certainly be considered very serious with us. The most important of these is perhaps the manner in which the servants of all the families inhabiting the same house are lodged together in the upper or mansard story, with a separate entrance from the street, and thus

entirely apart from all supervision from their employers except when actually on duty. The immorality admitted to be notorious among this class in Paris it is not surprising to hear of under such an arrangement; but an almost equally serious objection to English minds would be the scandal and tittle-tattle which go on continually between servants of different families as to the doings of their several employers, for which the opportunities would thus be multiplied fiftyfold, and which would render all real privacy as to its own concerns an absolute impossibility for any family inhabiting such a house. . . . The provision of a separate servants' staircase with a servants' entrance on each flat would of course somewhat complicate the planning, but in houses on a tolerably large scale it could very well be managed; only it should be so placed as to be in the way of being a good deal overlooked by the residents, and not in a too removed and out-of-the-way corner, otherwise the facility for gossip, &c., would be almost as great as in the Parisian system.[143]

Within the flat that portion of it occupied by the servants would have to be kept distinct and removed from the rest. 'The three sections of an ordinary house – the dining and reception-rooms; the bed-rooms; the kitchen and domestic offices – must be distinct in themselves, and shut off from each other,' William H. White explained in 1876. 'The Parisian principle of plan . . . will not do for London.'[144]

Much of the debate over the moral impact of the introduction of flats to London assumed that the choice for the middle classes at any rate lay between a flat and a separate house. In fact a large proportion of Londoners occupied one or more rooms as lodgings in what had originally been built as single-family houses. William H. White reminded the RIBA in 1877 that 'within a certain radius of Temple-bar, and even of Regent-circus, the great mass of the residents are lodgers, who occupy a story, a set of rooms, or a single apartment in a house planned as a single residence'.[145]

It had been estimated in 1851 that three-quarters of the population of London either kept or dwelt in a lodging house of some sort – and this included many who were undeniably middle-class. The *Architect* in 1871 asserted that even in distant suburbs such as Highgate, Dalston, Clapham, and Kensington there were 'whole streets . . . full of houses let off from ground-floor to attic in single rooms'.[146] Such houses had been laid out as if they were to be occupied by single families, but in fact were often split up for multiple occupation from the start. 'Throughout every second or third rate street in London we perceive unmistakable signs that the houses generally contain as many families as they have storeys, and sometimes more,' wrote the *Building News* in 1868:

And yet every one of them has been planned exactly as if the builder thought it was to be occupied only by a single family. We are not alluding solely to those districts from which the wealthy inhabitants of a past generation have flitted and in which some inconveniences are almost inevitable, but to the rows upon rows of new houses which the builders well know will each be tenanted by several families, but which are planned after the old conventional plan, without a thought of the conveniences of the future occupants.

Even newly-built houses in Foley Street, near Langham Place, on the Portland Marylebone estate, were being occupied by several middle-class families each:

> None can say how very much of our want of social progress, of sickness, and of the daily
> slackening influence of family ties upon young men, with all its fearful results, are to be
> traced to the influence of homes where every office of the household has to be performed
> in the presence of all, to their great discomfort, and where domestic privacy is impossible.[147]

Yet the purpose-built self-contained flat was a rarity as late as 1880. 'In few points does
London . . . life . . . differ from that of the Continent more remarkably than in the almost
absolute ignoring by the former of all possibility of having more than one house under the
same roof,' according to *Dickens's Dictionary of London* of that year:

> Within the last few years, however, symptoms have appeared of a growing disposition on
> the part of Londoners to avail themselves of the Continental experience which the
> increased travelling facilities of the day have placed within reach of all, and to adopt the
> foreign fashion of living in flats. . . . At present almost the only separate *étages* to be found
> in London are those in the much-talked-of Queen Anne's Mansions, a good number of
> sets in Victoria-st, a few in Cromwell-rd, just between the railway-bridges, seven houses
> near Clarence-gate, Regent's-pk, known as the Cornwall Residences, and a single set in
> George-st, Edgware-rd. Of all these, however, the last named, with a few sets in Victoria-
> st, are still almost the only examples of the real self-contained 'flat' . . . In the case of the
> Queen Anne's Mansions . . . the self-containing principle has been deliberately set aside,
> and a kitchen and coffee-room have been built for the use of the entire establishment.[148]

The blocks that were built caught on so slowly that over a decade later 'Goth', writing in
the *Building News*, could still refer to them as passing eccentricities, unlikely to change the
fundamental nature of the Englishman's home:

> That the 'flat' system of living answered for a time there is abundant evidence in the huge
> blocks of residences in London at the present day. How the holders of flats now find things
> I do not know; but one can see many buildings practically empty, that must be white
> elephants to their owners. I doubt whether it is found that flats let on a long term, and
> should imagine that the suites of rooms change hands very frequently, and that were it
> not for the large floating population of London, their owners would be great losers. . . .
> It may be a matter of taste, but to those with a real love for a home, the flat must seem but
> a poor substitute for a house that may be called one's own.[149]

'The apartment-house has disadvantages: among them the gregariousness of the occupants,'
concluded the *Building News* in 1900. 'It is very doubtful, we think, whether the English race
will ever abandon their own small castles.'[150]

THE OFFICE BLOCK

If the block of flats, like the model dwelling, faced resistance from its supposed beneficiaries,
the commercial equivalent, the office block, was accepted by all as a self-evident necessity.
While converted town houses continued, and continue, to provide satisfactory quarters for

33 '"That the 'flat' system of living answered for a time there is abundant evidence in the huge blocks of residences in London at the present day."' Albert Hall Mansions, R. Norman Shaw, 1881.

small establishments, the increasing scale of activity of nineteenth-century insurance, banking, and other businesses came to demand larger and more impressive buildings, both to house their various operations and to serve as architectural expressions of their wealth, respectability, and reliability. Sometimes these buildings had space to spare to let as offices to other firms; as the century progressed speculative office blocks were built wholly for subletting.

With the possible exception of the Barbican scheme, the post-1945 reconstruction of the City has produced little of architectural interest. By contrast the Victorian rebuilding of the City brought structures as arresting in their architecture and novel in their plans as they were impressive by their bulk. The new banks, insurance buildings, and office blocks were significant not merely as new building types, but as offering opportunities for stylistic innovation and visual display.[151]

The altered external appearance of the City reflected its change from a more heterogeneous nature to the rigorously specialized one that it had come to adopt by the middle of the century. 'Except for business purposes, the City may be said to be now uninhabited,' the *Building News* reported in 1857:

> Those whose business lies there . . . follow the example of the sun – drive home daily to set, and to sit down to dinner in the far-distant west. . . . Nevertheless, the City does not exhibit any symptoms of architectural atrophy – quite the contrary. The semi-public structures . . . which, as banks, insurance companies, offices, chambers, or however else designated, have been there erected within the last year or two, have done more for its architectural character than had been done by its professedly monumental edifices . . . Many buildings which, when first erected, were considered 'notabilities,' are now looked upon very differently, or with perfect indifference. Warehouses and other large establishments for wholesale business are now made to contribute, in no small degree, to the adornment of the City, and though not exactly a new class of buildings, they open a new field of employment to architects.[152]

Mid-Victorian critics were torn between admiration at the audacity and dismay at the taste of the new City architects. The *Architect* in 1871 was more favourable than most when it contrasted the splendour and originality of their new commercial buildings with the retrograde architecture of the fashionable residential quarters:

> . . . There are few spaces in Europe of equal size which can compare for modern architectural interest with the mile radius round the Exchange. The edifices in which the larger City merchants are housed by day are palaces compared with the cold and monotonous dwellings which even our most aristocratic families inhabit at the West End. It may be that the exigencies of business-life, and the necessity which seems to grow stronger every day for putting on a good outside appearance, account for much of the elaborate and, one may say, lavish expenditure which has been made on buildings only intended for mere business purposes.[153]

The office building as a specific type was a nineteenth-century invention and its proliferation a Victorian phenomenon. Edward I'Anson (1812–88), probably the best-known City architect, commented on its novelty in a paper read to the RIBA in 1872:

> When I first began to build on the new London Bridge approaches, previous to 1840, City offices as now constructed were not thought of; the houses were built as shops and dwellings, or as warehouses, and it was the same in Moorgate-street. Since that time, however, a distinct type of construction has been evolved, which is now, perhaps, nearly perfect.[154]

Among 'remarkable and suggestive modifications in town buildings . . . made within the present century', T. Roger Smith and W.H. White, in a paper read to the Society of Arts in 1876, cited the specialized office building:

> The huge blocks of offices for merchants and professional men now to be found in the City . . . are comparative novelties . . . Little more than fifty years ago a great many merchants resided east of Temple Bar often over their counting-houses. Even at that time a few houses were let in separate floors, and used as offices; but buildings erected expressly for offices were unknown, and one of the first houses planned and constructed for that purpose was a stack of offices in Clements-lane, built about 1823. During the last twenty years the growth of this class of building has been enormous.[155]

Hitchcock argues that the increasing willingness of banks, insurance firms, and other businesses to indulge in architectural display after 1840 marked the end of the Georgian feeling that such pursuits, while honourable and of great use to society, did not in themselves carry much prestige.[156] Suspicious as Hexter and Kitson Clark, to mention but two, ought to make us of any explanation based on the rising middle classes, who seem in every successive age to be coming into their own at last, the argument is a plausible one, so long as we bear in mind that the Victorians strove to invest *every* aspect of life with distinctive architectural expression.[157] Commercial buildings in the City gave Victorian London some of its most impressive architectural monuments. The increasing size of individual business enterprises and the increased number of clerical employees demanded more space than the largest converted dwelling could supply. Changing aesthetic tastes combined with growing self-confidence and assertiveness on the part of City firms to ensure that architects would be encouraged to take full advantage of the larger sites and taller elevations.

In the forties and fifties the most popular architectural mode was the Renaissance palace, following Barry's splendid models in the Travellers' and Reform Clubs. The style was appropriate to buildings of great bulk, and carried both the fashionable connotations of Pall Mall and historical references to the merchant aristocracies of the Italian Renaissance.[158] The largest new structures in the early Victorian City were built for banks and insurance companies; only in the late fifties and sixties did office blocks as such rival them in size and pretension.[159]

The two decades from 1857 to 1877 saw the City transformed by the erection of office blocks of unprecedented size and elaborateness. Cannon Street became 'from the mercantile view, as grand in its way as Pall Mall is in the patrician and . . . the West End phase of life'. The new buildings in Gracechurch Street formed 'a very fair example of what we may call the City style of architecture . . . generally conceived in a rather loud key, exhibiting the maximum of showiness with the minimum of real art', according to the *Architect* in 1871; 'carrying a feeling of *cash* about it . . . redeemed . . . by a general impression of good workmanship and the presence of sound, honest material'.[160]

THE DEPARTMENT STORE

Depot, emporium, bazaar, warehouse – none of these seem to possess the slightest descriptive power. Whiteley's is an immense symposium of the arts and industries of the nation and of the world; a grand review of everything that goes to make life worth living passing in seemingly endless array before critical but bewildered humanity; an international exhibition of the resources and products of the earth and air, flood and field, established as one of the greatest 'lions' of the metropolis.[161]

Whatever the literal truth of that tribute to the Universal Provider, which appeared in an anonymous guidebook published around 1887, it captures both the aspirations and the significance of the new phenomenon of the department store. Although not a London invention, it reached here perhaps its highest form of development.* London had always been a centre of consumption, much of its manufacturing industry being geared to the production of luxury goods to be sold to Londoners. The lavish display of its shops, with their brilliantly lighted show-windows and obsequious assistants, was already the marvel of foreign visitors in the eighteenth century. What the Victorians did was to expand and institutionalize a number of pre-existing tendencies and put them all under a single roof.

London had no department stores in today's sense in 1850, although several large drapers, such as Shoolbred's, founded in 1820, Swan & Edgar (1812), Dickins and Jones (1803), and Marshall & Snelgrove (1837), had more than one department. The seventies and eighties saw these and other establishments expand into full department stores, joined by large new foundations like William Whiteley's (1863), the Civil Service Stores (1866), and the Army and Navy Stores (1871).[162] Harrods, which began as a grocery and provision dealer, joined the group and became, with Whiteley's, one of the two giants of late Victorian retailing.[163]

The late Victorian department store was designed to attract a middle-class clientele, and to do so emphasized 'specialization of the merchandising function . . . specialization in buying, selling, display, design and advertisement'.[164] It stressed quality of service, 'choice and individuality' to attract its customers. For Sir Osbert Lancaster's Great Aunt Bessie, 'the Army and Navy Stores fulfilled all the functions of her husband's club . . .'[165]

Whiteley's in particular aimed to offer within its walls a comprehensive imitation of life

---

* The Bon Marché in Paris, which opened in 1852, was long regarded as being the first department store, but Alison Adburgham regards both Kendal Milne in Manchester (founded in 1831) and Bainbridge's of Newcastle (1830) as having become department stores in the modern sense before 1850. Adburgham, pp. 137–40.

34 'Whiteley's in particular aimed to offer
within its walls a comprehensive imitation of life
itself.' Whiteley's, Westbourne Grove, 1900.

itself. It quickly expanded from its original character as a drapery establishment, steadily adding to the kinds of goods it sold: moving outward from ladies' clothing to gentlemen's outfitting in 1869, tailoring, boots, and hats in 1872, stationery in 1873, furniture, china, and glass in 1875, and ironmongery in 1876.[166] A food department was begun in 1875.[167] It meanwhile proceeded to offer one after another of the assortment of services that came to be associated with the great English department stores, opening a refreshment room and a house agency in 1872, and a dry cleaning service two years later.[168] A banking department followed in 1873, and a theatre ticket agency in 1879.[169] In 1881 alone Whiteley's added 'nine new departments: pictures, pianos, florist, fish, wines and spirits, beers and table waters, railway tickets, forage, and hire and exhibition'. The last named 'undertook to equip ceremonies public and private, to cater for shows and entertainments, and to provide goods and services however exotic and extravagant'.[170] In 1892 it established a laundry, featuring the special practice 'of segregating servants' washing from that of the rest of the family, marking it in blue with special labels and packing it separately'.[171] By 1906 there were 159 departments in all.[172]

But the proper London department store is more than a collection of things to buy: it is a total alternative environment, a vision of abundance, a succession of surprises, a place to go to be cosseted, flattered, and amused. Not merely providing its customers with the latest fashions and novelties, it served as a meeting place and promenade, a home away from home. Offering even more plate glass and mirrors, more brilliantly flaring gas jets, and a more successfully contrived illusion of luxury and joy than the gin palaces, theatres, hotels, and restaurants, it served less to rival the home than to complement it, providing ideas and opportunities for domestic embellishment.[173]

Every major neighbourhood had its own collection of shops, with one or more department stores as the dominant feature. 'A resident of Westbourne . . . finds in its principal street all the shops which he desires,' wrote Sir Walter Besant:

> The ladies are not obliged to go to Regent Street and Bond Street for the newest fashions and the most costly materials, for they can find these things on the spot. In the same way there are centres, High Streets, at Islington, at Hackney, at Clapham, at Brixton, where everything can be procured. These places are quite independent of the City and of the West End.[174]

Each shopping centre had its special clientele and its place in the fashionable hierarchy. 'Walworth is as much above Bermondsey New Road as Lewisham or Holloway would consider themselves above Walworth,' according to Booth; 'and a widening gulf separates these from shops in Kensington, in Oxford Street and in Regent Street.'[175]

If the département store as an institution had established itself by the last third of the century, its most impressive architectural expressions were not to come until the very end of Victoria's reign and in the twentieth century. For the most part Victorian department stores expanded by acquiring adjacent shops and throwing existing premises together.[176] The first department store in England to be built from the start as such was the Bon Marché at Brixton in 1877.*

Contemporary architectural journals were more distressed by the structural deceit implicit in their ground-floor shop-windows than impressed by the novel arrangements within the establishments. 'The shop-front, as we now understand it, is essentially a modern institution,' complained the *Building News* in 1881:

> ...What do we find? Consecutive miles of plate-glass – the huge sheets varying in size according to the ... prodigality of the tradesman; but inevitably glazed within the narrowest possible strips of brass, iron, or wood, which look like umbrella-ribs, or whalebone ... Every sign or notion of structural support is indefatigably burked; the party-wall is disputed to the last inch by this crystal demon; the piers, iron stanchions, or columns ... are incased in looking-glass, converted into sham show-cases, or concealed in some other equally ingenious way; so that the vast masses of brick-and-mortar above them become literally and truly 'the baseless fabric of a vision'.[177]

Yet it admitted that 'shop-windows, like the Stage, are a mirror of the times we live in. . . . there can be no question as to their attractiveness. If our country cousins come to pay us a visit in London, do they not devote their first morning to the shops in Regent-street in preference to the Royal Academy?'[178] The shop-window was the outward manifestation of the abundance within, just as the department store symbolized the varied pleasures of the new metropolis.

LONDON FOR THE LONDONER

To what extent did the ordinary Londoner – as distinct from the architectural journalist and the time-traveller from the 1970's – benefit from and enjoy the new buildings, institutions, and possibilities for pleasure and instruction that Victorian London offered? The notable rise in real incomes of the last third of the century meant that more of the population could participate in the advantages of urban life – whether this be a small house of their own in the suburbs, seats in the pit of one of the new music halls, education at one of the new board schools, a bank-holiday excursion to the newly-secured Epping Forest, or acquiring some cheap but attractive treasure at the burgeoning multiple shops or the expanding department stores. With the development of the Saturday half-holiday, more and more could come 'up-west' by tram or underground to gape at the vast new buildings, enjoy the Royal parks, visit the South Kensington museums, promenade along the Embankment, stare at the brilliantly-lit contents of the plate-glass shopfronts, take a cheap meal at one of the new tea shops if they could not afford the dinner at one of the monster restaurants (2s.9d. at Simpson's, 3s.6d. at the Gaiety, 2s.6d. at the Tivoli or the Criterion, or 2s.8d. in the Ladies' Grill Room of the Holborn Restaurant),[179] then go off to one of the many music halls (1s. for a seat in the pit at the Alhambra, Leicester Square).[180] Admittedly these prices were not low for a family trying to subsist on less than 20s. a week, but for the Englishman living above

---

* Adburgham, pp. 169–71. That a suburban location was chosen for such an important venture is yet another indication of the early decentralization of metropolitan retailing, and the separateness of the outlying districts.

the poverty line – and the great majority of them did – late Victorian London had a lot to offer.

So, of course, had late Georgian London: even in the eighteenth century Dr Johnson could exclaim over its inexhaustible variety. But the variety of the 1890's was different in kind from the variety of the 1770's. It derived in large measure, paradoxically, from the very techniques of mass-production that ought to have imposed a deadening standardization instead. But by making cheap and abundant what had once been dear and scarce, the new technology made London the prototype of the modern consumer society. Vulgar, competitive, raucous, often cruel, it yet did more to free than to oppress.

The exuberant inventiveness of its architects, the skill and daring of its engineers, the ingenuity of its entrepreneurs, the energy of its builders, the zeal of its reformers combined to create a city such as had never before existed. While retaining, even into the twentieth century, a fundamentally Georgian fabric, London had freed itself from the discipline of Georgian values. 'Taste' had become a matter for individual judgment; originality had replaced correctness as the goal of the artist. Such qualitative changes were immensely speeded by quantitative leaps. Growth in numbers, in wealth, and in productive capacity permitted a degree of specialization not only in the production of capital and consumer goods, but in the service industries commensurate with the growing demand for objects and experiences at once abundant and various. As the biggest, richest, and most sophisticated expression of Victorian civilization, London magnified and intensified both its virtues and its vices.

Yet parts of Victorian London represented not the denial but the persistence of its Georgian past. The prodigy buildings of the Embankment, the towering blocks of mansion flats, the palaces of commerce and pleasure lining the new thoroughfares of the City and West End were undeniably spectacular and portentous. But the spirit of the eighteenth century remained alive if not well, in particular on the aristocratic leasehold estates, in the speculative building industry, and in the new suburban developments to the west.

CHAPTER FOUR

The Preservation and Extension of Georgian London

LEASEHOLD ESTATES

It was not just the physical presence of Georgian streets and buildings that frustrated attempts to create a genuinely Victorian London, but the persistence of earlier institutions, practices, and attitudes. The 1830's and the decades that followed may have witnessed revolutionary changes in aesthetic values, demographic patterns, political organization, social aspirations, and economic practices; but some things remained the same: notably the pattern of land-ownership, the practices of estate management, and the structure of the building industry. The ground landlords and the speculative builders, working within the framework of the leasehold system, succeeded not only in preserving the character of existing Georgian neighbourhoods far longer than would otherwise have been likely, but in imposing an essentially Georgian character on new suburban developments. Georgian London persisted in spirit as well as body.

The great estates west of the City remained in the hands of the Russell, Grosvenor, Portman, and Cavendish-Bentinck families or their connections, and their agents maintained and refined the practices of management they had employed in the seventeenth and eighteenth centuries. Smaller holdings – like the Howard and Cecil estates south of the Strand, and the Foundling Hospital estate west of Gray's Inn Road – pursued similar policies. They all employed the 99-year building lease and the 21-year repairing lease, both with comprehensive restrictive covenants designed to maintain the character of the original building plan.[1]

The very existence of the older leasehold estates worked to keep most of Georgian London intact. The strict covenants of their leases operated to prevent significant structural alterations and to discourage changes in the use to which the buildings were put. Their comparative success in enforcing high standards of construction in the first instance and stringent repairing covenants thereafter resulted in houses that even at the expiration of their original leases were structurally sound: valuable enough in themselves to be relet on new repairing leases with no more than minor alterations in appearance. To the extent to which the policies

of management had kept the estates attractive to their tenants, they encouraged the maintenance of older patterns of life in parts of central London that might otherwise have
drastically changed in character. Beyond this, by their continuing prestige they provided
models for imitation by the developers of the newer estates to the west, which continued to
be planned, laid out, and managed along essentially Georgian lines through the greater part
of the reign of Victoria.

Such conservative policies were not universally applauded at the time. Leaders of aesthetic
opinion deplored the persistence of eighteenth-century architecture in Harley and Baker and
Gower streets; those for whom 'Metropolitan Improvements' meant schemes for easing the
flow of London traffic raged at the aristocratic obstacles to that traffic in the form of gates
barring free access to what would otherwise have been useful thoroughfares; while the
enforcement of structural and occupational covenants kept individual tenants from making
the most economic use of their property, and architects from exercising the freedom they
would have liked in putting their designs into effect.

Yet the older estates did not survive the Victorian era unchanged; nor were all of the
changes brought about by forces outside the control of the ground landlords. Some estates
were more willing to come to terms with change than others. The Grosvenor estate, for
instance, adopted a policy of active architectural innovation – between Victoria Station and
Hyde Park Corner in the sixties, and around Grosvenor Square in the eighties and nineties
– and thereby maintained and enhanced the social desirability of both neighbourhoods. The
Bedford estate, by contrast, maintained the outward physical appearance of Bloomsbury
while failing to preserve its residential character. The Bedford Office took yet another policy
with respect to the Covent Garden estate, actively encouraging the transformation both of
its physical appearance and its social and economic character. The Portman and Portland
estates in Marylebone maintained their architectural qualities better than the Grosvenor
estate, and the social composition of their tenants better than the Bedford estate. Others
followed decades of somnolent conservatism with spurts of comprehensive redevelopment:
the Norfolk estate south of the Strand, which remained a seventeenth-century backwater
throughout most of the nineteenth century, completely rebuilt itself in the eighties and
nineties; the Cadogan estate from the seventies onward startled fashionable London with its
new 'Queen Anne' streets in the reddest of red brick and the most exuberant terracotta.

The Bedford and Grosvenor estates represent, perhaps, the two extremes of policies
possible on well-managed properties in central London. Both sets of policies were deliberate
and well thought-out: far from merely permitting the radical physical transformation of
large areas south of Oxford Street and around Grosvenor Place, the Grosvenor estate
actively promoted them; far from maintaining Bloomsbury's aesthetic qualities through
unthinking inaction, the Bedford estate worked to preserve its atmosphere and appearance
with persistence, determination, and imagination. Both had, to say the least, financial
resources adequate to enable them to resist temporary economic pressures, and sufficient
confidence in the rightness of their policies to stand apart from the shifts in architectural
taste: the Grosvenor estate led advanced architectural fashion, while the Bedford estate
worked valiantly to preserve what few others at the time thought worth preserving.

THE BEDFORD ESTATE: BLOOMSBURY

Bloomsbury had even in the eighteenth century been something of an anomaly: a residential neighbourhood with aspirations to fashion located far from St James's and Piccadilly and bordered by extensive districts of poverty and decay. The excellence of its planning, the spaciousness of its layout, and the vigour with which the Bedford Office worked to maintain its character made it, in 1837, still one of the most attractive quarters of London. A large portion of it, including most of Tavistock Square and the adjacent streets, built to the high standards of Thomas Cubitt, was barely a decade old; a portion of Gordon Square remained uncompleted. And yet the estate was already uneasily aware that genteel tenants were increasingly reluctant to occupy its spacious and well-planned houses.[2] Outside observers regarded it as an old-fashioned quarter that had seen its best days.

The *Builder* commented in 1844:

> The wealthy classes of this great metropolis are always in locomotion; the streets and squares now covering Lamb's-Conduit-fields, which have almost all been built since 1800, are undergoing the changes common to all cities increasing in wealth and population. At the time they were built they were eagerly sought after by the gentry, and Russell-square had its ducal resident [the Duke of Bolton]: retreating before the tide of population, their place was supplied by dignitaries of the law, medical men, and merchants, for convenience-sake; but time is bringing further changes – the houses are now being rapidly deserted – are converted or converting into shops, lodging-houses, and chambers, and in a few years, when age begins to stamp its mark upon them, the last traces of aristocratic, commercial, or professional opulence will vanish from among them.[3]

A guidebook published in 1852 remarked that Bloomsbury 'constitutes a kind of miniature or secondary west-end . . .'[4] but *The Landlord's and Tenant's Guide* for the following year reported that 'the tide of fashion – ever receding westward – has retired from this once distinguished neighbourhood . . . now for the most part given up to lodging-house keepers or professional men'.[5] The *Building News* noticed a more general shift of function of the older residential quarters in an article on Bloomsbury Square in 1861: 'Professional men find the large rooms which the houses in . . . [the older squares] contain very convenient', it observed, 'and for that consideration consent to pay a rent which as private residences they would be unable to command'. It accounted for the 'sober, dingy appearance' that the squares then possessed as being 'the prevailing character of everything legal and professional'. Some private families were to be found lingering 'here and there in these once aristocratic quarters. But their transition from dwelling-houses to offices is none the less certain . . .'[6] The same journal admitted later in the decade that 'the Bedford estate, by the precarious title of Russell-square, still lies on the frontiers of the semi-fashionable world . . .' Yet its residents were being lured away to Tyburnia and Belgravia, while 'the southern streets of the Bedford estate are becoming yearly more and more shoppy, and the Euston-square terminus and that of the Midland menace it from the northern quarter, so that it will at length become a trading district like the Bedford Covent Garden estate'.[7] Russell Square, pronounced the *Architect* in 1872, 'is unquestionably the worse for its age . . .' as a consequence of the move of 'richer citizens' to the suburbs.[8] Even so the *Builder* the following year listed among its inhabitants 'a baron, a baronet, an alderman, and a member of Parliament, some physicians, and other professional men'. Bedford Square boasted 'a member of Parliament, and a consul-general, but most of the houses are occupied by medical men, professors of singing, &c., and artists. There is an Insurance Company and a Ladies' College, but no shops have yet intruded upon the privacy of the place.' Bloomsbury Square was 'given over to solicitors and architects for their offices, and to lodging-house keepers'.[9]

The decline affected the fashion, not the gentility of the estate; even a Bloomsbury boarding-house was a perfectly respectable establishment:

> There are boarding-houses in Bloomsbury [according to a guidebook of 1888], where are to be found medical and other students of both sexes and several nationalities, American folk passing through London, literary parsons 'up' for a week or two's reading at the British Museum, brides and bridegrooms from the provinces, Bohemians pure and simple, and the restless gentlemen who are 'something in the City', but no one knows what. . . .
>
> Some of the quiet Squares in the Bloomsbury district are very desirable resting-places in London, and we know of more than one boarding-house in this quarter at which we ourselves should consider it a privilege to stay.[10]

Edward Walford observed that it had become 'a mark of high breeding' to pretend not to know where Bloomsbury was, citing 'Mr. Croker's inquiry in the House of Commons, "But where *is* Russell Square?"' Yet he quoted Albert Smith to show that the Bedford estate retained a marked superiority to the streets and squares to the east of Southampton Row. To the landladies of the district between the Foundling Hospital and Red Lion Square, 'left stationary, whilst time has flown by them, like an object in the tranquil side-water of a stream', Great Ormond Street was still 'the focus of the West-end. . . . they still regard Russell and Bedford Squares as their *Belgravia* . . .'[11]

While the squares and principal streets of the Bedford estate maintained their precarious gentility, some of the lesser streets towards and across its borders had not. In 1876 the *Architect* reported that the smaller houses there were 'almost wholly given up to a poor class of lodging-house keepers'. The area between Gower Street and Charlotte Street had 'numerous houses with rich panelling, decorated plaster ceilings, wood dados, inlaid mantel-pieces, ornamental staircases, &c., occupied by people who have not the remotest appreciation thereof . . .'* Meanwhile, according to the *Building News*, the lawyers who once lived in Bloomsbury had 'found other more attractive suburban homes beyond the range and din of town life'. While admitting that the neighbourhood retained 'an air of antiquated respect-

---

* *A*, XVI (1876), p. 33. 'In Bedford, Russell, Tavistock Squares, and in one or two other squares in the immediate vicinity, each house with few exceptions is tenanted by a single family . . . but in the bye streets round those squares the population is principally composed of lodgers.' [William H. White], *Houses or Homes? An Architect's Appeal to the Duke of Bedford*, quoted in *A*, XVII (1877), p. 328.

ability, removed from the thoroughfares of business and shops', it doubted the wisdom 'of rebuilding in their original integrity for single families the old dwellings which now occupy the squares and streets of the Duke of Bedford's estate. . . . This part of the metropolis is losing in its residential character every year . . .' As they stood, the houses left much to be desired:

> Having inspected many of the interiors of houses in the locality of Russell and Bedford Squares, we can testify to the inadequacy of many of them in domestic conveniences. The bulk of them are without proper water-closet provision; these closets are often placed under the stairs, without light, with no ventilation of any kind, and with scarcely room to turn, while the halls and rooms are spacious and lofty. The kitchen conveniences are certainly below the standard expected for such houses, bath-rooms are exceptional, and few of the old houses are provided with heating or kitchen boiler ranges.[12]

In addition, 'the bedroom accommodation is in many of them deficient in proportion to the size of the house; everything is sacrificed to the sitting-rooms'.[13]

The Bedford Office could do nothing to remedy such deficiencies until the leases fell in. But as they did, it systematically required structural alterations before it would grant new repairing leases. In 1857 the *Building News* reported that the estate was having houses re-roofed and faced with Portland cement, as their leases fell in, in Tottenham Court Road, Tavistock Street, Great Russell Street, and Caroline Street.[14] 'As the leases run out . . . very great improvements are being effected, under the direction of Mr. [Charles] Parker, surveyor and architect to . . . the Duke of Bedford,' the journal reported:

> On the eastern side of *Southampton-row* eight houses and shops are in various stages of progress, the fronts of some of which have been entirely taken down and rebuilt, others are being thoroughly renovated, and the whole are to be made uniform in design, as regards their street elevations, which is being effected by facing them with Portland cement . . .

Here we see how far building practice lagged behind advanced architectural theory: uniformity of elevation had for the past two decades been almost as universally condemned as stucco facing; the Bedford estate in 1857 was bringing its property up to the standards of the 1820's. It was not being particularly retrograde in so doing, for similar policies were being followed by most other ground landlords and speculative builders in the fifties and even sixties. The *Building News* itself gave cautious approval:

> In reference to the cement facings of our street buildings, it may be urged that ultra-Purists in architecture may object to this mode of external embellishment; we may, however, remark that when the structures to which we advert are completed, they will present a much better appearance, architecturally, than the dull, tame, expressionless old brick fronts, which in many of our streets appear like walls perforated with holes for their window and door openings, the former being destitute of architraves or other dressings round them.

35 *above* ' "The Bedford estate, by the precarious title of Russell-square, still lies on the frontiers of the semi-fashionable world . . ." ' Russell Square, west side.

36 'In 1857 the *Building News* reported that the estate was having houses re-roofed and faced with Portland cement, as their leases fell in, in . . . Caroline Street.' Caroline Street, west side, at the corner of Tavistock Street (later Bedford Avenue).

No 'excessive external embellishment' was applied, 'but the whole is being done in the most appropriate manner, with moulded architraves round the windows, and terminated by a bold cornice, having its corona supported by Ionic blocks'. Plate-glass windows, 'in two squares each, instead of eight as formerly', were installed, 'by which much more light will be admitted into the various rooms'.[15]

Not until 1875, when the original 99-year leases for Bedford Square fell in, could the estate begin to do anything substantial about its houses north of Great Russell Street, and then, and for many years thereafter, only for the property along the western edge of Bloomsbury. It would be the very end of the century before the leases in Russell Square and its vicinity would expire. In the meantime it did what it could to raise the standard of occupancy of the houses in Gower Street, in particular, insisting on heavy repairs in exchange for new leases, and attempting, with only limited success, to replace lodging-house keepers with single family occupants.[16] Gower Street, 'one of the dullest, gloomiest thoroughfares in town. . . . [with its] depressing vista of . . . blackened house-fronts, their monotonous elevations wholly unbroken or unrelieved . . .'[17] so depressed the Victorians that the efforts of the estate to rehabilitate it were probably foredoomed. The *Building News* was sceptical as to Bloomsbury's social potentialities:

> It is said that the Duke of Bedford means, if he can, to stem the tide of fashion which has set in so long towards South Kensington. The leases are falling in on his property in Bloomsbury-square and the neighbourhood, and he means to build fine houses there in the hope of attracting fine people to that once fashionable but now less favoured district. . . . it is doubtful if he will overcome the objection which most persons will entertain to living so far from the parks. They will be close to the theatres, it is true; but they will be a long way from the Row, a long way from Bond-street, and, above all, a long way from Pall-mall and the clubs. . . . the ladies won't like the first, their husbands won't like the last.[18]

Shifts of aesthetic fashion in the seventies provided, for once, some help to the Bedford Office. The Queen Anne style was becoming popular for new domestic buildings, and encouraged a greater appreciation of genuine late Stuart and early Georgian architecture. Although it would be some time before the far plainer late Georgian that constituted most of Bloomsbury would again be admired, the *Building News* gave it grudging acceptance as early as 1880:

> The architectural exterior of the houses [in Bloomsbury] is, by the caprice of fashion, somewhat more in keeping with modern taste than it was a decade ago; the shabby hue of the brick fronts with their square windows and faded window drapery, the wide doorways, with here and there some carved work in the style of the Adams, take us back to a period when internal convenience was more studied than it is now. Internally, many of the houses show indications of former wealth: the cornices and ceilings are in some cases excellent examples of the style of the beginning of the present century. . . . The fireplaces are often designed in the best style of this age, the statuary marble mantel being enriched by the

light and elegant festooning and fluted ornaments common to this period. . . . Blooms-bury-square . . . shows signs of reconstruction.[19]

The *Builder* was generous in its praise of the efforts of the Bedford Office:

> The constant improvement of the Bloomsbury District, as opportunity serves, – by the care of the Bedford Office, – is a public advantage. To allow a neighbourhood to degener-ate to mere lodging-houses or rough business premises, and eventually, perhaps, to be given over to squalor and dirt, till some public Act of Parliament or local authority is required to remove the nuisance, has been too often the fate of localities which only commenced their downward career by being unfashionable. Here rigid care in the con-struction of new buildings is being exercised to prevent such a calamity overtaking one of the most healthy and one of the most convenient neighbourhoods of London, while the improvement of most of the hitherto objectionable districts adjoining has done and is doing much to render this again one of the most pleasant quarters of London.[20]

It later noted the remodelling of Gower Street:

> . . . Great improvements were made some little time since in a number of the houses on the west side of . . . [Gower] street, in regard to sanitary arrangements and additions necessary for modern ideas of comfort and decent living. The attempt made at the same time to give a more important appearance to the front of a good many of these houses, by framing the doorways with stone pilasters and architraves, has not been so successful; the additions thus made being, architecturally speaking, as ugly and badly-designed as they could well be . . . Very recently some of the larger houses on the east side of the street have been taken in hand, and subjected to a thorough refitting internally, without any similar attempt at stone-casing the entrances . . . These more lately 'revived' houses are excellent residences of their class, with a good deal of pleasing variety in the arrangement and planning of the principal rooms, and they have another attraction little suspected by the casual passer-by . . . quite a plantation of trees, some of them very fine ones. In the building alterations . . . the most religious care has been taken not in any way to injure these trees, which are a precious possession to the site.[21]

Ten years after the same journal again decried the alterations, this time with a greater sense of the aesthetic value of the original façades:

> In Gower-street . . . the houses originally all had those ornamental fan-lights, variously and often very gracefully designed, which were a characteristic of the period when they were built. Nearly all these have been removed and blank sheets of plate-glass sub-stituted. The doors of a number of the houses on the west side have been encased with heavy clumsy-looking stone framework, which quite destroys the original character of the houses, and on the east side an attempt has been made to give new dignity to some of the larger houses by absurd flat stone pilasters plastered against the walls. Why could they not let the old brick fronts alone? However plain, they were in much better taste than these clumsy additions.[22]

The Bedford Office was learning how hard it was to keep up with advanced architectural ideas, and that responding to the criticisms of the seventies was not the way to please the critics of the eighties and nineties.

Such critics came, though, to regard Bloomsbury more sympathetically, and sometimes used it as a stick to beat whatever excess of contemporary architecture seemed to deserve chastisement. Here, for instance, is the *Building News* in 1889:

> In the miles of stock brick and stucco of Bloomsbury one sees little to suggest that the designers of that gloomy locality ever had any but the most restricted views of architecture; but although the houses and squares do not inspire us with enthusiasm for the building of those days, they were at least the practical outcome of honest building and unsophisticated workmanship. The interiors and planning of these acres of town houses have at least one virtue – they are examples of commodiousness, convenience, and comfort, which are wanting in modern town houses. These merits must be set against their plainness and bare formality. But the era of these residences marks what we may call the great builders' era of the latter end of the 18th and commencement of the present century. . . . In Bloomsbury-square, a once fashionable neighbourhood . . . we have evidences of that careful internal planning and decoration which distinguish the earlier years of the Classic Revival. The houses in Tavistock-square and Woburn-place have the genuine Cubitt ring about them – massive, well built, and comfortable.[23]

So, just as the expiration of the Russell Square leases approached, it began to occur to architects that the dull, gloomy monotony of familiar Bloomsbury might have unsuspected virtues. Only when its integrity came to be threatened did people dimly recognize it for the treasure of architecture and town planning that it was.

The Grosvenor estate had been one of the pioneers in the introduction of the luxury flat to London. By contrast it was not until the nineties that blocks of flats began to appear in Bloomsbury, on the site of demolished substandard mews property west of Gower Street, and between Bedford Square and Great Russell Street. In the long run these flats probably did more to keep middle-class families resident in Bloomsbury than any amount of rebuilding of the impractically large houses in the squares. At the time, however, the *Building News* feared overcrowding and a change in the old residential quality of the neighbourhood:

> The tendency to a great activity in 'improvements' on the Bedford Estate seems to be taking a form which may have a very prejudicial effect on what is at present said to be the healthiest district in London. A great many tall buildings for houses in flats have recently been erected on sites between Gower-street and Tottenham Court-road, which, if fully occupied, must considerably increase the population per acre in this part of Bloomsbury; but these are entirely out-done by a huge block which is just being completed in Charlotte-street, between Bedford-square and Oxford-street. . . . If this goes on, the architectural effect of the old Bloomsbury squares, which in its way is quiet and pleasing, will be entirely spoiled . . .[24]

Despite such fears the new blocks of flats, away from the principal streets and squares, did

37 *above* 'Gower Street, "one of the dullest,
gloomiest thoroughfares in town . . . [with its]
depressing vista of . . . blackened house-fronts,
their monotonous elevations wholly unbroken or
unrelieved . . .".' Gower Street, east side, 1910.

38 '". . . a huge block which is just being
completed in Charlotte-street . . . If this goes on,
the architectural effect of the old Bloomsbury
squares, which in its way is quiet and pleasing,
will be entirely spoiled . . ."' Bedford Court
Mansions, 1894.

comparatively little to change the outward appearance of Bloomsbury. The demolition of the east side of Russell Square and the refacing of the blocks on the other sides with terracotta ornamentation, on the other hand, completely altered the character of that part of the estate. The change involved another fruitless attempt by the estate to catch up to late-Victorian architectural fashions. The *Builder* found the project totally misguided:

> The manner of improving the houses is more than questionable. 'It is proposed,' we are told, 'not to rebuild the houses' (this applies to the squares mainly) 'but to treat their fronts architecturally with porches, bay-windows, friezes, cornices, and window dressings, all in light buff terra cotta, new railings and balconettes will complete the exterior. Each block is being treated as a separate unit, the centre and wing houses being carried up an additional story, imparting variety to the present rather monotonous skyline, as well as affording needed additional bedroom accommodation to some of the larger class of houses where the reception rooms are now somewhat disproportionately large.'

The estate was, that is to say, proposing to do something about the accumulated criticism of decades as to the monotonous façades, dull skyline, and shortage of bedrooms in its streets. The *Builder* approved of the additional bedrooms, but found 'the proposal to tinker up the house fronts with terra-cotta dressings . . . as absurd as it is unnecessary, and a foolish expenditure of money . . . The houses as they exist have a certain character of their own which had much better be left to them.'[25] The east side of the square was in due course to be occupied by the present Russell Hotel and the late Imperial, a 'vicious mixture of Art Nouveau Gothic and Art Nouveau Tudor', according to Pevsner in 1952.[26]

THE BEDFORD ESTATE: COVENT GARDEN

The Bedford Office took a more active role in the replanning and rebuilding of the Covent Garden estate during the same period. At the start of the century the buildings and the street pattern were much as they had been when the estate was originally developed in the seventeenth century. The houses had, of course, long since ceased to be occupied singly, and large numbers had had their ground floors converted into shops.[27] Beginning with the erection of Charles Fowler's new market buildings in 1828–30, the estate methodically rebuilt, refronted, or demolished the decaying buildings, pushed through new streets, cleared away slum property, arranged for the building of model dwellings, and in general transformed the district into the specialized mercantile neighbourhood that it remained until the transfer of the market to Nine Elms in 1974.[28]

Between 1856 and 1865 the estate contributed large sums to a programme of street improvements in Covent Garden, including £15,000 towards the construction by the Metropolitan Board of Works of Garrick Street, forming an important route onto the estate from the west. It encouraged lessees to rebuild and repair extensively on the renewal of leases, although the original structures tended to remain under the new façades.[29] In connection with the building of Garrick Street the estate itself extended Burleigh Street from Exeter Street to Tavistock Street and pushed Hart Street westward to join Garrick Street.[30] The *Building News* described in 1875 some of the improvements made over the

39 *above* 'The *Builder* . . . found "the proposal
to tinker up the house fronts with terra-cotta
dressings . . . as absurd as it is unnecessary, and
a foolish expenditure of money . . .".' Proposed
alterations to Russell Square, north side. *Builder*
LXXII (1897), after p. 330.

40 '"The piazza round Covent-garden is about
to be rebuilt from the designs of Mr. Henry
Clutton . . ."' The original piazza in 1877, just
before demolition.

previous quarter century:

> Within the last twenty-five years most of the changes have been made; old and dilapidated tenements have been pulled down, and nests of vice and gambling-houses cleared by the progress of sanitary reform . . . We allude to 'King-street' . . . Its houses have been modernised exteriorly. Hardly half a dozen of the original brick fronts are to be seen. Stuccoed fronts have, in many instances, replaced the old façades, and there are a few pretentious new stone-fronted buildings.[31]

Many of the smaller courts and back lanes still formed densely-crowded slums, but they would all have disappeared by the end of the century.

The best-known feature of the estate, Inigo Jones's Piazza, became a victim to the general redevelopment. The *Architect* reported in 1877:

> Some of the streets around Covent Garden Market are about to undergo extensive improvements, the Duke of Bedford having decided upon the rebuilding of a large number of the houses in the thoroughfares on the several sides of the market, whilst it is also intended to carry the piazzas entirely round four sides. . . . The new buildings, as a matter of course, are to be of a superior character to those which they will replace, and the new piazzas in front of them will be more worthy of the place.[32]

The proposal was, as the steward of the estate had predicted, 'the subject of much public criticism and discussion'.[33] The *Building News* reported on the beginning of the reconstruction in 1877:

> The piazza round Covent-garden is about to be rebuilt from the designs of Mr. Henry Clutton, architect to the Duke of Bedford, and the frontages of the surrounding property are to be erected from Mr. Clutton's elevations, although independent architects may be employed for the internal arrangements. Work has already commenced at the corner of King-street . . . while the Bedford Hotel, at the top of Southampton-street, has been in progress some little time . . . Mr. Clutton is engaged by the Duke to remodel . . . [St Paul's] church . . . Messrs. Cubitt, we believe, are about to rebuild the northern portion of the square. The style chosen by Mr. Clutton is an exceedingly simple form of the Renaissance, in accord with the market buildings and Inigo Jones's church of St. Paul.[34]

Later the same year, it decided that the destruction of the original Piazza was not the wanton act that later generations have sometimes thought:

> On the north side we observe the block of property . . . being pulled down, including a long frontage of the old piazza or arcade. Observing the destruction of the latter, our attention was directed to the very flimsy and inferior construction of the old groined ceiling of plaster, and the half-decayed timbers above. On a former occasion we noticed the extensive bulging of the front and portions of the arcade, and we think the Duke has not too soon commenced the work of restoration. . . . We are glad to find that the new structures will be worthy of the locality and its historic associations – that the original

idea of Inigo Jones, to surround the square with a piazza, is intended in the new scheme
. . . The general features of the new façade will accord in style, if not in sentiment, with
the age of the old buildings.[35]

Further redevelopment came at the end of the century in connection with the formation
of the Aldwych and Kingsway by the London County Council. The present eastern end of
Tavistock Street, running behind the Waldorf Hotel and the Strand and Aldwych Theatres,
replaced a cluster of congested courts. The Duke sold most of the ground on the north side
to the L.C.C., which rehoused the displaced residents in new blocks. Similar demolitions and
building took place in the courts north of the Drury Lane Theatre and Russell Street.[36]

THE GROSVENOR ESTATE

When Thomas Cubitt was negotiating with both the Bedford and the Grosvenor estates in
the early 1820's, he found the former far more active in its planning and rigorous in its
controls. On the latter he took much greater initiative than did Lord Grosvenor's agents in
laying out and developing Belgravia and Pimlico. The accession of the second Marquess of
Westminster in 1845 produced sweeping reforms in the management of the Grosvenor
Office, although it never reached the level of thoroughness and efficiency of the Bedford
Office.[37] Even so, it was by the 1860's taking a more active, or at least more conspicuous
role in the redevelopment of its estate than the Bedford Office was in Bloomsbury. This is
not to suggest that the Bedford estate was less than vigilant in enforcing its leasehold
covenants, or that it neglected opportunities for improvement and rebuilding whenever
leases expired; but that the Grosvenor estate went beyond the limits of normal estate management to become one of the most energetic agents for the transformation of Georgian
into Victorian London.[38]

At the accession of Victoria the built-up estate of the Marquess of Westminster consisted
of some well-established streets running west from Park Lane and south from Oxford
Street, centring on Grosvenor Square, the most aristocratic address in London; and a ribbon
of eighteenth-century development running south from Hyde Park Corner, backing on the
very new and very grand stuccoed terraces of Belgravia; equally new but less grand streets
extended beyond towards the Thames. The Grosvenor Square region, while immensely
more fashionable than Bloomsbury, was held, if possible, in even lower regard for its
architecture:

> The most aristocratic streets at the west end of the town have very few attractions indeed
> for the admirers of architecture, [wrote the *Civil Engineer* in 1843] being far more remark-
> able for the absence than for any display of taste. They have a certain air of opulence about
> them, not to be mistaken; but it is entirely in 'undress;' so that nothing can be more
> homely and insipid than the 'magnificent squares' – as they are often bouncingly termed –
> in that quarter of the metropolis. Grosvenor Square is no exception, for if it contains some
> mansions above the average in point of size, it also presents some that are of more than
> ordinary ugliness.[39]

As late as the 1850's the architectural policies of the estate, under the direction of a dynasty of architects named Thomas Cundy, were unexceptionably conservative. When the leases of houses on the south side of Grosvenor Square fell in during that decade the resulting rebuilding displayed 'dignity and severity of style . . . with some suggestion of the Georgian façades they were replacing'.[40] The *Building News* in 1858 reported two new houses being built in the square, 'from the designs of Thomas Cundy, Esq., architect and surveyor to the estate . . . in the Italian style, the plain facings of which are to be of white Suffolk bricks, with moulded cement dressings to the windows, which will be surmounted by an enriched cornice . . .'[41]

The building of Victoria Station on the borders of Belgravia and the falling in of leases in nearby Grosvenor Place in the sixties provided the occasion for more drastic alterations, with a new street plan, new building types, and a dramatically different style of architecture. The *Builder* in 1865 thought the massive operations then going forward on the Grosvenor estate justified the concentration of urban landownership:

> A clearance has been made of several streets, and Grosvenor-place has been extended in a straight line to the Victoria [the present Grosvenor] Hotel; this whole district being now laid out with direct routes leading to the Palace and to Westminster, by Victoria-street, an open space being reserved for plantation [Grosvenor Gardens], and the projected buildings planned by the architect in a style to correspond with Belgravia, so as to form a suitable connecting link with the Westminster improvements. . . . Such changes, made at the seeming sacrifice of large rentals, when carried out, as in this instance, with skill and judgment, are sure to pay in increased returns, and the interests of owners and occupiers are both served; but this can happen only on large estates. The great obstruction to improvements in the ancient portions of the metropolis, is the minute and interminable subdivision of property and of interests . . .[42]

In creating a formal way from Hyde Park Corner to the new Victoria Station the Grosvenor estate was responsible for one of the more impressive metropolitan improvements of the decade. Grosvenor Gardens, adjacent to the station, not only brought the glories of the French Renaissance to the West End but was one of the early experiments designed to introduce French flats to a suspicious English public.

'A limited company is being formed for the erection of "*maisons meublées*" at Grosvenor-gardens,' the *Builder* reported in July 1865:

> The elevation of the proposed buildings, as well as of all the adjoining buildings, has been designed by Mr. T. Cundy, jun. . . . who has also laid out the garden inclosures in front of the houses. The ground-floor and basement of the building, as in Paris, will be let off in shops, and a portion of the ground-floor will be let for a *restaurant*, the proprietor being bound to supply the residents in the apartments. The upper part of the building will be the '*maisons meublées*,' and will comprise about 200 rooms. These will be so arranged that any number may be let off as a separate 'apartment;' and as there will be several entrances direct from the street, a tenant taking any considerable number of rooms might have the sole use of one of such entrances, thereby securing entire privacy.[43]

That 'restaurant' was still sufficiently foreign to require italicizing, that the plebeian word 'flat' was not used, and the assurance that some of the residents, at least, would not have to share a street entrance with any others suggests once again how deep-seated were the prejudices to be overcome before Londoners would accept flatted living; as well as how the Grosvenor estate had become the patron of the avant-garde.

The new houses in Grosvenor Place served both as a repudiation of the eighteenth century and a demonstration of the superior taste and refinement of the nineteenth:

> If the shade of Sir Charles Grandison ... could see the many changes wrought in the aspect of London ... it would be, perhaps, most astounded at those now progressing on the Grosvenor estate ... The cramped, low, many-paned plain brick houses which Clarissa, Belinda, and Pamela filled with chintz, china, mirrors, cabinets, and card-tables, appear seedy and unattractive to the last degree by the side of the lofty, airy, ornamented dwellings for which their descendants have created a demand.

The project exemplified the kind of coherent redevelopment possible only on large, well-managed leasehold estates:

> A magnificent scheme has been laid down, and time, money, and space have been given to carry it out. Unfettered, to any considerable extent, by the tedious and sometimes inconsiderate claims, or requisitions, of owners of intermediate properties, Lord Westminster has been able to make new roads, leave garden spaces, or build mansions, exactly on the positions recommended to him by his architect ... the new district is the well-considered and comprehensive scheme of a trained mind, instead of the thwarted, curtailed vexations which too many improvers' plans become through such opposition.

The new streets would secure more efficient social segregation, with the poor removed from back streets and mews and either placed under tidy supervision in new model blocks or expelled from the estate altogether:

> ... The poor he [the Marquis of Westminster] has not forgotten. Beside the snug houses occupied by the wealthy in this fashionable quarter, there were mews, and small dark streets of small smelly houses, in which dwelt the industrious poor who ministered to their rich neighbours, in the shape of small tradesmen, workmen, and workwomen, laundresses, &c., as well as stables for horses, and dwellings for coachmen. These have shared the fate of more important structures, and have been swept off the face of Pimlico. Their inhabitants, however, have not been uncared for. With the present demolition of the mews, the coachmen found their occupation removed, if not gone; there was, therefore, no necessity to provide for these; and the small shops, too, could scarcely be required in a region now bared to a desert; but the working classes who found homes in the locality have been provided for by the erection of two model lodging-houses in the Commercial-road, Pimlico, out of means leant for the purpose by the Marquis.

Not only were the poor kept decently away from the rich, but different degrees of wealth were separately provided for, and appropriate shops provided to serve their respective needs:

41 *above* 'Grosvenor Gardens . . . brought the glories of the French Renaissance to the West End . . .' Grosvenor Gardens.

42 'The new houses in Grosvenor Place served both as a repudiation of the eighteenth century and a demonstration of the superior taste and refinement of the nineteenth . . .' Grosvenor Place, looking up from Ebury Street.

. . . The whole scheme is a wide piece of comprehension. In the first instance, mansions are built for the ultra wealthy; a smaller class of house, equal as to taste and locality, is provided for those equal in degree, though not in requirements; first-class shops are brought into the district to provide for them; their dependants are provided for; and a bank established; the result promising to be an ornament to the metropolis, and creditable and profitable alike to the Marquis, the purchasers, the speculators, the architect, the tradesmen, and the builders.[44]

The *Architect* described the new buildings as

very preferable . . . to much of the street architecture of Paris. The roofs and chimneys are in many cases very striking, and there is a reasonable diversity between the various blocks of buildings, without any straining after effects of variety, although they must certainly be accused of imitating the effect of large public buildings instead of blocks of houses.[45]

The *Building News* also regretted the deceit involved in disguising the individuality of each house in order 'to make each block like one public building . . . but this seems to be inseparable from speculating building. As speculating building, these works are a step far in advance of what has yet been done . . .'[46]

During the eighties the estate embarked on the massive rebuilding of the streets around Grosvenor Square in the newly fashionable red brick and terracotta. 'It was a matter for thankfulness,' R.W. Edis told the Society of Arts in 1884, 'that one large owner of land in London – the Duke of Westminster – set a good example in his own property by encouraging in every way a departure from the old fogeydom of street design, and the use of modern improvements in building construction and materials.'[47] The *Daily News* wrote with enthusiasm of the transformation of the estate:

Pass by the corner of Gilbert Street, up Duke Street, round by Stalbridge Buildings, Lumley Street, through Grosvenor Square to Mount Street, and you will find many excellent specimens of a kind of architecture which seems destined, at no distant date, to transform large tracts of central and western London. The supersession of the flat, dull, and mean skylines of the old houses by steep, bold gables and broken roofs; the employment of balconies, arcades, and projecting windows; the feeling for colour; the grouping of wall spaces, with a view to the distribution of light and shade – all these are more or less characteristic of the new Domestic architecture of London. In a few years Mount Street will become an architectural gem – especially if the suggestion of building a quadrant, or crescent, between it and Grosvenor Square [the present Carlos Place] be carried out. It is true that the actual builders of the Mount Street new houses are scarcely free agents, and that the ground landlord, the Duke of Westminster, is the prime mover in this process of reconstruction. Still, the duke deserves all the praise due to good taste . . .

Nothing can be more striking, in this gradual transformation of London ugly into London beautiful, than the displacement of the wretched houses on the western side of Duke Street by the present really fine range of buildings of red brick, with their basements of grey granite, pilasters of red, window casements of terra-cotta, steep, central gable, bay windows, and balconies.

Here, as in the Grosvenor Place improvements, the working classes were moved into special, supervised buildings, and kept discreetly separate from the wealthy inhabitants of the rebuilt streets:

> The Duke Street and Mount Street buildings, portioned off into sets of chambers rented at two to three or four hundred a year each, are, however, less significant of the change in public taste than the artisans' block dwellings in their immediate neighbourhood. The Stalbridge and Balderton buildings behind Duke Street are palaces in comparison with the houses which they have superseded. With the recreation-ground which . . . will be opened to the occupants of these blocks, this new class of 'composite house' is a visible testimony to the popular craving for air, space, and light.*

Given such ambitious schemes, one can understand the assertion made by Francis E. Masey: 'It is . . . from the large owners of house property in London, with autocratic powers, such as the present Duke of Westminster, that any great structural improvements are to be hoped for.'[48] In 1892 'J.E.T.' in the *Building News* singled out Mount Street for special praise, stressing the active role played by the estate architect, Eustace Balfour, and the ground landlord himself in determining its architectural appearance:

> Old smoke-begrimed Mayfair is gradually disappearing, and in its place is growing up a neighbourhood of picturesque streets. All these charmingly-designed buildings, whether they be shops, flats, or private houses, and which meet the eye at every turn, have in every case been submitted to the personal inspection of the duke before their erection, and his judgment in rejecting some designs and approving others is exemplified by the pleasing result. The buildings . . . form one of the latest demonstrations of the vast strides London street architecture has made towards the picturesque.[49]

'We all know, almost every Londoner knows, that the gradual rebuilding of a part of London has been effected by the Duke of Westminster with unquestioned success . . . on a settled plan, and almost automatically . . .' Arthur Cawston told the RIBA in 1893.[50] 'In the central and more wealthy districts of London there is a vast improvement in street architecture,' Sir George Laurence Gomme boasted in 1898:

> Any one acquainted with the rebuilding of Lord Cadogan's estate at Chelsea, and of the Grosvenor estate in St. George's will concede this. The shop property and private houses

---

* Reprinted in *A*, XI (1888), pp. 167–8. 'The Duke of Westminster opened on Saturday a new garden in Duke-street, Grosvenor-square, laid out by him on part of his estate from which old, worn-out tenements had been removed. It comprises a little more than one-third of an acre, and consists of grass and plane trees, with broad, asphalted paths. This open space is part of a general scheme of improvement, which embraces also the erection by the Improved Industrial Dwellings Company, under building leases, of large blocks of working-class dwellings. These will accommodate some hundreds more persons than the improvement will have displaced.' *BN*, LVII (1889), p. 657.

built within the last few years in Mount Street, Audley Street, and the neighbourhood are of the most interesting types . . . fortunately rebuilding means, as a rule, improvement in style.[51]

Redevelopment continued steadily as the century came to an end. The *Builder* in 1896 described extensive demolition and rebuilding in the area between North and South Audley Streets and Park Lane.[52] In 1899 the *Building News* reported that the Davies Street entrance to Oxford Street had been widened.[53] Claridge's Hotel in Brook Street was rebuilt in conformity to the new style, which to this day gives that part of London an unmistakable architectural identity.

Both the Duke of Bedford and the Duke of Westminster took advantage of the expiration of leases on their estates to enforce systematic rebuilding, both with the aim of reinforcing their residential character. Both combined the destruction of substandard mews and working-class dwellings with the erection of model block dwellings and the creation of new open spaces. Both encouraged the refacing of town houses to bring them in line with current architectural fashions. Both strove either to remove the poor from the estate entirely or to house them in new, sanitary, supervised blocks. Of the two, the Westminster estate proceeded with more sweeping demolitions, more comprehensive programmes of rebuilding, and more striking architectural innovations. The line of buildings from Hyde Park Corner to Victoria Station remains, with gaps, to this day a monument to the fashion for French Renaissance of the sixties, while the area between Oxford Street and Berkeley Square still memorializes the passion for red brick and terracotta that gripped London in the late Victorian years. The Bedford estate, in contrast, lost its enthusiasm for heavy stone door-casings after imposing them on a single block of dwellings in Gower Street; and, fortunately, stopped covering houses with terracotta after its experiment in Russell Square.

The Westminster estate was not only bolder in its schemes, but more successful in their outcome. 'In place of the odd corners where, less than twenty years ago, poverty lurked,' Charles Booth observed in connection with the streets around Grosvenor Square in 1902, 'we now have private houses of the best class, well-arranged mews and some working-class dwellings, which really are models'.[54] His description of the district between Russell Square and Langham Place – which included, admittedly, a large area off the Bedford estate west of Tottenham Court Road – was less enthusiastic:

> Though no longer fashionable, the bulk of this district is fairly well-to-do; and the difficulties of the clergy in dealing with it are due, not so much to poverty as to the fact that the population consists largely of residents in furnished apartments and lodging-houses, with a considerable admixture of foreigners. There is also a large working-class element, respectable, but non-churchgoing.[55]

In 1892, according to the *Building News*, the new flats in Mount Street, 'notwithstanding their size, and consequently high rental . . . are already occupied, even before their actual completion'.[56] Five years later the *Builder* reported that in Bedford Square, 'we are informed that houses are almost going begging . . .'[57]

It would be unfair to attribute either the success of the one or the failure of the other to the quality of management of the respective estates. The Grosvenor estate had all the advantages of location, the Bedford estate none. It was one thing to build a street of mansions with Belgrave Square immediately to the rear and the grounds of Buckingham Palace to the front; quite another to maintain the character of an enclave of first-class houses surrounded on every side by socially inferior districts. It was one thing to raise the standing of streets adjacent to Oxford Street, Grosvenor Square, and Park Lane; quite another to do the same thing in the vicinity of New Oxford Street and Tottenham Court Road. What can only be said is that the Grosvenor estate took every advantage of its magnificent geographical situation, while the Bedford estate did everything that could reasonably be expected of it to counteract the drawbacks of its own location.

As for Covent Garden, for all the continuing attacks on 'Mud-Salad Market' by *Punch* and others, the Bedford estate, over the long run, successfully adapted the estate to the changed commercial needs of the age. The market and its environs continued to serve London reasonably well, with the streets and buildings left pretty much as the Bedford estate sold them in 1914, for another 60 years; by the 1970's the whole estate seems worthy of being preserved intact: could anything better vindicate the practices of its former ground land-lord? Functionally successful and aesthetically pleasing, it now seems one of the parts of London we can least do without: for the first time since the seventeenth century, a place to show foreign visitors with pride.

THE CADOGAN ESTATE

It requires an effort of the imagination to keep in mind that the greater part of Chelsea was, for most of the Victorian period, an area of poverty. Its present position as perhaps the most desirable residential neighbourhood in London comes, of course, in large part from its concentration of Georgian and early Victorian houses designed for working and lower middle-class occupation: small enough to be occupied by servantless professional families, and of an architecture that, if only with the discreet alterations whereby an early (or even mid-) Victorian façade becomes late Georgian, accords with expensive modern taste. But long before the very rich began to covet converted workmen's cottages the social cleansing of Chelsea had begun; and the Cadogan estate, from the 1870's onward, played a central role in luring wealth and fashion somewhat closer to Sloane Square and the King's Road.

To do so it adopted an architectural style that, for urban domestic purposes, marked the first sharp break with the late Georgian classical tradition. Down to the seventies Kensington and Bayswater were still being colonized with recognizable modifications of the stuccoed, porticoed terraces that were already covering Tyburnia and Belgravia in the 1820's. Architects and critics universally condemned them, but attempts to establish an alternative style, such as Gothic or Elizabethan, failed to create more than isolated curiosities, such as Lonsdale Square in Islington or St Ann's Villas, Norland Road, Notting Hill.[58] Only with Norman Shaw and the 'Queen Anne' did a startlingly different style first compete with and then defeat the once ubiquitous Italianate. Since Sir Osbert Lancaster has taught us to call it 'Pont Street Dutch', its association with the rebuilt Cadogan estate is stronger than ever.

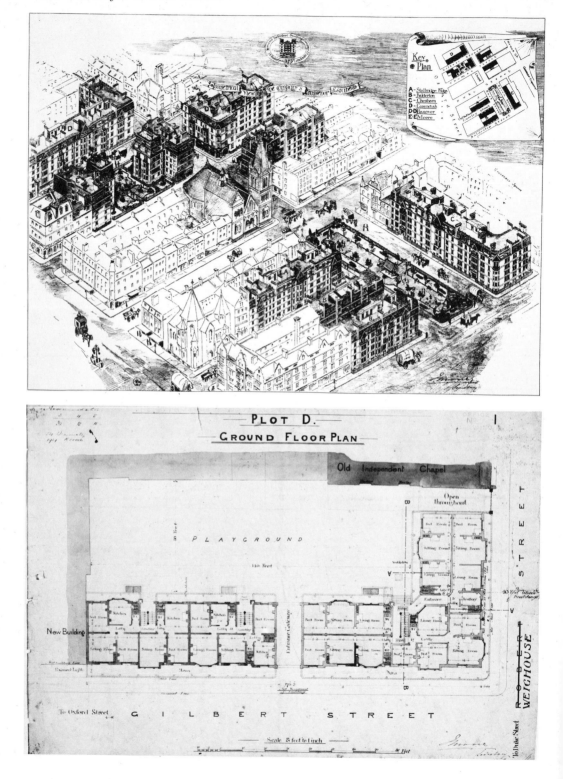

43 *left* '"The Stalbridge and Balderton buildings behind Duke Street are palaces in comparison with the houses which they have superseded."' Model dwellings on Grosvenor estate.

44 *left, below* '"With the recreation ground . . . this new class of 'composite house' is a visible testimony to the popular craving for air, space, and light."' Ground floor plan of Cavendish flats, Gilbert Street.

45 '. . . attempts to establish an alternative style, such as Gothic or Elizabethan, failed to create more than isolated curiosities . . .' Addison Road.

'QUEEN ANNE is by no means dead, as the style is about to be employed for the whole of the houses to be erected on the Cadogan estate, at Chelsea, where it is said red brick and green trees are to reign triumphant,' the *Building News* informed its readers in 1876. Lord Cadogan's architect, William Young, was among the builders taking plots. 'Every variety of the style is to be allowed; indeed, the more diversity of design the better, provided the style itself is in some sort kept to – the design in each case to be approved by Lord Cadogan.'[59] Here, at last, seemed an appropriate response to the demand of critics for a new urban style: one that would emphasize the individuality of each house, provide an interesting skyline, stress vertical rather than horizontal lines, permit a varied pattern of windows that could express something of the reality of the rooms they lighted, and replace the hated sham of stucco with the honesty of brick and the deep-red tones that so pleased the taste of the seventies. Beyond that its association with William and Mary and with the reign of Anne made it seem a *national* style. Even its connections with the Netherlands were more palatable than those of architecture that could only recall the Catholic Italians and the pagan Romans. Furthermore, Amsterdam, Antwerp, and Bruges had shown that similar styles were perfectly compatible with an urban setting. A row of such houses would possess unity of colour, building material, and style; while at the same time permitting, indeed demanding, individual variations in the treatment of each house. The *Building Nëws* thought it particularly appropriate for London:

> The best work of late has been done by the English revivalists of the 16th and 17th centuries, and it is almost patent to everyone that the Gothicists have lost ground very much of late for various reasons, not the least of which is that they are no longer the sole adapters of brick and vernacular ideas of domestic construction and comfort. . . . There is more than a mere sentimental reason why 'Queen Anne' or seventeenth century ideas have obtained such a footing in London, and that is, that a very large part of the Metropolis is already built in that age, and any attempt to Gothicise a street has led to failure. A very slight modification can easily transform the old brick fronts of many of the streets in London into respectable Queen Anne. . . . Again, the stone fronts in London have not been unqualified successes: they are constantly becoming begrimed with soot . . . It is very certain . . . that for London architecture brick has become again a favourite material . . .[60]

By adopting the new style the Cadogan estate placed itself in the forefront of advanced taste. No London estate of the latter decades of the century, with the possible exception of the Grosvenor estate, enjoyed more favourable treatment by the architectural press.

In creating a new garden square named after the freeholder, the Cadogan estate showed its intention of laying out its new development along the approved lines of the surrounding districts, however revolutionary its architecture might be. 'The houses in Cadogan-square will be faced with red brick in conformity with a rule laid down by the estate company, but this will be relieved by Portland stone . . .' according to the *Building News* in 1877. 'The houses are not designed in any particular style, though something is borrowed from the classic elegance of last century . . .'[61]

However alien to classical architecture 'Queen Anne' appears to us, it really did evoke a shadowy England of the seventeenth (or sometimes eighteenth) century for those who experienced it when it was new. The *Building News* was enchanted with the transformation that Norman Shaw and his followers had wrought on the Chelsea Embankment and Cheyne Walk:

> Still true to its tradition, the modern architecture of Chelsea is a revival of the old Classic of the 17th century . . . Proceeding up the river the steamboat passenger . . . sees an extensive row of large, new-built red-brick houses fronting the river, and recalling in their features the style of the Stuarts. . . . these new buildings . . . present more than usual interest to the architect. Few . . . can have failed to have noticed also a block of bright red houses in a massive vernacular style of brick, with narrow windows, small panes, and white sashes, putting one in mind, but for its spick-and-span freshness, of the old brick farm-houses and town residences of William the Third's era, with their tiled roofs, white-painted dormers, and sturdy English unimaginative plainness. We seem only to want the periwigs, laced coats, or spreading hoops of the time.[62]

For the *Builder*, too, the transformation of Chelsea called forth expressions of mixed nostalgia and delight in the present:

> What a surprise it is to be taken to Sloane-street . . . and to find, if old Hans-place, with its many memories, poetic and artistic, is all but the same, in its immediate neighbourhood, on the ground so long neglected . . . the red brick houses now being all but completed, which occupy what is called Cadogan-square . . . the houses of dear old friends replaced by magnificent mansions for, if not magnificent people, the possessors certainly of magnificent means.[63]

The demolitions for such new houses involved the sweeping away not only of picturesque architecture and old memories but of a large body of working-class inhabitants. 'An open-air indignation meeting was held on Monday night,' reported the *Building News* of 24 September 1886, 'at the junction of Cale, Markham, and College-streets, on what is known as Chelsea-common, to protest against Earl Cadogan's "inhuman policy in breaking up workmen's homes to fill his own pockets". The meeting was organised,' it explained, 'by working-class people who will be affected by the proposal of Lord Cadogan to demolish the cottage property on this part of his estate for the purpose of erecting superior modern houses, together with some artisan dwellings.' Over 4,000 would be displaced, while the new model dwellings, 'to be separated from the better class of dwellings by a mews', would house no more than 400.[64] Down to the end of the century, the residents of the vast new Pont Street Dutch houses lived in close proximity to the older Chelsea poor. 'Rich and poor here live very near together,' Charles Booth observed in 1902:

> The newly built region to the west of Sloane Street, which looks hardly less smart, though it is probably very much less wealthy, than Mayfair or Belgravia, is separated only by a narrow borderland of shabby gentility from a group of mean streets reminding one of

parts of Mile End or Bethnal Green. The poverty in them is of a respectable kind, not marked by the squalor or vice of Hoxton, of Somers Town or Lisson Grove, or such as is establishing itself in parts of Fulham or at the World's End, in Chelsea . . .[65]

H.L.W. Lawson referred specifically to the Cadogan estate when he rhetorically asked the Select Committee on Town Holdings in 1887, 'Has it not happened frequently in London of late . . . that the working-class property is not replaced by better working class property, but is pulled down to make room for residential property of a higher class?'[66]

If the social consequences of the estate's policy raised questions, the aesthetic ones were greeted with pleasure and emulation. Landlords of adjacent estates encouraged the new style. The *Building News* hailed the Queen Anne invasion of Kensington and Chelsea as a triumph for the principle of individualism:

Need we bring to the notice of the reader the new brick buildings rising on the east and west sides of the Royal Horticultural Gardens site at Kensington, in Queen's Gate and Prince's Gate, Sloane-street, in Cadogan-place, Chelsea, Egerton Gardens, and other parts, which present that individuality of expression to which we have referred? In these wide West-end streets the Classic or Italian style has held supremacy. The frontages have been planned on straight, rectangular lines, as in Cromwell-road and adjacent cross streets . . . But gradually this uniformity is being broken through; Flemish and Low Country features in red brick and terracotta are taking the place of the stone and stucco ornamentation.[67]

In a paper read to the Architectural Association Francis E. Masey cited 'the mansions of Chelsea and of Harrington and Collingham Gardens . . . as brilliant exceptions to a very dull general rule', of architectural mediocrity in suburbs.[68] 'Another extraordinary change in the face of London which has occurred . . . is the taste for red brick houses of bizarre and fantastic pattern, terraces and rows of which are springing up in all directions,' wrote Percy Fitzgerald in 1893. 'Of this new style there are some elaborate specimens of terra-cotta and brick blended to be found in the new Cadogan Square.'[69] Arthur Cawston held up the Cadogan estate as an example of the value of comprehensive planning to the RIBA the same year, citing a piece of ground whose value increased in five years from £85 per annum to £900, 'because the whole neighbourhood has been developed in a statesmanlike manner . . .'[70] The 1897 edition of Edward Walford's *Old and New London* found Cadogan Square, 'in the variety and splendour of its architecture . . . an agreeable contrast to most of the older squares of London'.[71]

The planning and architecture of the Cadogan and adjacent estates did not call forth universal admiration. The *Building News* found the quaintness excessive:

The rows of red brick houses or mansions in Cadogan-square or Lennox Gardens . . . built in a sort of Queen Anne or 17th-Century Renaissance, show how well we may spoil the best architecture by crowding rows of tall houses together, and how even the most varied elevations may defeat the good intentions of the designers. Here we find all kinds of 'cleverness' in picturesque planning, the recessed bay windows, the 'ingle-nook' porch,

46 '"The houses are not designed in any particular style, though something is borrowed from the classic elegance of last century . . ."' 50 and 52, Cadogan Square, 1886.

the wide squat doorway, the small-paned window, three-panelled door, a variety of quaint bits and details in carved brickwork, all jumbled together in capricious confusion. The old builder of Queen Anne date was never so ridiculous as to use the same features in a street row of houses as he did in a country villa . . .[72]

Whatever the aesthetic or social merits of its policy, the Cadogan estate managed to combine the estate management practices of Georgian London with the aesthetic values of the Victorian age to its own economic advantage. While the Grosvenor and Bedford estates worked to preserve their older residential character and social prestige, the Cadogan estate, through a comprehensive and imaginative rebuilding scheme, enhanced both. But it was to be the last major success of its sort. The *Building News* was correct in perceiving the fundamental incompatibility of Queen Anne architecture with traditional urban squares and terraces. The one demanded individuality and variety, the other subordination and uniformity. There were to be economic and demographic as well as aesthetic reasons for the decline of the town house in the twentieth century, but the appeal of the detached villa had already in the nineteenth doomed the Georgian terrace house to a lingering death. That it died so slowly and so splendidly is due in large measure to the efforts of ground landlords like the Dukes of Bedford and Westminster and Earl Cadogan.

GROUND LANDLORDS AND SPECULATIVE BUILDERS

Georgian principles of estate management persisted on the older estates in the built-up areas to a remarkable degree. Similar policies prevailed on the more outlying estates that were developed for the first time in the nineteenth century.

The pattern of landownership on the outskirts of London involved a comparable prevalence of large estates, whose owners ordinarily maintained control by granting building leases rather than disposing of the freehold. When they did sell the freehold, the buyer often granted leases instead of selling it off in small plots. The Northampton estate in Clerkenwell and Islington, the Eyre estate in St John's Wood, the Bishop of London's estate at Paddington, were all in process of development along traditional lines by 1837.

As the century progressed, estates farther out underwent the same process: the Eton College, Church Commissioners, and Maryon-Wilson estates in Hampstead; the Ladbroke estate at Notting Hill, the Smith's Charity and Gunter estates in Kensington, the Dulwich College estate in Camberwell, the Rolls estate at Stoke Newington, and countless smaller properties. In general, the larger the estate and the richer the landlord the more likely it was to be comprehensively planned at the outset and to have its character maintained thereafter by the enforcement of covenants and by well-considered rebuilding projects at the expiration of leases; such estates were more likely to have middle-class residents. Working-class neighbourhoods were more likely to grow up in districts characterized by fragmentation of ownership.*

* F.M.L. Thompson correlates the markedly lower social tone of West Hampstead from the rest of the parish with the prevalence of comparatively small freehold properties in the neighbourhood. *Hampstead: Building a Borough, 1650–1964*, Routledge & Kegan Paul, 1974, pp. 80–1. The notorious slums on the property of the Marquess of Northampton and the Ecclesiastical Commissioners show that large estates were not necessarily either well-managed or middle-class.

The quality of planning and the firmness of control of the earlier-developed estates tended to be superior to that of those farther out. Percy Hunter, speaking to the Architectural Association in 1885, contrasted the developments on the great estates in Bloomsbury, Marylebone, Mayfair, Belgravia, and Bayswater with those more recently built up in the outer suburbs. The former estates insisted on well-planned and soundly-constructed houses, and the districts showed 'evidence of general design and subordination . . .'. He found less of those qualities 'in the chaotic growth of Outer London during the last thirty years . . .'. The local authorities were 'unable to provide the guiding hand which is manifest on the great ducal estates'. The ground landlords were also culpable:

> . . . The freeholder himself, in addition to being a less wealthy man, and holding perhaps only one or two acres, instead of many, has, in the race for ground rents, become to a certain extent speculative too. Hence, among many adjoining owners there is but little or no unity of arrangements, while in the competition for public favour among their tenants, the leaseholding speculative builders, we get that free trade in architectural styles resulting in all those various and fearful combinations of white brick, red brick, Bath stone, stucco, slates, and tiles, according to the changing fashions of the years.[73]

That 'anomalous being', the speculative builder, wrote John W. Papworth in 1857, 'need not be a builder, or a tradesman in any branch of building: indeed, the persons whom I have known succeed best, were a sailor . . . a chandler's shopkeeper . . . and a footman . . .'[74] Yet in London the typical speculator, at least in the first instance, was a member of one of the building trades. Only when – as often happened – he went bankrupt, did his creditors, building merchants or private investors, take over the responsibility for his building agreement. On other occasions an investor from outside the building industry might be directly involved from the start, either as a partner or associate of a builder, or as the holder of an agreement or lease, sub-contracting for the actual construction. 'Advances are not unfrequently made to builders,' wrote Alfred Emden in 1885, 'under an arrangement to share in the profits derived from the buildings . . . such arrangements . . . do not necessarily constitute a partnership . . .'[75]

The size of building firms and the scale of their operations varied greatly, with some large and a great many small ones. The average size of building ventures remained little larger than it had been in the eighteenth century, until the boom of the 1880's. Thomas Cubitt was exceptional both in the massive scale of his activities and in his use of a large permanent body of employees instead of the more usual subcontracting to fulfil his agreements.[76] In the 1870's 80 per cent, and in the 1890's 60 per cent of the firms in London were building fewer than six houses a year. At the top of the scale in the nineties, Watts of Catford was putting up 400 houses annually.[77]

To an abundance of landowners eager to participate in the unearned increment that urban growth offered them, and an abundance of builders ready to risk their all in covering such land with houses, there was added a complementary abundance of investors, virtually forcing their money on the builders. The buoyant supply of capital for house-building matched the supply of land and labour.

The opportunities for investment open to the thrifty Victorian were far more limited than those of his twentieth-century descendant. Anyone who wished to earn a greater return on his savings than he could from Consols without undue risk was almost forced to invest in mortgages, ground rents, or improved ground rents.[78] 'The supply of capital for house-building certainly ebbed and flowed,' H.J. Dyos has concluded, 'but there is no clear evidence that it was ever checked in such a way as to impede development at all seriously; there is, on the contrary, rather more evidence of over-building in periods of easy money than of under-building when money was tight.'[79] Most observers agreed that demand for houses played a less important role in determining the amount of building than did the supply of investment capital. 'The amount of building would not depend on whether the houses were wanted or not,' Thomas Fatkin, secretary and manager of the Leeds Permanent Benefit Building Society told the Royal Commission on the Housing of the Working Classes. 'There are speculative builders who, if they could get the money, would put up houses even if they knew they were going to be empty for a long time.'[80]

A few professional builders made a practice of retaining a sizeable proportion of their houses as a permanent investment. But the Select Committee on Town Holdings was convinced that Edward Yates in south London was exceptional in following such a practice, most building being done by speculators who built 'to sell and build again'.[81] Whatever their intention, however, Howard Martin, a London surveyor, told the Committee that 'few builders now succeed in selling all their houses, and they have to keep a permanent staff on the estate to do the current repairs for tenants, superintend lettings . . . and so forth . . .'[82]

The speculative builder had a variety of capital resources at his disposal. His personal savings were rarely of much consequence in this connection, except perhaps as a help in making the first plunge into building for the market. But commentators stressed the absence of capital of most speculators and their total dependence on credit. The system of cross-contracting known as 'blood for blood', by which building craftsmen exchanged their specialized labour in one another's houses, was described by a surveyor in 1857 as one 'which no longer prevails . . .' having ceased to be common after 1810.[83]

The large-scale developer – who either purchased the freehold or, more likely, entered into a building agreement with the ground landlord – often helped to finance the speculations of his subordinate builders.[84] By granting mortgages and purchasing profit rents, James Burton was largely responsible for the success of the early development of the Foundling Hospital estate in the 1790's.[85] Thomas Cubitt made a practice of financing the smaller builders working under his supervision in Belgravia and Pimlico.[86]

In various ways the landlord often contributed substantially to meeting the costs of construction. The operation of the leasehold system itself, together with the practice of demanding no more than peppercorn or reduced 'grass' rents for the first several years, made it frequently unnecessary for the builder to pay any money at all for the land. The capital that a speculator would otherwise require was thus substantially reduced. James Noble, writing in 1836, recommended that, 'particularly where open spaces have to be enclosed, as well as *sewers* and *roads* formed, which occasions very heavy outlays by the Builder', the landlord give him 'every encouragement in respect to the allowance termed a grass, or a pepper-corn rent, and also the *progressive* payment of the reserved or full rent, so as to give sufficient time for the covering of the ground . . . without actually forcing the market . . .'[87] Those landlords who provided roads, sewers, and other amenities for their estates similarly relieved their builders of heavy capital outlays. In quite another way, those landlords who failed to impose or to enforce stringent regulations as to the quality of building also reduced the builders' needs for capital. Outright loans were a common, but far from universal device.[88] Writing in 1788, a governor of the Foundling Hospital attributed the success of the recent developments on the Portland and Bedford estates to the 'immense sums' lent by the ground landlords to the builders.[89] '. . . The real speculator,' wrote John W. Papworth in 1857, 'is often the landlord who lets ground and advances money, in the hope that the speculative builders would put a good deal more money . . . in the shape of carcasses on his ground . . .'[90] Some landlords, like Eton College, short of liquid capital, made no advances to builders on their estates. Others followed the example of the Duke of Norfolk, who facilitated the rebuilding of his estate between the Strand and the Embankment by granting loans at four per cent.[91]

Among outside institutions, banks in London rarely invested in speculative building. Building societies were, at least down to the 1870's, a far more important source of capital. Insurance companies, up to the 1880's at least, provided a substantial quantity of capital.[92] The National Provident Institution indirectly contributed to the development of the Chalcots estate in South Hampstead by lending Eton College £12,500 in 1865 to enable it to buy up the leasehold interest of 80 acres, so that they could be relet on building lease; it lent a further £2,000 in 1869, like the first at four and a-half per cent.[93]

Probably the bulk of the financing, particularly of the small to medium-sized builder, was done by solicitors for their investing clients.[94] Early in the century John Nash pointed to 'attornies with monied clients', building speculators, and builders' merchants as the 'artificial causes of the extension of the town . . .'[95]

The prospective investor in a building speculation could choose any one of a number of devices. The most cautious could purchase ground rents for a low rate of interest, no more than four per cent.[96] If he wished a higher yield, he could purchase improved ground rents at 20 years' purchase or rack rents at about 17.[97] He might also lend on mortgage, ordinarily at five per cent, on the security of the freehold land, house property, a building lease, or sometimes no more than a building agreement. In London, a lease was granted only when the house was built, if only in carcase. The correspondence of Thomas Batcheldor, the procrastinating registrar of Eton College, contains many letters from builders in Chalcots protesting against his lethargy in executing their leases when they had finished their houses:

> . . . You have no conception [Richard Nation wrote Batcheldor in 1864] of the injury it is to Builders to be kept out of their Leases after they are entitled to them – they are utterly dependent on borrowed money to a certain extent, which a prudent man generally engages before-hand – No advances can be made until they have their Leases – In the presence [sic] instance I have actually £4000 deposited at my Bankers – which had been there for sevl. Months . . . which we cannot touch until we have the Leases.[98]

THE ARCHITECTURE OF FASHIONABLE SUBURBIA

Unless he lived in one of the newer suburbs there was every likelihood that the early or mid-Victorian, whatever his aesthetic convictions, lived in a Georgian or Regency house. The intensity of the hatred of Georgian architecture by the Victorians may in part be accounted for by the fact that they lived surrounded by it. It was too solid and valuable to be swept away, and was in any event usually protected by the terms of a building lease that would take many more decades to expire. 'Ex Stirpe' complained of the situation to the *Builder* in 1864:

> It is a sad fact, that while stately piles are being reared for commercial purposes, – while banks, insurance offices, and mercantile buildings vie with each other in nobleness of form, and richness of decoration, our private houses, – our homes, – are mean and plain, and sometimes even have actual appearance of poverty. Long brick walls, black with dirt and smoke, with rows of oblong holes for windows (certainly improved of late by the introduction of plate-glass), doors conspicuous only from their plastered jambs, areas in front protected from the pavement by hideous iron railings, – these form the fronts of our streets, gloomy, uninviting, nay, even repulsive. There is one variety, but that is worse even. I allude to stuccodom; the head-quarters of which are near Regent's Park, and a large and, alas! rapidly increasing colony gathering round the British Museum.[99]

Even if the Victorian lived in a Victorian house, the chances were that it was Georgian or Regency in plan and spirit. The architectural innovations of the early Victorians mostly involved industrial, commercial, or public buildings; urban residential areas continued to be built much as they had in the eighteenth century. 'The early years of the Queen were marked by the gloom and incompetence in matters of art which characterized the Georgian period of history,' Sir George Laurence Gomme wrote in 1898. There was 'no new inspiration to add picturesque details to the bricks and mortar which took the place of green fields and trees'.[100]

The design of speculative housing lay with the builders, whose views on architecture remained traditional. '. . . The public need again and again to be reminded,' wrote the *Builder* in 1858, 'that what is really the architectural talent of the day, has nothing to do with what becomes the character of London architecture.' Most of what actually went up reflected the taste of the speculative builder and his judgment as to what would sell:

> Whatever be the commodiousness of certain houses, the *art* about them, in vicinal Cubitopolis, or Tyburnia; in suburban Islington, or Hackney; in transpontine Camberwell, or distant Greenwich, bears kindred likeness, whereto the cement-man has given much, and the artist and architect nothing save what has become distorted in transmission, or by the manner of its use. Houses are built even without drawings . . . The utmost that the builder gets in the way of architectural skill is comprised in the assistance of one of his own order, who is able to draw a rough plan and an elevation that will allow any kind of ornament he has on hand to be used, and without regard to proportions or congruity.[101]

'. . . While London architects are extensively employed in our provinces,' the *Architect* complained in 1873, 'London itself is, as a rule, built up without architects.'[102] Builders felt it 'best to conform to the existing type of house-planning as less costly and more likely of being remunerative. . . . leaseholders are content with building as their forefathers have done.'[103]

It was only at the end of the century that stylistic incongruities were at all apparent in the residential terraces of West London. The persistence of Georgian principles of street planning in the offices of the great estates made them insist on uniform façades. Even where they did not, builders were reluctant to depart from traditional designs, while householders preferred the anonymity and respectability of the standard London terrace. Economic considerations discouraged innovation:

> . . . A speculator building for undetermined clients only too rightly assumes that marked differences in the styling of his product from what is already familiar are not going to be pleasing to any considerable number of lessors or buyers. . . . moreover, real novelty whether technical or aesthetic always tends to cost more in building.

Social snobbery likewise dictated architectural conservatism:

> Most families who moved into Victorian terrace houses were out to better their social standing; hence, quite as in the 20th century, they had a strong preference for house types long associated with assured social position. . . . the members of the urban middle classes, male and female, wanted houses not too unlike the Georgian houses of the older portions of the West End . . . with little or no individual differentiation of individual houses from their neighbors.[104]

To the rage and dismay of aesthetes and moralists alike, Victorian builders continued to use stucco with as much enthusiasm as their Regency predecessors. A letter to the editor of the *Building News* in 1858 condemned two new squares on the Southampton estate, near Primrose Hill, for their deceitful exteriors:

> When will our builders leave off building these ugly stucco erections, which are a source of constant annoyance to the inhabitants, who have to wash or paint them every three or four years, and begin to build houses of colored bricks, which would be a pleasure to look at and to live in, and would not cost any more to make?[105]

The basic unit of Georgian London and the more fashionable extensions of Victorian London, the uniform terrace, grew less acceptable to advanced taste. 'We shall have no more of rolling out eight or ten houses into one sham façade,' exclaimed one writer in 1864; 'but in its stead, that charming individuality of architectural effect which we have so often admired as distinguishing each separate house in the fine old cities of Belgium and Germany . . . [where] each dwelling presents us with as marked an individuality of character as its inhabitants.'[106]

Functional inadequacies lurked behind the aesthetic shortcomings of the Georgian town houses. The recurring complaint about them was that in addition to being drab and gloomy, they were low, and their lowness meant that they lacked bedrooms. It was not so much that families were growing larger, although the fall in infant mortality, especially in middle-class families, may have had something of that effect, as a fundamental change in the attitude toward privacy and the importance of the individual personality. Victorian town houses had more separate bedrooms than houses designed for the same class in the previous century, and for that reason tended to be at least one storey taller. A writer in the *Builder* commented on the altered attitudes and their architectural consequences in 1864:

> The *quatrièmes* and *cinquièmes* of Parisian houses, which but recently we ridiculed with considerable hilarity, have now become indispensable in our own ordinary dwellings. . . . all private residences in the endless new streets, terraces, and squares of Belgravia, Tyburnia, and Westbournia, are provided with extra floors of bed-rooms; thus affording sleeping accommodation more in accordance with our present ideas of comfort, propriety, and health.[107]

The bedroom was designed only for sleeping: the bed-sitting room was regarded as a foreign, or at best effete aristocratic perversion. 'The Parisian uses his bedroom by day, and only eats in the dining room,' W.H. White explained to the Architectural Association in 1875; 'the Londoner often sits all day in his dining-room and only sleeps in his bedroom.'[108] To combine sleeping and sitting in one room struck the *Architect* as unwholesome, immoral, and contrary to the well-understood principle that every important function of life required a separate room:

> There are two ways of looking at a bedroom. It may be viewed as a sleeping place simply, or it may be regarded as a private sitting-room with a bed in it. This last is the view generally taken by the fashionable world. In such sitting-room bedrooms upholstery assumes an almost tyrannical position. The sofa, not merely with spring seat but with spring back and arms, draped to the ground temptingly, spreads abroad its luxurious undulations, easy chairs, all springs, low and capacious, invite you to be lazy. There are little tables for your refreshments, reading stands for your novel. The writing table is . . . crowded with the knick-knackeries of stationery . . . there are houses where the ministrations of luxury reach beyond the intended refinement to a condition of piggish laziness . . .
>
> Haply for the race there are those who take a very different view of what a bedroom should be. . . . With folk that are wise enough to sleep in rooms so furnished the bedroom is just what its name implies, a place for bed, and not a parlour or place for talk. If we intend to live in two rooms, and receive our friends in the bedroom, as the kings and nobles of the thirteenth century often did, and as the French do to this day, then there may be provision made to meet the requirements of a parlour, but until this has become a habit with us the clearer we can keep our sleeping places of furniture and hangings, and stuff of all kinds, the better for our health in all ways.[109]

If bedrooms, plain and fancy, proliferated, bathrooms remained a rarity even in fashionable neighbourhoods. 'London houses . . . are almost invariably without bathrooms,' according to T.L.W. in the *Building News* for 1873.[110] The suburbs were better equipped in this respect than the West End, according to the *Builder* later in the decade:

It is refreshing to both mind and body to observe how general of late years it has become to supply a bath-room to all new houses of 100*l.* a year rent and upwards. Indeed, in some of the fresh suburban neighbourhoods they are put to houses of even 50*l.* rent. There is no doubt it pays the builder to do so, for in most dwellings there is some dressing-room, or small room in a wing, where a hot and cold bath can be placed, and respectable tenants will pay 5*l.* or 10*l.* extra rent in a moderate-sized house to secure the benefit.

I only wonder that landlords do not more generally and actively set to work and supply baths to the old houses as fast as they become vacant, or before. In St. John's-wood, for instance, how very few of the houses have the convenience, except those built within the last five or ten years. The same at Bayswater and Notting-hill and Brompton, until we rise to residences of 150*l.* a year or more. Many of the houses in Westbourne-terrace, Cleveland-square, and similar localities, though producing 200*l.* to 300*l.* a year on lease, are still without bath-rooms. But in the new neighbourhoods, even when not especially fashionable, such as St. Peter's-park (Paddington), Shepherd's-bush, Brixton, &c., we find bath-rooms in fresh houses down to 50*l.* rent, or occasionally lower.

It would be curious to inquire what proportion of the fashionable town-houses about Wimpole-street, Bryanstone-square, May-fair, and other West-end parts, are still unprovided.[111]

Though internally enlarged, diversified, and improved, the town house persisted in its old external dress. Even in 1873, on the eve of the Queen Anne revolution in domestic design, the *Architect* lamented 'the almost universal absence of architectural character . . . in the London town-houses; the dwellings of the nobility and gentry constituting no exception to the melancholy rule'. Yet stucco, both in London and the suburbs, was in decline. The 'cast consoles, balustrades and capitals, heavy cornices and vertical streaks of pilasters' that had formed the 'hideous elevations of compo-fronted houses' 20 years earlier were being supplanted by façades employing 'variegated brick-work . . .'[112] And before long the Cadogan and Grosvenor estates would be leading the way into a new red-and-pink world, so that the Victorian could not only work, worship, shop, and play in appropriately Victorian buildings, but conduct the rituals of family life there, too.

R.W. Edis described the last stage of the London town house in a call to action at the Society of Arts in 1884:

Brickwork ought to be frankly accepted as the natural material of the town, and a better material than stone for all domestic and non-monumental purposes. Terra-cotta ought to be cultivated as a legitimate refinement upon brick, easily dealt with, inexpensive, and highly effective artistically. Glazed brickwork ought to be also made use of, if only as a self-cleansing surface in an atmosphere overloaded with defilement. 'Italian palaces and Gothic fortresses' ought to be equally refused admission into modern London streets; both being equally inappropriate, inconvenient, and ungraceful in the circumstances of London life. Our own Elizabethan or Stuart modes ought to be rather studied, as likely to turn out better for our own modern requirements than any styles of antique times, belonging to other lands, other climates, and other peoples. Our houses ought to tell the story on their faces plainly of English convenience and English comfort within . . .[113]

But the revolution had come too late. For better or worse, fashionable residential London had already been built in Italianate stucco, fixing the appearance of Tyburnia and Bayswater, Belgravia and Brompton, Kensington and Notting Hill for at least another century.

TYBURNIA AND BAYSWATER

Hyde Park served throughout the eighteenth century as an effective barrier to westward expansion, or, to put it another way, seemed London's natural western boundary. To the south, Brompton preserved the appearance of a country village, and Chelsea, Fulham, and Kensington were separate communities, each with a character of its own. In the 1780's Henry Holland had been involved in the Hans Town development, a portent of intensive residential building in the southwestern suburbs, but by and large the area was one of market gardens, with ribbon development along the principal roads to the west. North of the park there was even less to be seen. Paddington was an isolated village, and there was a cluster of low-class housing around the Kensington Gravel Pits, near today's Notting Hill Gate.

Yet Paddington and Pimlico were the obvious areas for expansion for fashionable London. Lying within the gravel belt that permitted easy drainage, and adjacent to the most desirable residential areas, with the Royal Parks in convenient proximity, both areas were admirably suited for intensive residential development of the most ambitious sort. Distant from centres of employment, they would not have done as working-class quarters, and were inconveniently far from the City and the Inns of Court for the business and professional classes, for whom Bloomsbury and Islington were in any event making ample provision. Convenient to Mayfair, St James's, and Westminster, they seemed designed for the wealthy and leisured who kept their own carriages.

Both the omnibus and the underground railway were in the future when the Bishop of London north of the Park and Lord Grosvenor to the south laid out their estates for building in the boom years of the early 1820's. With the layout of the Bedford estate in Bloomsbury to emulate and surpass, and the terraces going up around Regent's Park as architectural models, the way seemed clear to make the western suburbs an even more spacious, more leafy, more aristocratic West End. The land was held in large estates by substantial land-owners; the mechanism of building contracts containing strict architectural controls, and 99-year leases with stringent repairing and occupation covenants had been proved to work well in London conditions. The way seemed open for applying all the lessons in town planning learned from the best eighteenth-century experiments, and to produce an ideal urban environment, limited only by the capacity of the aristocracy and the upper middle classes to absorb the new housing. The remarkable thing is that, with temporary and inevitable setbacks, the audacious schemes succeeded, economically, socially, and aesthetically.

Belgravia, Pimlico, Brompton, Chelsea, Kensington, Tyburnia, Bayswater, even Notting Hill, while of varying social prestige, remain largely intact for our inspection and enjoyment. Still overwhelmingly residential, unlike the eighteenth-century West End, retaining to a great degree their original buildings (though often much altered within), they have survived the social revolutions of the twentieth century remarkably well, housing the well-to-do of our age behind the same walls that housed the very rich of Victorian London. Belgravia has altered least, architecturally and socially. South Kensington, after deteriorating in the late Victorian years and early twentieth century, has come back with notable strength: if it is impossible even now to regard the streets around the western extensions of the Cromwell Road with any great enthusiasm, the whole area is pleasant to live in. North of the Park has never been quite as fashionable as it set out to be, but in its architectural splendours, and still more in the imaginative layout of its estates, it surpasses even Belgravia.[114]

While undeniably suburbs, and described as such throughout the Victorian period, Bayswater and Kensington were never 'suburban' in the way Clapham or Highgate or Norwood were. They did experiment with streets of detached and semi-detached villas, but for the most part maintained the terrace and variants of the communal garden square as their predominant building pattern. If architectural devices such as the spacing of windows and the use of heavy, pillared porticoes in front of each entrance stressed the individuality of the separate houses in a terrace more than Georgian practice had allowed, they preserved the architectural uniformity and the subordination of the individual house to the whole terrace. Houses were taller, ornament was coarser, and the effects were more flamboyant than strict eighteenth-century taste would have permitted: yet the new districts were recognizable extensions of Marylebone and Mayfair, more fashionable Bloomsburys, Greater Georgian London. Their aesthetic backwardness led to their being mostly ignored by the architectural journals of their day. Hitchcock has complained of the difficulty of finding contemporary prints or drawings of the new terraces as they arose. They were considered at best too commonplace for comment, at worst representations of all that was unfortunate in the lease-hold system and the speculative building industry. They were not 'architecture' at all. Yet an occasional comment survives in print.

'A few days ago I came along the new town of London called Hyde Park Gardens,' wrote a correspondent to the *Builder* in 1844, 'and I was much pleased to see that the architects in general are anxious not only to imitate, but to outdo, the ancient Grecians, Romans, &c., in the decoration of buildings. I could not help thinking that the inmates must perceive the pleasure the passers-by feel, in looking at the nice façades of their dwellings . . .'[115] If the architecture of Hyde Park Gardens looked back to the Regency for its inspiration, its physical layout set the tone for much subsequent terrace development. For its houses, reached from the north by a separate carriage road, looked out towards Hyde Park separated from it by communal pleasure grounds, reached directly from the houses themselves. Other 'gardens' that later appeared in Bayswater and Ladbroke Grove and in many parts of Kensington had the pleasure grounds almost completely hidden from the street. Their advantages from the point of view of the privacy and exclusiveness of the occupants of the adjoining houses was great: if the pleasure of the casual pedestrian was diminished, the arrangement substituted inward-looking Victorian domesticity for Georgian aristocratic display.[116]

Only in Tyburnia did a guidebook published in 1851 discern 'that studied symmetry and variety in street-planning which the classic taste of Wren and Evelyn vainly endeavoured to introduce into the city after the fire, and for which the size of the suburban estates, and vast scale of the operations on them, might be supposed to present opportunities unequalled in modern times.'[117] William Gaspey described Tyburnia in 1852 as 'one of the most elegant and *recherché* districts in which the abodes of rank are situate, not even surpassed by the attractive drives and promenades of aristocratic Belgravia.' It had become 'a favourite *locale* of the titled and rich'. To the west lay the even newer Bayswater, then in the course of rapid development. Bishop's Road, 'a spacious and handsome avenue of stately houses . . . extending to *Westbourne-grove*, Nottingham-hill [sic], and the country beyond', together with Eastbourne Terrace, Westbourne Terrace, and Gloucester Road, 'comprehending double rows of elegant mansions . . .' were already in existence.[118]

The collections of villas that already existed between Gloucester Terrace and Kensington Park Road were by the end of the decade engulfed in a continuous development which included some semi-detached houses, but which consisted mostly of terraces, all in florid, neoclassical stucco.[119] Alfred Cox described the 'very modern houses and mansions' of Tyburnia as occupied by 'members of Parliament, wealthy merchants, and professional men'. It had 'sprung up . . . within the last dozen years . . .' and showed great 'regularity of appearance . . .'. Architectural fashion, however, had left Tyburnia far behind: 'The fine squares, spacious streets, and lofty houses, have a striking appearance; but the uninterrupted uniformity of "compo" decoration of the flimsiest kind fatigues the eye, and will not bear critical examination.'[120] Bayswater, a mile west of Hyde Park Gate, was even newer, and consisted of three-quarters of a square mile of 'numerous wide and even roads . . . *detached family mansions, stately gentlemen's residences*, and *villas*, with large gardens and lawns in front and at the rear . . .' They were 'occupied by the middle and upper classes, including families of almost every denomination', who could worship at two 'noble and well-built' churches and three chapels, and travel to central London 'at all times . . . by any of the many excellent omnibuses on the routes . . .'[121]

The *Building News* in the latter part of the decade carried almost weekly bulletins on the rapid progress of building north of the Park and beyond. 'A very large amount of building operations, principally of a first-class description, are now in very active progress on the Bayswater estates,' one issue in 1857 reported:

In *Leinster-square, Palace-gardens*, of which George Wyatt, Esq., is the principal proprietor, architect, and builder, very great progress has been made, not only in the buildings, but also in the grounds, which are laid out with great taste, and already . . . planted with choice shrubs and flowers. The first-class residences now in hand . . . will comprise family mansions of the best description, great care being taken to have them built in the most sound and substantial manner, and appropriately decorated. . . . In these houses more than usual ingenuity seems to have been brought to bear in the planning of the basements for domestic comfort and convenience; for, in addition to commodious kitchens and sculleries, with a profusion of fittings to them, there is a housekeeper's-room and butler's pantry to each, two wine cellars, beer cellar larders, and servants' waterclosets, together with a cistern capable of holding 300 gallons of water.

Other builders were putting up houses of similar pretensions in Princes Square, Inverness Terrace, and Leinster Terrace.[122]

'Amongst the town mansions and smaller residences now in progress in the metropolis,' it observed later that same year, 'none are more distinguishable than those now in hand on portions of the *Bayswater and Paddington Estates*, and that are severally being built by Mr. George Wyatt, Mr. [Charles] Chambers, Mr. [Thomas] Pocock, Mr. [William Lloyd?] Edwards, Mr. [J.V.?] Scantlebury, Mr. [G.F.J.] Tippétt and Mr. Austin.' Henry de Bruno Austin, of Cleveland Square, was building 'on a very extensive scale, and many of them adapted for the various requirements of a town mansion of a nobleman or wealthy commoner. The principal block now in progress by Mr. Austin will . . . be finished externally in a very ornate style of embellishment . . .'[123] He had earlier been described as building 'several first-class dwelling-houses, which form the north-eastern end of *Westbourne-terrace* . . . together with numerous others in *Cleveland-square* . . .' The most ambitious of Austin's ventures formed a portion of the most impressive feature of the Bayswater of that period, the present Lancaster Gate, then known as Upper Hyde Park Gardens, designed by Sancton Wood. Austin built 30 houses in the westernmost section of the terrace, while Messrs Rigby were responsible for 70 to the east, including those surrounding Christ's Church at the centre.[124] 'The style . . . is that known as the French Renaissance, with features on it resembling those so gorgeously illustrated in the Palace of the Tuileries . . . with the omission of the sculptures.'[125] Even 10 years later the *Building News* thought Lancaster Gate the handsomest terrace in London, 'or, as private residences, in any city in the world'. Its houses were 'elegant rather than grand, not arresting attention by overgrown pavilions shooting up at every corner', like those in Grosvenor Place. Scorning the then-fashionable novelties of 'polished granite' and 'many-coloured material . . . they have an air of quiet and assured gentility that we fail to find in any of the rows of residential buildings at present progressing in other directions.'[126]

Behind the impressive terraces facing the Park, street after street of only marginally less pretentious houses were going up in the late fifties. The *Building News* was able to report in 1858 that, 'notwithstanding the many complaints we hear made about the slackness and depression of the building trades . . . there are no fewer than *ten* new squares in active progress in the suburbs of our enormously increasing metropolis', including four important ones in Bayswater and Paddington. Kensington Gardens Square, also by Austin, would consist of 98 first-class houses, with 22 stables in connection, and a garden 'to be filled with flowers and shrubs, thus giving a more refreshing and cheerful aspect than the paved *places* of most continental towns and cities'.[127]

Early in 1859 the *Building News* reported 'hundreds of workmen . . . at present engaged in the building and finishing' of houses in Bayswater and Notting Hill, 'most of which are of a very superior description, and many of them on such a large scale, that they may justly be called town mansions'. The districts, together with Kensington, were 'forming the abodes of the wealthy and more aristocratic portion of the population of the metropolis'.[128] Later that year it again commented with admiration on the 'immense works which have been lately built, and are now in progress' in Bayswater:

47 *right* '. . . double rows of elegant mansions . . .' Westbourne Terrace and nearby fields.

48 *below* '"The style . . . is that known as the French Renaissance, with features on it resembling those so gorgeously illustrated in the Palace of the Tuileries . . . with the omission of the sculptures."' Lancaster Gate, 1866.

Large squares and terraces of palatial residences have been reared as if by magic, which rival, and in many instances surpass, the finest of those in the hitherto aristocratic localities. The long range of Westbourne and Gloucester terraces are now in their turn eclipsed as completely as they outshone their predecessors, and the tide of wealthy householders has flowed still farther westward.

Already some of the area was changing in character from residential to commercial, if commercial of a most genteel sort: 'The main artery, Westbourne-grove, which divides this important suburb is now rapidly undergoing a change – the semi-detached villas are demolished, and shops are raised at the eastern end which are unsurpassed by any in London.'[129] By the sixties Westbourne Grove and Gloucester Road had become a fashionable shopping district, where William Whiteley and lesser retailers provided Bayswater with many of the ingredients of a coherent community centre. One of the earlier and more attractive of the suburban retail districts, it not only served the immediate locality but attracted customers from all of genteel London.[130] 'The splendid mansions raised in the vicinity [of Westbourne Grove] have awakened the West-end shopkeepers to the necessity of keeping pace with them, and the long array of magnificent and well-stocked shops even already obviate the need to "go into town" for the most expensive goods,' the *Building News* observed in 1860.[131] 'Places that were considered rural and retired only ten years ago, have become centres of commercial activity,' wrote the *Builder* in 1863:

> Westbourne-grove, only recently a double line of semi-detached villas, with gardens before and behind, is now a thoroughfare of good shops. The Queen's-road [the present Queensway], in everybody's remembrance quite a lovers' lane, as far as quiet and leafy shades could make it so, is now as business-like as Edgware-road, one side being an uninterrupted succession of smart shops, and the gardens in front of the houses on the other side being one by one covered over and converted into shops also.[132]

The shops benefitted from the prosperity of the surrounding streets. George Augustus Sala, writing in 1879, found

> the vast majority of the promenaders . . . in Westbourne Grove . . . exceptionally well-dressed. . . . Westbourne Grove is . . . the centre of the new prosperous and refined district. I suppose there are fewer pawnbrokers' shops in the region lying west of the Edgware Road than in any other part of London. When you have passed the canal bridge there are absolutely no slums . . .[133]

A splendid row of houses faced the Park:

> . . . Commencing at Lord Grosvenor's mansions, near the Marble Arch, and continuous along the whole park border nearly as far as Notting-hill Gate, the ranges of noble mansions, in terraces, have been completed along the Bayswater-road [the *Builder* reported in 1869], which, facing the park and Kensington Gardens, and fronting the south, make them the most favoured residential abodes; shrubbed flower borders, and the open views of forest scenery, together with a dry sandy soil, offering attractions which no other suburb can rival.[134]

In the Bayswater Road, wrote 'Quondam' in 1872, unlike the main road to Kensington, 'no paltry ranges of mean shops border the road, nor sever the continuous sylvan view; because on this line successive ranges of noble terraces have been erected within the last forty years . . .'[135] *Dickens's Dictionary of London* found the Uxbridge Road 'certainly the finest approach to London . . . being everywhere broad and straight. . . . At the end of May, when the foliage is at its brightest and freshest, and the road is alive with handsome equipages, its beauty is remarkable.'[136]

NOTTING HILL

Notting Hill never rivalled Bayswater in fashion or pretentiousness. 'The district of Notting Hill is almost entirely the product of the present generation,' W.S. Clarke wrote in 1881:

> Thirty years ago . . . there was a line of shops good, bad, and indifferent – chiefly the latter – called High-street. There were also a few houses on the London side inhabited by private people, foreigners, adventurers, or respectable confidential *employés* of West-end commercial houses. Beyond the street on the Uxbridge-road, here and there a house testified to the latent intention of speculators to build more; but the whole area to the north of that road had not left the guardianship of the cattle-feeder, the dairy-man, or the gardener.[137]

The early development of Notting Hill antedated that of Bayswater, and began at the same time as that of Tyburnia. In 1823 the architect Thomas Allason prepared a building plan for the Ladbroke estate, which included the line of the present Ladbroke Grove. Although it was not carried out in its original form, its proposal for villas backing onto private communal gardens set the tone for the ultimate layout of the estate. Before the collapse of the first period of activity a number of houses along and just north of the present Holland Park Avenue were erected.[138] Building on the Norland estate to the west began in 1839 and was nearly completed by the early fifties. Its most impressive feature was and is Royal Crescent, facing Holland Park Avenue.[139]

Meanwhile building had resumed on the Ladbroke estate under the direction of the solicitor Richard Roy. In the early 1850's Charles Henry Blake and Samuel Walker began the imaginative succession of terraces and crescents that characterize the district, following the designs of Thomas Allom.[140] A sharp rise in interest rates in 1853 brought the builders of Notting Hill to bankruptcy and their uncompleted houses to ruin.[141] 'On the north-eastern portion of the ill-fated Notting-hill estate, we regret to observe a very great number of buildings still standing in a deplorable condition,' reported the *Building News* in 1857, 'some in carcase with their roofs on, others partly roofed in, and some in rough carcase with some of their walls not yet up to their eaves, presenting a most melancholy instance of the waste of capital.'[142] Ladbroke Gardens in 1860 was a 'desert of dilapidated structures and decaying carcases. . . . few . . . would care to dwell in that dreary desolation, – with the wind howling and vagrants prowling in the speculative warnings around them.' Lansdowne Road North was 'another sickly plant . . .' although the 'neglected carcases on the north side of the road have been taken up by a few enterprising men, and several are now even quite completed, forming roomy and desirable residences'.[143]

The sixties saw building resumed and the imaginative scheme realized. 'On the northern slope of Notting Hill a new and fashionable town has been erected within the last fifteen years,' wrote George Rose Emerson in 1862; 'even now some of the roads have scarcely emerged from the "carcass" condition, in which, for several years, through the failure of a building speculation, they stood.'[144] Hitchcock finds the resulting development 'the finest Early Victorian layout in London in the semi-urban manner . . .' Its spacious plan combines terraces and semi-detached villas arranged in great sweeping curves, enclosing huge communal gardens:

> The finest effects . . . derive from Allom's masterly handling of the cross views. . . . The operatic grandeur of Bayswater gives way here to something richer, more varied, and more humane. . . . Allom created the masterpiece of Early Victorian planning, retaining the most vital elements of the Georgian tradition and at the same time vigorously renewing it.[145]

The *Survey of London* praises 'Allom's brilliant scenic display', and finds 'his strange sort of grandeur . . . still evident . . . He adopted a more flexible, more romantic approach than the architects of South Kensington or Bayswater.'[146] 'Nothing could have been better conceived, and never was enterprise more rewarded,' wrote W.S. Clarke in 1881. The gardens, crescents, roads, dales, and parks that came to form Ladbroke Grove and Norland Town to the west were 'worthy examples of the converting process which within living memory has turned fields into palaces and many grades of well-ordered habitations.'[147]

By the nineties social as well as architectural fashion had left Bayswater and its western extensions far behind. 'How curious . . . are the feelings aroused by the Bayswater region!' exclaimed Percy Fitzgerald in 1893:

> Here we find wastes of 'compo' mansions, terraces and squares in abundance . . . There is a general pretentiousness – from the uniform, stuccoed balustrades, the languid trees, and dusty folliage. 'Middle-class' folk live in these would-be palaces and terraces. Mixed up . . . with this affected state, we find streets, rows of flashy shops, and all the vulgar incidents of traffic, omnibuses, carts, etc.

He found 'a curious general stagnation' in the 'tame yellow houses' of Westbourne Terrace, and nearby 'streets and shops of a poorish sort.'[148] But Charles Booth thought that the region was regaining some of its earlier prestige:

> The district on the north side of the Bayswater Road, with its continuation southward by Holland Park and Campden Hill . . . has all gained in recent years. The tide of fashion and favour which for some time flowed towards Brompton exhausted itself in the Wild West of Earl's Court, and there has been some reaction in favour of Bayswater and Tyburnia, as well as the opening up of new ground in Holland Park and on Campden Hill. . . . In few parts of this district are there any signs of decay . . .[149]

Sir Osbert Lancaster remembers Edwardian Notting Hill as an unchallenged stronghold of

49 *top* '''worthy examples of the converting process which within living memory has turned fields into palaces and many grades of well-ordered habitations.''' Kensington Park Gardens looking east. Lithograph by T. Allom, 1853.

50 *above* '''. . . there has been some reaction in favour of Bayswater and Tyburnia, as well as the opening up of new ground in Holland Park and on Campden Hill.''' Houses in Holland Park.

upper-middle-class respectability: '. . . the squares and terraces . . . had once formed the very Acropolis of Edwardian propriety . . . [housing] eminent K.C.s and the Masters of City Companies . . .'[150]

BELGRAVIA AND PIMLICO

Shepherd and Elmes included two plates of Belgrave Square in their *Metropolitan Improvements* (1827–31). The latter observed:

> This extensive area is now covering with mansions and handsome houses, laid out with beautiful plantations, into two spacious squares, a crescent, and several detached villas. This great undertaking, equal in extent and value to many cities . . . [is] destined (say the projectors) to be the future residences of the highest class of the fashionable world . . .[151]

John Britton wrote:

> In 1825, the principal part was engaged by the *Messrs. Cubitt* for building, who immediately commenced with raising the surface, and forming streets and communications . . . Their operations were soon followed by other powerful parties, and a mass of fine buildings has been raised within this short space of time, beyond all precedent; – many of the houses are already occupied, and others engaged by noblemen and persons of rank.

He, like most contemporaries, was impressed by the structural qualities of Cubitt's building:

> The streets and squares are paved, Macadamised, and lighted, on the most approved principles; the houses are constructed with the best materials, and . . . every thing seems to be provided for the domestic comforts, as well as for the luxuries of its gay inhabitants. . . . The surveyor for the ground landlord, Mr. Cundy, as well as the architects and builders engaged in this great plan, are all gentlemen of high respectability and integrity; and will not easily degrade their own characters by doing any thing dishonourable themselves, or by suffering others to do so.

Belgrave Square, ten acres in area, was the principal feature of the estate:

> The whole of the houses are large, lofty, and every way spacious, with stuccoed fronts, porches, balustraded balconies, and those in the centre of each side are decorated with columns . . . It is not, however, in the exterior, that the chief merit of these mansions consists, but rather in the size and style of their principal apartments. At the four corners of the Square are to be as many insulated villas, or mansions, with spacious gardens and shrubberies.
>
> This novel feature will greatly improve the character and appearance of the Square, by increasing its area, opening its approaches, and extending the plantation beyond the real boundary lines of the four rows of houses. We may easily anticipate the pleasing, and indeed beautiful effects, which will ultimately be produced from this plan.[152]

The boom that had prompted such elaborate schemes was already over when Elmes and Britton wrote. Houses begun in the early twenties were still untenanted in the forties, and

Eaton Square was not completed until 1853. Pimlico took even longer to finish.[153] Contemporaries were sceptical as to its prospect. Brady's *New Pocket Guide* for 1838, while admitting that the 'rage for building speculations, on a *superb* scale', that was creating Belgravia, seemed to be 'sanctioned by the votaries of fashion, and the possessors of rank and wealth', and that Belgrave Square itself was already 'tenanted by nobles and gentlemen of fortune, with the view, it is presumed, that this must shortly be the *court-end* of the town', was uncertain about its future. 'If the tide of fashion *continue* to flow this way, all this may answer; but we take leave to *doubt*.'[154]

Fashion did continue to move into Belgravia and even beyond, but the anti-classical reaction brought its architecture and planning into disrepute while it was still being built. 'Youngest and most gorgeous of our squares is Belgrave Square . . .' wrote one critic in the early forties. '. . . We should have better liked less uniformity in the architecture. We prefer individual character in the houses: we do not like to see them merely parts of an architectural whole, like soldiers, who are only parts of a rank.'[155] The *Building News* in 1857 found 'Belgrave and Eaton squares, and the rest of Belgravia . . . in point of architectural quality . . . only a very few degrees less insipid and uninteresting' than Baker, Harley, and Gower Streets.[156] '. . . There is not much majesty in the modern elevation of Belgravian squares and wide streets,' it observed the next year; 'but it is at least the best evidence our city affords of symmetry in stucco.'[157]

The economic and social success of Belgravia was, by the fifties, assured. Alfred Cox reported that the '*Grosvenor Place* district, or *Belgravia*', included 'elegant modern houses of recent construction, many still in progress; crescents, terraces, and mansions of the aristocracy'. He noticed 'the high social position' of the residents of Belgrave and Eaton Squares. 'The regularity of the designs of this newly-built neighbourhood gives it on the whole a more imposing air than the district of Tyburnia.'[158] 'The north side of Belgravia, or that portion of it lying between Knightsbridge and Chelsea, is extremely *recherché*,' according to William Gaspey, writing in 1851.[159]

Pimlico, composed of 'respectable if dullish examples of post-Georgian design suited to the rather unfashionable clientele for which . . . [it] seems from the first to have catered',[160] was less so, but perfectly successful on its own terms: 'the south side, between Belgrave-place . . . and Vauxhall bridge . . . though less distinguished,' Gaspey wrote, 'still abounds in handsome squares and spacious streets, residences in which only opulence can command. *Eccleston* and *Warwick-squares* are recent erections upon a superb scale.'[161] A newspaper article in 1877 described Pimlico, or 'South Belgravia', as 'genteel, sacred to professional men . . . not rich enough to luxuriate in Belgravia proper, but rich enough to live in private houses – for this is a *retired* suburb'. Its inhabitants were 'more lively than in Kensington . . . and yet a cut above Chelsea, which is only commercial . . .'[162] Comfort and propriety reigned:

The genteel part live in a small space, the immediate neighbourhood of Gloucester, Sussex, Cambridge, Sutherland Streets – while Lupus Street is the sweet south that borders this paradise of rest. This is the abode of gentility – a servant or two in the kitchen, birds in the windows, with flowers in boxes, pianos, and the latest fashions . . . People are here

51 *top* "'This great undertaking . . . destined (say the projectors) to be the future residences of the highest class of the fashionable world . . .'" Belgrave Square, north side, from Shepherd and Elmes, *Metropolitan Improvements*.

52 *above* "'. . . the whole neighbourhood must necessarily both from the character of the buildings and the privacy of the approach to them, be occupied by noblemen and gentlemen exclusively.'" Kensington Palace Gardens, northern entrance, 1845.

always dressed in their best, and though not the cream of the cream, can show on occasion broughams and pairs . . . Where people do not live in their property they are artists – they teach the piano, singing, dancing, drawing, languages, or are in the City . . .[163]

By the nineties Pimlico had declined to such an extent that Charles Booth could describe it as being perhaps the most deplorable middle-class neighbourhood in London. The area west of Tachbrook Street, between Victoria and Lupus Street he described as 'singularly unsatis-factory . . .' Although there was no extreme poverty and a great deal of physical comfort and even wealth, the streets and squares were yearly deteriorating:

> Even the well-to-do occupants seem often to take little pride in their houses. At best it is a depressing district, passing . . . from . . . shabby gentility to . . . gradual decay and grimy dilapidation which is apt to overtake houses built for another class, and altogether unsuited for their present occupants: short of paint, the plaster peeling and cracking; sordid and degraded dwellings, they remain a nightmare in the memory.

Prostitution abounded, particularly near Victoria Station and in small hotels in Vauxhall Bridge Road. South of Lupus Street there was more poverty, mitigated by 'some of the best model dwellings in London'. St George's Square had 'an out of the way charm of its own which, making little pretence after fashion, seems to defy decay . . .'[164]

KENSINGTON

Kensington's history as a significant London suburb dates from the building of the palace there by William III and the creation at the same time of Kensington Square.[165] Not until the Great Exhibition of 1851 and the subsequent development of the land directly to the south of the site as a cluster of museums and public institutions did massive housing speculation begin. The extension of the Metropolitan Railway through Notting Hill Gate to Gloucester Road and South Kensington in 1867, and the related building of the Metropolitan District Railway to Westminster and the City – together forming what became the Inner Circle – made the new streets and squares easily accessible from the rest of London.

Already, and indeed by 1837, the wedge of streets and squares between Brompton and Kensington Roads had been laid out. The pretty houses in Montpelier Square date from 1837.[166] The houses were mostly quite small, and the district was reported to be popular with people in the theatre and the arts.

Shortly thereafter, far out in West Brompton, the Boltons on the Gunter estate were laid out by George Godwin, the estate surveyor and editor of the *Builder*. Semi-detached and placed about an oval crescent, they combine the formality of the urban garden square with the house-form of the villa suburb.[167] A far more ambitious scheme involving detached residences was the row of mansions in Kensington Palace Gardens, built on Crown land in the late forties and early fifties.[168] Alfred Cox, writing in 1853, was impressed by the high degree of privacy and social segregation that was there achieved:

> The houses adjoining the new private road are all magnificent detached mansions; the approach is by a lodge and gates, and the whole property being under the control of the

Commissioners of Woods and Forests, the possibility of injury to the houses by the subse-, quent erection of inferior buildings in the vicinity is precluded. The situation is perfectly open and healthful, and the houses, which command interesting views of the palace, gardens, &c., can never, therefore, suffer deterioration. There is not a single mean tenement or offensive object to injure the prospect, and the whole neighbourhood must necessarily, both from the character of the buildings and the privacy of the approach to them, be occupied by noblemen and gentlemen exclusively.[169]

But for the most part the district was genteel rather than fashionable, semi-rural rather than suburban, and something of a health-resort. 'Brompton and Chelsea . . . are low-lying districts,' Cox explained. 'The air of the former, being moist and mild, has the reputation of being beneficial to consumptive persons.'[170] Brompton, 'pleasant and salubrious . . . for the purity and health-bestowing qualities of its air, has been by some assimilated to Montpelier', according to another guidebook. 'Elegant villas, groves, terraces, rows, and squares in this district, well populated, indicate the absence of poverty and the existence of wealth, or at least of competence.'[171] 'It is difficult for those of the present generation who only know the district as it now stands, with its spacious roads, stately houses, and numerous public buildings,' wrote Edgar A. Bowring in an article on South Kensington in 1877, 'to picture to themselves its appearance a quarter of a century ago . . .' At the time of the Exhibition, 'the whole frontage to Hyde Park consisted of a few old-fashioned houses, to most of which large gardens in the rear were attached . . .' Most of the area was devoted to market gardens. '. . . The secluded region of Brompton Park, with its fine old trees, and quaint dwellings which formed the favourite abodes of leading actors, occupied the site of the now world-known South Kensington Museum; and, in short, silence and solitude reigned through-out . . .'[172]

The Exhibition brought concerted and pretentious development. Sir Charles James Freake (1814–84) had already finished Prince's Terrace, between Knightsbridge and Kensington Gore, by mid-1851. The purchase by the Commissioners of the Exhibition in 1852 of nearly 70 acres south of the Park from the Harrington and Gore House estates stimulated building in the surrounding fields. The Commissioners' land south of the Cromwell Road and west of the Albert Road (later Queen's Gate) was advertized for lease the following year; the income was to serve as an endowment for the institutions to be erected on the remaining land. Meanwhile a developer named Elger had taken over Freake's speculation in Prince's Terrace, and proceeded to build behind it Prince's Gardens and Ennismore Gardens, on land belonging to the Earl of Listowel.[173]

By the late fifties, the transformation of the fields south of the Exhibition site into a fashionable suburb, rivalling Tyburnia and Bayswater, was well under way. In 1857 the *Building News* reported that Charles Aldin, of Clapham, had 'erected ten very large and superior dwelling-houses' on the southern side of Kensington Gore.[174] By the following year he had 'made very rapid advances in providing suitable residences for the more aristo-cratic stream of our London population . . .' Behind a 'block of eleven shops and dwelling-houses in the Gloucester-road . . . Mr. Aldin has just erected, further to the south, a large block of twelve first-class residences, which are five stories in height . . . forming excellent dwellings for large families.'[175]

Meanwhile Freake was building at Prince's Gate 'six first-class dwelling houses . . . of considerable architectural beauty . . .'[176] His houses in the Cromwell Road were of the Italian style, 'and there is a considerable amount of picturesque beauty displayed in their design, they not being of the ordinary monotonous horizontal street outline "against the sky." The end houses are carried up to a greater altitude, and thus comprehend an extra story.'[177]

In 1857 the *Building News* described the 'very large block of first-class mansions . . . in various stages of progress . . .' being built on the Harrington estate at the northern end of Prince Albert's Road (Queen's Gate) by William Jackson, of Pimlico. He had leased a large section of the Earl of Harrington's estate, on which he was to build 300 first and second-class houses.[178] By the following year Jackson had built another 'large palatial mass' at the north-west corner of Prince Albert Road.[179]

The *Builder* was as pleased as its younger rival at the metamorphosis of Brompton into the district of tall Italianate mansions that it has remained into our own time. 'In the progressive increase of London, no quarter has advanced so much in style and finish as the district lying between the Old Brompton and Kensington roads,' wrote 'Vox Querens' in April 1858. The site was well drained, 'and the altitude is quite sufficient to raise it above the fuliginous and swampy influences of Pimlico and Belgravia . . .'[180]

In Kensington, 'amongst the great speculative builders who are now expending almost fabulous amounts of capital', none were more important than Freake, Jackson, and Aldin,

> who within the last two or three years have erected buildings of a most princely character [reported the *Building News* in 1859]. In fact, these gentlemen with a fearless speculative energy may be said conjointly to have created a new town composed of dwelling-houses of a highly superior class, that for splendour of detail and internal conveniences, more than rival the *palazzi* of the nobles of Venice, Verona, Milan, Mantua, Florence, Genoa, and other cities of Italy, in the most palmy days of their prosperity.

Freake was operating to the east of the 1851 Commissioners' land, and Jackson and Aldin to the west, 'on ground formerly belonging to the Earl of Harrington, and other proprietors'.*

The style of 'this large and important "*new town*" at the south-western suburb of our great metropolis' was Italian, 'in various modifications of its development from the severe details of Palladian characteristics to the ornate embellishments of the later Renaissance features, as adopted by some of the more eminent French architects'. Although delayed by a

---

* *BN*, V (1859), pp. 879–80. For Freake, Aldin, and Jackson, see Summerson, *The London Building World of the Eighteen-Sixties*, Thames and Hudson, 1973, pp. 16–17. In 1869 the *Builder* honoured the three as 'the original founders of this great quadrangle of fashion . . . Mr. Freake, who built Princes-terrace and the Exhibition-road, with the adjacent squares; then Mr. Jackson, who commenced the Albert-road, Queen's Gate-square, and adjuncts; and afterwards Mr. Aldin, who completed the whole extent, as far as Mr. Jackson's present works in Gloucester-road, and at Stanhope-gardens.' *B*, XXVII (1869), p. 629.

prolonged industrial dispute, Freake's operations on the north side of Prince's Gardens were progressing, as were those of the other two builders:

> . . . Mr. Aldin . . . has been pursuing his works without interruption in the face of the 'strike,' with an average number of upwards of 400 men in various branches. At present, Mr. Aldin is carrying up two extensive blocks on the western side of Prince Albert's-road . . . and on the western side of what is to be called Queen's Gate Gardens . . . he has erected and nearly completed a large range of dwelling houses . . . The interior of these structures are all planned with suitable conveniences for families, and range at rentals from £150 to £300 per annum. In Petersham-terrace and the Gloucester-road, Mr. Aldin has also erected some very superior and substantial edifices . . .[181]

Jackson's operations were mostly along the western side of Prince Albert's Road, and along the Kensington and Gore Roads. In other countries, the article remarked, such 'vast undertakings' would be directed by governments, 'and not by private individuals, as in England...' It was confident 'that ultimately something great will be accomplished, as a general whole . . .'[182]

Lovers of the picturesque and proponents of the Gothic as the new universal style were less pleased. A. J. Beresford Hope attacked the 'large houses and straight streets' of the new developments in South Kensington in 1861:

> No doubt they were improvements in the buildings compared with what they might have been some years ago. The height is greater in Tyburnia than in Belgravia, and in Brompton-Kensington than in Tyburnia. There is an improvement also in the roofing. Still there are many points which do not admit of so much praise. The material is almost confined to compo. The distribution of streets is that miserable one of right angles, square blocks, mutations of palaces, terraces, in short, where we want houses. There was no harmony in them with ancient London. They were the last specimens of every thing which, if they meant to make the metropolis picturesque, they ought to avoid.

He recommended the lavish use of polychrome brick, and of gables to form an interesting and varied skyline.[183]

'Westward still the tendency of the town continues to advance,' observed 'Quondam' early in 1863. In 'the truly noble quarter of South Kensington', builders had 'expended large amounts in ranges of costly mansions flanking the Exhibition, the Prince Albert's and the Cromwell roads, as well as the splendid squares and terraces in close propinquity . . .'[184] By now the Park and Gardens were entirely surrounded by buildings and builders. Even to the west, 'cooping in and eating into Holland Park, girdled and regirdled with hideous lines of railway viaduct, horrid with shrieking engines, and veiled in clouds not only of steam but of smoke, London is closing in beyond Kensington, and speeding, almost as fast as a snail can crawl, down the western roads.'[185]

The position of the *Builder*'s editor as surveyor to one of the principal Kensington landowners may account for some of its enthusiasm. In 1868 it dealt with that landowner's transformation of the Redcliffe estate, between the Old Brompton and Fulham Roads, from

53 'Meanwhile Freake was building at Prince's
Gate "... first-class dwelling houses ... of
considerable architectural beauty ...".' Prince's
Gate.

market gardens into a new and expensive suburb. The central feature of the estate, most of which was owned by the Gunter family, was Redcliffe Gardens, 'on either side of which very capital semi-detached villas are being erected'. In Redcliffe Square there was to be a church, a necessity for any fashionable development.* The building was proceeding admirably:

> The builders have carried out their operations with great spirit and activity; they have constructed the whole of the roads and sewers, and there are now erected on the estate . . . about 550 houses, shops, and stables. The houses have been built with a view apparently to suit a variety of tenants, as the rents commence at 50*l.*, and range from that amount up to 160*l.* per annum. About 400 more houses . . . are yet to be erected, many of them of large size. With a good service of omnibuses, and two railway-stations, viz., the Chelsea Station [on the West London Extension Railway], at the south end of the estate, and the West Brompton Station, at the north end . . . which afford ready communication with the City, this district can scarcely fail to come into good use, and give a good reward to the builders for their enterprise and skill.[186]

The *Building News* was more impressed with the quantity than with the quality of what was going up in 'Brompton, or, as residents prefer to call it, South Kensington . . .' The conservatism of the mid-Victorian speculative builder, that makes the district so attractive today, infuriated those who took architecture seriously in the 1860's:

> . . . In the neighbourhood of the Cromwell-road, a great deal of building is going on. We use the word building advisedly, for there is little enough that can be termed architecture. The row of houses called Queen's Gate, overlooking the Exhibition of 1862, is lofty and conspicuous, but it is neither grand nor picturesque; indeed, the neighbourhood presents an aspect of monotonous mediocrity, than which scarcely anything can be more offensive.[187]

Cromwell Road, 'a healthy and open locality, rather aristocratic in its entourage from its neighbourhood to South Kensington', was being steadily developed during the seventies and beyond. One builder, W.H. Cullingford of Phillimore Gardens, was reported to be investing a quarter of a million pounds in the erection of 50 houses along the road.[188] The *Building News* remained unimpressed:

> We have lately noticed the rapid advances being made in the localities of Kensington and Brompton in what may be called the *haut ton* architecture of the day. In the neighbourhood of Earl's-court-road, Cromwell-road, and Gloucester-road, we may notice rows of mansions and houses of white bricks, stone, and compo, five, six, and seven stories in height, that have been erected within the last year or two, but displaying very mediocre

---

* 'In . . . rising localities, wheresoever four or five hundred houses have been completed, and even before they are occupied, a district church or chapel of ease is sure to arise. . . . Private proprietors, at Onslow-square and Earles-court . . . have set apart sites for churches; such liberality proving in general not prejudicial to worldly interests.' *B*, XXI (1863), p. 85.

design. . . . There is a meretricious unentertaining character about it that would only suit the humdrum or the wearied follower of fashion, and would be almost agony to the *genus irritabile* of poets and painters.[189]

It deplored the 'dismal and insufferable . . . monotony' of the 'favoured locality' of the Gloucester, Cromwell, and Earl's Court Roads:

We might almost imagine we were within the precincts of some convict establishment or military barrack – that railing, wall, and barricade formed the limits of our existence in their interminable prospect. We suffer a sense of oppression as we cast our eyes down the miles of stereotyped perspective of Cromwell-road or Queen's-gate, in which balustrade and hackneyed fenestration in stock brick and stucco are supreme, the flat stretch of wall being only broken by Ionic porches, which look like sentry-boxes in the lengthened vista.[190]

By the time W. J. Loftie published his history of Kensington in 1888 the red-brick revolution had extended itself from the Cadogan estate to the westernmost outposts of Kensington, bringing colour, contrast, and surprise:

. . . Behind and beyond Cromwell Road, a little to the south and west, we come upon a wholly different region. It is not as an inhabited country yet ten years old: but 'here,' as a flippant traveller has been heard to remark, 'Queen Anne has gone mad.' Street after street, and square after square, are built in red brick and terra-cotta after designs by various eminent architects of the school founded by Mr. Norman Shaw, but far outstripping his views, and plunging into the wildest extravagances of what may be called eclectic art. . . . the architect . . . takes features from any ancient or modern building which he thinks may look picturesque. The result is not quite satisfactory, although some of the houses – or rather palaces – in Harrington Gardens and Collingham Road are very handsome, very commodious, and probably very costly. The architects too often seem to me to err, first, by bringing in foreign models, and, secondly, by forgetting that they are building not country but town houses.[191]

What Loftie was seeing was, in fact, the last significant generation of the London town house. For although isolated terraces of expensive town houses are still being built both north and south of the Park, the kinds of families for which they were built were coming to prefer, even in late Victorian London, the luxury flat or the suburban villa.

Kensington, meanwhile, became more and more assimilated to central London. The commercialization of its main thoroughfares was already taking place in the mid-Victorian period. Kensington High Street, like Westbourne Grove in Bayswater, became a shopping street of importance not only for the adjacent residential area, but for London as a whole. Joseph Toms had a 'Toy and Fancy Repository' there as early as 1854, and was in 1862 joined by Charles Derry. John Barker left Whiteley's to open his store in the High Street in 1870, by which date Pontings was there as well.[192] The *Architect* in 1870 reported that the street was receiving an 'improved line of frontage', taking 'an easy curve up to the Metropolitan

District Railway Station. The new buildings are of white brick with stone and compo dressings, and are four storeys high.'[193] A decade later Kensington High Street, 'although still irregular in architecture, and bearing on its front the aspect of a past', was described as 'one of the most fashionable and popular promenades in London', by W.S. Clarke:

> The real shopping interest, from a lady's point of view, commences about Young-street, and extends (on that [south] side only) to Wright's-lane, where it altogether ends. Within this space, and on that side of the way, the shopkeepers vie with one another in tempting the fair passengers who make it their promenade between four and six P.M. during the London season. But it is from half-past eleven till one that most of the shopping is really done by ladies and carriage-folk generally. Regent-street, Oxford-street, and Bond-street may prove more expensive, but can hardly be found more choice, as may be seen any day between May and August by a visit at the right houses of the High-street of Kensington.[194]

The *Building News* remarked in 1882 on the speed with which Kensington had attached itself to the expanded metropolis:

> The enormous increase of buildings and population in Kensington is familiar to most people, though few are aware how very recent is the period during which North, West, and South Kensington have sprung from the respectable and comparatively old-fashioned parent village. In those days, the quiet and respectability of old Kensington attracted many residents; but, except perhaps in the neighbourhood of Campden-Hill, these attractions have gradually been assimilated to the garishness of the modern extensions. It is not more than a dozen years since the mass of houses now constituting Earl's-court was fields and market gardens. West Kensington, extending from Hammersmith to Shepherd's-bush, was scarcely known even by name – almost the only house in it being a melancholy cottage about the middle of the lane, on the gateway of which was the legend that it was the office for the West Kensington estate, and that lots might be had for building purposes. But it was not a prepossessing locality, and few could then have imagined that the Hammersmith extension of the Metropolitan Railway would so soon have brought with it a new town.[195]

W.J. Loftie exulted in the density and extent of Kensington's urban development in 1888:

> . . . To me there does not exist in the world any scenery more impressive than the view from the summit of Campden Hill. The sea of houses surging up and over all the hills round about, the innumerable chimneys, the endless streets, stretching to the horizon on all sides, with here and there a dark tree, or the faint glimmer of a green lawn, to remind you that these things exist – such a scene is a marvel on the earth, a wonder unwitnessed elsewhere; for we must remember that though there are great cities in our own and other countries, there is no city now in existence worthy to be even compared with London; and certainly none where standing actually in the outskirts, as on Campden Hill, we still see a complete horizon, all of houses.[196]

But Kensington was already past its peak. It had never seriously threatened the pre-

54 *top* '"There is a meretricious unentertaining character about it that would only suit the humdrum or the wearied follower of fashion . . ."' Cromwell Road.

55 *above* '". . . behind and beyond Cromwell Road . . . 'Queen Anne has gone mad'."' 11–15, Collingham Gardens, 1887.

56 'Kensington High Street . . . became a
shopping street of importance not only for the
adjacent residential area, but for London as a
whole.' Looking west, 1893.

57   '"The sea of houses surging up and over all the hills round about, the innumerable chimneys, the endless streets, stretching to the horizon on all sides . . ."' Addison Road.

eminence of Belgravia, much less of Mayfair; and by the late Victorian period was being deserted by the large, prosperous, and respectable families for whom it was intended. As early as 1878 the *Estates Gazette* reported that builders were finding it hard to attract purchasers for big houses there, and were subdividing them for multiple occupation.[197] The *Builder* in 1892 alluded to 'the decrease in value during the last ten years of houses in South Kensington...'.[198] Percy Fitzgerald remarked in 1893 that 'these vast Kensington houses are now found too costly to maintain, except for persons of large means'.[199] As a result, 'South Kensington, with its palatial mansions ... which sprang up at a season of "inflation", when every one was, or fancied he was, growing rich', was now 'somewhat out of fashion and deserted ...'.[200]

Booth's survey, on the other hand, found none of the deterioration in Kensington that he observed in Pimlico and Westbourne Park. Rents were 'steady, except in the western portion, where the nearness to the exhibitions at Earl's Court has lowered them ...'. Indirect evidence of the departure of the carriage-keeping class was the appearance in some mews in Kensington – as in Bayswater – that were 'intended for private servants' of 'drivers of shop carts or cabwashers'. The only patches of poverty in the parish were 'small village remnants of labourers ... Poverty is being crowded out of the greater part of this district [i.e., West London as a whole], and is crowding into Kensal New Town and Fulham ...'. The dominant population of Kensington and Brompton was 'a middle class verging on fashion and wealth'.[201]

The spirit of Georgian London, having grown ever more attenuated as it pushed its way westward from St James's, Mayfair, and Marylebone, finally vanished in the distant outposts of Kensington in the nineties. The Georgian Revival was then in its healthy infancy, but that was something else entirely. For practical purposes the future lay with the most extreme denial of Georgian urbanity: the villa suburb.

CHAPTER FIVE

The Villa and the New Suburb

'For my own part,' said he, 'I am excessively fond of a cottage; there is always
so much comfort, so much elegance about them. And I protest, if I had any
money to spare, I should buy a little land and build one myself, within a short
distance of London, where I might drive myself down at any time, and collect
a few friends about me and be happy.'
Mr Robert Ferrars, in *Sense and Sensibility*

THE GROWTH OF OUTER LONDON

'In every age and in every country the spirit of the time is shown in the homes of the people,'
Ernest Newton told the Architectural Association in 1891.[1] 'The influences which our
common everyday surroundings have upon our characters, our conceptions, our habits of
thought and conduct, are often very much underrated,' R. Barry Parker observed to the
Society of Architects in 1895.[2] Such surroundings were, for the comfortable middle classes,
increasingly taking the form of a detached or semi-detached house set in a garden, and
hidden by a fence or shrubbery from a suburban street.

Middle-class suburban villages, scattered villas, and ribbon developments along the
principal roads had surrounded eighteenth-century London. Islington, Hackney, Highgate, Hampstead, and Hammersmith north of the river, and Clapham – the most famous
of all Georgian suburbs – to the south housed significant numbers of City merchants and
professional men who travelled daily to their work by public coach or private carriage or
horse. But the dormitory suburb in the modern sense and on a large scale was a nineteenth-
century innovation.

Low-density suburban development depended on the existence of a number of social and
technological prerequisites, most of which had come into being by 1830. Safety of life and
property was a prime consideration in selecting a residence in pre-Victorian England.
Suburbs had traditionally and quite rightly been associated with lawlessness, with the forces
of riot and disorder, since they lay outside the jurisdiction of the primitive forms of watch of
the cities and boroughs. Gas lighting – first installed in Pall Mall in 1807, but a common
method of street lighting from 1816 onward – the establishment of the Metropolitan Police
in 1829, and, equally important, the general softening of manners that took place in the
nineteenth century, made suburban living less of a risk for the middle-class subject of
William IV than it had been earlier.* The omnibus, first introduced along the New Road

---

* 'What has the new light of all the preachers done for the morality and order of London, compared to what had been effected by gas lighting!' *Westminster Review*, 1829, quoted in John Timbs,
Curiosities of London, 1885, p. 372.

Map II   London and environs in 1834.

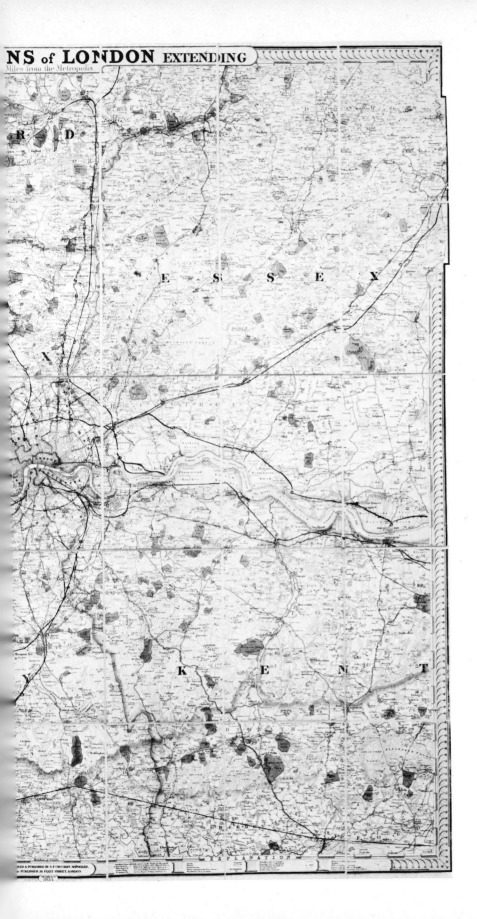

from Paddington to the City in 1829, by providing a genteel alternative to the private carriage, made it feasible for the gentleman of limited means to reside farther than walking distance from his place of business. The Thames steamboat provided a less genteel but cheaper conveyance for those living in riverside suburbs. By the fifties the suburban train would extend still further the possibilities of residence. The omnibus and the train permitted middle-class neighbourhoods to dispense with mews, and households to be run with only female servants.

Whatever the causes, the proliferation of scattered settlements was a more significant portent than the development of terraces and squares in Islington, Bayswater, and Kensington: unprecedented in form and structure as well as astonishing in extent.

'On every hand the extraordinary growth which the closing half of the present century has witnessed continues to develop; but . . . the southern side of the river . . . offers the most wonderful contrast to what it presented 60 years ago,' observed the *Building News* in 1893:

> In 1833 the only portion laid out in streets was comprised within the curve of the Thames, and bounded by a line drawn from Lambeth Palace by Newington, and ending at Bermondsey. All lay open beyond this 'pale.' Battersea Fields by 'Nine Elms,' and Vauxhall Gardens, and so away to Kennington, existed as an open tract, stretching to Deptford and Greenwich.[3]

'The expansion of London during the Nineteenth Century is in itself a fact unparalleled in the history of cities,' wrote Sir Walter Besant in 1899:

> I have before me a map of the year 1834 . . . showing South London as it was. I see a small town or collection of small towns, occupying the district called the Borough Proper, Lambeth, Newington, Walworth, and Bermondsey. In some parts this area is densely populated, filled with narrow courts and lanes; in other parts there are broad fields, open spaces, unoccupied pieces of ground. At the back of Vauxhall Gardens, for instance, there are open fields; in Walworth there is a certain place, then notorious for the people who lived there, called Snow's Fields; in Bermondsey there are also open spaces . . . without any buildings. Battersea is a mere stretch of open country.[4]

Ribbon development lined roads leading out from London in every direction. A writer in the *Builder* for 1844 described the vogue in the early years of the century 'for a kind of nondescript building, termed country box or cottage, and the roads of our suburbs were soon lined with these things of Liliputian dimensions, divided into four, six, or eight cells, in which people eat, drank, and slept, and performed the ordinary routine of idle life, protecting themselves from the balmy breath of heaven by bulwarks of rheumatic-looking trees and sickly shrubs . . .'.[5] A guidebook published in 1838 reported: 'From Kensington to Hammersmith is now almost one continued street, chiefly of modern buildings . . .'. At the same time existing villages were swelled with new residents from the metropolis. Hammersmith was 'crowded with houses of all sizes. Many of them are substantial well-built family residences, especially in the main street, and towards the Thames, which is here skirted by handsome villas . . .'[6] Norwood was 'studded with villa residences, large and small, and of various degrees of elegance . . .'.[7]

By the early Victorian period the accumulation of isolated detached residences, terraces along the principal roads, and the gradual expansion of existing villages was swamped by large-scale speculative building in the outer as well as the inner suburbs.[8] The *Builder* in 1844 quoted the *Globe* on the 'immense speculations in building which now give life and activity to the metropolis and its environs'. The parish of Lambeth, where 'the prodigious increase of houses is really astonishing', was said to have increased since 1822 by an 'almost incalculable' amount:

> Kennington-common, Stockwell, Brixton, South Lambeth, Wandsworth-road, Vauxhall, and the more remote parts of the parish, are formed into streets and rows of first, second, and third-rate buildings. Several squares have been formed and churches erected. Much taste is displayed in the architectural style of the suburban villas and cottages; but amidst this mass of buildings which strike the eye in almost every direction, hundreds of houses remain unoccupied. How so many private residences can find occupants is a question not easily solved. . . . the houses already built are more than enough for the inhabitants of Lambeth, Wandsworth, and Camberwell for the next 20 years.[9]

The *Globe* was not alone in its conviction that builders were absurdly overestimating the demand for suburban houses. 'The villa mania is everywhere most obtrusive,' exclaimed the *Morning Herald* in 1848:

> No one who has recently travelled with his eyes open . . . in the environs of this overgrown metropolis, can have failed to observe that houses are springing up in all quarters . . . Money is scarce; the whole nation is in difficulties; but houses spring up everywhere, as though capital were abundant – as though one-half of the world were on the look out for investments, and the other half continually in search of eligible family residences, desirable villas, and aristocratic cottages, which have nothing in the world of the cottage about them except the name.[10]

The outer suburbs in the fifties were still dominated by large villas set in extensive grounds. 'Denmark-hill is a gentle eminence,' wrote one guidebook, 'on which several fine mansions, some modern and a few ancient, are erected. . . . similar in character . . . are *Herne-hill* and *Champion-hill*, which are studded with gentlemen's seats, and from the elevations of which fine views are gained of the picturesque landscapes of Kent and Surrey.'[11] The same guide describes Peckham Rye as 'a favourite resort for invalids. . . . there is not in the immediate neighbourhood of London a more open and agreeable country than Peckham-rye, *Nunhead*, *Forest-hill*, and the adjacent localities.'[12] Norwood was 'the most picturesque district in . . . Lambeth. . . . situate in a delightful vale . . . The surpassing beauty of its scenery has tended to attract residents, and during the present century building has rapidly progressed here, terraces, villas, and hotels, having been erected; but . . . speculation has not been permitted to injure the landscape. Norwood still abounds in large uncultivated tracts of forest land . . .'.[13] Once improved bus and train services had come into effect, and still more with

58 *top* 'Hammersmith was "crowded with houses of all sizes. Many of them are substantial well-built family residence, especially in the main street . . .".' Hammersmith Broadway and Queen Street, *c.* 1840. Oil painting by J. Pollard.

59 *above* '. . . detached and semi-detached villas extended . . . into Shepherd's Bush and Hammersmith . . .' Lime Grove, Hammersmith, *c.* 1895.

the coming of the tram in the seventies, Lambeth saw dense housing and commercial developments supplant the large individual villas. After 1860 only in the hillier neighbourhoods like Norwood and the area near the Crystal Palace were new large detached houses built; the rest of the parish was covered with the ordinary products of the speculative builder.[14]

Suburbia was steadily moving northward as well as southward. In surveying the suburban progress of the North West from the top of Primrose Hill in 1862, George Rose Emerson recalled that at one time 'at its feet were swamps intersected by green lanes, leading from Marybone fields and Tottenham Court':

> Sixty years ago even the hill was as secluded and rural, as completely removed from the hum and bustle of a great city, as any Sussex or Devonshire hillock. Now, as we look Londonwards, we find that the metropolis has thrown out its arms and embraced us, not yet with a stifling clutch, but with ominous closeness. . . . St. John's Wood, spruce and trim, invades us on the right, and on the opposite side are huge railway stations, circular engine-factories, house upon house, and street upon street. We turn away from London, only to find that bricks and mortar are fast invading the pleasant Hampstead fields . . . A huge cutting [the London and North Western main line] traverses the valley at our feet, and pierces the bowels of the green hill . . . But the tall trees crowning the ridge of Hampstead Hill are yet untouched . . . and we willingly forget, that farther eastward, the once green slopes of Holloway are crowded with houses, and that castellated prisons rear their dismal and defiant towers.[15]

The fields at Gospel Oak were 'nearly covered with terraces and crescents; and Kentish Town is throwing out lines of bricks and mortar to meet its neighbours, Hampstead Heath and Downshire Hill'.[16] Farther east were Hackney, Clapton, and Dalston which together constituted 'one of the handsomest suburbs of London. There is still an old-fashioned air about Hackney itself . . .' which still retained traces of the days when it was dominated by the villas of prosperous City merchants. '. . . Dalston has thrown out long lines of handsome villas across the fields and orchards on the south-west; Clapton has developed itself on the north-east . . . and down in the [Lea] Marshes . . . are now large hives of manufacturing industry.'[17] Victoria Park had greatly increased the value of nearby property: 'A new town of handsome villa residences has sprung up where before were open fields, waste lands, or miserable rookeries tenanted by a squalid, criminal population'.[18] Westward, too, detached and semi-detached villas extended beyond the more urban developments of Bayswater and Kensington into Shepherd's Bush and Hammersmith, where Brook Green had 'degenerated into a common sewer . . . arched over'.[19]

Each new extension of building called forth expressions of wonder at the ever-increasing size of London, regrets at the destruction of the countryside and familiar village landmarks, apprehension lest the building industry really had at last overestimated the market for suburban villas, and disapproval of the architectural, sanitary, and structural qualities of the houses going up. 'Belsize Park . . . has succumbed to the march of bricks and mortar, and permitted the inroad of labyrinths of streets that will ultimately bear comparison with

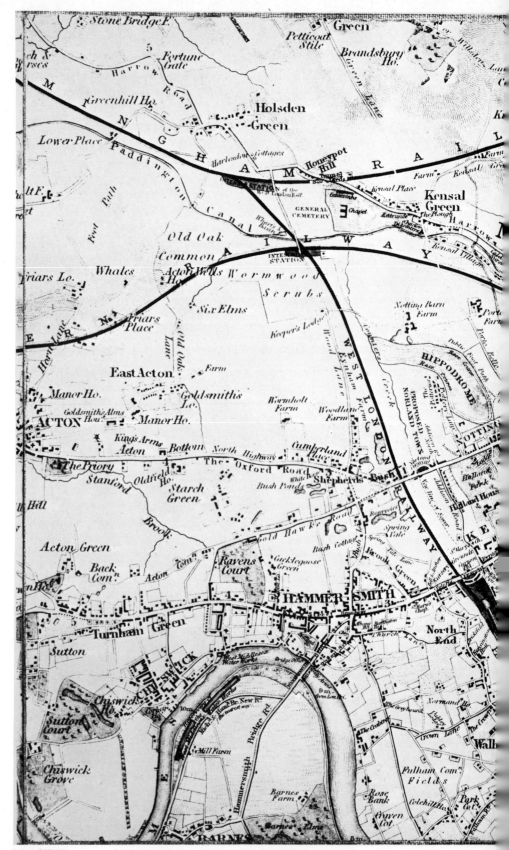

Map III Western suburbs in 1840. Section from B.R. Davis, *Map of London and Surroundings,* 1

Belgravia,' reported the *Builder* in 1863. The once-secluded residents of Maida Hill 'look upon a new neighbourhood of streets that has completely walled them in, known as the Warrington Estate'. The Edgware Road provided the new suburbs to the north west a convenient concentration of shops: 'The commercial aspect of Edgware-road now only ceases a short distance from Kilburn-gate, and beyond that obstruction it again takes possession of the highway for a length of road nearly reaching to Willesden-lane'.[20]

The early Victorian period saw much ribbon development along the main roads, with large undeveloped areas in between. Later the emphasis changed to one of filling in the gaps. 'There has been a very curious contrast between the mode of the growth of London from 1834 to 1867, and that from that date to 1881,' the *Builder* for 1885 pointed out:

> In the former period, while several broad and compact districts were built over, and while the central nucleus increased very largely, one particular feature was the pushing out of lines of buildings along the course of the main roads, by as much, in some of them, as from three to four miles. During the last fourteen years of the time compared, on the contrary, extension along the lines of road has been generally but little marked, a stretch of about a mile and a half along the Edgware-road, and around the railways there intersecting, being the most noticeable. But the intervals between the lines shot out in the earlier period have been busily filled up during the latter: so that the growth of the solid nucleus, with but few interstices left open, has been nothing less than prodigious.[21]

Perhaps the explanation in part is that three to four miles was about the maximum practical walking distance, and that the earlier new suburban residents had relied on private carriages or omnibuses running along the major roads. From the sixties onward, suburbanites either lived close enough to their places of employment to walk, or clustered around the different railway stations.

The workmen's train had not yet become a serious inducement to the artisan class to move out along the main lines of railway, and railway suburbia in the sixties remained middle class and low in density. 'The present tendency of building [in suburban Surrey and Kent] is to expand along the course of their railways, not in dense lines of streets, but in villa or even cottage residences, each furnished with a breathing-ground in the way of garden or paddock,' observed the *Builder* in 1868. It found much to admire in 'the wholesome and rational style of building which is now dotting over the district between Camberwell and Croydon'.[22]

Denser development was on the way. 'Where does the flood of London humanity intend to stop?' asked the *Builder* in 1870:

> Many of us are old enough to remember the opening of the Finchley-road some seven-and-thirty years ago, and even later, when the Swiss Cottage was the solitary goal of Cockney pleasure-seekers – the *ultima thule* of London civilisation in that direction. . . .
>
>   All before you, and around you, to a quadrant of the compass, were fields, gardens, and farms, with breezy Hampstead up the hill on the right, and the pleasant village of Kilburn away on the left.

The speculative builders had changed all that:

Pursuing our way . . . down West-end-lane, we find that they have not begun to move much there as yet; but, after crossing the two railway bridges, to the east of which the Midland Railway passes under the Hampstead and City Junction Line, we come upon the outpost works of advancing London. . . .

'Where will London end?' we said to a respectable-looking man who was surveying the situation . . .

'Goodness knows,' was his reply. 'Building plots are snapped up as if they were so many gold nuggets. You go to-day, and all but settle; only you think that you'll consider for a day or two. By the time that you have made up your mind some "early bird" has dropped down at the land agent's and gobbled up the morsels that you had set your heart upon.'

To the east Belsize Park was already 'covered with goodly houses wherein the well-to-do of the City and town rest in the bosom of their families, after their day's labour and their double ride on that valuable . . . convenience, the Metropolitan and St. John's Wood Railway'. Farther out building was more scattered:

The strip of country between the Finchley-road and Kilburn . . . is of an undulating character, well wooded, and the atmosphere remarkably clear. The landscape, fieldwards, is studded with the residences of the wealthy, and hundreds of the semi-detached villa community are daily taking root in the soil. . . .

Looking across the valley in the direction of Kilburn, stakes in line are driven into the earth, marking the outline of future 'roads', 'avenues', 'terraces', and so on.[23]

The built-up area was still more extended when James Thorne's *Handbook to the Environs of London* appeared in 1876. 'Monotonous streets and lines of villas are fast encircling the town,' he wrote of Croydon, 'the neighbourhood of which being pleasant and picturesque, and within easy reach of the city, is a favourite residence for men of business, who may be seen flocking to the morning trains in surprising numbers.'[24] Between Croydon and London, and near the Crystal Palace, lay Penge:

Fifty years ago Penge was only spoken of as a common, and the maps show hardly a house upon it. By the Crooked Billet, on the Beckenham road, there were a few dwellings . . . the old canal was bought and converted into a railway in 1839, and Penge Common was fixed on as a convenient stat. for Norwood and Beckenham. Then 'the plague of building lighted upon it;' spread more rapidly when Penge Place was taken for the Crystal Palace, Penge Wood was absorbed partly in the palace grounds, and the rest, doubly attractive from its proximity to that popular resort, given over to the builder; and culminated when a Freehold Building Society bought what had been spared of the Common for distribution among its members. Now, Penge is a town in size and population, in appearance a waste of modern tenements, mean, monotonous, and wearisome. It has 3 churches, many chapels, schools, hotels, taverns, inns, 'offices' of all sorts, shops, 4 or 5 rly. stations, and whatever may be looked for in a new suburban rly. town.[25]

Sydenham, 'of old only known as a genteel hamlet of Lewisham, famed for sylvan retreats,

60 *top* '"The commercial aspect of Edgware-
road now only ceases a short distance from
Kilburn-gate . . ."' Toll gate at Kilburn, 1860.

61 *above* 'Sydenham . . . "has grown into a
district of villas . . .".' Seymour Lodge, Sydenham
Hill, *c.* 1880.

charming prospects, and once for its medicinal waters', also owed its recent growth to the move there of the Crystal Palace: 'It has grown into a district of villas, detached and semi-detached cottages, terraces, so-called parks, and streets . . . it has lost its rural character, and is assuming every day more the aspect of a suburb of London.'[26]

West of London what had until recently been separate villages were now linked with the metropolis by continuous building. Of Fulham, Thorne wrote: 'The line of houses is now virtually unbroken from London, and Fulham has become a portion of the outer fringe of the great city'.[27] In nearby Hammersmith, 'the builder has very nearly supplanted the gardener and farmer; the mansions are for the most part pulled down, occupied as schools or institutions, been subdivided, or given place to factories . . .'. It had become an industrial as well as a dormitory suburb, boasting 'large engineering establishments, distilleries, lead mills, oil mills, a coach factory, boat-builders' yards, and brick fields, besides the extensive pumping works of the West Middlesex Water Company'.[28]

From time to time London seemed overbuilt not merely from an aesthetic, but from a practical economic point of view. In 1881 it was stated that of the 4,800 houses built in the previous ten years in East Dulwich, 40 per cent were then unoccupied.[29] At the annual meeting of the Northern and Eastern Suburban Industrial Dwellings Company the following year, the chairman justified a reduction of the rents being asked in Tottenham by pointing to 'the large amount of over-building which had been going forward in various directions around London during the past year or more'.[30] The *Building News* argued in 1884 that 'a cursory inspection of any residential locality such as Richmond, where agents' boards are sadly thick on the field', indicated a general glut of houses.[31] By 1886 the fall in suburban house rents had become general:

> The fall is more noticeable in the class of houses ranging between £25 to £50 rental, to be accounted for by the excessive production of houses of this class. . . . In the neighbour-hoods of Camberwell, Peckham, Brixton, Dulwich, and Lower Norwood, the house agents boards may be counted by the score in any road. On a very desirable and eligible building estate, the Tulse Hill Park Estate, a row of superior houses of recent construction are announced 'to be Let or Sold,' and many of the old and substantially built residences along the main Brixton-road are also in the market. . . . Houses hitherto let at £50 and £45 have been reduced £5 or more, and small houses letting at £36 are reduced to £32. In East Dulwich – though this has been a blighted district ever since the jerry builder left his mark on it – houses of £28 and £30 may now be had at £25 . . . In the north and west suburbs the like reductions have taken place.[32]

In 1887 the effects of earlier overbuilding had at last brought a diminution in the volume of new building. '. . . Round London speculating building seems to stagnate very consider-ably,' wrote the *Building News* of 24 June 1887. 'Indeed, it would appear that the unhallowed jerry-building system has . . . almost extinguished itself by reason of its greedy over-production, like some monster form, suffocating in its own filth.'[33] Building went on regardless, according to the *Builder*:

62 'In nearby Hammersmith, "the builder has very nearly supplanted the gardener and farmer . . ."' Hammersmith Green, *c.* 1875.

... House property in or near London ... does more than stand still in value; on the whole it depreciates. ... The abundant supply of money enables builders to go on opening up new districts and erecting new houses. New houses have always an attraction for many people, and a few modern additions, such as electric bells, attract residents. In a word, the supply exceeds the demand . . .[34]

'London of to-day is, as to its greater part, a new city,' wrote Charles Eyre Pascoe in 1888:

There are persons still living who remember when its western limits reached but a short distance beyond the now thickly populated districts of Pimlico and Paddington. Those limits now extend almost to Kingston in Surrey, and to Brentford in Middlesex, having long since encroached upon Fulham, Shepherd's Bush, and Kilburn. . . . Elm Park, one of the last unoccupied spots between London and the old gardens of Cremorne, is now covered with streets and terraces . . . In the north-west . . . the mansions on Fitz-John's Avenue . . . In the far east, rows and rows of neat little houses appear all the way down the road to Ilford. On the Surrey and Kentish side, even to Sydenham and Chislehurst, Wimbledon and Croydon, the work of building progresses, enlarging to a wonderful extent the area of modern London.[35]

As the century came to an end the character of modern suburbia had already been established. With the rise in the standard of living in the last third of the century more and more families could afford suburban residence. The building of a tramway network, the forthcoming electrification not only of those tramways but of the steam underground and mainline railways, and the building of the deep-level tubes were about to give Greater London something very like the public transport system that it has today. The motor car and the motor bus had yet to appear in any significant numbers, but the bicycle had already made feasible residence at some distance from the railway. The suburban villa was becoming not merely potentially but actually the home of the ordinary Englishman. 'There is a great flood . . . which has overtaken London and our great cities with houses and dwellings for the middle and working classes,' the *Building News* observed in 1900:

Go where we will – north, south, east, or west of this huge overgrown Metropolis – the fungus-like growth of houses manifests itself, stretching from town to suburb and village – as from the southern suburbs to Herne Hill and Dulwich, and from Streatham to Croydon. In every direction we see the same outward growth of dwelling-houses of a small and unpretending class – generally a repetition of a type of house that has been found to meet the requirements of the middle class and artisan. The larger and more commodious residence of fifty years ago is being pulled down, or swamped by this tide of small houses: where one large house existed ten or a hundred or more have been built, absorbing the acres of gardens and private park lands. This is one of the social revolutions of the age . . .[36]

THE SUBURB AND THE COUNTRYSIDE

The multiplication of suburbs did nothing to make them more attractive to people with aesthetic or intellectual pretensions. 'That crowd of half-bred towns that belt about London

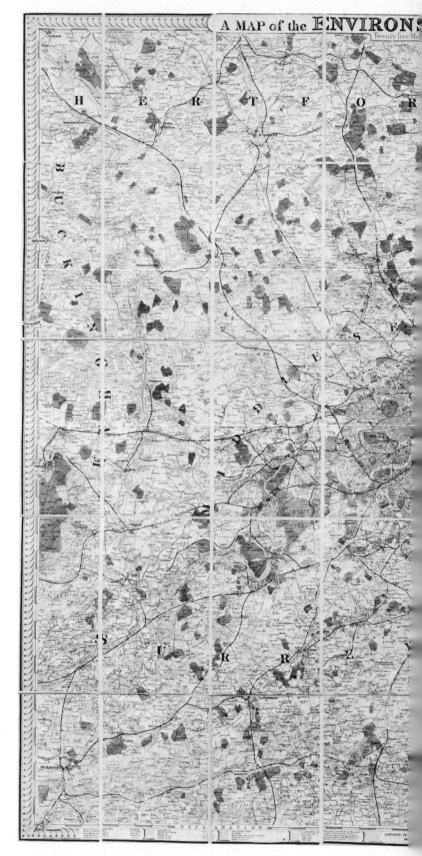

Map IV   London and environs,
c. 1885.

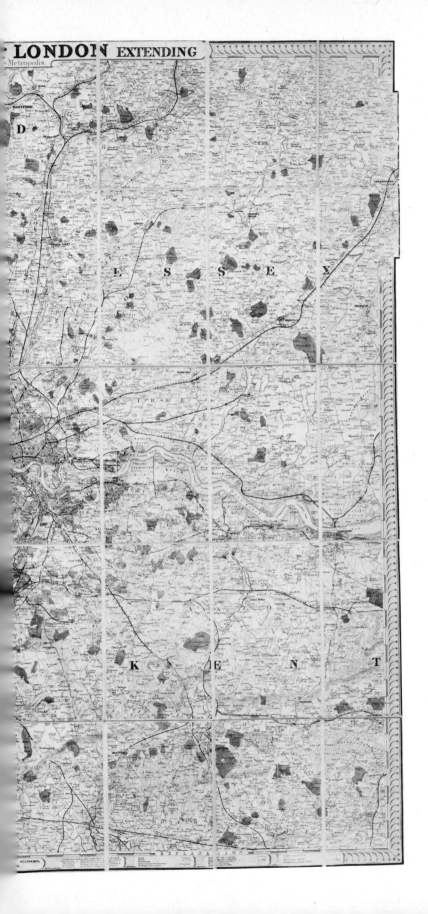

LONDON EXTENDING
Metropolis.

and are known usually by the name *suburbs* has always been to me the occasion for distinct and unmitigated hatred,' wrote one contributor to the *Architect* in 1876. 'A modern suburb is a place which is neither one thing nor the other; it has neither the advantage of the town nor the open freedom of the country, but manages to combine in nice equality of proportion the disadvantages of both.'[37]

In fact the suburb has to be understood not as a failed attempt to be either town or country, but as an environment fundamentally different from either, with distinctive attributes and needs. But while suburbs were not, and did not try to be *like* the country, in their early stages they were very *close* to the country. The new Victorian suburbs occupied a different kind of landscape from that which surrounds them today. Just as the Victorian office block or church or hotel looked very different encompassed by low terraces of Georgian brick, from the same office block or church or hotel surrounded by later Victorian structures, or by Edwardian classical or new Elizabethan glass; so each new suburb must be pictured surrounded and interpenetrated by the open countryside.

The situation in the Green Belt today, where occupants of houses built in 1939 on the fringe of then-expanding developments still have the countryside literally at their doorsteps was, if only temporarily, the experience of the early dwellers in each new Victorian suburb. The grimness of much Victorian suburban architecture was mitigated by the immediate presence of open fields. One or two villas, even one or two streets of villas, set apart from the town, could never have been as oppressive in isolation as they became when surrounded by street after street of duplicates of themselves. Even today, by looking for stylistic discontinuities, the visitor in most London suburbs can visualize what had once been the boundary between town and country: where a row of Wimbledon Transitional suddenly turns into Bypass Variegated (to borrow two more of Sir Osbert Lancaster's useful categories), there, one can be reasonably certain, the suburban dweller for many years looked out directly on green fields. '. . . Those of us born since 1939 tend to forget how intense a reality, and not merely a myth, the memory of the encircling farmland still is for our elders,' Nicholas Taylor writes of London suburbia.[38]

The unbuilt-on outskirts of London were not, to be sure, necessarily idyllic in appearance: it was not all a question of neat cottages looking out on smiling meadows. However unprepossessing Battersea may be today, its builders cannot be accused of blighting a beauty spot, as Sir Walter Besant reminds us:

I myself remember the old Battersea Fields perfectly well; one shivers at the recollection; they were low, flat, damp, and, I believe, treeless; they were crossed, like Hackney Marsh, by paths raised above the level; at no time of year could the Battersea Fields look anything but dreary. In winter they were inexpressibly dismal.[39]

But the same author also points out how much natural beauty elsewhere had been destroyed:

It is difficult, now that the whole country south of London has been covered with villas, roads, streets, and shops, to understand how wonderful for loveliness it was until the builder seized upon it. When the ground rose out of the great Lambeth and Bermondsey Marsh – the cliff or incline is marked still by the names of Battersea Rise, Clapham Rise, and Brixton Rise – it opened out into one wild heath after another – Clapham, Wandsworth, Putney, Wimbledon, Barnes, Tooting, Streatham, Richmond, Thornton, and so south as far as Banstead Downs. The country was not flat: it rose at Wimbledon to a high plateau; it rose at Norwood to a chain of hills; between the Heaths stretched gardens and orchards; between the orchards were pasture lands; on the hill sides were hanging woods; villages were scattered about, each with its venerable church and its peaceful churchyard . . . the loveliness of South London lay almost at the very doors of London: one could walk into it . . .[40]

One cause, in fact, of the early growth of London's suburbia was the sheer beauty of much of its immediate surroundings. John Ruskin, whose family moved from Hunter Street near Brunswick Square to a semi-detached house at Herne Hill in 1823, thus later describes his childhood memories of the locality:

The view from the ridge on both sides was, before railroads came, entirely lovely: westward at evening, almost sublime, over softly wreathing distances of domestic wood; – Thames herself not visible, nor any fields except immediately beneath; but the tops of twenty square miles of politely inhabited groves. On the other side, east and south, the Norwood hills, partly rough with furze, partly wooded with birch and oak, partly in pure bramble copse, and rather steep pasture, rose with the promise of all the rustic loveliness of Surrey and Kent in them, and with so much of space and height in their sweep, as gave them some fellowship with hills of true hill-districts.[41]

Places within walking distance of London that possessed scenic attractions, and particularly if they also had mineral springs, usually passed through the stage of popular spa before the residential phase, although the two ordinarily overlapped. Thus Norwood in the 1830's still commanded 'extensive and agreeable views', and retained 'a *few* agreeable walks . . . out of the dusty high road inclosed right and left, so prevalent for several miles on the Surrey side of the bridges'. It had 'several good houses of entertainment for visitors, aristocratic or plebeian. . . . the place has . . . always been famous for holiday excursions and pleasure-parties, and the resort hither has of late years been much increased in consequence of the discovery of the mineral waters, called the *Beulah Spa* . . .'.[42]

Every new suburb had a period when the countryside was at worst a short distance across the brickfields and building sites. The 'handsome houses and genteel semi-detached cottages' that by 1862 had replaced the 'delightful rural walks' that once lay between King Street, Hammersmith and Shepherd's Bush, together with the 'rows of showy villas' in Hammersmith Grove, and the 'new stucco villas' stretching towards Gold Hawk Road, still enjoyed 'interspaces of corn-fields and garden ground . . .'.[43] In the early fifties, 'people living on Maida-hill looked out of their windows upon fields that stretched away to Pinner and Harrow . . .'.[44]

63 'The grimness of much Victorian suburban architecture was mitigated by the immediate presence of open fields.' Crystal Palace and surrounding houses from West Norwood. Percy Fitzgerald, *London City Suburbs*, 1893, p. 183.

The *Building News* in 1874 pointed out both the extent and the precariousness of the rural qualities of suburbs north and south of the Thames:

If the . . . 'Northern Heights' . . . Highgate, Upper Holloway, Highbury, &c. – have their special charms of bracing atmosphere, elevated position, fine views, and open situation, so, also, has Southern London special peculiarities of an equally inviting kind. Although Southwark, Lambeth, and Clapham are flat and low, as a rule, Camberwell, Denmark and Herne Hills, East and West Dulwich, and, beyond them, the rising ground of Sydenham and Norwood, are full of retreats as diversified in surface, and even more favoured by sylvan characteristics. Norwood, and the localities between Camberwell and Sydenham, are rich in wooded scenery, though here and there the speculative builders and kin societies called 'Building Societies' are depriving the glade or the meadow of its pastoral sward, and the thicket and grove of their folial richness.

By moving to the rural outskirts, suburban pioneers destroyed the beauty that had attracted them there in the first instance. The *Building News*, while rejoicing in substantial gentlemen's seats set in extensive grounds, condemned the proliferation of smaller suburban residences for the less well-to-do, a distinction understandable on aesthetic if not on social grounds:

We noticed one of the mushroom class of depradations in our last, its tendency to over-spread every yard of open ground, to denude the open pasture, field, or wood of every vestige of its verdure, and to substitute . . . frail tenements . . . This class of house property – houses of rentals from about £28 to £40 – seems to perfectly overwhelm the suburban dweller.

What strikes the modern reader is the same reflection that strikes him when he observes what remains of such districts of suburban housing: the enormous size of the lower middle-class population in mid-Victorian London, able to command the rudiments of genteel living for a rent of £28 upwards annually.* But the *Building News* was less impressed by the number of Londoners able to afford the luxury of suburban living than dismayed by the density at which they were housed: 'We can point to estates and localities, once open and healthy, which have given place to these close-set nests of brick and mortar, in the neighbourhoods of Brixton, Clapham, and Camberwell; but as houses so built readily let, any remonstrance appears to be useless'.[45]

As the grounds of private estates were covered with new developments, the semi-rural quality of many suburbs disappeared. 'Only a few years ago it was possible to distinguish the invasions of the speculator-builder by the number of private estates which were dotted over the landscape,' the *Building News* recalled in 1896:

Between them were acres of woodland or meadow or old residences of a past generation with their acres of land. But this partial invasion of the landscape may no longer be seen; the building estates have coalesced or joined, and what before was a varied mixture of old

* £28 is the rent mentioned again and again as the minimum at which a suburban house could be had by a middle-class tenant.

and new have now become a mass of dwellings. Even the hilly slopes of the 'Northern Heights,' and the hills stretching from Brixton to the Sydenham ridge are more or less covered . . .[46]

Some suburbs kept their links with the countryside down to the end of the century. Denmark Hill, 'a fair attractive district, with distinct charms of its own', retained into the nineties a juxtaposition of rural and residential scenes:

The air here seems ever mild and salubrious; there is an abundance of old trees by the roadside, with pleasant fields stretching far away. There are gentle ascents by Denmark Hill and Dulwich, quaintly named Dog-kennel Hill and Redpost Hill. Here are comfortable-looking mansions, of old-fashioned and formal cut, that seem to doze on in tranquil fashion. The speculative builder has not, as yet, done much mischief . . . The fair country seems to commence here, for the long, densely-crowded rows of town houses stop abruptly at Camberwell Green, whence there spread out at once the inviting rural roads to Sydenham and Dulwich.[47]

Dulwich preserved its rural qualities throughout the century:

Notwithstanding the active building operations that of late years have fenced in London and its suburbs . . . Dulwich has not yet wholly lost its rural aspect, and tracts of meadowland are yet to be found within its borders. From the high grounds of Champion Hill, Denmark Hill, and Herne Hill . . . through the whole length of the intervening valley, and up the opposite slopes to the summit of Sydenham and Forest Hills, may still be heard the song of birds; while the beauties of the place are spread out in groves and pleasure-grounds, green lanes, and flowery meadows.[48]

THE BUILDING PROCESS

'Where, when, how will the continual growth, frightening in its speed, of London . . . come to an end?' asked a French visitor in the eighties:

. . . One cannot take five hundred steps in one of the innumerable suburbs . . . which daily attach themselves more firmly to the centre until they lose themselves intimately and entirely in it, without coming upon a field that one had seen three months before, quiet, grassy, populated with sheep or cows, but whose appearance has in so little time altered completely. Turned over from top to bottom, cut into deep trenches, covered with heaps of mud, piles of bricks, stacks of timbers, in the midst of which are working bustling navvies and people loading or unloading the tip carts, you see quickly rise there, – the works stop only on Sundays, – not a single isolated house, but the beginning of a new street. This changed scene, which seems magical by the brief time that it requires, – the English dwelling, of such light construction that a heavy step on the floor will shake it from top to bottom, is built in a few days, – is taking place simultaneously . . . to all points of the compass. If you return in a few months, you will find the street finished, with pavements on each side, lit by gas . . . And don't be thinking that the houses . . . remain long empty; most of them are rented, *occupied*, before they have been completed, while the carpenters, plasterers, roofers, and painters are still working on them, well before the plaster inside the rooms is dry and the walls papered.[49]

The physical operations involved in the creation of each new suburban development were everywhere much the same. 'A stranger walking a few miles around London would see sights that would surprise him,' 'A Kensalltonian' informed the *Builder* in 1880:

> Here . . . are carts and wagons laden with building materials, endeavouring to gain access to a field; the wheels are sunk axle deep in the mire, wagoners smacking their whips and beating their horses unmercifully, but all to no purpose; the destined place for unloading is, by mud and mire, rendered inaccessible. Building operations have commenced in this field. As the stranger approaches, he sees a mass of brickwork on either side of an impassable road, that is destined to be called a street at some future day; the walls of the houses, though newly built, look very shaky . . .[50]

At best the appearance of a newly-erected building estate lacked the neatness and order that we have come to associate with the Victorian suburb. 'In the suburbs of London . . . may be found a number of building sites that, at this time of the year, are little better than mud ponds,' wrote the *Building News* in January 1884. 'Houses have been built on one or both sides of a roughly-formed roadway cut out of the meadow or field, which may have received a layer of rough gravel, and in this condition the estate is left till nearly all the houses are built or let.'[51] Building sites were always unattractive, and sometimes contained potential threats to the health of future residents. 'In dozens of suburban spots round the metropolis, colonies of houses have arisen upon land, which a few years ago had been used for brickmaking or gardens . . . such land was not only damp and ill-drained, but was saturated with animal and vegetable matter to such an extent as to become perfectly unhealthy for house-building,' according to the *Building News* in 1883. 'The land is flat, badly drained, and is generally flooded in rainy seasons. Such sites are abundant in Essex . . . they are generally the first to be invaded by the speculative builder.'[52]

The failures of over-ambitious speculations often left whole developments in a desolate, half-completed state for years on end. 'A few years ago, in perambulating the then outskirts of London,' the *Builder* recalled in 1866, 'it was no unusual thing to find, in localities now centres of thriving suburban districts, a row of unsightly carcasses. Roofless, unglazed, ruinous-looking masses of bricks and mortar would stand, sometimes for years, proclaiming their dismal tale of materials unpaid for and too credulous mortgagees denuded of their cash.'[53]

The completed building estates that emerged from the mud and disorder pleased no one but the landowner, builder, and tenants. By their rawness, their uniformity of architecture, and their lack of softening foliage to mask the harsh lines of the new façades they did nothing to lessen the regrets for what they had replaced, whether market gardens or pasture land, the private grounds of an old-fashioned detached mansion or a village street. Yet for their new tenants they offered a delightful alternative to something far less salubrious in central London.

64   *top*   '"Norwood, and the localities between Camberwell and Sydenham, are rich in wooded scenery, though here and there the speculative buildings . . . are depriving the glade or the meadow of its pastoral sward . . ."' Gipsy Road, Lower Norwood. Fitzgerald, *London City Suburbs*, p. 12.

65   *above*   '"And don't be thinking that the houses . . . remain long empty; most of them are rented, *occupied*, before they have been completed, while the carpenters, plasterers, roofers, and painters are still working on them . . ."' Speculative terraces in process of construction.

SUBURBAN ATTRACTIONS

Critics have tended, both in Victorian times and since, to argue that the suburb was something forced on an unwilling or at least helpless and apathetic middle class: that just as rising land values and the unhealthiness of central London compelled it to migrate to the suburbs, the kind of communities and the kind of houses its members moved into once they got there were such that they had to accept willy-nilly. The *Architect* for 1883 painted a pathetic picture:

> . . . The house-hunter in the suburbs of London is like the pioneer on the American prairie, an explorer without a guide in a perfect wilderness, knowing nothing, trusting nobody, taking every risk as he best can, hoping against hope, and relying at the worst upon his liberty to try again. . . . [Suburbia] is a *terra incognita* . . . in which house-hunting . . . has become . . . an adventure of despair.[54]

By any ordinary standards, the middle-class family looking for a house to rent in the London suburbs enjoyed a buyer's market in almost any period down to the Second World War. Supply consistently exceeded demand, and there was no difficulty involved in moving to another house or another suburb if one was at all displeased with what one had. 'Many, at any rate,' according to Professor T. Roger Smith, 'of those who resided in the outskirts were remarkably ready to migrate from one quarter to another, so much so that not a few systematically changed their dwelling every three years.'[55]

The choice that such a situation ostensibly gave the prospective tenant or buyer was, many argued, illusory, as in fact all houses produced by the speculative builder were essentially the same. Suburban houses 'are planned generally, without the slightest regard to the different requirements of tenants; they are cast in the same mould and stereotyped in feature', asserted the *Building News* in 1883. 'Every suburb of the metropolis is overrun with these ready-made houses. The needy tenant has no choice – he is obliged to take the stereotyped dwelling . . .'[56] 'It is amazing, certainly, amid the diversity that exists, how few houses are to be found in the suburbs that really satisfy the householder,' said the same journal six years earlier:

> The builder of a row of houses or a colony of detached villas selects what he considers a tenantable model, and builds them wholesale . . . His doorways are placed in set positions that experience has approved, and his offices are planned after all the conventional ideas of tenants have been consulted. He often gets his elevations drawn for him to suit his own whims, or they are allowed to follow his notions, and to conform to his idea of cheap construction and ornamentation.

However standardized the design, the products seemed to please prospective buyers, possibly because 'all the conventional ideas of tenants' really were incorporated into the plans:

> Though pretentious and vulgar they let well in spite of their architectural defects. At Finsbury-park, Holloway, Dalston, Chalk Farm, Hampstead, Kilburn, on the north; Norwood, Streatham, and Brixton, on the south; and Kensington, Hammersmith, and Battersea, on the west, we meet with houses and villas of this class by the hundred . . .[57]

Because the new tenants ought not to have liked such houses, it was assumed that they did not. Such thinking about popular taste is still common among those who would like to combine aesthetic elitism with social egalitarianism, and for whom nothing is more distressing than the thought that the majority may really prefer mediocrity to excellence. 'It is claimed by some that the suburban resident is not really a free agent and that his choice is limited by his ignorance of the alternatives, or even that he is given no choice at all,' writes J.M. Richards in *The Castles on the Ground*:

> Is it really the case, however, that an innocent and unwilling public is made to accept whatever villainies the speculative builder chooses to force upon him? The speculative builder can no doubt be blamed for much, but he is a business man supplying a demand and, as business men must, he instinctively reacts to the nature of the demand.[58]

The above passage was first published in 1946, just about the time that the buyer's market in middle-class housing had come, perhaps once and for all, to an end. The astonishing rise in prices during the early 1970's for perfectly ordinary pre-war semi-detached houses may not necessarily mean that they still represent what the middle classes would most like for themselves, but it does indicate that they are willing to settle for them, and to pay a great deal of money for the privilege.

By contrast, in the period before 1939, and certainly in that before 1901, when there was always an oversupply of middle-class housing in the London area, and when builders were doing their utmost to cut costs and add features like electric bells and stained glass windows in the front door to attract the elusive buyer or tenant – and going bankrupt with great regularity in the process – the argument that they were wilfully ignoring the real desires of their public is too contrary to common sense to be accepted without a great deal of supporting evidence. The repeated assertions of architects and critics that such was the case sound too much like wishful thinking to be fully convincing.

A more productive line of enquiry would be to ask what sort of satisfactions the houses actually built, purchased, and inhabited did provide: what aspirations were fulfilled, what values expressed, what kinds of behaviour encouraged.

The home occupied a central place in any Victorian system of values. Ernest Newton, speaking to the Architectural Association in 1891, argued that it was, in an age of crumbling beliefs, the only remaining object of national worship:

> Nowadays, when all religions are assailed, and we believe in nothing very strongly, it is almost impossible to make our churches express anything more than a sort of galvanised enthusiasm; we reproduce old forms as symbolical of certain legends, although we are not quite sure whether we believe them or not . . . Belief in the sacredness of home-life, however, is still left to us, and is itself a religion, pure and easy to believe. It requires no elaborate creeds, its worship is the simplest, its discipline the gentlest and its rewards are peace and contentment.[59]

The suburb provided an environment where home-life flourished as nowhere else. On the eve of the Victorian era the suburb and the suburban villa enjoyed the esteem of aesthetes and moralists alike. It was in connection with James Burton's villa in Regent's Park – conceived, as Summerson has pointed out, as the prototype of the garden suburb – that J.B. Papworth wrote of the importance of the home in English culture:

> The desire to congregate about him in his dwelling and domain all the means of domestic comfort, is a prominent feature of the character of an Englishman; and he there lays up his chief resources against the cares of life. His home is the depository of his most interesting pleasures, the anticipated enjoyment of which gives energy to his mind, and cheers his exertion towards the accomplishment of his undertakings: he eagerly embraces its pleasures and repose during the intervals which he can spare for recreation, and flies to it as a welcome retreat from bustle and the toils of life, when desirous and prepared to transfer them to more youthful energies. Thus the suitableness of his dwelling becomes . . . the measure of the Englishman's enjoyments . . .[60]

It was to achieve just such ends that villa suburbia proliferated.

PRIVACY

'Few modern authors can mention a suburb without a snarl, as if suburban meant much the same as sub-human,' Michael Robbins has observed. 'It is apparently common ground that in suburbs . . . there is no sense of community . . .'[61] A frequent charge made against the dormitory suburb is that the absence of meeting rooms, clubs, and other social centres throws the individual back on the tender mercies of the nuclear family, lurking behind the garden gate. Sir Walter Besant deplored 'the life of the suburb without any society; no social gatherings or institutions; as dull a life as mankind ever tolerated'. The early Victorian exodus to the suburbs destroyed 'the old gregarious and social life of the City . . .'.[62] The effect of suburban isolation was universal boredom:

> The men went into town every morning and returned every evening; they had dinner; they talked a little; they went to bed. . . . The case of the women was worse; they lost all the London life – the shops, the animation of the streets, their old circle of friends; in its place they found all the exclusiveness and class feeling of London with none of the advantages of a country town. . . . in the new suburb of Stockwell there were no interests [in common]; the wife of the small wholesale merchant would not call on the wife of the retail dealer; the wife of the barrister would not call on either; there was no society, and so for fifty years the massive dulness of the London suburb continued.[63]

The Thurber cartoon of the suburban husband approaching his house which has somehow merged into the threatening head of his wife lying in wait for him represents both the situation and the explanation. It was not, as architectural and social critics would have us believe, that facilities for communal activity were omitted in order to save the builder money and maximize rents. The landowners were perfectly willing, even eager, to subscribe money and donate land for the erection of churches. But, while a church could and did serve as a community centre, its main function was, from the point of view of the estate developer, to lend an air of respectability to the property. And apart from the church and the barest minimum of public houses (and sometimes not even that), the opportunities for a social life away from the separate houses in the ordinary suburb were extremely limited.*

Such a state of things was agreeable to the residents themselves; far from being regarded as a deprivation it was one of the advantages of suburban living. The flight to the suburbs involved the temporary rejection of the rest of society, of that part that extended beyond the immediate family of the householder: the most satisfactory suburb was that which gave him the maximum of privacy and the minimum of outside distraction.

'This is the justification for the suburb: the island is small; the population is great; each man to be a full man needs a dwelling of his own and some soil that is his to work on,' writes Michael Robbins: 'The suburb is the most economical way of supplying these needs'.[64] J.M. Richards stresses the suburbanite's need to withdraw into his own private fortress:

> It is in keeping with his ambition to take root, to reduce his responsibilities to a kind his eye and mind can encompass, to contrive for himself an environment . . . in which he is master. . . . the outside world is barred as far as possible from intrusion into the suburban jungle.[65]

The spirit of suburbia is 'nourished . . . especially in the treasured privacy of house and garden'.[66] Nicholas Taylor has more recently argued that 'the need for privacy . . . remains paramount: the need of the nuclear family to keep the casual passer-by at arm's length'.[67]

For the more prosperous residents of Surbiton, Ealing, and Sidcup, 'privacy and seclusion were at a premium', we are told by Alan A. Jackson; 'the fine villas of the First Class season-ticket holders were hidden in elaborate nests of evergreen trees and shrubs, approached by sinuous gravel drives which . . . provided convenient warning of visitors'.[68] For the less affluent the semi-detached house 'offered white collars and artisans the chance of escape from the often intrusive gregariousness of the inner suburban terraces and more than a suggestion of the detached privacy so long the prerogative of the middle class'.† For the suburban householder of the inter-war period, everything in life was 'centred around the new home, which he sought to make a shelter from the harsh realities of the world, a controllable, predictable environment for himself and his family'. The consequences of such withdrawal were not entirely pleasant:

* The late Victorian period saw some improvement in this respect: 'Of late years . . . the suburbs have developed a social life of their own; they have theatres, they have lawn tennis clubs, they have bicycle clubs, they have dances, dinners, subscription balls, concerts, and receptions.' Besant, *London in the Nineteenth Century*, p. 263.

† Ibid., p. 133. The passage refers to the period after the First World War. Jackson's book shows that while suburbia in the twentieth century has expanded tremendously in area and in the proportion of the population inhabiting it, the qualities it possesses and the values it reinforces remain those of the Victorian period.

For the family, social life was restricted, the deprivation often self-imposed. Housewives in particular led a strangely isolated, lonely existence during the time the rest of the family was away at work or school. . . . Women who had lived in a Surrey suburb for over a year hardly knew their neighbours' names and contacts were minimal: 'People just nod, and pass on'.

. . . Many of the new suburbans in any event wished to 'keep themselves to themselves' . . . they chose . . . to sink into the comfortable anonymity which still remains a strong feature of London suburban life, rarely extending their acquaintance beyond immediate neighbours.[69]

Even on the commuter trains, 'most preferred to travel alone . . .'.[70] For those with middle-class upbringings, the social fragmentation was perhaps in accord with their expectations and wishes; but for those who made the move from the inner-city slum to the suburban council estate, the change from the warmth and gregariousness of the one to the loneliness and isolation of the other must have been felt as a serious loss.

However ambivalent the response of the suburbanites of the twentieth century to the enforced privacy of their new environment, for the Victorians the privacy, and indeed the dullness of suburbia were among its chief attractions. One of the advertized features of the villas set in Regent's Park was that it was 'so planted that no villa should see any other, but each should appear to possess the whole of the park, and that the streets of houses which overlook the park should not see the villas, nor one street of houses overlook those of another street'.[71]

Regent's Park was designed to give sylvan privacy to the very rich; the adjacent Eyre estate at St John's Wood succeeded in giving it to people of more modest means. Though Georgian in its conception – the original building plan dates from 1794 – it provided the prototype for Victorian suburbia. Its detached and semi-detached Italianate villas, hidden behind high garden walls and luxuriant vegetation, offered the withdrawn seclusion and social homogeneity that its later imitators aspired to achieve. It introduced the semi-detached house to London. John Shaw (1776–1832), whose son of the same name was to supervise the early development of the Eton College estate, was the architect in charge.[72] The younger John Shaw told the Bursar of Eton College in 1845 that the Eyre estate was 'one of the most important and valuable Properties connected with the Metropolis . . . the Roads being wide and the houses of a very superior Class'.[73]

Its residents made it 'their place of retreat from the showy fashionable or dingy trading resorts of the great metropolis', Cox observed in the 1850's. Each house had its own garden, from one-eighth to one-half acre in extent, 'with, in a small proportion of cases, stabling thereon, the precincts of each house rendered private and exclusive by plain brick walls about five feet in height. These universally-used brick walls pervade the entire district – it is its peculiar characteristic: securing agreeable privacy to each resident . . .'.[74] St John's Wood offered the suburban ideal: an escape from both the business and the public pleasures of the town, privacy to the individual and family, closeness to nature, but a nature safely enclosed by man-made walls, and social exclusiveness.

66 *top* 'The suburb provided an environment where homelife flourished as nowhere else.'

67 *above* '"... The outside world is barred as far as possible from instrusion into the suburban jungle."'

Seclusion did not necessarily mean propriety, for the neighbourhood had from its earliest days an equivocal reputation, which seems not to have disturbed its opulent and industrious residents, but which lent it a piquant form of specialized function: a site for discreet and expensive vice. Cox in 1853 darkly admitted that 'St. John's Wood was once resorted to by dissipated men of affluence for the indulgence of one of their worst vices'; but assured his readers that 'a little light has . . . dispelled the greatest part of their dark, demoralizing scenes, and left respectable inhabitants unannoyed', protected as they were by their own garden walls.[75] The privacy such walls afforded also promoted blameless artistic endeavours. In 1833 Thomas Smith had noted the presence of 'a number of artists . . . in this neighbourhood . . .'.[76] Clarke in 1881 thought 'the seclusion that distinguishes the residences in St. John's Wood . . . favourable to the pursuits of art and literature, and makes it in some respects the very best locality for individuals so engaged'.[77]

'We may wander for hours past these villas, along the Maida Vale and Grove Road, still confronted by high walls,' wrote Percy Fitzgerald in 1893, 'while we speculate what sort of persons live within, and whether they enjoy their seclusion.' He thought it would be 'impossible for . . . a bachelor who has removed from the pleasant bustle of St. James's Street to take up his abode here permanently without . . . giving way to its influence. He would become gradually retiring and silent in his ways . . .'.[78]

Elsewhere the suburban villa served as a refuge not only from the discomforts of the city but from its moral temptations. By living in the suburbs, Charles Pearson argued in 1846, 'our habits are improved, and . . . our morals are improved'.[79] But separateness and dispersion were seen as ends in themselves, whatever their effect on moral conduct.

Even the communal garden square was criticized as offering less privacy than the walled garden of the individual house. A letter to the editor of the *Building News* in 1858 condemned the developers of those parts of London still being laid out along traditional urban lines:

Will you allow me to enter my protest against the rage which now prevails among builders for the formation of 'squares' in the suburbs! . . . after travelling five miles from the Bank, we begin to grow impatient of gardens desecrated to semi-public use, and to demand a plot, however small, for the special delectation of our own family. Surely at places like Highbury, Camberwell, Brompton, or Bayswater, removed so far from either the Strand or Cornhill, we may be spared the infliction of 'rows' of brick-and-mortar walls even in squares, and may be excused for spurning the offer of a common parade-ground, where no plot is left to the private dwelling except the compulsory 10 feet by 10 at the back . . .

. . . The ground wasted for supposed general use would in most cases be enough, if allotted in separate portions, to render each house semi-detached at least.

It so happens that I have had peculiar opportunities for ascertaining the exact wants of persons seeking good suburban residences; and for the benefit of builders, I distinctly state that detached houses, beyond all comparison, are the most in request, and command the best rents and prices. What is it that makes St. John's-wood the most pleasant looking to the eye of all the suburbs to London but the circumstance of nearly every house having a good piece of garden ground about it![80]

Critics condemned high-density building quite as much in the name of privacy as for sanitary and aesthetic reasons. '. . . The absence of privacy and security from a besieging fortress of a thousand eyes render the boast of an Englishman's home only a name,' thundered the *Building News* in 1874. 'See what a few yards more of garden or back yard would do.' Even in terraces the front doors ought to be kept separate from one another:

> It is very common to see in a row of houses the doors placed in pairs with a single pier . . . between them. Sometimes there is not even a visible division, the stone landing or steps being made to extend the whole width of the two doorways . . . The idea is . . . hardly compatible with our English notions of comfort and privacy. . . . it is unquestionably more in accordance with our taste to place the doorways of adjacent houses as far apart as possible. The collision of neighbours and friends at the threshold of one's house is not always pleasing . . . Not only do separated doors add to the privacy of a row, but the interposition of the passage and hall becomes a highly useful separation between two houses. Nothing can be more unpleasant . . . than the sounds of the next house.[81]

Privacy was invariably assumed to be a requisite for the middle-class home. The *Building News* thought 'a certain amount of retirement and seclusion . . . necessary for the resident middle class'.[82] The rapture with which W.S. Clarke viewed what must even then have been some pretty unpromising suburbs makes his *Suburban Homes of London* (1881) of comparatively little value in determining what such districts were really like, but it remains of immense help in determining what the suburban house-seeker was looking for. Again and again Clarke praises a district for its withdrawn seclusion and privacy, never for its lively social life or its abundant community activities. Thus, speaking of South Croydon, 'there is an air of peaceful seclusion and floral beauty pervading the villas hereabout that make one almost wish to be one of the dwellers therein'.[83] Of St John's Wood, 'there is no place where persons are more isolated'.[84] The railway had given 'to all classes the opportunity of working in cities and towns, and living in the country a more private life than was possible in our provincial towns a hundred years ago, or even now'.[85] In the hardly more critical *London City Suburbs* the following decade, Percy Fitzgerald found 'a certain sense of dreamy solitude, an air of contented happiness and tranquility' in the roads linking Dulwich with the Crystal Palace.[86]

THE FAMILY AND THE DWELLING

'Despite the ridicule which those who fancy themselves fast and *beaux esprits* may attach to the idea of a family man, we believe he is happier and a better citizen than the man about town,' the *Building News* asserted in 1861. 'The superior prosperity, and internal peace, and obedience to the laws of Englishmen is mainly due to the large proportion of them being domesticated, as compared with the people of other countries. Men who marry and give pledges to fortune are the safest and solidest pillars of the State.'[87] In the repeated comparisons drawn between London and Paris the point was again and again made that London was designed for the family and the home, Paris for the single man and the café. 'In one very important point Paris and London differ . . .' observed the *Architect* in 1869. 'Paris is . . . an out-of-doors city. Its gardens, squares, boulevards, &c., are almost the sitting-rooms of a great part of the population.'[88] In London, sitting rooms were its sitting rooms: the middle classes typically entertained at home, and looked with disfavour at those who took their pleasures in public places. In condemning 'uncomfortably small' rooms in the houses of suburban London, the *British Quarterly Review* in 1879 pointed to the dire consequence: 'Houses are so cramped that peace and comfort is [sic] sought for in places of public amusement, and fathers and sons betake themselves to the public-house'.[89]

In a discussion at the Architectural Association following a paper describing Parisian blocks of flats, one speaker remarked on 'how widely the domestic arrangements and requirements of the French differed from our own. In order to make our houses like those of the French we must change our nationality. In France family life appeared rather to be sinking, whereas in England it was the reverse'.[90] '. . . Interminable lines of houses, the vast majority of which are inhabited by one family only, stretch away from central London in every direction,' William H. White reminded the RIBA in 1877:

> Such a system which gives to each family not only the superficial area of a plot of land, but also the whole cube of space above it, must be a right one. Any one conversant with habitual phases of life in Paris and London will freely admit the advantages of a system that grants to the head of a household the partly poetical license of breathing his native air on his own ground.[91]

The splendour of Haussmann's boulevards made many ask why London could not have such delightful promenades as well. The *Architect* thought them morally unsuitable for the English:

> Many circumstances . . . combined to enable people to dispense with such great lines of approach as are to be seen abroad. Nor can it be denied that their absence is not altogether an evil. If in London we possessed such agreeable roads as the Paris boulevards we might have a vast number of *flâneurs* among us. Just as the hard English weather makes hard English men, the narrow streets of the City compelled people to reside beyond the walls, and at a later time made them seek their homes in the country or by the sea. An immense amount of dawdling and frittering away of life must be put down to the broad ways of Continental cities.[92]

Each villa was designed to afford maximum privacy from outsiders, from the servants, and from the other members of the family. 'The house itself is a small community no less specialized than the town where it lies,' according to Rasmussen. 'Each member has his own course marked out, and when he sticks to it he can live at his ease and the different members need not interfere with each other's affairs.'[93] In a paper read to the Architectural Association in 1891 Ernest Newton admitted that 'absolute privacy, when required, is undoubtedly necessary, and is, in fact, one of the charms of home . . .'.[94] Robert Kerr told the RIBA in 1894 that 'the English idea of domestic comfort depended very much upon privacy, especially as to the complete separation of the family from the servants . . . the family as one class demanded and were entitled to their own privacy, and the servants as another class demanded and were entitled to theirs'.[95]

The greatly increased number of bedrooms in Victorian as compared to Georgian houses of the same class is eloquent testimony to the value placed on privacy within the family. The *Builder* in 1864 was quite smug on the point:

> . . . When we reflect upon the scanty supply of sleeping apartments which it was usual to construct in an ordinary London house of the annual value of from £80 to £120 a year, at the time that Regent-street was built, and which scarcely ever exceeded in number two principal bedrooms and three or four attics, it becomes difficult to conceive how the last generation bestowed themselves in their sleeping arrangements. . . . our present ideas on the subject render increased accommodation in this respect absolutely necessary.*

Smaller houses had smaller rooms, but nearly as many of them. 'The houses we see all around us are, like ready-made articles, to meet a general demand . . .' the *Building News* observed in 1900:

> Even the smallest of these must have a stereotyped number of conventional apartments, to imitate as far as possible a gentleman's residence. There must be the two reception-rooms with their offices, and three or four bedrooms, lavatory, and bathroom, all squeezed within four walls . . . the average tenant is contented if he can get a house like his better-off neighbours, even though the rooms are not much larger than good closets, and the speculative builder satisfies his want.[96]

Whatever his motives, the Victorian householder pursued the end of functional subdivision into as many single-purpose rooms as possible, with as much zeal as his great-grandchildren pursue space and openness. The one generation put in partitions and closed doors as single-mindedly as ours removes and opens them.

INDIVIDUALISM

'It cannot be doubted that individualism . . . is a prevailing characteristic of modern English architecture,' the *Architect* asserted in 1872. 'It is . . . to this very individualism that . . . is due most of the undoubted life and vigour which animates the profession . . .'[97] Did the suburb contribute to or did it inhibit the individualism that is supposed to have characterized not only architecture, but the whole of Victorian society?

Nicholas Taylor argues that it strengthened individualism. Even in the ordinary sprawling lower-middle-class London suburb he perceives 'freedom, diversity and individuality – the

---

* *B*, XXII (1864), p. 94. 'A modern Englishman seeing typical London houses from the eighteenth century wonders how it has been possible to live in them. In those days the house was much more made for show than nowadays. . . . The reception-rooms were the chief thing . . . In comparison to these stately rooms the more intimate rooms were rather scarce . . . But in the course of the nineteenth century the English house got a stamp of its own and at an early period the demands of comfort increased rapidly. . . . The houses of the rich no longer consist of a suite of drawing-rooms but of a series of separate rooms each with its special purpose just as the owner . . . has a very extensive wardrobe consisting of a special plain suit for each possible occasion.' Rasmussen, *London: the Unique City*, pp. 294–5. See also *A*, LVI (1896), p. 173.

ability of ordinary families to do their own thing . . .'[98] To the extent that it offered greater possibilities for personal privacy, the suburb testifies to the growing value placed on the separate individual. 'All these related aspects of privacy, intricacy, cultivation and micro-climate are in the end . . . a matter of identity – of each family's possession of its own special territory,' Taylor insists.[99]

But while suburbia did not exclude eccentricity it did not encourage either romantic alienation or rebellion. It stressed the separateness of the individual more than his distinctive-ness. For the genuine nonconformist central London or one of those suburbs – St John's Wood, Hampstead, Bedford Park – that catered to the artist or intellectual would provide an appropriate environment. The ordinary suburb assumed, if it did not impose, at least outward conformity of behaviour; but in its planning and in the symbolism of its archi-tecture it tried to see to it that such conformity took place by individuals and families cut off from the obtrusive society or inspection of their fellows.

Insofar as individualism is encouraged by architectural variety, it was perhaps least evident in villa suburbia. For the constant and often fruitful experimentation with different styles, building plans, and constructional techniques one would turn to the railways, to new industries, to the City, to retail trade, to the large country house – even to public buildings – before one would turn to domestic housing. The most that might be argued – and even here we have the warning of Henry-Russell Hitchcock that the impression is illusory – is that the villa suburb was somewhat less hostile to architectural experimentation and innovation than the neo-Georgian districts like Bayswater and Kensington.

Why this should have been so is not immediately evident. Certainly the small scale and narrow profit margins of the ordinary speculative builder are part of the answer; together with the responsiveness of the building industry to the demand of a large public that knew, or thought that it knew, what it liked. The abundant evidence of the kind of house this vast body of patrons encouraged suggests that while it might be willing to contemplate variety, experimentation, and innovation in public buildings, railway stations, theatres, hotels, and department stores, it drew the line when it came to something so vital and personal as the home.

Yet the villa suburb was itself an extraordinary innovation; and if Hitchcock is right to remind us that the prototypes of the suburb and the detached and semi-detached villas that constituted it were late Georgian,* their acceptance and proliferation were a Victorian phenomenon: they moved from being the toy of the isolated aesthete to being the dominant and preferred environment for the whole of the English middle class. What can only be said is that having made the move from the urban terrace to the suburban villa the middle class exhausted its capacity for adventure.

While suburban architectural styles and house plans have changed during the period from

* 'The villa architects of the late Georgian period . . . either continued to practice or had very similar successors in the 40's and early 50's. Most villa work tends to fall into place as part of the suburban operations of speculative builders. The Picturesque modes of the 20's and 30's were in general corrupted and standardized by builders of the 40's, not creatively developed. Cottage and villa books deteriorated in quality and even, it would seem, decreased in quantity.' Hitchcock, I, p. 412.

the 1830's to the 1970's; given the magnitude of the social, economic, and technological revolutions that have taken place in those years, the astonishing thing is how little the suburban environment has changed from then to now. J.M. Richards would say that it is precisely the function of the suburb to be a kind of womb or comfortable cave into which to escape from the disconcerting revolutions in the 'real' world. Dyos and Reeder argue that for the Victorian middle classes the flight to the suburb was a way of postponing facing the reality of the urban crisis of their own times.[100] Whatever it was, something of their hopes and fears and aspirations were embodied in the brick and stucco of the houses into which they withdrew, whether to escape from an intolerable outside world or to worship at the shrine of domesticity, perhaps to strengthen themselves for the task of making that world less intolerable.

'The Picturesque,' Nicholas Taylor argues, 'was *par excellence* the image of the Victorian suburb . . . an anti-civic aesthetic, a rejection of a collectivized palace front, in which ten and twenty houses had been treated as a single unit around a central pediment . . . It preached instead the gospel of individuality . . .' But if, as he says, '*Rus in urbe* meant every man possessing his own distinctively composed villa amidst his own shrubbery',[101] the villa suburb would have remained, as it began, a retreat for an eccentric, affluent minority. Only through standardization of its component parts could suburban living be made available to any sizeable portion of the population.

Whatever their deficiencies as to variety, villas were by definition separate, and offered greater opportunities for individual treatment than did the terrace. The objections to terrace development were aesthetic and moral as well as hygienic and emotional. They precluded varied and interesting skylines, masked the identity of the individual house, and, by grouping separate dwellings together into a single unifying composition, were deceitful. The *Builder* in 1861 reported a lecture at the Architectural Exhibition by A.J. Beresford Hope, who described himself defiantly as a 'Northern Goth', in which he attacked London terraces, urging that the skyline be dealt with, 'boldly as the most important feature of the whole building', and that each house be constructed 'as in itself a unit standing by itself, looking, of course, more to its height than to its width'. One of the most persistent aspects of the Victorian reaction against classicism was its emphasis on the vertical as opposed to the horizontal. Terrace houses

> could never be satisfactory. Do what you will, there was something about it that betrayed the sham. In building a town, even if it were necessary to make a street as straight . . . as an arrow, it would be better to break up and destroy the uniformity of the terrace. The idea of causing it to resemble a palace front could never be realised . . .[102]

Earlier condemnations of growing London had held up the country village as the proper alternative to metropolitan sprawl. The Victorians, no longer regarding London as a parasitic drain on the economy and aware that it needed the population it had, saw the suburb as a more appropriate solution. But it would have to be a suburb without recognizably urban characteristics: of this they were certain. Bayswater and Kensington, however successful as building speculations, did not provide a model for the way London's excess population ought to be housed. The *Building News* in 1863 condemned the terrace house as an improper suburban residence:

> . . . We cannot omit to remark of the lamentable want of taste displayed in the erections in the outskirting suburbs of London. We have only to name Bayswater, Norwood, Islington, Brixton, and some other suburbs in proof. What we greatly deplore is the trumpery allotments which have been dealt out to builders, and the closely-packed streets and terraces which have arisen. Instead of detached or semi-detached villas, of decent proportions, between which, glimpses of country, and light and air could have been obtained, we have barbarously-stuccoed streets and terraces, of most contemptible architecture, stereotyped *ad infinitum*. . . .
>
> . . . It is a mistake to make a suburb a closely-packed town, instead of giving it the character of what it should be. It is this system which is driving people further away from London in quest of country residences, instead of offering them semi-detached country-looking villas within moderate distance from town.[103]

A writer for the *Cornhill Magazine* was equally opposed to the terrace house as a deprivation of the individual identity of the occupant:

> To have to live in a row of houses built by contract, all at the same time, and all exactly alike, in which it is impossible to tell your own dwelling, except by looking at the number on the door, has always seemed to me one of the chief objections to life in a town, and one of the most pathetic and aggravating of the minor troubles of humanity. . . .
>
> I hold that by submitting to, or worse still, by rejoicing in, a tame uniformity in our domiciles, we, of our own accord, deprive ourselves of one of the highest privileges of reason, and degrade ourselves by submission to one of the necessities under which instinct labours. . . . To man alone is the privilege given of impressing . . . a stamp of individual peculiarity on his home.[104]

St John's Wood, 'a forest of villas, of nearly all sorts and sizes', sometimes carried individualism to the extremes of eccentricity in its architecture as well as in the manners of its residents. 'Here we have one [house] in the pseudo Greek style,' reported the *Building News* in 1857; 'there, another in very indifferent Italian; at the next turn the feudal castle is represented in miniature, with its central tower carried up to a most preposterous height, and surmounted by frowning battlements; again, the quaint Elizabethan rises, with its eccentric peculiarities . . .'.[105] Cox had earlier in the decade found the architecture 'a strange medley: the examples of each order . . . are a little equivocal'. The builders had 'confused the various prevailing orders of architecture'.[106]

Summerson finds 'the variety in mid-Victorian suburban design . . . perfectly astonishing'.[107] Yet to mid-Victorian critics, most villa suburbs seemed nearly as dull and monotonous as those laid out in terraces, squares, and crescents. 'Full as are the suburbs of London of villas and mansions standing . . . in their own grounds, there is comparatively little good architecture displayed in them,' complained the *Building News* in 1866:

> . . . While both city and country teem with buildings of very great merit and perhaps

unprecedented originality, the neutral ground of the suburbs furnishes but scant evidence of the existence of any architectural talent whatever. Often have we wandered St. John's Wood-wards, often ascended Primrose Hill, and continued our career through the vale of Maida, past Notting Hill and so through Holland Park, in the hope of seeing something really good, with, if possible, a dash of originality about it, but rarely indeed were we rewarded for our exertions. Everywhere the detached and semi-detached villa, the mansion, even the abomination known as a cottage *orné* bears the mark of dull sameness, unless, indeed, it breaks out into a wildness of style in which grotesqueness is more noticeable than originality.[108]

By the seventies some builders were taking such criticism to heart. Queen Anne was beginning to appear in the more fashionable western suburbs, while speculators in others began to imitate some of the architectural experiments that were already enlivening central London. Inevitably they got it all wrong, or so at least the critics insisted. The *Building News* in 1875 condemned the 'want of taste and frequent extravagance' in the architecture of the London suburbs:

It is what we may designate the serio-comic burlesque of the architectural drama. Its prevailing characters are ridiculous travesties of church doorways and windows, mimic Gothic pillars and arches, caricatured translations of Venetian façades, and a variety of the decorative paraphernalia of every Classic and Gothic school. . . . it is the pushing to extreme the more sensuous elements of our architectural styles . . . We see the same tendency in women's attire, and among the less educated tastes of every class of society.[109]

But even architectural extravagances lent themselves to repetition, and a high degree of standardization continued to characterize most London suburbs.

The *Building News* saw the logic behind the unvaried plan of the suburban house:

The stereotyped house in a row, with its conventional arrangement of entrance, passage, and stairs, its front and back parlours, and projecting offices in the rear, appears to be the nearest approach that can be made to economical house construction. It may be varied a little, but the extent of the variation is small, and the internal arrangement of the apartments remains much the same.[110]

Yet it asked, in defiance of all economic rationality, for custom-built houses, which would certainly have provided greater employment for the architectural profession, whatever the effects on costs.

'In looking at the rows of villas and tenements which skirt the roads of our suburbs,' it wrote in 1884, 'we cannot avoid remarking the dull and wearying sameness of treatment, both in plan and elevation, as if individuals had tastes precisely the same, or were cast in one mould.'[111] The *Builder* similarly condemned the 'rows of showy houses . . . in long broken lines, as monotonous and uninteresting as the lives of their inhabitants'.[112]

The fear and loathing of monotony is a predominant and recurrent feature of Victorian architectural criticism. Much of what struck later generations as a wilful desire to shock or

Semi=detached Villas
Nightingale Lane S.W.
erected by
George Jennings Lambeth
Sanitary Engineer

built of Red brick &
'Parkstone' cream Terra-cotta.

Thos. E. Collcutt f·r·i·b·a
architect

68 'Queen Anne was beginning to appear in the
more fashionable western suburbs . . .'
Semi-detached villas in red brick and terracotta
in Nightingale Lane, S.W., by Thomas E.
Collcutt. *British Architect*, 18 May 1883.

69   '. . . a high degree of standardization
continued to characterize most London suburbs.'
Tooting.

even a passion for ugliness may have stemmed from a wish to introduce a note of individuality into an otherwise uniform suburban environment. But it was the architect, not the speculative builder, who was usually responsible for such outbreaks of romantic individualism. The latter, whether from his own or his customers' conservatism, or from the economic advantages of putting up identical buildings, continued to build houses – even detached ones – more or less uniformly in rows. 'People tenant these houses because they cannot pick and choose, and the speculative builder is content to reproduce them,' complained the *Building News* in 1893. External style was no better than internal design:

> It is either a sort of builder's nondescript style, in which a carver and a tesselated tile manufacturer are permanently engaged on the job; or a travesty of 'Queen Anne,' or 'modern' Renaissance, or Gothic . . . Monotonous repetition of features . . . is one of the saddest things in this fearful spreading of tenements and middle-class dwellings. Ugly corners, where there is a turn in the road, and hideous roofs and chimneys and gables, fill us with dismay as we tread such neighbourhoods as Putney, or Richmond, or Wimbledon, or Brixton . . .[113]

Michael Robbins warns us against what he calls 'the architectural fallacy': that the aesthetic qualities of buildings directly reflect the character of their occupants. It 'has been a vulgar error . . . to suppose that because the Victorians put up ugly buildings they must have been insensitive and unintelligent.'[114] We are perhaps less likely today to dismiss Victorian buildings as ugly than we were in 1953, but the architecture of Victorian suburbia was undeniably repetitious and monotonous. The fallacy would be to conclude that people lived stereotyped lives in the stereotyped buildings.

The economies of scale and standardization were such that custom-designed houses were, and could have been, possible only for the rich. While the building industry was probably the most traditional of any in its technology, and the least mechanized, its products struck contemporaries as typifying modern mass production:

> Glancing at a few of the many suburbs which skirt this huge city [wrote the *Building News* in 1874], one thing becomes . . . conspicuous . . . namely the 'manufacture' (we cannot call it building) of a class of houses of moderate size to supply an unceasing demand. . . . The trade of house-manufacture must indeed be a flourishing one when we see whole rows of brick shells and flimsy partitioning run-up in the course of a few weeks, decked with all the ready-manufactured devices of the mason and plasterer . . . The manufacture of bricks themselves is not one wit more mechanical than the manufacture of the . . . dwellings . . .[115]

It understood the necessity of mass production, while regretting its consequences:

> Multiplication of the same pattern is to the builder of suburban houses what it is to the manufacturer. They can be built cheaper and quicker if the same plans and templates, window-frames and sashes, the same stone dressings, the same fastenings and ironmongery are used, than if each of these things undergoes modification to suit individual taste. . . . The builder knows exactly the width and number of bricks and closers required

70 '"Monotonous repetition of features . . . is
one of the saddest things in this fearful spreading
of tenements and middle-class dwellings."'
Woolwich Road, Greenwich.

71 *below* 'Many a high street reflects the
successive periods of settlement . . .' High Street,
Lower Norwood, in the 1890's. Fitzgerald,
London City Suburbs, p. 189.

for each pier; he can tell the number of bricks required for each house; he can order ornamental stringcourses and cornices wholesale, as he can his iron guttering and his railing. . . . All this multiplication of the same details and fittings enables a considerable reduction to be made in the cost of erecting a few hundreds of houses. No one doubts this. On the other hand, the same number of men and women of diverse tastes and habits are compelled to dwell in them. Many hundreds, nay thousands, of individuals of different habits and requirements are forced into the same number of houses erected on the same plan, and with the same accessories.[116]

The ordinary Victorian could not afford to live in an architect-designed house. The gloriously varied outlines, colours, shapes, textures, and decorative details of Victorian buildings that were designed separately suggest that those who could afford it valued individuality of appearance highly. That cheap housing was universally condemned for its monotony – more than for its want of taste, for instance – suggests the high value placed on variety and distinctiveness.

The builders of speculative suburbia tried to produce an effect, if not of variety, at least of separateness in their houses. Even in terraces, by replacing the flat cornice unifying all the houses in a row with a roofline giving each dwelling a separate gable facing onto the street, by projecting bays, and by many other devices, they emphasized the identity of each individual house.[117] Like so much else in Victorian culture, the villa suburb tried to make available to the many pleasures that had until then been confined to the few. And if the mass-produced detached villa in Upper Norwood failed ludicrously in its attempt to be a baronial castle or a ducal hunting lodge, the aspiration and the gesture remained.

SUBURBAN ANONYMITY?

Another charge laid against the suburb is that not only is every house like its neighbour, but every suburb is like the next one: that not only does the architecture work to impose a uniform life-style on every resident, but that the community as a whole is equally lacking in identity. 'There is a notion that all the Middlesex suburbs are exactly the same,' Michael Robbins has written, and that 'if you are set down in one you may go a long way before you have any idea where you are.'[118] The *Builder* in 1879 decried the 'poverty and chill aspect of the *suburbs*' of London, and the drab uniformity of its approaches on all sides: '. . . what can there possibly be of less interest or promise than the lines of roadway leading into the great metropolis . . . lined on either side for miles with rows of ordinary street houses, no way differing from those in the heart of the City itself . . .'.[119]

As surrounding villages became dormitory communities, contemporaries regretted the erosion of features that had made them distinctive. For them what was remarkable was the inundation of separate, traditional villages by a standardized suburbia. In retrospect, the addition to suburbia of islands of traditional village environments seems more significant; even the remains of earlier suburban dwellings gave an architectural variety and richness lacking in communities developed entirely at one period. Many a high street reflects the successive periods of settlement in a way that American suburbs rarely and Australian

72 *above* 'Other villages retained their
pre-suburban character intact.' High Street,
Edgware, *c.* 1888–90.

73 '"... the delightfully shady Grove ..."'
Camberwell Grove in the 1870's. Edward
Walford, *Old and New London*, VI, 283.

suburbs never do. Edward Walford noted such a mixture of periods and styles in the Beckenham of the eighties:

> The chief street of Beckenham is long and winding, and the houses are largely intermixed with fields and gardens, looking as if they were built at a time when space was plentiful. . . . But modern 'Tudor,' 'Jacobean,' and 'Queen Anne' houses are rapidly superseding the ruder, and perhaps not less picturesque, erections of bygone times: one old inn is blossoming into a railway 'hotel'; a new row of shops, with a bank at the corner, styles itself the 'Parade'; and modern grandeur is gradually driving away the air of quiet and homely respectability which has up to this time given a character to Beckenham.[120]

Other villages retained their pre-suburban character intact. Probably '. . . few rural villages, even in Yorkshire or Devonshire,' Walford informs us, 'are more sequestered than West Wickham, which almost adjoins Hayes and Keston Commons . . .'[121] Some suburbs showed a greater mixture of old and new features than others. Hackney retained much of its eighteenth-century character long after it had been deserted by the prosperous classes, while Camberwell in the eighties was valued for its early-Victorian qualities:

> The rustic air about Church-street, the principal thoroughfare; the really charming Green . . . the noble road fringed with trees leading to Peckham; the delightfully shady Grove, and the pretty walks up Denmark Hill and Champion Hill towards Dulwich and Herne Hill, offer attractions which are not often to be met with.
>
> Then, Camberwell is not 'new;' it has a history . . . it is not like its neighbour Brixton – a creation of yesterday. Thirty or forty years ago Camberwell was the City tradesman's *beau idéal* of a suburban retreat; and there are plenty of houses still standing which give one a good idea of his taste. A large garden with plenty of fruit-trees was indispensable . . .[122]

The new villas near South Croydon station benefitted from still-rural surroundings. '. . . The old field-paths, like net-work, for which all the neighbourhood of Croydon is remarkable, are still preserved, enabling one to pass through between two houses from one part to another in most curious and pleasant pilgrimage.'[123]

'Each suburb,' Michael Robbins observes, 'and each district of each suburb, has its own personality, each on a different step in the social scale and each with different kinds of interests.'[124] Percy Fitzgerald argued that each suburb had '"a note" of its own', which gave 'a tone to the whole district', affecting 'even the character and pursuits of the natives'.[125] The *Building News*, in its review of *London City Suburbs*, agreed:

> London has never become one homogeneous mass, and the annexed districts attached to London proper retain in a marked degree their distinctive characteristics. Westminster and Islington, Knightsbridge and the 'Borough,' Chelsea and St. John's Wood, Hampstead and Brixton – all continue to hold an individuality of their own, such as writers like Dickens and Thackeray delighted to take note of. There are . . . over a score of High-streets in our ever-growing, ever-absorbing London still retaining their identity, and recalling the days when the great centre to which they mostly led remained an almost detached city, the country coming up to its very gates.[126]

J.H. Westergaard argues in a recent study that 'the outward spread of Greater London . . . does not involve the submergence of local identity. Old communities are transformed, and new ones emerge: they have a distinctive character and a degree of local economic independence much greater than is often assumed'.[127]

Two suburbs – one old, one new – that no one ever accused of faceless anonymity were Hampstead and Bedford Park. Hampstead was, then as now, the most attractive of the suburbs. 'The Hampstead-road, as we advance towards the pretty village after which it is named, assumes a more beautiful aspect, and on either side elegant villas, cottages, and mansions meet the eye,' according to Gaspey in 1851. '*Hampstead* is extremely picturesque, and the salubrity of its air, the loveliness of its scenery, and its magnificent heath . . . render it a favourite abode with invalids and with persons of rank and fortune.'[128] It preserved its older character better than most suburban villages: 'Hampstead is now nearly joined to London by rows of villas and terraces', wrote George Rose Emerson in 1862; even so, there 'still attaches to the older part of the town a certain stately air of dignified respectability, in the red-brick spacious mansions . . .'.[129] Even its newer buildings were picturesque enough to please contemporary critics. The *Building News* for 1876 specifically excluded Hampstead from its general condemnation of suburban architecture:

> One of the few localities about London which has become the favoured haunt of artists, and which has defied the rule of speculative builders, is Hampstead. By nature irregular and hilly, it has resisted to a certain extent those elements of uniformity and monotony which characterise the flatter districts of the West-end. Here, it is impossible to build a row of houses that shall be at once regular in height and uniform in feature. . . . there is an irregularity which has particularly favoured the artistic *penchant*, and those in search of the picturesque.[130]

A new suburb which avoided the reproach of stereotyped Philistinism was Bedford Park, at Turnham Green in Chiswick. Designed in large measure by Norman Shaw in the Queen Anne style, and laid out in a moderately picturesque fashion, it sought to provide an appropriate environment for the intellectual middle classes. Shaw 'arranged round a village green a significantly secular-looking church, an arty pub, a row of generously glazed shops and the tree-lined entrance to radiating avenues of red-brick, Dutch-gabled houses, self-consciously evoking the atmosphere of some mythical early seventeenth century village'.[131] The owner of the estate, Jonathan Carr, Jr., proposed 'to supply for the middle classes that which the Shaftesbury-park Estate [in Battersea] has partially done for the labouring classes – namely houses well planned, conveniently arranged, and constructed with regard to both stability and architectural character', according to the *Building News* in 1876. At the time 18 houses, designed by E.W. Godwin, had already been erected, whereby 'architectural effect is simply obtained in an inexpensive way by the use of good materials picturesquely handled . . .'.[132]

Developments in Bedford Park's neighbouring districts were doing more to submerge the character of existing villages than to add new picturesque features to the landscape. Acton by the eighties had changed from 'the quiet, out-of-the-way village of half a century ago' to 'a very populous place, owing to the building of villas, consequent on the opening of the railways. It now possesses two or three churches; it has Congregational, Anabaptist, Wesleyan, and other chapels, a lecture hall, and also its Local Board of Health, public library, and reading-room'.[133] Much, too, had changed in Teddington: 'rows of spruce villas and neat terraces have sprung up along the roads to Hampton Wick, and all over the upper end of the village, which must soon call itself a town . . . .'. Established local businesses suffered: '. . . grand "hotels" and magnificent "stores" . . . have fairly driven out the keepers of its hostelries, and threaten to swallow up the "small trader" class'.[134] Richmond, which had long been 'pretty, refined, and exclusive', was by the eighties, 'a simple London suburb, differing only from Peckham Rye by the superiority of its situation, and its long-continued reputation . . .'. Builders were 'superseding the quaint passages and narrow streets by rows of hideous villas . . .'.[135]

The Queen Anne revival and perhaps the perspective that only the passage of time can give were making critics in the eighties more aware of the virtues of genuine eighteenth-century architecture. If the solid mass of Georgian houses in central London continued to look grim and depressing, the detached villas and gentlemen's dwellings in the surrounding villages came to seem quaint and picturesque. Such relics of Georgian suburbia were by then falling victim to more intensive development. 'It is impossible to walk through any of the London suburbs outside the radius of four miles from Charing-cross without being struck by the rapidity with which the few remaining houses of the last century are being demolished . . .' reported the *Builder* in 1883. While it granted that 'the houses of our well-to-do forefathers of a hundred years ago had . . . few claims to be considered in any high sense as works of art . . . they had their merits, notwithstanding . . .'. The new houses replacing them had 'not a trace of the reserve and quiet aristocratic bearing of the old'.[136]

The *Building News* in 1888 deplored the monotonous 'straight lines of frontage . . . along which one elevation is repeated *ad nauseam* . . .' in Hampstead, Fulham, Walham Green, West Brompton, Putney, Richmond, 'and even at those once pretty villages, Beckenham and Bromley in Kent'.* In those suburbs 'whole estates of ancestral age and beauty [were] being ruthlessly destroyed at the hands of land-grabbers and builders . . .'. Putney had 'lost many of its claims to the consideration of the artist and lover of the quaint and picturesque. . . . the spirit of modern enterprise is transforming the once irregular lines of the High-street . . . into one of cockney-like primness and uniformity'.[137]

Ernest Newton found 'a walk in the suburbs of London' a depressing experience. 'North, south, east or west, they are all the same,' he told the Architectural Association in 1891:

There are only two styles of suburban houses, the gabled and the ungabled. The gabled is the most popular. . . . The height is generally considerably greater than the width. The

---

* It is only fair to say that a resident of Bromley, Kent, wrote to reassure the readers of the *Building News* that while the village was being transformed by an 'abundance' of speculative builders, '(with a few isolated exceptions) we are free from the long rows of cold, barrack-like villas of stereotyped design and without relief. Among the many large estates now being developed you will hardly find two houses of the same elevation . . . in no rising suburb will, I think, be found more variety or picturesque effect.' *BN*, LIV (1888), p. 553.

GROUP OF VILLAS ON HERNE HILL, CAMBERWELL.

74 *above* '"Thirty or forty years ago Camberwell was the City tradesman's *beau idéal* of a suburban retreat . . ."' Villas on Herne Hill, Camberwell, 1825.

75 *above, right* 'A new suburb which avoided the reproach of stereotyped Philistinism was Bedford Park . . .' Villas by Norman Shaw at Bedford Park.

76 *right* '". . . an arty pub, a row of generously glazed shops . . ."' Shops and inn by Norman Shaw at Bedford Park.

BEDFORD·PARK· is ·within· 50·Yards· of·
·TURNHAM·GREEN·*RAILWAY·STATION*·
·ents £45 to £85 per Annum·Good·Drainage & Gravelly·Soil·
Architect·to·the·Estate· R·Norman·Shaw· ·R·A·x·
·or PARTICULARS· for Houses & Plots· apply to The Office on the ESTATE
·: Messrs·Carr·Fulton & Carr, 17ª Vigo·Sͭ
·gent·Street·or·to·Messrs·Terrell & Honey· 70ª Aldermanbury·City·E·C·

windows, of which the front mainly consists, are of impossible proportions. There are, of course, a stone bay, with wooden sashes; a porch, rich with brown graining, going halfway up the house; and bricks the colour of a London fog, with wiry streaks of red running through at intervals. A purple slate roof, with a formidable spiky iron ridge, tops the whole . . . Houses of this kind are stereotyped, and have enclosed London like a forest; thousands of people live in them and call them home, and I suppose they may also be considered as expressing the spirit of the age.[138]

SOCIAL SEGREGATION

For all but a fortunate few suburban householders architectural distinctiveness was an ideal more aspired towards than realized. What the majority got was a degree of separateness, brought about by the detached or semi-detached nature of the house, the walls or hedges dividing front and rear gardens from the neighbouring ones, architectural features emphasizing the identity of each house, and an interior plan that enabled the different members of the household to isolate themselves from one another. Beyond that the nature of the suburb itself diminished the possibilities of contact with people of other social classes: if the suburbanite was not wholly cut off from his fellow man, he at least had the comfort of seeing for the most part only men or women more or less like himself.

'. . . Residential location and relocation may be seen as strategies for minimizing the social distance between the individual and populations which he desires to emulate and for maximizing that from groups which he wishes to leave behind,'[139] Duncan Timms tells us:

> Residential differentiation and the resulting segregation of populations serve many purposes. Physical isolation symbolizes social isolation and decreases the chances of undesirable and potentially embarrassing contact. Furthermore, segregation may provide a means of group support in the face of a hostile environment . . . residential differentiation characterizes both the pre-industrial and the industrial city, both the laissez-faire and the planned, both the capitalist and the socialist.[140]

However universal the tendency towards residential differentiation, Victorian London achieved it to an unprecedented degree. The new suburb was a highly efficient means both of functional and social segregation: functional in that it enabled home-life and work to be carried out in two distinct and often distant places, social in that it enabled each class to be tidily sorted into its own homogeneous neighbourhood.

Suburban living did not necessarily involve social segregation. 'More obviously than the freely composed landscape garden,' Nicholas Taylor writes of the eighteenth-century villa communities along the upper Thames, 'the freely associated dwellings of different people of different classes were an expression of the distinctively English tradition of liberalism or Whiggery . . . The suburban village became a living parable of free thought and free trade.'[141] But here as elsewhere the social mingling that took place in the eighteenth century was more a matter of necessity than choice. There were simply not enough villa-dwelling gentlefolk to make a socially exclusive suburb possible. Even in London itself, the best neighbourhoods would have seemed shockingly 'mixed' to later generations.

77 'Richmond . . . was by the eighties, "a
simple London suburb, differing only from
Peckham Rye by the superiority of its situation,
and its long-continued reputation . . .".' Lower
George Street, Richmond.

The urban estates of the eighteenth century distinguished, more carefully and efficiently than those of the seventeenth, between streets of first, second, and third-rate houses; they permitted shops only in the narrower back streets, and prohibited offensive trades entirely. Yet all provided for several classes of society. Even Mayfair had its mean streets and narrow courts as well as a variety of services – from markets to mews – to benefit residents of the great houses in the principal streets and squares. Each estate was a varied, balanced community which excluded only the very poor and industrial nuisances on principle. Segregation, social and functional, took place between street and street, not between estate and estate.

The Victorian suburb went much further to reinforce the respectability and the social standing of the resident. '. . . The middle-class suburb,' Dyos and Reeder tell us, 'offered an arena for the manipulation of social distinctions to those most conscious of their possibilities and most adept at turning them into shapes on the ground . . .'[142]

The villas and terraces of Regent's Park were, at the outset, 'the retreats of the happy free-born sons of commerce, of the wealthy commonalty of Britain, who thus enrich and bedeck the heart of their great empire'.[143] In 1833 Thomas Smith described the 'detached villa residences, situated in large gardens', which had been erected 'in every variety of architectural elegance' in the adjacent St John's Wood, as being 'occupied by persons of the first respectability'.[144] Yet an early issue of the *Builder*, describing the neighbourhood of Regent's Park, and thinking, perhaps of Nash's Park Villages, but more probably of the poverty in the nearby Portland and Camden Towns, commented on 'an evident deficiency of tact in jumbling the poor and rich together, for the latter soon take fright as they find themselves environed by the former'.[145]

By the 1840's the rich were not content to have the poor decently screened off in a nearby mews or court, but wished to escape from their proximity entirely. From the 1830's commuting by omnibus and from the forties commuting by rail were possibilities open to the middle class, but, because of the relatively high fares, not yet to the working classes: any suburb beyond walking distance of central London became, therefore, necessarily safe from working-class contamination.[146] The *Building News* in 1858 quoted Samuel Huggins, *Notes of a Recent Visit to the Metropolis* as remarking that the residential streets and squares of London were 'now abandoned for the most part by the classes alone possessed of wealth and taste, for the suburban villa . . .'.[147]

The detached and semi-detached Italianate villas of St John's Wood combined social homogeneity with withdrawn seclusion. Alfred Cox, writing in 1853, was as impressed by the respectability of its inhabitants as he was by its physical beauty:

> There is as great a number of habitations within the limits of the district as is compatible with the umbrageous character of its interior, the rural character of the boundaries, and the wishes of the opulent and industrious professional men and tradesmen of London, who are for the most part its inhabitants . . .[148]

Its social exclusiveness was aided by a comparative absence of stables and mews. Such a situation was made possible by the excellent omnibus service that provided genteel transportation to and from both the City and the West End, and made the maintenance of a private carriage unnecessary. The absence of mews meant the absence of the necessarily lower-class population that lived in them and, more important still, the freedom from the danger that the mews might (if there were not enough demand for it to house horses and carriages) deteriorate into a miniature slum, contaminating the surrounding streets.[149] The Eyre estate was equally free of 'encroachments for supplying housekeeping requisites', the nearest shops being in the working-class districts of Portland Town and Lisson Grove.[150]

The estate found little difficulty in attracting residents of the utmost respectability. Even Lady Amelia de Courcy, in *The Small House at Allington* (1864), was perfectly content to move to St John's Wood on her marriage, and her sister, Lady Alexandrina, would have been happy to do likewise had her husband not refused to live north of the New Road. But for the most part the inhabitants were 'professional men, city merchants, and West End tradesmen, retired officers from India and the Colonies, and merchants from Australia'.[151] By the early eighties W.S. Clarke was conscious of social decline: 'The professional element was more abundant here in former days than at present, and the same remark applies to artists and students,' he reported. 'These gather about Brompton; still there are several famous names among the St. John's Wood residents'.[152] In that secluded district, 'there meet together, so far as locality is concerned, the eminent in every department of London life . . .'.[153] Perhaps more reliable is the description in Booth's *Life and Labour of the People in London*:

> The older part of St. John's Wood, south of Marlborough Road, is a very pleasant district. . . . North of Marlborough Road the district is rather newer and more pretentious, but much less attractive. As far as wealth goes there may not be much to choose between the inhabitants of the two districts, but as to character, a good deal. The older locality is largely artistic or Bohemian, and in parts somewhat questionable. The newer is 'solid and stolidly' middle class, whose men for the most part are men of business.[154]

He found some evidence of social deterioration. 'South of the North London Railway, in St. John's Wood and Maida Vale, the district tends to a lower social level' than in Hampstead proper. 'The best families go to Hampstead . . .'[155]

Whatever its social vicissitudes, and however justified its reputation of 'faint impropriety',[156] St John's Wood remained and remains one of London's most immediately delightful neighbourhoods. It retained its standing by combining the appearance of outer suburbia with the convenience of inner suburban location. Other inner suburbs found it harder to compete with the attractions of newer districts farther out.

Already in the 1840's a perceptible exodus of the middle classes was affecting the character of the older suburbs. 'The better class of houses, that is, houses of from 50l. a-year and upwards, do not let now so well as they used to do,' a correspondent wrote to the *Builder* in 1849:

> Those parties who can afford it are beginning to move off a little way into the country, along the different lines of railway. I know three or four instances of this within these last

twelve months. One party has gone to reside at Sydenham, from the neighbourhood of Cloudsley-square, Islington, and the other two to Penge, on the Croydon line, from Myddelton-square. Now, as new lines of railway are opened, and the facilities for residing a short distance from town increase, so will the houses in the [older] suburbs be deserted by the most respectable tenants, and the depreciation of house property in these neighbourhoods be *beyond all calculation* . . .[157]

The lower middle classes followed, moving into less distant and more closely-built suburbs of their own. 'Owing primarily to the establishment of omnibuses,' wrote 'Londinensis' in the *Builder* the same year, 'many thousand families of limited income have left the City to reside in the suburbs . . . in small four, six, or eight-roomed tenements, with but small gardens attached to them . . .'[158]

The suburbanization of rural Middlesex, Essex, Surrey, and Kent was directly related to the transformation of the City into a wholly commercial quarter. 'The picturesque hills of Surrey, near Dulwich and Norwood, are studded with the villas of citizens, who retire thither from the bustle of town,' wrote one guidebook in 1851:

Blackheath . . . continues to be a favourite resort in summer, and its buildings have increased since the access to it has been facilitated by the railway. . . . Hampstead and Highgate . . . with others on the north, and Dulwich, Camberwell, Clapham, &c., on the south, side of the river, consist, mostly, of the houses of tradesmen and others who daily visit the city in pursuit of business. This prevalent fashion among the Londoners of fixing their abode in the suburbs has been greatly encouraged by the easy communication afforded by the *omnibuses* and coaches which run to and from at all hours of the day, and till late at night. Owing to this circumstance, the . . . city proper . . . may now, indeed, be called a collection of shops and warehouses rather than of residences for families.[159]

The rise of rents in at least some districts of central London (Bloomsbury, certainly, remained comparatively moderate in its rents) gave another economic motive for suburban living. 'Within ten years there has been a considerable increase in the rents of houses,' reported 'Quondam' in 1865 in the *Builder*:

About the year 1850, the rent might have been computed, on an average, at 5*l.* a room per annum, unless in exceptional positions; – for an eight-roomed house, 40*l.* per annum; one of ten rooms, 50*l.*; of twelve rooms, 60*l.*; and so on; but as the capital has spread out and swollen, the original and central portions have assumed a value that could never have been anticipated. . . .

  In the outer boundaries of London, on all sides, there are still ranges of fair and clean-built dwellings, planned to suit persons of moderate income, at the rate of about 5*l.* a room; but these must be sought outside the circle, three miles from Charing Cross . . .[160]

'Solomon Set-Square' agreed that central London by the sixties was too expensive for the ordinary middle-class family:

Readers . . . will remember the very exhaustive discussion carried on by the daily papers some few years ago of the problem how to live in London on £300 a-year. The general conclusion arrived at was that, for a middle class family of average number, it was next to impossible to live upon that income. It was held that a middle class Londoner could not even marry on £300 a-year. . . . Since that discussion in the newspapers the times have grown far worse. . . . Now the middle-class Londoner, as a rule, does not live in London. . . . [but] carries his family into the suburbs . . .[161]

'The railways,' wrote 'An Unbeneficed District Surveyor' in 1873, 'have set us all moving far away from London – that is to say, the special middle class of Londoners . . . people with incomes ranging from three to five hundred a year':

The upper ten thousand and the abject poor still live and sleep in the metropolis. The middle classes . . . betake themselves to far-off spots, like Richmond, Watford, Croydon or Slough. True it is that the smaller fry content themselves with semi-detached boxes at Putney, Kilburn, New Cross, or Ealing; but the wealthier take a more extended scope, and are found to go daily to and from the capital as far as even Reading or Brighton.[162]

Each economic sub-group, that is to say, had its own particular set of suburbs to choose among.

Those wealthy enough to keep their own carriages could and did live beyond the limit of bus and train service; the improvement of transport facilities often lowered the social tone of a neighbourhood by making possible denser housing and commercial developments. When, in 1863, Herne Hill became an important junction for the London, Chatham and Dover, from which trains left for both Victoria and the line to Blackfriars and Holborn Viaduct, the standing of the neighbourhood as a wealthy residential district was doomed. In 1866 a loop line joined Denmark Hill to both Victoria and London Bridge. Both communities were soon covered with streets of cheap houses.[163]

Each suburb became associated with a particular type of resident. According to a guide-book of the early sixties, 'authors, journalists, publishers, &c., mostly incline to St. John's-wood . . . City men, such as stockbrokers, merchants, and commercial agents, affect Tyburnia, Bayswater, Haverstock-hill, Brixton, and Clapham . . .'.[164] Denmark Hill was described, 'not inappropriately', according to the *Architect*, as 'the Belgravia of South London'.[165] Dalston, Brixton, New Cross, Forest Hill, Walthamstow, and Tottenham were 'almost wholly peopled by clerks', according to Sir Walter Besant. 'Kennington, Stockwell, Camberwell, contain a large number of City tradesmen. Such suburbs as Balham, Sydenham, Highgate, Hampstead, Barnes, Richmond, and others contain the richer sort.'[166]

F.M.L. Thompson has shown how the Eton College estate at Chalcots, in South Hampstead, acquired its social character:

. . . The landlord's agent to some extent, but the speculative builders above all, were insistent on the desirability of building virtually one single type of house on the estate . . . The houses might vary in appearance and design . . . but inside they provided very much the same amount of accommodation, the typical mid-century middling-sized family house . . . They were solid, respectable, comfortable, unexciting; nothing grand or imposing. . . . The builders having created a supply of a particular kind of houses, the district was peopled by social groups suited to that type by their means, way of living, and aspirations. From the side of housing demand there was a very powerful urge for people of like condition to want to live in the same neighbourhood with their kind, to decline to be mixed up with their inferiors, or at the very least to keep away from noxious, unhealthy, or otherwise unpleasant areas. These were strong tides making for segregation.[167]

The social homogeneity of Chalcots, like that of St John's Wood to the west and Belsize Park to the north, was helped by the comparative absence of mews property on the estate. The mews that it did contain – behind Winchester Road, off King's College Road, and behind England's Lane and Ainger Road – gave it what little working-class population it had. An exchange of letters in 1871 with respect to a proposed church school in Winchester Road, 'so that the poor on the estate may receive a religious education',[168] reveals how consciously the ground landlord and the builders alike were directing their policies towards the creation and maintenance of a single-class neighbourhood.

John Roche and Arthur Lucas, who were building nearby, objected to the school, fearing that it would 'injuriously affect their Houses'.[169] The Rev. Thomas W. Peile, Manager of the St Paul's Parochial Schools in Hampstead, responded angrily, making explicit a number of considerations usually left unspoken:

> . . . There are already at least 50 families of working men residing on your estate i.e. in the Mews off King's College Road and in Kings College Road and in the Mews at the back of Winchester Road. which is now being extended by your Tenants Messrs. Lucas & Roche. I am sorry to find that the said Builders (the latter of whom is I believe a Roman Catholic) not only refuse to give a site for a new school . . . but also express great alarm lest you should grant us a building site any where near the portion the College has allotted to them.
>
> Messrs. Lucas & Roche are building Shops and Mews which will be inhabited by a class of people for whom school accommodation must be provided and yet they refuse a site for a school which would accommodate their own Tenants.
>
> . . . As a working class population already exists on this part of your property – and as arrangements are being made by your builders to *increase* the numbers of the working classes on this part of your property – there is a reasonable and legitimate cause why a site should be granted for the accommodation of the said working classes.[170]

Such reasoning clearly alarmed the estate's surveyor, George Pownall, as seen in his pencilled notes:

> Where do the children come from – no pressing necessity
>   Objections
>   from the tenants of Adamson Road who have laid out considerable sums

The houses being built on the Estate are not such as require School accommodation . . .
Damaging to the property in its present state

And, most significant of all: 'No more mews to be built –'.[171] No more mews were built, and the lower orders were kept at bay, although, one is glad to report, the College did grant an unfinished public house in Winchester Road to be used for the requested school.[172]

It would be misleading to exaggerate the social uniformity of any one suburb. The *Architect* reminded its readers that 'there are social distinctions of considerable range amongst the residents in any particular suburb, and . . . "wholesale Clapham declines the acquaintance of retail Clapham" emphatically enough . . .'. If anything, it found the degree of social mixture distressing: '. . . even in the open country it is not uncommon for a family of refinement and position to find themselves flanked on one side by a settler from Smithfield market, and on the other by a gentleman who is in the baby-linen line in High Holborn or the Strand . . .'.[173]

Owners and developers of building estates imposed building regulations that would ensure houses of a high minimum value that would attract affluent residents. 'Nothing but buildings of a superior class, including villas and high-class mansions, will be permitted to be erected,' the *Architect* reported with respect to the 200-acre Hatcham Manor estate at New Cross Gate, which the Haberdashers' Company laid out for building in 1875. 'A general architectural design has been agreed upon, and . . . the several elevations must be to a large extent uniform with it in character . . . the designs . . . must receive the approval of the Haberdashers' Company.'[174] The Company was subjected to a fair amount of criticism for insisting on architectural uniformity – this, after all, being 1875, not 1825 – but none for planning social uniformity.

Cheaper transport costs and rising real incomes were, by the seventies, enabling families of modest means to move into hitherto exclusive suburban districts. The *Architect* in 1873 was dismayed by

another kind of housebuilding going on in the country, beside the railway stations in the vicinity of London . . . This is the building of small houses in streets – actually in close rows along one side of the way and the other – with little back yards or so-called gardens such as people possess at Battersea or Islington. What can be the advantage in search of which poor clerks and shopmen bring themselves to travel backwards and forwards all the year round, by the first train in the morning and the last at night, between the counting-house or the counter in London and such a makeshift . . . as this, it is really not easy to see.[175]

Such invasions hastened the deterioration of the older suburbs. Those in the larger houses that remained took flight to more distant suburbs, and within a few years a socially homogeneous upper middle-class neighbourhood had turned itself into an equally homogeneous lower middle-class district. The *Building News* of 1881 saw the character of inner suburbia threatened:

The first evil . . . is the alarming intrusion of small houses upon the larger properties . . .

The danger threatens to become yearly so formidable as to drive the wealthier and professional class of residents farther out, and to make our suburbs huge wastes of brick and mortar devoted to small trades and lodging-houses. . . . [A] letter in the *South London Press* . . . cites the neighbourhoods of Stockwell and Herne Hill, where one dense mass of small houses exists, with narrow roads, and not one open space or public garden to be met with.

Similar inferior developments were transforming the physical appearance and social standing of Streatham, Brixton, the Dulwich Grove estate, Peckham Rye, and Wandsworth.[176]

If the *Building News* may have exaggerated the rapidity of social deterioration in certain suburbs, W.S. Clarke painted a picture of implausible stability. In so doing he accurately reflected the hopes of the prospective middle-class tenant. Brixton appears to especially good advantage:

It is due . . . to the absence of any drawback in the way of 'back slums,' that the wealthy tradesman, both in and out of business, has selected Brixton as his 'quarter.' It is too regular in its architecture, too new in its associations, to suit the artist, but this very regularity and newness have charms of their own to the man of business. Brixton, indeed, is best described by a word now somewhat out of date, but a good expressive word in its original signification – it is 'genteel.'[177]

Balham was equally attractive and socially homogeneous:

Proceeding along the main road from the station towards Upper Tooting, the road is fringed with a succession of very fine houses, all of which have extensive gardens, and not one of which would be of less rental than 100*l.* per annum, while the majority would be far in excess of that amount. . . .

It is one great recommendation of Balham that it has no back slums. All is of an 'eminently respectable' character, and no wonder it has been chosen as a place of residence by so many of the wealthy.[178]

The roads connecting Norwood Junction station with Woodside were 'fringed by dwellings that differ in value from 30*l.* to 80*l.* and 90*l.* per annum, and are very adroitly classified by keeping those of similar value in near neighbourhood, to the exclusion of others'.[179]

Workmen's trains, the extension of tramways, and rising real incomes were introducing more and more people to the pleasures of suburban living as the century approached its end. The maintenance, under such conditions, of a proper distance between the different classes of society required a degree of alertness and willingness to move on the part of the socially-conscious householder. It meant, as the *Building News* observed in 1890, abandoning what had once been gratifyingly exclusive districts to the lower orders:

We find suburbs, once delightful retreats for the busy City man, which attracted the *élite* of the professional and commercial classes, fast losing their fair name and reputation. Putney, Fulham, Richmond, Kew, on the west; Hampstead, Highgate, Hornsey, Finsbury, on the north; Clapham, Brixton, Dulwich, and Norwood, on the south, are already being irretrievably spoiled by the reckless speculator . . . while every acre of land is allowed to be crowded with from fifty to sixty houses, which is about the average density in many of the new localities, the higher class of suburbs are being brought down to the level of those in poorer districts. . . . The greedy landowner and the speculative builder are doing more to bring about an equality between the two classes than any other individuals, for they are rendering town and suburbs as much like one another as possible, by destroying those characteristics which people of means or of higher culture seek in their endeavour to obtain some approach to country life. There must be a limit to the increasing extension of the 'centre ring' of Greater London, the constant moving of the better-to do classes further out . . .[180]

Its fears for the continuing desirability of Hampstead and Dulwich and Richmond were exaggerated, but the quotation indicates both the fluidity of the character of suburbia at the time, and the intensity of the conviction that social segregation ought at all costs to be maintained. As each class moved from an inner suburb to one further out, it was replaced by a somewhat lower class of tenant also engaged in the process of outward migration: 'Southwark is moving to Walworth, Walworth to North Brixton and Stockwell, while the servant-keepers of outer South London go to Croydon and other places.'[181] Geographical mobility was maintaining, and perhaps even enhancing the degree of social segregation, even though the standing of particular districts might fluctuate. The abundance of property on the market, and the tendency of householders of every economic rank to rent rather than to purchase facilitated such responses to changes in the character of neighbourhoods.

If suburbs tended to deteriorate as they grew older, there also existed powerful forces to maintain the character of a district once it was established. On occasion residents would take concerted action to prevent the erection of dwellings for an uncongenial class. Thus, in 1881 the residents of Wanstead Flats, near Epping Forest, on hearing that a nine-acre estate was to be divided into 'small plots for the erection of cottage property and artisans' dwellings', jointly purchased the property for £9,000. 'The purchase has been made solely with the view of preventing the land being let in small plots, and it is understood that it will shortly be resold in lots suitable for the erection of residences of the villa class.'[182]

Even districts that did not take such dramatic action were likely to retain their character. W. Ashworth finds remarkable persistence in the proportion of the various social groupings in the different Essex suburbs from the time of their early development to the present. Thus West Ham has remained industrial and working class.[183] Leyton, Walthamstow, and East Ham have been lower middle-class dormitories from the start.[184] The energetic defence of Wanstead Flats by its early residents evidently proved successful, for Wanstead, together with Ilford, Woodford, Buckhurst Hill, and Chingford, remained distinctively middle class, with a character 'obvious to outward view in architectural style, rather larger houses, less dense layout and easy access to open space'.[185] A fourth type, with physical characteristics more like Wanstead but a population more like West Ham, was a council estate like Becontree.[186] '. . . Whether the place of work is close at hand or miles away,' Ashworth concludes, 'the influence of the local residential environment is . . . pervasive and tenacious . . . what is done leaves its mark socially as well as aesthetically for generations. . . .'[187]

78   *top*   '". . . those once pretty villages, Beckenham and Bromley in Kent."' High Street, Bromley, *c.* 1895.

79   *above*   '". . . Balham . . . is of an 'eminently respectable' character, and no wonder it has been chosen as a place of residence by so many of the wealthy."' Semi-detached villas at Balham, 1870.

CHALCOTS: THE ESSENCE OF SUBURBIA

Regent's Park and St John's Wood and Hampstead and Bedford Park, however well they embody one or another ideal suburban attribute, are all atypical because of the very excellence of the architecture or planning or, in the case of Hampstead, of their good fortune in retaining pre-Victorian qualities. A suburb which by its very banality is more representative is the Eton College estate. The one outstanding quality of Chalcots – stretching from St John's Wood to Haverstock Hill, from Primrose Hill to Belsize Park – is its mediocrity.[188] The Provost and Fellows of Eton College did nothing to startle the expectations or outrage the sensibilities of the builders or tenants on their estate. It is the unremarkable quality of the management and the indifferent nature of the results that give the estate its peculiar interest, just as a second-rate book often has more to tell the intellectual historian than a masterpiece.

Sir John Summerson has called the architecture of Chalcots 'catch-penny', the result of a 'commonplace . . . chain of events . . . a process which comes as near as possible to complete anonymity in its results, for it can truthfully be said that not one solitary soul was ever really interested in what the physical visible results would be'.[189] Hugh C. Prince has described the houses of Samuel Cuming, the principal builder on the estate in the forties and fifties, as 'nondescript . . . inoffensive . . . only remotely classical yet no more than vaguely romantic. They were built to please respectable but undiscerning clients'.[190] Kate Simon has called the productions of William Willett, whose late Victorian and Edwardian houses brought the original development to a close, 'dour, red-brick, lightless, airless, insane excrescences'.[191]

Yet Chalcots, despite its indifferent architecture and planning, was an unusually successful suburb. In a period characterized by a chronic oversupply of middle-class housing, Chalcots attracted and continued to attract the kind of resident for whom it was designed. While the Bedford estate was fighting its losing battle to keep its genteel tenants from deserting its elegant Georgian squares, the 'respectable but undiscerning clients' who constituted the bulk of the middle-class house-market moved into the anonymous Italianate villas of Chalcots and, as a class, remained there. Summerson has remarked on the unusual degree of social continuity in the neighbourhood. After describing the inhabitants of 1851, according to the census records of that year, as 'a mixed lot – small manufacturers, solicitors, a Congregational minister, an architect, a painter or two, widows bringing up families on small incomes', he pointed out that 'its character . . . remained much the same and so far as I can ascertain has always done so. Allowing for the changes which have taken place in the structure of society as a whole one can say that these houses are now inhabited by exactly the same type of people who lived in them a hundred years ago'.[192] There was a perceptible social decline by the early twentieth century. One resident, writing in 1918, observed that 'the character of the population has changed. This is no longer, to anything like the former extent, a neighbourhood wherein rising, or successful, professional and business men set up households and bring up families.'[193] Yet the decline was far from catastrophic, certainly far less than occurred in Bloomsbury. What generations of architects, surveyors, solicitors, and stewards strove vainly to achieve on the Bedford estate, Eton College seems to have managed without really trying.

The records of its estate show little evidence of serious planning, even of the landlord holding reluctant builders to higher standards of design, construction, or layout than they would themselves have wished. The history of the estate is one of mediocre management and mediocre builders proceeding according to an accepted pattern, a standard way of going about such things. If Bloomsbury was a magnificent failure, Chalcots was an undeserved success.

The ability of Chalcots to meet so precisely the wishes of its middle-class tenants may have come about not so much in spite of the passive policies of the ground landlord as because of them. The Georgian tradition of town planning, while it continued to be both applicable and applied to districts like Bayswater and Kensington, was irrelevant to the needs of villa suburbia.

Georgian estate planning imposed architectural uniformity but accepted social diversity. In any given neighbourhood the garden squares and principal streets would be designed for the better sort of resident, the back streets for the middling sort, and the courts and mews for the lower orders, decently screened from view. Chalcots permitted architectural diversity but achieved social uniformity. Its only exceptions to ubiquitous middle-class villas were a few shops, carefully restricted in area and location.

Chalcots succeeded without taking much thought for success. Its history suggests that, given sufficient size and a favourable location, a Victorian suburban estate planned and managed itself. What in practice this meant was that the kind of speculative builders that were attracted to an estate like Chalcots were competent and experienced enough to know how to put up houses that would appeal to middle-class tenants. F.M.L. Thompson stresses the unplanned nature of the Eton College estate:

> The urbanisation which it did . . . receive . . . was not imposed upon it by any master plan or any dominant developer; rather it just happened, piecemeal, in response to demand for suburban housing or more directly in response to speculative builders' ideas of what the demand for suburban housing was likely to be. The total effect was highly successful: a pleasantly leafy, prosperous but not ostentatious, middle-class district, with varied architectural styles which were in the main modest and unpretentious, which escaped the rigidity and monotony of a single-handed operation or an estate-office development. The pleasing features of the result owed only a little to estate management . . . they owed much more to the fortunate selection of builders who came on to the estate; and perhaps most of all to the persistent desire of middle-class families to live near the royal parks and among their own kind.[194]

Chalcots was fortunate in its situation, which enabled it to absorb some of the prestige of Regent's Park to the south, St John's Wood to the west, and Hampstead to the north. It failed to developed a distinctive character of its own and lacked even a name, for 'Chalcots' had meaning only for the antiquary.[195] The neighbourhood was variously identified in whole or in part as Haverstock Hill, Primrose Hill, St John's Wood, and South Hampstead, and its anonymity reflected the derivative nature of its layout and its architecture.

In order to derive full advantage from its promising site, Eton College did no more than

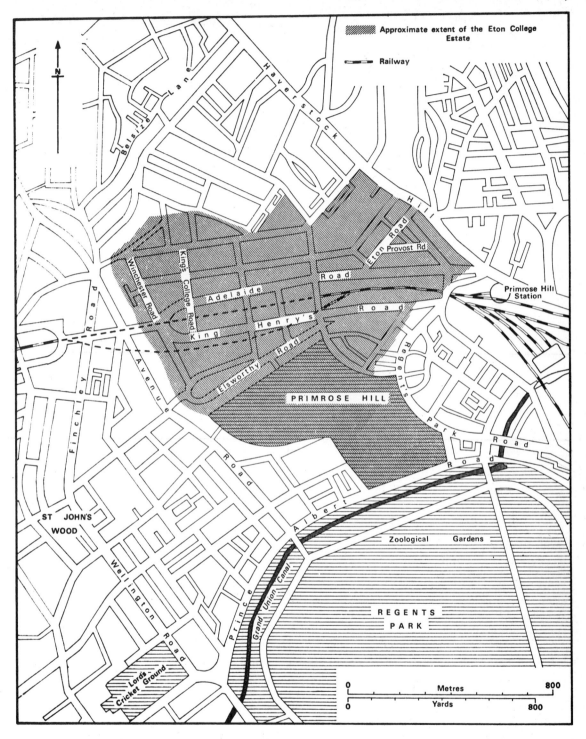

Map V   Eton College Chalcots estate, and surroundings. Dyos and Wolff, *The Victorian City*, I, 336.

any other large, responsible London landlord did, and far less than some. It hired a succession of surveyors, who proposed, modified, and abandoned a succession of spacious but un-original street plans; it had its solicitors draw up versions of standard building agreements and leases. It negotiated with a succession of developers and builders, who proceeded to erect detached and semi-detached villas in whatever style was currently in fashion. For amenities it encouraged the building of churches and an adequate number of respectably managed public houses. The houses were decently designed and substantially built, in accordance with the building agreements: not so much in consequence of their provisions, as because the builders and developers were accustomed to put up houses of that sort. One would imagine that the more respectable and better-established builders would be attracted to a sizeable, conservatively managed estate such as Chalcots. The dilatory behaviour of the Provost and Fellows, and particularly the bursar and registrar, with respect to the manage-ment of their London property – leading especially to delays in the execution of leases – did nothing to encourage builders and, it might be argued, made it impossible for any but a builder of some standing and considerable capital resources to indulge in the luxury of an Eton College speculation.

Unlike many ground landlords, the college offered no financial assistance to builders in the form of loans, purchases of improved ground rents, or contributions towards the expense of roadways and sewers. The builders did not seem to find the controls and coven-ants in the agreements irksome, although they inevitably increased their costs. There were disagreements as to the rate of rent per acre, the amount of time during which the full rent would be replaced by a peppercorn and a 'grass' rent, and the time allowed for the houses to be built; but there is no evidence that the builders were either trying to skimp on the dimensions or quality of materials, or that they were trying to crowd more and smaller houses onto their plots than the agreements allowed – both recurring problems on the Bedford estate.[196] From the point of view of the developers and builders, the situation called for precisely the large – but not too large – substantial houses on a spacious plan that the agreements called for. None of this is surprising, since there is every indication that most of the initiative for the layout and quality of construction came from the building developers themselves. The surviving estate plans that did originate with the landlords and their agents either proved impractical or were modified out of recognition in the negotiations with the developers.

The leasehold covenants served not so much as obstacles to bad building as encourage-ments to good, and an implied guarantee that the rest of the estate would be built to similar standards.[197] What mattered was less the conscious policies of the ground landlord than the continuing existence of a market for the kind of houses being erected, the willingness of substantial builders to speculate on the estate, and the seemingly inexhaustible pool of capital available to support middle-class housing developments in London.

The earliest plan for Chalcots would have made it a northward extension of Regent's Park; the actual development began as an eastward extension of St John's Wood, and ended as a southern continuation of Hampstead. Perhaps its success derived from its ability to reflect the aesthetic and social character of all three.

The Crown architects had in 1811 suggested that what was to become the northern portion of Regent's Park, land adjacent to the Eton College estate at Primrose Hill, could be 'most advantageously disposed of for Villas, having each an allotment of from two to five, ten, or a greater number of Acres'.[198] John Nash similarly proposed that the whole of the Park 'be let in parcels of from four to twenty acres, for the purpose of building villas . . .'.[199] The handful of villas actually built in the park is only a fragment of the original conception.[200]

The first plan for Chalcots, dated by Noel Blakiston 1822, proposed a similar layout. It argued that 'the Estate from its proximity to London and from its elevated situation is so well adapted for the erection of Villas with a small Quantity of Land attached thereto that it would be eagerly sought after by the wealthy Citizens of the Metropolis – and builders would readily speculate in taking the plots'. It proposed that the whole estate of about 230 acres, except for 14 acres on Primrose Hill itself, be divided into 77 building lots, all larger than half-an-acre.[201] Two years later John Jenkins produced a building plan that divided the whole of Chalcots, including Primrose Hill, into 75 large plots, to be served by four new roads.[202] Primrose Hill was never developed, and was in 1842 granted to the Crown in exchange for property in Eton.[203]

By 1826, when the college obtained a private Act authorizing it to grant 99-year leases on Chalcots, the building boom of the twenties had collapsed, and it was becoming evident that Regent's Park was not going to become a garden suburb for the very rich. More modest and realistic plans for Chalcots were thus called for, and the estate brought in the younger John Shaw (1803–70) to supervise operations. In March 1827 he prepared a scheme for the small part of the estate immediately adjacent to Haverstock Hill, providing for 34 detached villas set in plots of at least half-an-acre. None of the villas was to face directly on Haverstock Hill, along which trees were to screen its traffic; instead three new roads were to be formed. Each house was to contain at least 12 'squares' of building, i.e., 1,200 square feet, well above the minimum nine squares for first-rate houses specified by the London Building Act. Although a notable retreat from the grandiose intentions of the earlier plan, Shaw's scheme contemplated far larger houses than were ultimately built on the site.[204]

A later map, dated 1829, shows a less ambitious street plan and a smaller number of villas, 14 in all, on either side of the new road paralleling Haverstock Hill. Later additions in pencil show two alternative routes for a projected road bisecting the estate and linking Chalk Farm with the Finchley Road, together with the line of the London & Birmingham Railway and the portal of the Primrose Hill tunnel.[205]

In the same year printed 'Proposals for Building', with a coloured plan on the back, were prepared. They called the attention of builders to 'this very desirable Property, which is too well known to render necessary any description of its eligibility, in all respects, for Villas and respectable Residences, combining the advantages of Town and Country'. The college proposed to offer 'in the first instance . . . that part of the Estate adjoining the Hampstead Road at Haverstock Hill . . . containing about Fifteen Acres, in lots of not less than half an Acre, for the erection of single or double detached Villas'. The college would form the roads, which were intended, '(should the Buildings go on) to be continued and connected with other Roads, particularly with the new Turnpike Road from Mary-le-bone to Finchley, now

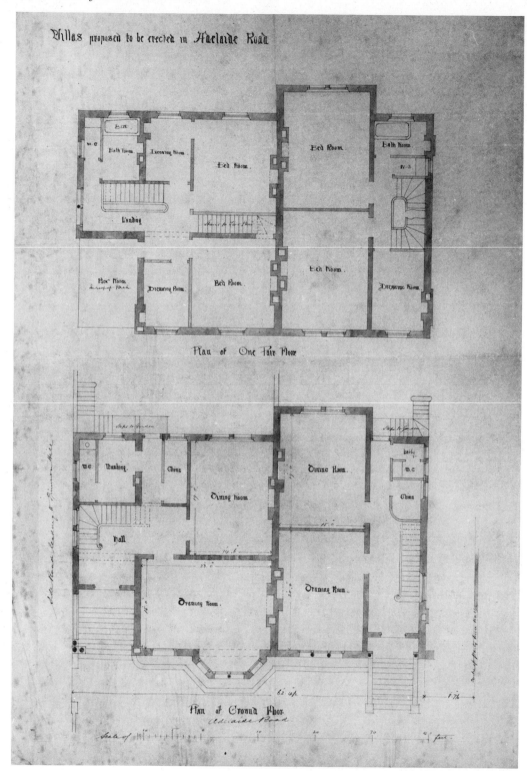

80 '. . . large – but not too large – substantial houses on a spacious plan . . .' Plan of villas in Adelaide Road. Photo: S.G. Parker-Ross.

in progress'. Even without such connections, 'the Roads at present proposed will afford very desirable Frontages for Buildings, having the advantage of adjoining the main Hampstead Road, and being at the same time secluded from its publicity'. There was no mention of the dimensions of the houses or their rates of building, except that they were to be 'substantial and respectable private Houses', whose plans, elevations, and structural specifications would require the approval of Mr Shaw.[206]

The result must have been disappointing to all concerned. As Summerson puts it, 'some rather wretched pairs of villas sprang up on one side of the estate. Nothing more happened until 1842.'[207]

It was 1840 before Shaw presented the college with a comprehensive plan of development. His proposals are interesting both as an expression of the ideas of suburban planning held by an experienced early-Victorian architect, and as an indication of how hard it was for any landowner rationally to direct the growth of London. For no portion of Shaw's plan was put into effect, since it proved to be as unacceptable to speculative builders as the plan of 1822 had been. The landowner could only exercise his power within the limits imposed by geography, fashion, the structure of the building industry, and the state of the money market.

Shaw was able to report that building on the portion of the estate fronting the Hampstead Road was virtually complete. 'Before making any further advance,' he wrote the bursar, 'it is highly important to consider . . . what will probably be the most beneficial mode of appropriating the Estate generally to the purposes of building, so that whatever may be done shall be upon a definite plan'. To that end he enclosed a plan containing a comprehensive pattern of streets and building lots. Negotiations were already in progress for the sale of Primrose Hill, but the plan showed that part of the estate marked out in building plots like the rest. So long as arrangements were made 'for definite and sufficient access into the Estate' from Regent's Park, Shaw thought the preservation of Primrose Hill as a public open space would 'materially benefit the Estate, while by securing the Roadways I have alluded to, it will not lead to any alteration in the design of the *residue* of the Estate'.

The plan represents an intermediate stage between the extremely spacious scheme of 1822 and the relatively compact layout that the building developers ultimately gave to the estate. In laying down the lines of roads, Shaw 'endeavoured to suggest the best Communications to the most important points, and to secure double frontages to each line as far as practicable'. There were to be no more than three major east-west roads, compared with the five actually built, and two north-south roads, where there were eventually to be four. Apart from the comparatively narrow building plots for the houses already completed along Haverstock Hill, the plan provided for a total of no more than about 215 lots, nearly three times the number contemplated in 1822, but far fewer than there were eventually to be.[208]

The two indispensable amenities for any respectable housing estate were a church and a public house. William Wynn, the first substantial developer on the estate, gave it its first public house, the Adelaide Tavern, at the eastern end of Adelaide Road in 1842. In requesting the assistance of the college in his application for a license, Wynn pointed out that there was up to then 'not 1 public house [on the estate] . . . and taking the improvements altogether with the new park and Adelaide Road being a principal thoroughfare to the park the house will be an improvement to the estate'.[209] Three years later Shaw authorized Samuel Cuming to build a second 'Hotel or Tavern' in Adelaide Road, 500 yards distant from the Adelaide Tavern:

> . . . Its being restricted from being inferior to the *1st* Rate Class of Building will I think [Shaw wrote to the bursar] insure its respectability and Mr. Cuming who would be most interested in maintaining this respectability (considering his large Building Engagement) thinks such an house essentially necessary for the convenience of the large neighborhood which will be established: He is also desirous of ascertaining if the College would be willing to give a site for a Church on the new Line of Road . . . he tells me there is very great want of a place of worship and . . . he feels confident he could obtain the necessary funds for its erection.[210]

Shaw had given considerable thought to the need for a church in his 1840 report:

> From frequent applications made by the Residents on the Property, and in the Neighborhood, I find that there is a general demand for a Chapel on the Estate, there being no place of worship within a very considerable distance; Mr. Wynn the builder of many of the houses and other persons have led me to believe that it would be profitable even as a speculation to establish one, and that if the object could be entertained or promoted by the Provost and College such a subscription would be made by the neighborhood as would with their aid accomplish it.
>
> Undoubtedly the existence of such a building on the Estate would most materially lead to the formation of a neighborhood around it . . .[211]

The church that was finally erected, St Saviour's, was located in the triangular enclosure, north of Adelaide Road, formed by Provost and Eton Roads and Eton Villas. Samuel Cuming was the largest of the original subscribers, pledging £200, and the college donated the site.[212] The church, in the Early English style, was completed in 1856, except for the tower and spire, which were added later.[213] In 1870 the college conveyed a freehold site at the junction of King Henry's and Elsworthy Roads to the Ecclesiastical Commissioners for the erection of another church, St Mary's, completed in 1873.[214]

Leases generally prohibited the use of houses as other than gentlemen's private residences, except in streets designed from the outset for shops, notably King's College and Winchester Roads, and England's Lane.

The initiative for setting out the actual pattern of streets lay with the building developers, notably Samuel Cuming. Cuming, who dominated the operations on the estate from the mid-forties to the fifties, continued to build until his death in 1870. The difference in the scale and density of construction between the plans of the ground landlord and the proposals of the building contractor reflected the customary conflict of interest between landlord and speculator, whereby the latter, with his better knowledge of the house market, would scale down the ambitious designs of the former. Even so, the actual development carried out the surveyor's basic intention: that it consist of streets of villas, of the same order as those that were making the Eyre estate such a speculative and social success.

Shaw considered communications with St John's Wood of the utmost importance, and laid great stress on pushing a road across Chalcots to join the Finchley Road. For that reason Adelaide Road was developed several decades before the parts of the estate to the north or south of it. The printed building proposals of 1829 had promised through communications with the Eyre estate. Ten years later negotiations were in progress with William Kingdom, 'a Gentleman . . . of great respectability, and considerable Property', who had recently engaged in a speculation on Lord Holland's estate in Kensington, to construct the entire road and to build at its two ends, in 'a style of Building somewhat similar to the Terraces of the Regent's Park, or of the Oxford and Cambridge Terraces [Sussex Gardens, Paddington]; there can be little doubt of the new Road', which would be called Eton Terrace, 'becoming a splendid addition to the projected improvements of the neighbourhood'. Shaw was willing to reduce Kingdom's ground rent from £35 an acre to as low as £20 if he would at his own expense build the road, 'intended to be 400 feet from the Center of the Railway and Tunnel and extending the whole length of the North side of it', and from which 'branch roads may be formed . . . in many directions', since it would 'so materially enhance the value of the Estate generally'.[215]

The negotiations with Kingdom fell through, but the following January Shaw was proposing to 'communicate with Colonel Eyre with reference to the access proposed to the St. Johns Wood Estate . . . which . . . will afford a mutual benefit to the *two* Estates'.[216] On 14 July 1845 Shaw reported that Adelaide Road had by then been formed 'to the extent of about 1500 feet', one third of the way to the Finchley Road, and that arrangements had been made with Colonel Eyre for the junction of the two roads. He urged that the road and sewer 'be formed *at once*, & not progressively . . . and in this Condition Mr. Cuming acquiesces; indeed it is to his own interest with reference to his selling or letting the houses now building upon the Land he has taken, as there naturally exists a feeling in the Public, either that the Road may not be continued, or that many years may first elapse'.[217]

He wrote confidently the following January: 'when this new line is . . . opened I feel assured that the remaining frontages of the College Land will be advantageously disposed of, and the whole Estate greatly increased in value'.[218] He contemplated two more roads running west from the Hampstead Road north of Adelaide Road, but did not intend to extend the Private Road (later College Road) farther northward. There was also to be a road 'on the Chalcotts Estate running parallel with the Marylebone & Finchley Road at about the same distance from the boundary of the two Estates', which became Winchester Road.[219]

The building agreements with Cuming, like those with later developers on the estate, left him a fair amount of freedom to determine the details of his operations. For example, in his first agreement, he contracted to build 'not less than 8 single or double detached houses of not less than the 2d. rate on that part of the plan marked A', with similarly loose specifications for the other four plots. 'Plans of each house and a general Specification of the same [were] to be submitted to, and to be subject to the approval of the Surveyor to the estate before it is commenced and no house [was] to be built inferior as respects materials and workmanship to those now building by Mr. Cuming [under an agreement made previously with William Wynn] on the estate.'[220] A standard covenant required that 'a space of at least 15 feet . . . be reserved between the main walls of each single or double detached House'.[221]

The surveyor found nothing to object to in Cuming's operations. In July 1845 he wrote to the bursar: '. . . I passed some hours yesterday in going over it [the Chalcots estate], and was very much pleased with the New line of Road which is now complete up to Mr. Cuming's last take, and with the houses he has built, & is building, which are of a superior description as he proceeds.'[222] Late in 1850 he reported that although 'there has been generally a cessation of building during the last two years . . . what has been done at Chalcot I am happy to say has been well done, and the Houses are of a respectable class & character'.[223]

The subsequent building history of the estate lasted into the twentieth century, as Adelaide Road was joined by King Henry's and Elsworthy Roads to the south, and Fellows Road and Eton Avenue to the north. Cuming was joined by a number of other large-scale developers from the fifties onward. George Frasi, a civil engineer from Canonbury, agreed to take over 12 acres comprising what was to become Fellows and Winchester Roads in 1853, promising to build between 40 and 104 'single or double detached dwelling houses or Blocks of dwellinghouses of the second rate . . .'.[224] James Fotheringham and Thomas Renton took on another four-acre plot south of Adelaide Road the same year, agreeing to build shop buildings and semi-detached houses.[225] Frasi was declared a bankrupt in December 1855, after having expended £10,000 on the estate. His agreement was taken over by Frank Clemow, who owned the well-known Anderton Hotel in Fleet Street, and Mary Ann Angell, a 'spinster' who lived in Canonbury Square.[226] Meanwhile Fotheringham's and Renton's agreement had been taken over by Robert Yeo, a builder, of Belsize Road.[227]

The *Building News* in 1857 took notice of the high degree of building activity in and around the Eton College estate: 'On various separate estates situated on this [Haverstock] hill . . . a very large amount of building operations are now in very active progress, notwithstanding the continued "tightness of the money market".' It specifically commended the work of Robert Yeo, who was then building 'a very large detached villa' at the corner of Winchester and Adelaide Roads.[228] It had already praised Cuming's houses in Adelaide Road: 'It is worthy of remark that these residences are owned, and have been built, by *one* proprietor, Mr. Samuel Cuming . . . who has already erected upon both sides of the road an immense number of similar buildings, to the extent of upwards of half-a-mile.'[229] The following year it reported that Cuming's villas were 'all finished, and either sold or let; several more are in very active progress, and in various stages of advancement'.[230]

Towards the end of the fifties many of the builders on the estate found themselves in serious difficulty, and were unable to carry out the terms of their agreements.[231] Clemow and Miss Angell were forced to give up the greater part of their land,[232] leaving Robert Yeo the most active builder. In May 1861 Shaw was complaining of the difficulty of getting offers for the remaining land.[233] Early in 1862 the situation changed for the better. 'I have two *very important* proposals for building Land to submit to you,' Shaw wrote to the registrar in February of that year.[234] The *Builder* may have heard rumours of the offer, for on 8 February it expressed concern about the loss of open space on Primrose Hill:

PRIMROSE HILL. – Those who feel how inestimable, in every point of view, is such a tract of open ground, will regret to hear that the whole northern side of the hill, from the wooden paling which passes across near its summit, to the railway, including about fifty acres of land, is now likely to be covered with houses. . . . The northern portion is now offered on building leases, with the other part of Chalcot Estate, extending over the fields as far as Belsize . . . the contemplated building over Chalcot Estate will render every acre of open space more and more valuable to the public.[235]

The land required was on agricultural lease, and in order to acquire the leasehold interest of its tenant, Giles Clarke, the college proceeded to raise the necessary £12,500 on mortgage from the National Provident company.[236]

On 19 May 1863 Robert Yeo took three plots in King Henry's Road, totalling more than four acres. He agreed to build by 1868 between 28 and 42 detached or semi-detached houses at the rate of eight per year.[237] On 9 June 1863 Thomas Yeo and Powell Warner, solicitors, agreed to take the whole of both sides of King Henry's Road eastward from Primrose Hill Road, together with an adjacent portion of Ainger Road. In the former they contracted to build between 50 and 70 villas, in the latter 'Shops or Terrace with Mews in rear', all to be completed by 1869.[238]

Once the 80 acres leased by Giles Clarke had been resumed by the college plans for building development went forward with all deliberate speed. On 7 August 1865 the college solicitor Clement Uvedale Price was 'attending on Mr. Pownall in his Office, and discussing with him what ground should be resumed at Michaelmas next and the various applications he had received . . .'.[239] George Pownall had succeeded John Shaw as surveyor to the college in 1863.[240] On 16 March 1866 Price was 'attending the College entering into explanation of the various proposals to take the greater part of the Estate . . .'.[241]

Jacob Hibberd's building agreement, dated 16 March 1866, covers the north-eastern portion of the estate, south of England's Lane. He agreed to build 'not less than One hundred and fifty Dwelling houses or Shops and Eighteen Stables . . .' by Michaelmas 1880. The shops were to be along England's Lane and Haverstock Hill; the rest of the buildings were to be gentlemen's private residences.[242] On the same date John George Bettinson covenanted to build 'not less than thirty detached or semidetached houses' along the south side of Fellows Road, from Merton Road to Primrose Hill Road, at the rate of five a year.[243] Land not immediately required for building was let to a Mr Smith for grazing purposes at £50.[244]

Samuel Cuming also shared in the new building ground, taking four sizeable plots east of Merton Road and south of King Henry's Road, at a rent rising to £420. He agreed to build at least 70 detached or semi-detached houses at the rate of seven a year.[245] Cuming died on 13 January 1870, leaving his brother John and his son Samuel to carry on his building commitments.[246] Cuming had in fact not begun to build any of the houses in the agreement, 'as he had not completed the buildings under a previous agreement . . .'. Unlike other builders on the estate he was more than solvent at his death, leaving 'an only Son well provided for in addition to providing for his daughters . . .'.[247]

The north-western corner of the estate went to Daniel Tidey, who was also building

81 *above* '"... what has been done at Chalcot I am happy to say has been well done, and the Houses are of a respectable class & character."' Backs of houses, looking north from Adelaide Road, with spire of St Saviour's Church, 1968. S.G. Parker-Ross.

82 *right* 'The *Building News* in 1857 ... specifically commended the work of Robert Yeo, who was then building "a very large detached villa" at the corner of Winchester and Adelaide Roads.' Elevation and plan of Yeo's villa. S.G. Parker-Ross.

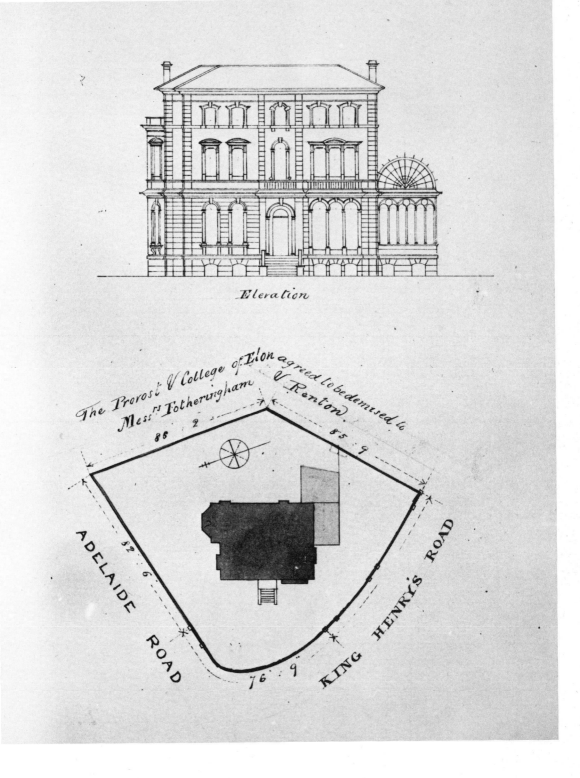

Elevation

The Provost & College of Eton agreed to be demised to
Mess.rs Fotheringham & Renton.

88 2

85 9

ADELAIDE ROAD

52 6

KING HENRY'S ROAD

76 9

extensively on the adjacent Belsize Park estate.[248] He was already at work on the latter estate, 'approached from the western side of the Hampstead-road . . . by a noble avenue of elm trees, and . . . very salubriously situated', in 1858. 'On the northern side of what is to be called Buckland-terrace, ten detached villas have been erected by Mr. Tidey, builder,' reported the *Building News* in that year. 'These buildings are all uniform in design, and of the ordinary suburban architectural detail, in which Italian features are most predominant.'[249] Tidey was also responsible for Queens Gardens in Bayswater.[250] On the Chalcots estate Tidey agreed to build at least 180 houses, at the rate of ten per year, at a rent rising to £1,200 annually.[251]

Jacob Hibberd agreed to take slightly more than an acre along the north side of Fellows Road eastward from Primrose Hill Road, on which he was to build at least 11 houses.[252] On 14 March 1867 J.G. Bettinson signed a building agreement for six sizeable plots on both sides of Fellows Road and Winchester Road, at a rent rising to £704. He would build not less than 140 detached or semi-detached houses, at the rate of 12 annually, or greater in proportion if he chose to build more than 140 in all.[253]

As a result of the different agreements, Price was able to write to the assistant registrar Richard Cope in 1867: 'With the exception of the land let to Mr. Welbourne at £50 a year the whole estate is now included either under agreements for leases or leases.'[254] Not quite 12 acres were leased for 14 years as the Eton and Middlesex Cricket Ground.[255]

The south-eastern corner of the estate, adjoining Primrose Hill, and including Primrose Hill Road and Ainger Road, was included in an agreement with Thomas and Frederick Burkwood Welbourn, builders, on 5 May 1868. They agreed to build 'not less than Ninety two houses and eighteen stables', at the rate of twelve per year, paying a rent rising to a maximum of £480 in the sixth year.[256]

By the end of 1869 Price was calculating for the new Bursar, W.A. Carter, the projected increase in rental under the several new building agreements, which by 1873 would amount to £2,791 10s. over the Michaelmas 1869 rental. 'It is right to add,' he cautiously concluded, 'that should any of the Parties fail before carrying out their agreements the whole of the yearly increase might not be received.'[257]

The caution proved more justified than the optimism, for the early 1870's saw a succession of bankruptcies among the contractors on the estate, bringing building virtually to a standstill. The solicitors' accounts for the early months of 1870 already suggest that something was wrong. On 8 February 1870 they were 'writing to Messrs. Pownall as to non-completion of Houses on Lease to Mr. Roche and Mr. Ronald according to the Covenant'. Since this land was included in Tidey's original agreement, he was himself clearly in difficulty, too. On 12 March Pownall 'approved of time being given for completion of Houses and also for any arrangement with Tidey's Assignee for carrying out the Agreement'.[258] In April 1870 the solicitors were 'drawing notice to Trustees of Tidey's Bankruptcy to disclaim building Agreement'.[259]

Before the year was over Bettinson's speculation, too, had failed.[260] Sir Walter Rockcliff Farquhar, Bart., of St James's Street, and John Roche, Gentleman, of Belsize Park Gardens, agreed to take over the greater part of Bettinson's agreement of 14 March 1867. The two had lent £9,000 to Bettinson on mortgage.[261] The new building agreement, dated 23 March 1871, was undertaken by Roche in conjunction with Arthur Lucas of Marlow Road, Buckinghamshire, timber merchant. They agreed to build at least 110 houses at the rate of 12 per year.[262] On the same day the college granted Roche a licence to hold the building agreement granted to Bettinson for the south side of Fellows Road, from Merton Road to Primrose Hill Road. The names included in the licence give further evidence of the kinds and varieties of investors in building speculations in Victorian London. They include Springall Thompson, Esq.; Frederick Thompson, Gentleman; and the Rev. Joseph Morrison Croker. John Roche turns out to be not merely a Gentleman from Belsize Park Gardens, but a slate merchant at Grand Junction Wharf, South Paddington.[263]

Jacob Hibberd, who had taken on a new agreement for a further plot of ground extending southward from England's Lane as recently as 1870, found himself also in the bankruptcy court by the spring of 1871.[264]

As of Michaelmas 1872 the gross rents from Chalcots – excluding those from the grass land – amounted to £4,458 16s. 5d. The solicitors estimated that, if existing building agreements were completed, the rent by 1880 would have reached £5,228 16s. 5d. Building agreements at the time were in the hands of John Roche, Messrs. Welbourn, Samuel Cuming, and Jacob Hibberd, although the last was in process of liquidation. The 20 acres formerly under agreement to Tidey were at the time unlet for building purposes, but were being let as grass land for £30: 'the land is so cut up that more rent could not be obtained'.[265]

On 18 December 1873 the trustee and creditors of the estate of Jacob Hibberd, in liquidation, entered into a new building agreement with the estate. The creditors were Springall Thompson, Esq., of New Square, Lincoln's Inn; and Frederick Thompson, Gentleman, of Raymond Buildings, Gray's Inn. Thomas Maynard, brick maker, of South Wharf, Paddington, was trustee. The agreement covered the greater part of the block bounded on the east by Haverstock Hill, on the north by England's Lane, on the west by Primrose Hill Road and Fellows Road, and on the south by Steele's Road. Hibberd had before his bankruptcy erected buildings sufficient to secure ground rents amounting to £358 10s., reducing the rent to be secured by the college from the original £648 to £289 10s. Springall Thompson, it developed, had lent a total of £23,000 to Hibberd between 1866 and 1870.[266]

Despite the severe setbacks that led to the different bankruptcies, building pushed forward and the *Builder* of 27 March 1875 was able to report: 'The Eton property is now largely built upon, and the appropriate names of Eton, King's College, King Henry's, Provost, Fellows, Oppidans, and Merton roads mark its position.'[267] It found little worthy of comment in the actual houses going up. 'There is nothing very interesting,' it remarked the following year, 'in the appearance of that extremely modern row of shops, Steele's-terrace . . .'.[268]

On 29 March 1876 Henry Rose, Gentleman, of Great George Street, Westminster, surrendered the agreement obtained by the late John Roche and Arthur Lucas to build 110 houses in Fellows and Winchester Roads. Roche had died 30 August 1873.[269] The following day Rose entered into a new agreement for virtually the same ground, on which he promised to build a minimum of 80 houses by 1882, at a rent rising to a total of £487 15s.[270]

On the same day Thomas and Frederick Burkwood Welbourn received an extension of time on their building agreement, they having completed no more than 53 of the 72 houses they were supposed to have finished by Michaelmas 1875, 'and they have not since erected . . . any other dwellinghouse or Stable . . .'. They were given a new schedule of construction with the whole to be built by Michaelmas 1882.[271]

In 1881 there appeared the developer who was to complete the building of Chalcots, providing the estate with some of its most splendid houses: William Willett. Widespread imitation and duplication in the form of 'Wimbledon Transitional' and 'Bypass Variegated' make it difficult to respond as seriously to Willett's houses as they deserve, but the suburban dream has rarely been achieved with greater magnificence.

The Chalcots Accounts of George Pownall and his son include an entry from January to August 1881, 'treating & agreeing with Mr. W. Willett to take 18 Acres of Land at a Maximum rent of £900 per annum . . . & preparing and settling the Plans of the Buildings to be erected . . .'.[272] Willett had been involved in the neighbourhood since 1869 when he took over from Daniel Tidey the responsibility for building a number of houses in Belsize Crescent. He was also extensively concerned with the development of the Cadogan and Holland estates in Chelsea and Kensington.[273]

Willett's first building agreement, dated 27 July 1881, covers much of the same ground as that taken by Daniel Tidey in 1866. Willett was to build not less than 200 dwelling houses by 1900. The ground ran the length of Eton Avenue – then known as Bursars Road – from Winchester Road to Primrose Hill Road and Belsize Park Gardens, and from the line of Lancaster Road to the backs of houses on the north side of Fellows Road. He was within three months to 'enclose the said pieces of land . . . with a post and rail fence . . . as shall effectually keep out cattle . . . And shall not . . . permit or suffer the said land . . . to be used for the feeding of sheep thereon.'[274]

The agreement was revised on 31 December 1885, adding a small piece of ground fronting Belsize Park Gardens, and making Eton Avenue run directly into England's Lane instead of forking into two roads at its eastern end. The rent was reduced to a maximum of £758, and the number of houses to 140, involving a considerable reduction from the original amount and number.[275] Willett proceeded steadily with his contract, and in 1886 there were complaints that the roadway in Merton Road 'had been cut up by the heavy traffic caused by Mr. Willett's carts'.[276]

Willett's final agreement, dated 18 December 1890, consisted of the former site of the Eton and Middlesex Cricket Ground, at the south-western corner of the estate, forming the site for the western end of Elsworthy Road. For a rent rising to a maximum of £650, Willett covenanted to build not less than 125 'Dwelling houses Shops or Stables', at the rate of 20 attached, 15 semi-detached, or 10 detached houses per annum. All were to be finished by Michaelmas 1905.[277] In fact, as of December 1895, no houses had yet been completed under the agreement.[278]

Willett's houses, built in association with his son William, were noted for their solidity, spaciousness, and attractive appearance. Their use of 'good bricks, tiles, and Portland stone' gave them 'an effect of warmth, colour, and interest. Variety of elevation was aimed at and achieved.'[279] They 'put Norman Shaw on the production line, going in for gables, tiled roofs, bay windows, red brick exteriors . . . deliberate contrasts in shape and elevation between adjoining houses. It was the effective beginning of twentieth-century suburban architecture . . .'[280] Neither Eton Avenue nor Elsworthy Road was completed until the early years of the twentieth century. The latter in particular has the appearance of a suburban road far more distant from the centre of things than it is, making it as representative of Edwardian suburbia as Adelaide Road was of the early Victorian sort.

Chalcots represents in miniature the whole experience of the creation of villa suburbia: the leisurely pace of development – it took over 70 years for 200 acres of desirable building land already on the fringe of built-up London in the 1820's to be fully covered with houses – the looseness of control on the part of the landlord, the frequency of bankruptcy among speculators, the mediocrity of planning and architecture; yet despite it all, the generally agreeable results.

What sort of appeal had Chalcots to the generations of solid, middle-class householders who chose to bring up their families there? First of all, it offered social homogeneity: the houses were all of much the same size and appearance, broken only slightly by the shop property in Winchester and King's College Roads and in England's Lane, and by an occasional mews. Secondly, it offered, in its detached or semi-detached dwellings, a degree of separateness and seclusion to each family. Thirdly, it offered dullness: two pubs, two churches, a few shops, nothing – even in the form of architectural extravagance – to compete with the attractions of the hearth.

One essential suburban quality, repellent to its detractors, cherished by its inhabitants, is that of make-believe, the denial of the economic basis of its existence, the exclusion of other classes and of any sort of manufacture, the relegation of essential trades to segregated back streets. The life that Mr Manning offered Ann Veronica was one possible only in a suburb, where she might find refuge from the 'great, ugly, endless wilderness of selfish, sweating, vulgar competition', as she ironically put it herself,

> a sort of beautiful garden close – wearing lovely dresses and picking beautiful flowers . . . While those other girls trudge to business and those other women let lodgings. And in reality even the magic garden close resolves itself into a villa at Morningside Park and my father being more and more cross and overbearing at meals . . .[281]

Wells saw the suburb as yet another instrument for the subjection of women: and indeed, insofar as the Victorian home was kept physically remote from centres of economic, social, and intellectual activity, the authority of the husband was more easily exercised. But the suburb threw the husband and father, too, inevitably back on the resources of his home in a neighbourhood that offered it little competition: only other homes like his own.

The most successful suburb was the one that possessed the highest concentration of anti-urban qualities: solitude, dullness, uniformity, social homogeneity, barely adequate public transportation, the proximity of similar neighbourhoods – remoteness, both physical and psychological, from what is mistakenly regarded as the Real World.

The qualities cited by most town planners in condemnation of the suburb: monotony, the compartmentalization of life, the separation of leisure from work, the absence of social mixture, the refusal to face the simplest facts, whether the real structural qualities of the house or the economic activities that support it, were just the qualities that the Victorian middle classes most cherished. Efforts to avoid such qualities while retaining the low density, gardens, and the like that seem desirable qualities in suburbs, have produced the hybrid garden cities and today's New Towns. Their failure to establish themselves as the standard environment of our time, while dormitory suburbs multiply, suggests that even today people who can choose prefer the artificialities of Golders Green and the banalities of Chalcots to the more moral and bracing atmosphere of Welwyn and Crawley.

CHAPTER SIX

Salubrious Dwellings for the Industrious Classes

... In its success is involved the triumph of the moral virtues and the elevation of the great body of the people. I have always felt that the best security for civilisation is the dwelling. It is the real nursery of all domestic virtue and without a becoming home the exercise of those virtues is impossible.
Disraeli on Shaftesbury Park, quoted in *Artizans Centenary, 1867–1967*, privately printed, n.d., p. 13.

THE ASSUMPTIONS OF PATERNALISM

The inherent internal contradiction in a society that glorified individuality yet required standardization, that longed to re-establish lost patterns of craftsmanship yet depended on the machine, that tried to reconcile a concern for the well-being of the mass of the people with aesthetic aims that could only be realized at an expense that would limit their products to a wealthy few, is not exhausted by an examination of its attitude towards suburban housing.

The Victorians found it hard to accept that there could either be more houses or better houses, not both – without a massive transfer of resources from other forms of investment – that lower density of suburban housing would either mean greater crowding at the centre or the destruction of more agricultural land and an increase in the cost of transporting the suburban population to and from work; that substantial, well-designed, individualized dwellings cost more than flimsy, standardized houses; that one of the consequences of the greater solidity and structural superiority of dwellings in Paris was a higher level of rents and an even greater degree of urban crowding than London suffered. It is of course in the nature of things to wish for mutually exclusive goods, and it is always easier to detect the incompatibility between such desires in an age removed from one's own. And the tension between the two forces produces something in-between as a result. But such tension is rarely between self-evidently evil ends and self-evidently good ones, even when the supporters of one side are inarticulate, and the supporters of the other side speak with eloquence, moral fervour, and persistence.

No one at the time had anything very good to say about the speculative builders, who were themselves generally too busy building (as well as too poorly educated) to speak for themselves. Since then S.E. Rasmussen as an architect and H.J. Dyos as an economic historian – together with a growing body of his students and disciples – have begun to rehabilitate the builders and developers who made Victorian London. A more persuasive defence of their activities is the actual London they built.

In apportioning praise and blame for the condition of life in Victorian London we must remember that builders built buildings (and roads, and sewers, and railway lines, and bridges, and other physical things); they did not 'build' poverty, inequality, disease, injustice, ignorance, and other social evils. Victorian reformers were themselves often guilty of looking too narrowly for causes of the evils of their time in particular institutions, laws, or practices rather than in their society, ideas, and institutions as a whole: whether in the Corn Laws, the restricted suffrage, the ecclesiastical establishment, drink, or – to take a particularly absurd and inadequate explanation which was nevertheless passionately believed by many who ought to have known better – leasehold tenure; rather than try to get at more fundamental causes: they were, with rare exceptions, whatever their party, in the literal sense, insufficiently radical. It is all the more necessary for historians to avoid the unthinking acceptance of the assumptions and mental processes of the people with whom they are dealing. Some Victorian culprits – like drink and the improvidence of the undeserving poor – we find quite easy, perhaps too easy, to discount. Others, like the jerry-builder and the slum-landlord, are easier for us, even today, to accept uncritically as sufficient explanations.

Even Pevsner has given support to the denigration of those who, however inadequately, provided new housing for the working classes:

> ... Socially the outstanding feature of these thirty or forty years [1801–41] is the growth of slums in the East End until they had reached the appalling dimensions and conditions branded as a shame for ever by Chadwick, Kay, Southwood Smith, and others in their *Report on the Sanitary Condition of the Labouring Classes* published in 1842. The unmitigated slum stretched from the River through Stepney and Poplar to Bethnal Green, Shoreditch, and Finsbury, and affected on the S bank Bermondsey and Southwark. The population of the last two rose from 109,000 to 203,000 and of the five boroughs on the NE from 223,000 to 505,000. ... well over one-third of the population of London in 1841 lived in slum conditions worse than any anywhere in London now.[1]

What Pevsner has written is perfectly true, but could mislead the unwary. For it presents as totally shameful what was a moderately admirable achievement by the London building industry: the creation, for the first time, and in considerable quantity, of housing designed from the outset for working-class occupation, with units small enough to make single-family occupation of individual houses at least a possibility.

In the eighteenth century, and in central London for long afterwards, the poor lived in single rooms in decayed houses designed originally for middle and upper-class occupation. Even the fourth-rate house as defined by the London Building Acts was too large and too expensive to be occupied as such by any but a reasonably prosperous family. The proper criticism to be directed against the landlords and builders of the new East End suburbs of the early nineteenth century is not that they built ugly, inadequate streets of cottage housing that quickly deteriorated into squalid slums, but that they did not build enough of them.

The assumption that it is wrong to build slum housing (or more accurately housing in which slums form themselves) is a converse fallacy to that entertained by well-meaning Victorian reformers, that demolishing slum property meant destroying slums. Actually, of course, by forcing the former inmates to move into already overcrowded housing it created new slums, even worse than the old.

The growing concern about the quality and quantity of working-class housing that came to dominate late Victorian social thought can be regarded as a necessary preparation for the twentieth-century welfare state. It can equally be regarded as a way of avoiding any but the most superficial examination of the fundamental problems of poverty and social justice.

From the unfair vantage point that hindsight allows, there were no problems – except those that were part of the human condition itself – that the Victorian poor faced that could not have been solved by more money – preferably a great deal of it – in their own pockets. That the Victorian poor were badly housed goes without saying. They were also badly fed, badly clothed, badly educated, and inadequately provided with medical care, sport, entertainment, travel, drink, art – all of the good things of life; they had insufficient leisure and inadequate opportunities for making the best of the leisure they had. Whether the extra money came as a result of their getting a bigger share of the gross national product or whether it came from an increase in the amount of that product to be shared – or, as has happened, a combination of the two – was far less important than that the poor got it. Only with adequate funds and the freedom to allocate them as they pleased could the poor have the same ability to make real their aspirations that the middle classes enjoyed. 'The reward each citizen earns . . . must be his own to do with as he will,' said Harold Laski in 1928:

> He may choose, as is so typical of America, to sacrifice the creature-comforts of his home to the possession of a motor-car; or he may wish, as is the case of many Londoners, to endure the discomfort of a long railway journey for the pleasure of cultivating his own garden. The more a man is tempted to experiment with his own standards of consumption, the better it is for society.[2]

Needless to say, no Victorian reformer argued in that way. If Macaulay could envisage a twentieth century in which farm labourers would earn 15s. a week and artisans 10s. a day, this could be dismissed as yet another example of his quantitative and materialistic conception of progress.[3] Underlying all Victorian and a great deal of twentieth-century social thought is the assumption of working-class improvidence, that the poor, unless properly guided, would spend any extra money unwisely. The paternalistic conviction that we know better what is good for you than you yourself do may quite possibly have been perfectly justified. It is not my purpose to examine the validity of the conviction, merely to point out its pervasiveness.

If the last two chapters showed how middle-class housing reflected middle-class values and aspirations, no one can expect working-class housing to reflect working-class values and aspirations. The unskilled casual labourer took whatever he could get. The skilled artisan had somewhat more freedom to choose, but far less than the middle-class householder. And much of what he had to choose from reflected not so much his own wishes as those of the middle-class philanthropist or reformer. Working-class housing in a distorted but unmistakable way reflected middle-class values as much as middle-class housing did: at its worst by showing what they were willing to tolerate, at its best by showing the kind of environment they wished to impose on the lower orders.

'Impose on' is a harsh expression; but 'provide for' is too weak, since it might suggest that the recipients had very much to say about what that environment would consist of. 'Since the poor rarely have much direct opportunity to call the tune in architecture,' Hitchcock reminds us, 'reports of their desires prepared by others (whether philanthropists or bureaucrats) are largely suspect . . .'.[4] It may be that the philanthropic housing of the nineteenth century and the council housing of the twentieth represented exactly what the working classes most wished for themselves. It may also be true that housing – rather than any of the other good but scarce things of life – was what they wanted more and better of. We shall never know: what we do know is that the middle classes thought they ought to wish it. Beyond that was the environmentalist's conviction that improved housing would create improved people, morally and intellectually as well as physically. Just as the detached suburban house was designed to make its middle-class occupants more middle class, so the hope of the supporters of improved industrial dwellings was that they would inculcate middle-class values in their working-class inmates.

'The problem of the housing of the poor,' William Emerson told the RIBA in his presidential address in 1900, 'should be so solved as to raise the working classes to a higher physical and moral level, and assist in redeeming them not only from the worst evils of poverty and misery, but from evil surroundings and wickedness.' Aesthetic virtue would combine with moral and physical improvement as architects worked to 'render the dwellings of the poor not only comfortable and sanitary but beautiful, so as to educate and raise their tastes'.[5]

SPECULATIVE WORKING-CLASS HOUSING

'Purpose-built' dwellings for the working classes, whether speculative or philanthropic, were a nineteenth-century innovation. Just as many of the eighteenth-century urban poor had to make do with the cast-off clothes of their social superiors, so they lived for the most part in the discarded dwellings of their betters. The West Indian occupant of a semiconverted terrace house in Notting Hill or Brixton is experiencing the same situation that the Huguenot occupant of a room in a deteriorated town house off Soho Square or the Victorian casual labourer in a once-fashionable court near Covent Garden did. Down to the twentieth century most working-class Londoners lived in houses that had not been built with them in mind; down to the nineteenth century all of them did.

Why that should have been is by no means self-evident. Farm labourers did not, by and large, live in converted yeomen's cottages, nor yeomen in portions of decayed country houses. And in provincial towns the working classes usually lived in cottages intended from the start for them.[6] Here, as in so many other ways, London was different.

Part of the difference was in its size and wealth: land was simply too scarce and valuable to be squandered on separate dwellings for the artisan class, much less for the really poor. Nor was it worth anyone's while to construct new dwellings for multiple occupancy for those unable to afford an entire house to themselves. Finally, the successive London Building Acts provided minimum standards of dimensions and building materials that placed even the smallest and cheapest type of house beyond the reach of anyone of less than middle-class status.

It was particularly in the outlying districts where land values were less and the Building Acts were either inoperative or loosely enforced that the first significant developments of speculative housing designed from the outset for working-class occupation took place. Pevsner's 'unmitigated slum . . . from the River through Stepney and Poplar to Bethnal Green, Shoreditch, and Finsbury, and . . . on the S Bank Bermondsey and Southwark',[7] was the result.

Cottages in such districts, though small, were even so likely to be cut up for multiple occupancy. 'The restraint imposed by the Building Act has, in the neighbourhood of London, tended much to produce a kind of house, called a fourth-rate house,' wrote I.J. Kent in the *Architectural Magazine* in 1834:

> . . . The smallest of these are built, principally for the occupation of the poor, in the suburbs of London, in inferior situations. These houses consist of two rooms; they have generally from 12 ft. to 14 ft. frontage, and are from 12 ft. to 14 ft. deep, having an access on the ground floor in front into the lower room, and steps outside at the back leading into the upper room. Three, four, or more have a yard and other conveniences in common. Dwellings of this description are rarely properly drained or ventilated, and therefore form nurseries for the cholera and all other diseases. They are usually let at from 3s. to 4s. per week each room.[8]

Some working-class housing got itself erected in more central, and even respectable parts of London inadvertently, at least from the point of view of the ground landlord. Inadequately drafted or insufficiently enforced building agreements might make it possible for the speculative builder to erect substandard dwellings in the courts or passages behind the larger houses he had covenanted to put up. Thus, in the first decade of the nineteenth century, the Foundling Hospital reluctantly allowed James Burton and George Payne respectively to put up some buildings 'of a very small and slight character . . .' between Tavistock Place and Bernard Street, and north of Compton Street, which quickly became noisome slums.[9] The loosely-drawn building leases on the Northampton estate in Islington and Clerkenwell contained no prohibitions of building on the garden grounds of the original houses; cheap tenements were accordingly built over such vacant ground in the 1830's.[10]

Other landlords were imprudent enough to grant leases with few or no stipulations as to any of the buildings to be erected. Lord Southampton let 50 acres of Camden Town with no more restrictions than a provision that the builder erect 500 third-rate houses, 'or a lesser number of superior rate, so as to be of the same value, within 14 years . . .'. The Portman estate let most of its land north of the New Road 'to a Builder of the name of Porter, without any restriction in the mode of covering it . . .'.[11] Both areas established themselves as working-class districts at once. Immediately adjacent to the elegant villas of St John's Wood lay Portland Town, 'composed of houses of the meanest description, and inhabited by persons of the humblest class of life . . .'. Thomas Smith reported that there had been 'some un-accountable oversight in the arrangements made for letting out this land on building leases . . . the Duke of Portland was exceedingly angry when he discovered the character of the buildings erected on this property'.[12] At the end of the century the local Wesleyan minister described Portland Town as 'an island of poverty in the midst of wealth . . .'.[13]

It was a commonplace of estate management that middle-class housing was always to be preferred to working-class, even though the level of ground rents might be the same. (Such rents depended more on the proximity of the estate to town centres or to centres of fashion than to the character of buildings to be erected on it.) The principal economic motive a landlord had for preferring low-density middle-class development to high-density working-class was the greater probability of the former maintaining its reversionary value throughout the course of the lease. James Noble warned landowners in 1836 that 'the inferior, or fourth-rate dwellings, merely secure a ground rental for the time being; and probably, from the introduction of indifferent materials, and slight character of construction, become prema-turely dilapidated, if not ruinous, before the expiration of a long building term; and conse-quently *an improved rent to the freeholder would be visionary* . . .'.[14]

F.M.L. Thompson has ingeniously calculated that the Belsize estate in Hampstead may have 'fixed the ground rent in relation to the expected value of the reversion when the 99-year lease expired, moving one up as the second fell so that the ground landlord's ultimate profit from the land should always remain approximately the same'.[15] As a result it charged ground-rents of around £50 per acre in middle-class districts like Belsize Park, Rosslyn Park, and Parliament Hill Road; but £82 an acre in the working-class district of Fleet Road.[16] But on other estates there is no apparent relationship between ground rents and the class of house.

The prevailing assumption was that landowners ought to try to persuade builders to put up as valuable and substantial buildings as possible. John Nash condemned landowners who, like the Duke of Portland and Lords Southampton and Portman, had permitted the erection of working-class housing on their estates. As of 1815 no 'speculation in buildings of any consequence' had yet taken place north of the New Road, but rather 'houses of cheap rent have become the object of builders' in that area. The practice of speculators in the northern outskirts was 'to take large tracts of ground by the acre, and to crowd as many streets and lanes into it as they can, in order to create so many feet lineal, to underlet for building; and the fruit of the speculation is the sale of the increased ground rents'. The result was houses 'of the meanest sort . . . built of the worst and slightest material . . .' and which would leave the ground landlord with 'his land encumbered with a heap of ruins' when the leases expired. Only by laying out neighbourhoods with large and substantial houses could landlords ensure the reversionary value of their property. 'Houses inhabited by the first classes of society last longer,' Nash explained, 'because their luxuries and comforts require that their houses should be kept clean and renovated; and the changes of fashion occasion so many alterations, that the houses of the first classes may be said to be rebuilt many times during the term of a building lease . . .'. No such forces operated with the lower orders, whose houses became therefore 'more liable to decay than those inhabited by the higher classes'. He pointed out that 'Mary-le-bone Park and the lands around it form the beginning of the ascent of the high grounds of Hampstead and Highgate . . . and it is to be lamented that houses of such a mean stamp as have been built at Somers Town and are now building on Lord Southampton's ground, should disgrace this Apex of the Metropolis, particularly as there is sufficient space on the lower grounds for any increase of buildings required for the lower classes . . .'.[17]

Even, or indeed especially, in cases where estates had succeeded in keeping working-class housing off their streets, there was a strong tendency for slums to appear along their boundaries. 'It is really singular to remark how often a single line of road or houses serves to form a distinct line of demarkation between the extreme conditions of society,' the *Builder* wrote in 1844 of the contrast between Bloomsbury and the district immediately to the north: 'a few steps beyond this assemblage of streets and squares and we enter Somers Town, a vast assemblage of "put up houses", already falling into decay, and inhabited by poverty in its hydra-headed form on the one hand, and by greedy shop-keepers on the other . . .'.[18] John Hollingshead remarked on the same phenomenon in 1861:

> If large factories and centres of industry invariably attract a crowded, dependent population, terraces and squares of private mansions do the same. From Belgravia to Bloomsbury – from St. Pancras to Bayswater – there is hardly a settlement of leading residences that has not its particular colony of ill-housed poor hanging on to its skirts. Behind the mansion there is generally a stable, and near the stable there is generally a maze of close streets, containing a small greengrocer's, a small dairy, a quiet coachman's public-house, and a number of houses let out in tenements. These houses shelter a large number of painters, bricklayers, carpenters, and similar labourers, with their families, and many laundresses, and charwomen. Each room, with a few exceptions, is the home of a different family . . .[19]

What was bad for the well-being of any given estate was not necessarily bad for London as a whole. Whatever the sanitary deficiencies of Portland Town and Somers Town, to the extent to which they existed at all they relieved some of the pressure on other working-class districts. Yet they bear witness to the truth that within the West End in particular working-class housing came about by accident rather than by design, and that the efforts of management on the best estates were to prevent its coming into existence and, if that failed, to replace it by something else as soon as that became possible.

The 'something else' might be middle-class housing or commercial buildings of some sort. Or it might be new thoroughfares or a line of railway. The former could ordinarily be achieved only at the expiration of the original leases, but the latter possibilities, since they counted as 'improvements', could take place at any time.

The railway – or tramway – suburb, whether in the form of the privately-built late Victorian communities along the line of the Great Eastern or the twentieth-century council estate, proved ultimately to be the only feasible way of housing the vast majority of working-class Londoners in a decent and sanitary fashion. For a variety of reasons, including the necessity for casual labourers to remain within walking distance of their employment and the inability of many of the poor to pay even minimal railway fares, the suburban solution to overcrowding was not, for many decades, generally practical: the exodus from central London long remained a middle-class phenomenon. But proposals to enable the workers to benefit from the new technology of the railway came very early.

In 1846 the *Surrey Advertiser* reported a scheme whereby ten villages, 'containing in each 500 cottage residences, with seven persons to each cottage', were to be built near Croydon, each village to cover 500 acres, and all together to house 350,000 people. 'It is said the [London and] Croydon [Railway] Company . . . have entered into an agreement to allow the members of these villages to be carried the whole length of the Croydon Railway, ten miles and a half, at three half-pence per head.'[20] In 1855 Charles Pearson, solicitor to the City of London, was calling for the establishment of a model working-class suburb at Hornsey or Tottenham, on the newly-opened Great Northern line, where land could be had at from £100 to £200 an acre.[21] The *Builder* expressed the hope in 1861 that 'by and by . . . numbers who now live in the courts, alleys, cellars, and garrets of the teeming hive London, may find their way, night and morning, to healthy rural villages, sub-suburbs, with the aid of the locomotive and far-seeing railway directors'.[22]

Long before the Great Eastern Railway introduced workmen's trains as such, suburbs with working-class inhabitants were being formed along its lines. In September 1856 the *Builder* predicted that 'another great offshoot of London will, before long, have been established in the green fields of Hornsey and Tottenham'. Much of the district was undergoing villa development, but in Edmonton there were 'rows of small cottages' in lamentable sanitary condition.[23] To the east of the City, the establishment of new industries – or old ones moving outward from London itself to escape its stringent sanitary regulations – was encouraging the growth of a substantial working-class population. The *Builder* in 1859 described a train journey from Fenchurch Street to Loughton, remarking on the rapid increase of population in Hackney, Homerton, Stepney, Poplar, Stratford, Plaistow, and other northeastern suburbs. The Great Eastern's locomotive works at Stratford had created, 'a large demand for houses suitable for the industrious classes', most of which were 'of small size, and without improvement on the usual plan'. The correspondent found the area, 'cut up in all directions by branches of railways . . . not very inviting: the numerous coal-waggons, the bustle, and unornamental nature of the stations, and other works', reminded him of the mining districts of Northumberland and Durham.[24]

James Thorne's *Handbook to the Environs of London*, published in 1876, contrasted Plaistow's respectable past as a semi-rural retreat for the City merchant with its current industrial and proletarian condition:

Unpleasant manufactures, driven from the capital, have settled down in the Marshes. The great Metropolitan Sewer, in the form of a huge grass-covered embankment, has been carried across the level, and through the vill. The construction of the sewer, the opening of the rly., and the proximity of great manufacturing establishments caused a large influx of the labouring classes. The gentry migrated. The handsome old mansions have been pulled down, suffered to go to decay, or diverted to other uses, and the grounds built over. The trees have been felled; the fields, changed into streets which lead nowhere, are left unfinished and fragmentary, and lined with mean little tenements . . . dirty, frail, and gardenless . . .

The old vill. has extended into the Barking Road, and spread out over the marshes, and has been met by straggling streets and houses from Hall Ville, Silver Town, Canning Town, and the Victoria Docks, manufacturing and shipping quarters, built on the marshes between the Lea and the Thames, and reaching back across the Barking Road towards Plaistow proper and West Ham. . . . these places . . . have grown up within the last few years about the great docks, chemical, creosoting, artificial manure, engineering and various other works, without order and without oversight; are dirty, incomplete, unfragrant, unattractive, but in many points of view exceedingly interesting.[25]

Stratford was another industrial suburb:

Stratford has become a considerable manufacturing district. Much of the land is low and marshy, and being well provided with rly. facilities, and the navigable Lea on one side of it affording ready access to the Thames and docks, it has become the home of many factories which find difficulty in obtaining sites so near to London. Besides the old-established corn-mills, distilleries, breweries, chemical and dye-works by the Lea, there are now extensive engineering establishments, print-works, jute spinning mills, manufactories of vestas and matches, printing ink, aniline colour, varnish, soap and candle factories, oil, grease, creosote, bone-boiling, paraffin, coprolite, nitro-phosphate, guano, and other artificial manure and gas and tar works . . .[26]

One can almost read the stereotyped list of 'offensive trades' in any West End lease: Plaistow and Stratford represented both the antithesis and the necessary complement to Bloomsbury and Belgravia.

The most astonishing of the eastern suburbs, perhaps, was West Ham. 'It is really a counter-part to the growth of some Northern towns,' wrote W.S. Clarke; 'or rather, like the amazing aggregations in America . . . it will not be long before the whole of the land between Edmonton, by Woodford and Wanstead, down to Stratford and Poplar, make a new phase in the development of English local life, and a unity more like a county than a borough.'[27] The *Builder* was equally impressed, if also dismayed, by West Ham, which finally acquired a corporation in 1886:

Half a century ago it was a straggling village of some five or six thousand inhabitants on the east bank of the Lea and near its mouth; and . . . might have remained so but for the Act of 1854, which placed many . . . restrictions on the manufactories existing within the metropolis. Their owners naturally sought a retreat where nobody could interfere with them, and found at West Ham . . . liberty to make smells and generally pollute the atmosphere, cheap land, and proximity to water carriage. So West Ham increased rapidly and became one of the busiest and dirtiest places in the kingdom . . .[28]

The East End suburbs became, more than a specialized neighbourhood, a vast specialized region, devoted to necessary but unpleasant industries and characterized by the less necessary qualities of poverty and ugliness, overcrowding and disease. The ugliness, at least, was long mitigated by the physical survivals of the area's earlier period, when it served as a rural retreat for affluent City merchants. Hackney in particular retained many of its qualities as an eighteenth-century commuting village long into the Victorian period. Clarke was not alone in testifying to its charms:

> [Visitors] exclaim in wonder at the large old-fashioned houses, the trees and gardens, the magnificent avenue of the old churchyard, and the resemblance of that part of Hackney called Mare-street and Church-street to an old English country town.[29]

Even in 1893 Percy Fitzgerald found Hackney quaint and picturesque, 'very much of the pattern of some remote town such as Folkestone, with its narrow straggling streets full of old red-brick houses, tiled roofs, gardens, tramcars, glimpses of "downs" and commons, and patches of green revealing themselves at sudden openings . . .'.[30] Charles Booth confirmed the picture of a Hackney still retaining vestiges of a genteel past:

> The nobility have indeed gone and left no trace, but the day of the merchants is scarcely over. A few of the old houses in Clapton Road are still in the occupation of wealthy city men, and many more have their residences on Stamford Hill . . .
> . . . Hackney . . . not so long ago . . . was a suburb of large houses surrounded by their gardens or even parks, interspersed with nursery gardens, watercress beds and ponds, and fields where cows might graze. Even now there is greenery enough left in corners to show how well the soil responded to cultivation.[31]

But it was present poverty rather than past gentility that Booth mainly treated:

> The general tendency during the last half century has been for Hackney to become a poorer and much more crowded quarter, but the change has not been uniform. The line of Mare Street and Clapton Road . . . divides the district into nearly equal parts, and almost all the poverty is to be found to the east of this line . . .

Here as elsewhere Booth was fascinated by the tendency for particular kinds of poverty to be concentrated in particular neighbourhoods, yet another manifestation of the forces 'sorting-out' London's population into geographically-segregated sub-categories:

> The unkempt poverty . . . by Hackney Wick and All Souls', Clapton . . . differs . . . from that of the poor streets which represent the old villages of Hackney and Homerton. In these outlying districts, where London stretches to her furthest limits on the North-East, there are very marked peculiarities . . . in the remoter portion of Hackney, in place of a general spreading outwards, it would rather seem as though the rejected from the centre had been flung completely over the heads of the rest of the population, to alight where no man yet had settled, occupying undesirable ill-built houses on the marshy land that is drained or flooded by the River Lea.

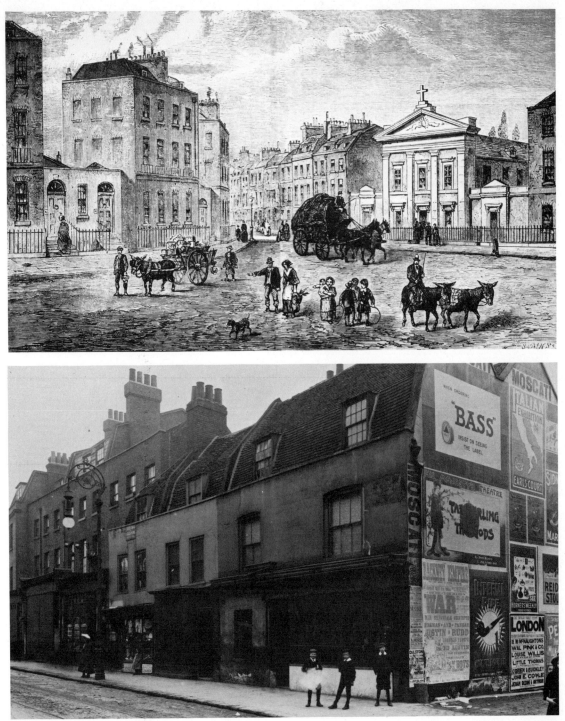

83 *top* '". . . Somers Town, a vast assemblage of 'put up houses,' already falling into decay . . ."' The Polygon, Somers Town, 1850.

84 *above* '". . . the resemblance of that part of Hackney called Mare-street and Church-street to an old English country town."' Mare Street, Hackney, 1904.

. . . The streets abutting on South Mill Fields were built for better purposes, but are falling to the social position of Hackney Wick, or even lower. . . . This district has been the refuge of shady characters, and a poor class is attracted by the low rents. It is a dismal, but not a rowdy district. . . .

The remainder of the district, to the west of Mare Street and between Wick Road and Victoria Park, is either lower middle or solid working class, and . . . the prevailing pink of the large map changes to red as we approach Stamford Hill or Victoria Park . . . from regular working-class inhabitants, with residential shopkeepers in the main streets, to well-to-do middle-class people with, here and there, little patches of extreme poverty.

From one point of view Hackney was simply going through the customary social and physical deterioration that seemed the lot of all but the most favoured suburbs. What made it remarkable was the sharpness of the fall, and the resulting physical juxtaposition of the remains of past glory and present disgrace. Nor had the process come to a halt:

. . . Hackney is becoming poorer. The larger houses are turned into factories. The better-to-do residents are leaving, or have left. In the homes and in the churches their places are taken by a lower middle grade. . . . Each class as it moves away is replaced by one slightly poorer and lower . . .

With this downward tendency there is a considerable augmentation in total numbers. The working-class population has increased greatly, and, in addition, room has been found in some parts for new comers of a very much lower degree. The same houses accommodate more people and, where there has been rebuilding, more houses stand upon the same land. The outward movement of the well-to-do has been checked to some extent in Dalston . . . and there has even been a tendency to return to the good old houses on the part of families driven south again by the working class invasion of Enfield, Tottenham and Edmonton.[32]

South of the river but even closer to the City, Rotherhithe was another centre of intense building activity. The *Builder* in 1878 cited 'St Helena' in that parish as 'a marvellous illustration of almost preternatural structural enterprise and activity', and an example of how a new working-class neighbourhood could be brought rapidly into existence:

Our new town, which includes about twelve roads and streets, and about 600 houses, the greater portion of them occupied, was laid out about a year ago, and the first brick laid . . . in September 1877! The new settlement, at present detached and rather out of the way, is situated between the Commercial Docks and the Greenwich Railway . . .

The new town . . . covers an area of between ten and twelve acres. It is built upon surplus land that had to be taken by the East London Railway Company . . . It was . . . bought by seven purchasers, who have erected the houses in the almost incredibly short space of time mentioned. Its streets include Fawcett, Cornbury, Reculver, Edale, Rutford, Goodson, and Alpine roads, with numerous cross connexions. Alpine road seems a curious misnomer, inasmuch as the land is as level as a billiard-table, and forms portion of a wide area on the south of the Thames, now occupied as market gardens, that before the embankment of the river in past ages was submerged by every tide. . . .

The whole of the houses on the estate, with the exception of five, and corner premises, are almost identically alike in plan and appearance. . . . The houses are 24 ft. from front to back, and have each 16 ft. of frontage. Each pair of houses has a coupled addition at the back, containing the kitchen, and behind it the wash-house, a pair of closets, the water-cisterns, with wooden covers over them, being at the rear of all. The front rooms have bay-windows . . . The ground-floor windows are filled with plate-glass; the entrance doors are recessed. These 'oriels' are covered with ornamental slates. The kitchens have also bay-windows. The houses are evidently intended to accommodate two families each, the first-floor back-room, as well as the kitchen on the ground-floor, being fitted with range, oven, and boiler. The rooms are small, but the houses, as regards internal accommodation, in pantry, cupboards, presses, &c., are better fitted than some of a more pretentious character, for which considerably higher rents are paid. The houses have in front a narrow strip inclosed by a coped dwarf wall, surmounted by a neat iron rail. The rents are 10s. and 12s. per week.

The *Builder* was not wholly amiss in calling it a 'new town' rather than a mere artisans' dormitory, for it was already showing some of the attributes of a balanced community:

Nothing has been done as yet . . . in paving or public lighting, but in many other respects the settlement is getting completed. Pillar letter-boxes have been established; legends over doors and windows indicate the places of business of butcher, baker, grocer, tailor, shoemaker, milliner and dressmaker, plumber and glazier, dealer in tinned goods and sundries, haberdasher, greengrocer, &c. 'Mangling is done here,' there are 'Lodgings for single men.' At one place bottled wines and spirits are sold, and at another beer . . . Two public-houses have been provisionally licensed. . . .

In fine, this yearling town from present appearances gives promise . . . to house a population of not much fewer than 4,000 inhabitants, or more than many market-towns, and will be entitled to take its place among the marvels of modern days.[33]

DETERIORATING NEIGHBOURHOODS

To the east and south of the City speculators worked to provide housing that was sufficiently cheap and nasty to be available for working-class occupation even when it was new. But elsewhere in London what was available for the working-class family or individual, and in particular for the very poor, was housing that had been originally intended for a higher social class but that had, for one reason or another, come down in the world. The decaying house and the deteriorating neighbourhood have usually been seen as symptoms of urban failure – whether resulting from bad planning, jerry building, inadequate enforcement of leasehold covenants by ground landlords or by-laws by local authorities, or some more pervasive sickness in the total community. And yet in the absence of a building industry that provided an adequate supply of new housing for the working classes, houses abandoned by the middle classes could only mitigate otherwise intolerable overcrowding. Anything that increased the number of houses and rooms available for the poor – however miserable the accommodation might have been from an aesthetic or sanitary point of view – at least kept a bad situation from getting worse.

Booth, in chronicling the deterioration of certain North London suburbs, pointed out that the decay of a neighbourhood was in practice consistent with an improvement in the quality of the lives of those who lived there: 'Those who come are poorer than those who go, and each district in turn grows poorer. Yet it may easily be that, as individuals, all are better off; that those who come are not so badly housed as before, while those who go have gone to better quarters.'[34] It was equally possible, of course, for both neighbourhood and individual to deteriorate: geographical, like social mobility, can as easily be downward as upward.

Hackney was not the only suburb to lose the attraction it once had for City merchants. Hoxton, according to a guide book of 1838, 'formerly a place of some consequence, as the numerous old mansions in it will testify. . . . has now . . . long since "fallen from its high estate;" its grand houses are converted into schools and receptacles for lunatics, and its modern ones are of the second and third-rate . . .'.[35] Kentish Town, once recommended by doctors 'as a salubrious place', still had 'numerous genteel residences' as late as the 1830's; but on the whole seemed 'on the decline, many of the best houses being unoccupied (August, 1836)'.[36]

The late-Georgian ribbon developments along the main routes connecting South London with the Thames bridges had by the nineties physically deteriorated as much as their architecture had declined in public estimation:

> Nothing gives such an idea of the hopeless monotony of certain portions of London [wrote Percy Fitzgerald in 1893] as the routes by the Old Kent Road and Westminster Bridge Road, that lead to Camberwell, Clapham, Greenwich, etc. Long rows of grim, shabby-looking houses – there are cast-off or 'second-hand' houses, like cast-off clothes – line these dismal avenues, which seem interminable.[37]

Most of the inner suburbs south of the river had long since lost their original inhabitants and genteel qualities. Peckham, for instance, was 'no longer the old Peckham: it is overrun with terraces and houses, and the "rye" or common has a stinted, impoverished, albeit neat and trim air'.[38]

Booth found the outward movement of successive social classes especially noticeable in north-eastern London:

> A great impulse has been given to this movement by demolitions in the inner circle in connection with the Holborn Valley improvements and the making of Rosebery Avenue, and by the extension of business premises in Central London; but concurrently with the need thus created for house-room for the poor, and the consequent invasion by them of the available districts most adjacent to their old homes and their centres of employment, there has been, on the part of the well-to-do middle class, a tendency to move further out, a tendency born of prosperity. Their places are taken by a lower section of the middle class or by well-employed members of the working classes, all fully contented with the

change they make; and under new conditions of housing room is made, in the general shuffle, for the outcasts from elsewhere as well as for natural increase; the whole result being a great additional population and a rapid change in the character of almost every part of the district.

To the extreme north 'the poorest and worst, in their desire for cheaper houses or less stringent rules, cross the London boundary, as do the rich in search of pleasant gardens and green fields'.

The extent of a neighbourhood's decline, Booth thought, was much affected by the quality of the houses and other aspects of the physical environment:

> The North-West corner, near Hornsey, is said to have been ruined by bad building . . . The clearances in Somers Town for railroad extension sent a whole colony of very rough people to the badly built streets near Junction Road . . . Of the Tufnell Park area, from which the rich are now going, it is said that if the new houses are of the same kind as have been put up in Corinne and Hugo Roads, the whole neighbourhood will inevitably go down rapidly; for the poor and rough will press into it from all sides.
>
> . . . The good condition in which Highbury Fields have been kept for the public use since their transfer to the County Council is said to have arrested general deterioration, although decline in some of the best parts immediately adjacent to the Fields may have been hastened; and in some other places the character of particular estates has been sustained by restrictions as to licensed houses.[39]

Camden Town which, as recently as 1870, had been 'a residential quarter of wealth and even fashion . . . had become largely a place of business; among the residents servants were rare, and in nearly every house there was a lodger'. Poverty was greatest to the north, while the better off lived in the southern part:

> With both the tendency is downward. The old residents of the better houses are being replaced by those who find their living partly in letting apartments, and young people of the prosperous working class move further out, leaving the dregs to be continually reinforced by new comers of a lower standing.[40]

Nearby Kentish Town had, on the other hand, been changed for the better by the coming of the Midland Railway in the sixties, demolishing the old slums and scattering their inhabitants; in their place introducing 'a good class of working men both as its own employees and by fostering the multiplication of local factories . . . As a result rents have risen, and the poor being pushed out have betaken themselves to Highgate New Town and other parts.'[41]

MODEL BLOCK DWELLINGS

The model dwellings for the working classes had architectural as well as social significance: wholly new responses to unprecedented challenges, like the railway station, the office block, the board school, and the public baths. They tended, in the early decades of their existence in particular, to be sited not in the developing outskirts but in the midst of long-existing neighbourhoods, and must be seen as belonging to the transformation of an older, Georgian London rather than to the creation of a new, wholly Victorian London in the suburbs.

Socially they contributed to the systematic sorting out and rearrangement of the various grades of Victorian society.* Not only did they put carefully selected groups of working-class families and individuals under one roof where they could be supervised and improved more effectively, but they were a way of separating the respectable, deserving poor from their unregenerate brothers and sisters. One had to be pretty far up the social pyramid to gain admittance to a model dwelling, and, indeed, to be willing to undergo the kind of surveillance that went on in them. While it would be an exaggeration to think of them as domestic panopticons, they were uncomfortable and uncongenial places for anyone intending to pursue a life of sloth and improvidence, not to speak of crime or vice. They could be regarded as training schools for the inculcation of middle-class virtues among the lower, but aspiring orders.

'Heavy and monotonous . . . having all the pretensions of warehouses and barracks . . . they do not even invite the class of tenants for whom they are intended,' the *Building News* charged in 1883. 'They have not even the stamp of domestic habitability to recommend them . . .'.[42] Grim, bleak, and forbidding, they resist even today our tendency to assimilate all aspects of Victorian culture in a warm, nostalgic embrace. The young and trendy may eagerly move into transformed rows of labourers' cottages, but there has been no comparable rush into Peabody Buildings. Yet they represented a vast improvement in housing to those fortunate and determined enough to move into them when they were new, making possible a decent life on a small income.

It is a commonplace that the gregariousness of the traditional working-class quarter stands in marked contrast to the passion for individual privacy that characterizes the middle-class suburb. The individual flat in a model dwelling, although not ordinarily entirely self-contained, did provide the individual and his family with a greater degree of privacy than was possible in the ordinary lodging-house. The *Building News* argued in 1857 for an even greater degree of separateness, even at the expense of centralized supervision:

> Several plans of model lodgings are talked of, but the working classes have not realised the benefit of such a class of accommodation. Most of what has been proposed is too benevolent, and not suited to the wants of the expected tenants. It must be so contrived that each tenant has separate access; but all the stairways and passages must be cleaned at the expense of the proprietor, and there must be no reliance on co-operation. Instead of relying on co-operation, the reliance must be that all the women will squabble if they can, and therefore they must, as far as possible, be kept out of each other's way. Doubtless this

* For a modern parallel, in the high-rise council flats on the Roehampton estate in the 1950's, 'the different types of building were used to segregate different types of family: the childless and the middle-aged in the tall blocks, the young families with children in the maisonettes, the big families in the houses, the elderly in the bungalows – each category marked off by broad swathes of grassland. In effect one could see, set out architecturally, a kind of built diagram of the housing manager's filing cabinet, with each particular size of family neatly classified under the same heading.' Nicholas Taylor, *The Village in the City*, pp. 174–5.

consideration very much restricts the accommodation which, under a co-operative system, might be afforded; but those who know how much the working classes stand upon their independence, and how little really the middle classes will sacrifice this for purposes of co-operation, will not be disappointed. Each tenant must be independent within his own domain, and there, if need be, allowed to make a pig of himself, to smoke and spit, to keep the place dirty instead of clean, and for himself and wife to enjoy the full privileges of the Great Unwashed.[43]

Such a policy did not prevail, most philanthropists believing that privacy and independence were privileges to be granted only to those who were middle class or who had learned how to behave in a middle-class fashion, even when not being watched.

Still, privacy was of great importance, even within the individual flat. In discussing a new model dwelling in 1875, the *Architect* urged that 'due provision' be made 'in its internal plan for the division of its living from its sleeping rooms, by proper lobbies for that privacy which even our ordinary common lodging-houses provide'.[44] 'A Country Architect' found the internal arrangements of some new blocks erected in Pimlico by Sir Sydney Waterlow's company somewhat better from the point of view of segregation of function and individual privacy:

> The tenements, rented from some seven to nine shillings a week, are an obvious improve-
> ment on the ordinary abominable English 'model-house' plan of reaching one room
> through another. 'Ebury Buildings' are happily provided with small entrance lobbies,
> affording some reasonable privacy for the poor inmates, who perhaps appreciate it even
> more than their wealthier neighbours. But the plan of even this improved block is very
> far from perfect: we found the parents' bed-room entered solely from the common parlor
> or living-room . . .[45]

'The poor . . .' wrote 'An Unbeneficed District Surveyor' in the same journal, 'crowd into the model houses; though hardly any of them are satisfactorily planned; making as they usually do, scant provision for the poor man's privacy'.[46] The unpopularity of the block dwellings was ascribed to their incompatibility with privacy and the separateness of family life. 'The working classes do not care for them,' asserted the *Building News* in 1896:

> However well constructed, the tenement block has not been appreciated – one main
> reason being the want of an independent street entrance, and the separate playground.
> Sentiment also has something to do with the dislike to the huge block. Every family is
> merely a fraction of a great whole, and is under a kind of control which is uncongenial to
> the working man's independence of action.[47]

Some critics questioned the desirability of segregating the poor and concentrating them in model dwellings.[48] Others protested against the regimentation which seemed an inescap-able aspect of block living. 'The gigantic commercial lodging-house scheme has . . . not answered expectations, any more than the gigantic hotel enterprise did,' concluded the *Building News* in 1883. '. . . What with enormous flats of tenements, the system of middle-

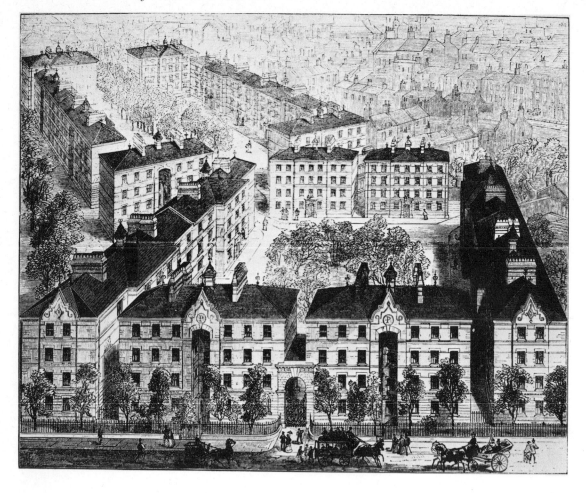

85 'Not only did they put carefully selected
groups of working-class families and individuals
under one roof where they could be supervised
and improved more effectively, but they were a
way of separating the respectable, deserving poor
from their unregenerate brothers and sisters.'
Peabody Square model dwellings, Blackfriars
Road.

men and the big coffee-room, with all the evils of a regime half mechanical and half military, the system has quite failed to meet with the sympathy of the people.'[49]

COTTAGE ESTATES

If blocks of model dwellings were the most original and visible responses to the problem of providing decent housing for the poor, the philanthropic cottage estates more accurately reflected the values of middle-class reformers. If the first were the prototypes of the modern block of council flats, the latter prefigured the twentieth-century council estate. The first was an attempt to develop a novel architectural form for the housing of a particular class of people; the second was an attempt to adapt the existing forms of middle-class suburbia to the needs of the working class. As such, the model estates indicate just what suburban qualities were regarded as so important that they had to be incorporated into a development stripped down to its essentials.

Opponents and proponents alike of suburban housing estates for the working classes agreed that the criterion for judging their value was the extent to which they strengthened family ties. Leslie Sutton argued in 1861 that they would weaken them:

> To compel the working classes to live at a distance from where they are employed is to impose upon them unnecessary expenditure, to impair family relations, and to encourage drunkenness. If a man cannot go home to his dinner he is in that respect keeping two establishments and compelled to incur additional outlay, while he is driven to an eating-house, or worse – a public house, where habits of estrangement from home are gradually fostered and a tendency to indulge in strong drinks encouraged.[50]

The *Building News* also thought that suburban living posed a threat to the working-class family:

> . . . Probably the greatest mischief that would result from the expulsion of the working classes to remote distances from the metropolis, would be the heavy tax it would impose, and the gradually weakening of family ties which it would introduce. Suppose the case of a city porter or a longshore man, or an operative, dwelling five or ten miles from London – the scene of his daily labors. He must lose time in railway travelling . . . and loss of time . . . is loss of money. . . . Further, the operative must take his dinner and tea from home – that is to say incur additional expense, and it is greatly to be feared, if he be fond of company and deficient in resolution, that he may be tempted to forsake his home and keep late hours.

To segregate the working classes into special districts could lead to a dangerous rise in class consciousness: 'The demarcation of classes is an enormous evil,' it warned; 'it creates class hatreds, and may at any time fan discontent into rebellion or revolution, as it has done ere now.'[51] Octavia Hill also opposed the tendency to concentrate the poor in homogeneous districts:

> . . . Miss HILL . . . warns the public against the consequence of creating colonies of poor

people in the neighbourhood of London, and recommends that there should be some deliberation before compulsory powers of purchase are granted, by which large bodies of the poor shall be forced *en masse* to migrate to suburbs where they will form necessarily new and numerous districts like the East End – that is, where acres and acres of houses are occupied exclusively by the poor.[52]

Most observers, though, thought a suburban cottage would strengthen the working-class family as much as the suburban villa strengthened the middle-class one. The *Building News* in 1892 called for an extension of the provision of cheap workmen's trains on such grounds:

Anything that will tend to encourage the working classes to go out into the suburbs rather than swell the already overcrowded metropolitan districts must be for the benefit not only of the working men themselves, but also the general community. In town a man gets a few small rooms in a densely populated neighbourhood; in the suburbs he can have his own house and garden . . . In town he gets a filthy compound in lieu of the breath of heaven, and if the atmosphere of the suburbs does not quite come up to rural standard, it is yet far superior to the air in mid-London. Out of town the working man's Sabbath may be a far better-spent day than otherwise. His wife may not have public washhouses whereat to cleanse the weekly linen heap; but she has her own copper and back garden for the necessary laundry operations. Workmen's trains are indeed one of the boons of the century, being a real blessing to the poorer section of workers in town, and one worth all the other imaginary benefits gained by agitation put together. It is surprising how artisans now move about backwards and forwards to their work. It seems now no uncommon thing for the majority of the workmen on a job to go daily, say, from South to North London and back, and it is pleasant to think that craftsmen and others one daily sees are living comfortably in their own clean homes and not suffering from the misery of overcrowded tenements.[53]

The segregated housing estates, whether speculative or philanthropic, that grew up in the mid to late-Victorian suburbs, with their comparatively high rents, were for the most part occupied by the skilled artisan classes. The *Architect* for 1874 observed that 'the journeymen of Maudslay's, or Cubitts', constituted 'a class of men who can contrive to have their modest establishment in the outskirts of the town, as if they were a sort of aristocracy of working people, collecting in a crowd at the railway station conveniently enough at half-past five in the morning, or a little earlier', just as their betters would be three hours or more later, 'and leaving their wives and youngsters comfortably at home till . . . half-past six, or a little later . . .'. It thought 'suburban townships' like Shaftesbury Park in Battersea an admirable arrangement for that class of family, affording them 'at the same time better air and cheaper land . . . with something like the benefits of country life'.[54] 'Results have shown that the well-to-do working-man or city clerk with small means prefers to take a two-storied dwelling with a sufficient area of ground in the rear, than to rent a flat,' argued the *Building News* in 1892:

In London we have ample proof of this preference. The many-storied blocks of dwellings are tenanted by single men or those with small families; the six or seven-roomed dwellings in our suburbs, such as those at Plaistow, Leytonstone, Loughborough Junction, are occupied by thousands who can just manage to pay out of their incomes the cost of a moderate railway journey.[55]

Speculators had for decades been providing houses of varying quality for the more prosperous of the working classes, but philanthropically funded building estates came only with the sixties. An early example was provided at Milkwood Road, Brixton, near the Herne Hill station of the London, Chatham and Dover, on 24 acres leased by the Suburban Village and General Dwellings Company in 1868. The railway provided cheap fares to Victoria, Blackfriars, and Holborn Viaduct for the new residents.[56] The company proposed to buy 'estates in all the suburbs near to and having direct railway connexion with London, and erect thereon complete villages'. Its cottages were to have 'from four to eight rooms with every domestic convenience, each house to have a piece of garden ground'. The notion that eight-room houses would be suitable for the occupation of working-class families was unrealistic, and a continuation of the London practice of building houses so large that they had to be divided into separate lodgings. 'Educational establishments, etc., will be provided, as also a limited number of shops.'[57]

The *Building News* commented on the proposal in 1866:

We are glad to learn that it is not intended to erect this village in unsightly, barrack-looking blocks, or to build up dull, monotonous ranges of inferior streets; but to have a variety of structures, adapted alike to the clerk and artizan, as well as to the everyday labourer; and by every sanitary improvement to make them . . . the abodes of cleanliness, comfort, and health. Dr. Burns anticipates the direct benefits will be rentals at least 20 or 30 per cent. below what is paid in our over-crowded and dirty London districts; the means of easy, frequent, and cheap access to town; houses giving from three to six rooms to the people, according to their need and means; with a direct purpose that there shall be secured to them all possible educational and moral advantages.[58]

The emphasis placed on health, the linking of educational and moral with sanitary ends, the intention to provide dwellings suitable for all groups from that of the clerk down to the unskilled labourer, and the stress on the value of architectural variety are all worthy of note. If the expectation that this type of development would directly benefit the poorest of the working classes proved a forlorn hope, the other aims typified the aspirations of all Victorian housing reform movements.

In March 1869 the Earl of Shaftesbury laid the first stone in the building of the Loughborough Park estate of the Suburban Village and General Dwellings Company, between Coldharbour Lane and the east side of Loughborough Junction.[59] The *Architect* reported that the houses, 'built in ornamental brick', would contain from six to ten rooms:

Lord Shaftesbury . . . dwelt upon . . . the enormous benefits which must accrue to the working men from having clean, well-ventilated, and wholesome dwellings, instead of being huddled together as they now were in crowded sties, the very atmosphere of which

86 *top* '"Heavy and monotonous . . . having all the pretensions of warehouses and barracks . . ."' Beaconsfield Buildings, model dwellings at Stroud Vale, Islington.

87 *above* '"It is surprising how artisans now move about backwards and forwards to their work."' Arrival of workmen's train at Victoria Station, 1865.

so depressed the vital system that drinking and all its hideous train of vices were almost forced upon the poor.

The emphasis the Victorians placed on ventilation and their conviction that intemperance played a central role in depressing the state of the poor are here curiously linked.

> He believed in the goodness of the scheme, as he believed in the excellency of most of the efforts which were now fortunately being made for the benefit of the artisan and mechanic, and all the upper class of handicraftsmen, and he thought the day was not far distant when as classes they could be pointed to as models of frugality, temperance, and industry.[60]

The company had given up the pretence that the estate would be occupied by any but the aristocracy of labour. Lord Shaftesbury's emphasis on the moral effect which the estate would have on its occupants is typical of Victorian environmentalism and their conviction that any real improvement in the lives of the poor would have to come from their own efforts as individuals. Better housing and the thrift necessary for house-ownership were means to their moral regeneration.

The company failed, and the plot was taken over by a private firm, the Milkwood Hall Estate, 'for the erection of a good class of houses . . . .'.[61] The *Architect* reported the following year that the estate was 'now almost covered with buildings, several hundreds of houses, suitable for tradesmen and others, together with large shops, having been erected within the last twelve months . . . .'.[62] W.S. Clarke, writing in 1881, described the majority of the houses on the Milkwood estate as 'very attractive and neat-looking . . .'. It was 'designed to suit moderate purses, the average rent being about 30*l*'. West of the railway were to be found other 'small houses of a similar character, while at Herne Hill, which is now becoming as thickly populated as Loughborough, is a host of houses also mostly of a small size'.[63]

The Artizans', Labourers', and General Dwellings Company was more successful in its efforts to build cottage estates for the working classes, although here, too, the beneficiaries were artisans rather than the very poor. Founded in 1867, its first major endeavour was the creation of the Shaftesbury Park estate on 40 acres lying between Lavender Hill and the railway line running east from Clapham Junction.[64] 'This estate . . . is now laid out in a series of oblong blocks or terraces, for the erection of 1,200 houses . . .' reported the *Builder* in 1873:

> The design of the houses partakes somewhat of the domestic Gothic or Tudor, though no particular style has been strictly followed by the architect. The houses are built in four grades, containing five, six, seven, and eight rooms respectively. The rents range from 5s.6d. to 9s.6d. per week, including rates and taxes; or, if the houses are purchased by the occupiers, the prices are from 150*l*. to 300*l*. each house. . . . The streets throughout the estate are to be planted with trees . . . forming miniature boulevards. About three acres have been reserved in the centre of the estate for recreative purposes, and a gymnasium. The estate will have its own schools, library, and baths. A site has also been reserved for a co-operative store. . . . A distinctive feature is that there are to be no public houses . . . and this feature, it is said, is highly approved by the working men themselves.[65]

The estate later reversed its policy as to sales, and reserved all its houses for letting on weekly tenancies.[66] The *Builder*, inspecting Shaftesbury Park in 1874, found 'long straight ranges of two-story buildings, varied by hoods over the doors, and occasional turrets . . . Externally, the houses seem well built, and have a very respectable appearance. There is a temporary lecture-room at the commencement of the estate.'[67] The *Building News* was more critical:

Out of a dreary waste south of Battersea Park not long since a low, swampy flat, over which the Thames periodically flowed, and cut off by a network of railways on one side, and on the other by the Wandsworth-road, has sprung up . . . a new neighbourhood – an 'artisans' city'. . . .

The houses are built in close-set rows, the entrances being in pairs, and the offices at the back forming semi-detached projections in the ordinary manner. Taking a first-class dwelling . . . we enter a passage . . . leading to a front room about 11 ft. 3 in. by 11 ft. 4 in., exclusive of a small bay-window. . . . The back room is about 12 ft. by 10 ft. 9 in. . . . the kitchen is about 9 ft. by 8 ft. . . . and opens into a small scullery or washhouse, fitted with a galvanised iron copper and a sink. Coals are provided for under the stairs. Upstairs there are three bedrooms . . . besides a small back room as bathroom, with a tap. The rooms are well lighted, and ventilated by valved air-gratings . . . The joinery and fittings . . . are certainly of a praiseworthy description . . . The rent of these 'eight-roomed,' or, rather, seven-roomed, houses is £26 – higher than we expected to find on this estate. Including the rates and taxes, the total annual cost will, we think, be above the figure the ordinary artisan can afford.

The three lesser rates of houses were all without bathrooms and proportionally smaller and lower in rent.

Generally, the construction appears to be sound . . . We should have preferred semi-detached blocks in some parts . . . The roads are narrow; the footpaths . . . are narrow . . . in regard to the anticipations of those who looked upon the estate as one in which a great deal more of the rural element might have been blended. Still there are many re-deeming points; the houses seem to be all taken by tenants who regard their own cleanli-ness and sobriety. There is a quiet and pleasing air of comfort about the place. . . .

Laudable endeavours to break the monotony of the houses have been attempted by the architect, in the form of projecting oriels and towers, capped by embattled parapets and steep-pointed roofs. They certainly to a degree take off the weariness of a long street . . .

More than half the estate is already built and occupied, and we are informed there is a continual influx of comers, both as tenants and purchasers.[68]

In 1877 Baxter Langley and William Swindlehurst, respectively chairman and secretary of the company, were sentenced for fraud at the Old Bailey 'for making illicit profits from the purchase of the Queens Park Estate [in Willesden] and for taking commissions for the purchase of goods and excessive prices . . . Despite angry protests, rents at Shaftesbury Park were raised twice in the year and the central open space built over.'[69]

W.S. Clarke commented in 1881 on 'the spirit of neatness and love for horticulture which all the tenants seem to have', at Shaftesbury Park. Although the ground was 'somewhat low . . . we do not know a more desirable place for a man with a small family and small means . . . Some agitation was recently caused by the raising of the rents, but even at the present enhanced prices they compare favourably with those surrounding the estate.' He found the houses 'prettily designed, though the repetition of the same pattern would somewhat pall, were it not that variety is introduced by the floral display which each occupant seems called upon to make'.[70]

The next project of the company was Queen's Park, an 80-acre site on the Harrow Road purchased from All Souls College, Oxford, and designed to accommodate no fewer than 16,000 residents.[71] '. . . Already, when not a single brick has been laid, applications for upwards of 1,000 houses have been made,' reported the *Architect* in 1874:

> The estate . . . will be made as attractive as possible. Four out of the eighty acres will be appropriated in the centre to a garden and recreation ground; the roads and streets will be planted . . . with trees, and special inducements will be offered to the inhabitants to lay out the gardens both front and back in as tasteful a manner as their time and means will permit. . . . The lecture-hall and institute will be a large building, and there will be co-operative stores, coal depôt, dairy farm, baths and wash-houses . . . There is to be no publichouse . . . and . . . every opportunity will be taken to promote and develop temperance principles. Reading rooms, discussion clubs, libraries, and other substitutes for the public-house will be a marked feature.[72]

The *Builder* reported that the houses would contain from five to eight rooms, and the rents would range from 5s.9d. per week to 26*l*. per year.[73]

A letter to the editor of the *Building News* described the condition of Queen's Park in 1883, noting in particular the prevalence of subletting:

> Publicans and pawnbrokers there are none, sinners are guarded against by a high standard of credentials in writing, and the rent must be paid 'in advance.' . . . The 1st, 2nd, and 3rd classes [of houses] are mostly occupied by *two* families, and in every alternate window there is a card 'Rooms to Let,' 'Unfurnished Apartments,' &c. The 4th and 5th classes are not so as a rule, but in them 'Young Men,' 'Single Men,' 'Respectable Men,' are in great demand. The houses are certainly better built than the typical 'speculator' would have the heart to do. The drainage is good, and the streets are 'well kept'; but as regards rents, they are about equal to the average suburban cottage of their respective classes . . .[74]

Later that year the *Building News* reported the completion of the houses on the estate, built at a total cost of £700,000.[75]

'. . . There is great competition for these houses . . .' Booth wrote of Queen's Park in 1899.[76] 'The occupants are of the regularly employed class: railway men or police, artisans, small clerks, and others.' The estate provided the same sort of retreat from urban temptations that the middle-class suburb did, not only public houses but cookshops and restaurants being excluded. 'The streets are very quiet at night; it is a district of home-life and of comfort; if other pleasures are sought they are found elsewhere, as is also the daily work of all the men.'[77]

The third major project of the company was the Noel Park estate at Hornsey. The *Builder* in 1883 reported the laying of the corner stone of one of the streets by the inevitable Lord Shaftesbury. A total of 2,600 houses, ranging from four to eight rooms, were planned, at a rental from 6s. to 11s.6d. weekly:

> The Hornsey estate . . . will compare favourably with any workmen's colony that we know. . . . It is expected that within four or five years the land will all be covered, and it is intended to build a very large proportion of fourth and fifth class houses in order to meet the great demand among the poorer members of the industrial classes for houses which they can afford to occupy without the necessity of taking in lodgers.[78]

Such expectations proved premature, and building was suspended in 1887. The Great Eastern Railway refused to issue workmen's tickets from the adjacent Green Lanes Station, offering instead third-class monthly season tickets at a 25 per cent reduction. The General Manager explained that the railway's policy was against 'the granting of these workmen's tickets from any other districts than those from whence they issue at the present time'. To issue them from Green Lanes 'would do us a very large amount of injury, and would cause the same public annoyance and inconvenience . . . as exists already upon the Stamford Hill and Walthamstow lines.' The more expensive tickets would attract 'a better class of people' to Noel Park. He thought that 'no one living in Noel Park could desire to possess the same class of neighbours as the residents of Stamford Hill have in the neighbourhood of St. Anne's Road'.[79] The fares proved too high and the estate too distant to attract enough tenants, and Noel Park was not finally completed until 1929, although most houses had been finished by 1907.[80]

In 1890 the company, after concentrating for several years on the building of blocks of model dwellings in central London, turned its attention again to the suburbs. It purchased Leigham Court at Streatham Hill, an estate of 66 acres, on which it proposed to build 1600 workmen's cottages similar to those on its earlier estates.[81] The *Building News* thought it an unwarranted invasion of middle-class territory:

> The residents of Streatham Hill must deplore the recent spoliation of the fine wooded park belonging to Leigham Court . . . Why such a locality should have been selected for the purpose of dwellings for the working classes, so far away as it is from the centre of their labour, and right in the midst of a superior residential neighbourhood, we cannot imagine. It is a great pity this beautiful site should not have been secured for a different class of residences . . .[82]

Actually the Leigham Court estate was designed for a somewhat higher class than Shaftesbury Park or Queen's Park. Its houses, for instance, all had fitted baths. On the other hand the company provided 539 maisonettes and 18 flats as well as 427 separate houses, thereby retreating from its earlier intention to make an individual house, however small, available for all its tenants. For whatever reason, it found it harder to attract tenants to Streatham Hill and Hornsey than it had to Battersea and Willesden.[83]

PROPOSED LIBRARY AND WORKING MEN'S CLUB

VIEW IN ELSEY ROAD

88 *top* 'The *Builder*, inspecting Shaftesbury Park in 1874, found "long straight ranges of two-story buildings, varied by hoods over the doors, and occasional turrets . . .".' Shaftesbury Park Estate, Battersea.

89 *above* '"Why such a locality should have been selected for the purpose of dwellings for the working classes . . . right in the midst of a superior residential neighbourhood, we cannot imagine."' Streatham Hill.

By the end of the century the general rise in the standard of living, the extension of tramways, soon to be electrified, the prospect of tube railways, and the great increase in the number of workmen's train services suggested that in the future suburban living would no longer be confined to the middle and artisan classes. The decision of local authorities to build working-class housing not only raised the question whether they were to take the form of model blocks or separate cottages, but whether they should be built in central London or in the outskirts. 'The housing of the working classes is one of the many vital questions awaiting the decision of our municipal authorities,' observed the *Building News* in 1899:

> By the large areas that have been opened by street and other improvements, an immense population of the poorer classes have to be provided for. The question whether they are to be housed in buildings near the old sites, or are to be provided for in our suburban districts, is one of great importance, not only to the classes themselves, but to the residents of our fast-filling suburbs. The extension of the tramway system, and the proposal to keep the cars running through the night, as well as the facilities afforded by the completion of the Central London and other underground railways, seem to favour the erection of dwellings in outlying districts; but the result is not reassuring, as the effect of these erections is likely to drive the commercial and professional citizens further out. . . . The high-block system is an eyesore to any suburb, as can be proved by anyone going to Camberwell, Brixton, Fulham, and other localities.[84]

Later the same year it reported the decision of the London County Council to build an estate of 1,200 houses at Tooting Common, to be let at 4s. and 5s. per week.[85] The future policy of the Council, which would so transform both the suburbs of London and the lives of vast numbers of Londoners in the twentieth century, was already being set. The *Architect* mused on the implications of such a policy:

> It has yet to be seen whether the working classes who have become habituated to residence in town would be satisfied with suburban quarters. . . . No doubt compensation could be found for the excitement of town, but there is no question the British workman is conservative and likes to live near the place where he is occupied. It would, therefore, be well to consider the erection of houses beyond the limits of towns as an experiment, and before launching into extensive operations like those proposed by the London County Council, to watch the effects on the first tenants and to be guided by experience. The working classes are not to be coerced even for their own advantage.[86]

But of course the working classes had been coerced for their own advantage as far back as anyone could remember. That was what Victorian philanthropy was all about.

Twentieth-century social policy would pursue similar lines. The new council estates would be Shaftesbury and Queen's and Noel Parks on a grander scale, farther out, with rising standards of space, amenities, and perhaps even architectural excellence. Residence would no longer be confined to the aristocracy of labour; public houses, while few and far between, would not be banned as a matter of principle; and in general the differences – increasingly psychological rather than physical – between middle and working-class neighbourhoods would be blurred as affluence worked its way down the social ladder. The suburban experience, with its pattern of commuting, its jealously tended gardens and its separating hedges, its tedium and its isolation, its cosiness and its dominating domesticity would become the normal mode of existence for the Londoner and the Englishman at large. The hopes that the suburb would become the means for the moral and intellectual regeneration of the working classes were not, by and large, to be realized, although the pleasanter middle-class vices have trickled down to corrupt the suburban worker and his family.

CHAPTER SEVEN

Grand Lines of Communication

TRANSPORT AND URBAN GROWTH

The studies of Fogel in America and Dyos and Kellett in England make one hesitate to attribute urban growth to the coming of the railways, or indeed to any changes in the technology of transport. Railway extensions, Kellett has shown, usually followed rather than preceded suburban development, and at best served to reinforce population movements already in progress. Beyond that we must keep in mind that the Victorians, like every generation before them but unlike ours, walked.[1]

If changes in the forms of transport cannot be regarded as a primary cause of urban growth, they did help determine the precise forms such growth took, even if here, too, they reinforced what was already happening. It was the existing artisan population that made it necessary for the Great Eastern Railway to extend its service of workmen's trains far beyond the statutory obligation: but that service in turn encouraged still further working-class migration to the north-eastern suburbs.

New road schemes, too, succeeded where they adapted themselves to existing flows of traffic and to existing patterns of land-use. The failure of New Oxford Street to participate in the prosperity of its namesake, the failure of the Embankment to relieve the congestion of the Strand and Fleet Street suggest, quite as much as the total failure of the West London Railway in the 50's to attract passengers, or indeed any sort of business, that London has a mind of its own, pursuing inscrutable ends according to a logic that eludes the cleverest entrepreneurs and planners.

Whether the new bridges and thoroughfares, railways and steamboat lines, omnibuses and tramways that intersected Victorian London in increasingly complex patterns are to be regarded more as causes or as symptoms of more fundamental organic changes, they undeniably represented the most startling novelties in the London environment. They contributed not only visual shocks but movement, unfamiliar noises and smells, and altered both the pace and the rhythm of urban life.

STREET IMPROVEMENTS

It will help to understand the enthusiasm with which the Victorians went about cutting new roads and at the same time widening and straightening old ones if we bear in mind that, to people of taste and discernment, roads were good, railways bad. 'The greatest danger to the

health of London, to its architectural appearance, and convenience for traffic, is to be appre-
hended from the penetration of railways,' exclaimed the *Building News* in 1860. 'If the capital
is to be anything more than a mere railway station and goods depôt, it is high time that a
system should be devised for the restraint and guidance of railway engineers and projectors.'[2]
New streets, on the other hand, were unalloyed blessings:

> Railways do not, like the Holborn Viaduct and the Thames Embankment, give us open
> new streets in exchange for narrow, close, and unhealthy old ones; nor do they, like the
> Viaduct and the Embankment, bring into favourable prominence fine old structures,
> formerly hidden in narrow streets, or create favourable sites for new public edifices. . . .
> A line of railway passing through a vast city such as London causes incalculable evil: it
> not only defaces existing thoroughfares, but renders the creation of good new ones
> impracticable for all time.[3]

Today, of course, it is just the opposite. In order to understand the emotional response to
schemes for new metropolitan railways we must remember the reaction to the proposed
motorway box of a few years ago: vehemently opposed by all lovers of the good, the true,
and the beautiful. In Victorian London proposals for cutting through new thoroughfares
evoked the same automatic responses that proposals for improved mass transit systems
receive today: instinctively favourable ones from environmentalists, extreme scepticism
from those who perceive their impact on municipal budgets and the level of rates. As a result
we build destructive urban motorways today but feel guilty about them, and dream of
high-speed, non-polluting urban railways: the Victorians built railways but knew in their
hearts that roads were better. Much the same sentimental energy that goes today into railway
preservation societies then went into books about old coaching inns and 'the romance of
the road'.

Insofar as street improvements destroyed the existing urban fabric that was one more
advantage: since the urban fabric was, after all, usually nothing but the hated inheritance of
Georgian London. New roads provided new building sites, and the occasion for more
contemporary architecture to mitigate and mask the dullness of the Georgian city. To an
age obsessed with ventilation, broad, straight avenues brought life-enhancing country
breezes.

In 1815 wide, straight streets existed for the most part within fashionable residential
quarters, comparatively unencumbered with traffic. The main north-south and east-west
routes and the principal business and shopping streets were narrow and irregular, and if
occasionally of reasonable width were sure to turn abruptly into a narrow bottleneck. Even
the main roads leading out of the central built-up area – like the Kensington Road and its
western extensions – were subject to sudden narrowings and turns that impeded through
traffic.

Some of the schemes proceeded with all deliberate speed. Others went forward in a
piecemeal and sporadic fashion, as leases of property along the route expired. Some had to
wait until the new century to be completed; others remain unfinished to this day. If the

cumulative effect was enormous, at any given time Londoners were more aware of the persistence of some old impediments to circulation than the removal of others, and perhaps most conscious of the disruption caused by improvement schemes being carried out. The *Daily News* thus described the upheaval produced by the improvements going on in the City in the sixties:

> For some years past a very large section of the City has been in possession of surveyors and masons, undergoing processes of demolition and reconstruction; familiar thoroughfares have been closed, familiar streets have disappeared in clouds of dust, familiar lines of traffic have been diverted into tortuous byways, and one of the chief thoroughfares of the metropolis has been a fine high road through a waste and howling wilderness, with a long vista of hoarding stretching on either side, and behind it ruin and desolation. But the inconvenience has been borne in faith. The present has been put to trouble that the future might profit, and now we stand on the threshold of that future. . . . at length the promise of a new London is ripe for realisation.[4]

Throughout the century the cry was that London was about to be choked to death by its traffic: it never was, but then neither did any of the street improvements visibly reduce congestion, much less inaugurate the New Jerusalem that was regularly predicted. In the nineteenth century as in the twentieth, traffic increased to crowd the facilities designed to ease it.

If Regent Street was derided for its architecture, it was universally admired as an example of traffic engineering. If in its latter aspect it was not more imitated than it was, it was for want of funds, not want of will. Most of the principal thoroughfares and many subsidiary streets in the City and West End today – Charing Cross Road, Shaftesbury Avenue, Queen Victoria Street, Cranbourn Street, Northumberland Avenue, and Holborn Viaduct to name a few – were Victorian improvements. Other, older thoroughfares, such as the Strand and Fleet Street, were widened and straightened. Whenever possible street improvements were planned to pass through congested and insanitary districts, partly to minimize the cost of acquiring property, but also so that they could combine the ends of speeding traffic and demolishing slums.

Thus Victoria Street was designed to 'join the Vauxhall-road, and materially widen the vicinity of Buckingham Palace', but in connection, 'the "rookery" which has existed for so many centuries in Westminster, Tothill-street, York-street, and Castle-lane, is all to come down . . .'.[5] The building of New Oxford Street was the occasion for the demolition of the most notorious slum in the western part of London:

> The locality called the Rookery, which is situate on the line of the new street that is to connect Oxford-street and Holborn . . . and which for many years has been the resort of the abandoned of both sexes, is about to be removed for the improvements in this neighbourhood. Sixty houses . . . have been sold by private contract . . . The purchaser of the property . . . has great difficulty in getting rid of the inmates, and in some of the houses, though the roofs have been taken off, they still remain.[6]

Some critics pointed out that abolishing slums did nothing to abolish poverty, but simply moved the poor from one congested district to increase the overcrowding in another. 'I cannot conceive,' the Duke of Bedford wrote in 1844, 'what becomes of all the poor people who are compelled to leave their houses and lodgings for the improvements of the town.'[7] Or as the *Building News* pointed out in 1883: 'Desirable as reconstruction is, it may prove less of a boon to the poorer class of tenants. Rebuilding often means overcrowding. . . . We widen the streets, but we condense the dwellings.'[8]

Yet the customary early-Victorian response to such demolitions was one of satisfaction. William Gaspey thought New Oxford Street an unmixed blessing:

New Oxford-street, a splendid pile of buildings similar in character to the erections in Regent-street, is of recent date, and has arisen upon courts and narrow streets in the rear of Holborn, Broad-street, and High-street, St. Giles. To form the more western portion of it, an execrable neighbourhood has been cleared away . . . familiarly known as the *Rookery*. This labyrinth of dark and dismal alleys was, perhaps, not only the most wretched, but the most disreputable district in London. There, ventilation, sewerage, cleanliness, were sanitary adjucts totally unknown . . . which metropolitan *Inferno* disappearing, in its place and on its site New Oxford-street, nearly the most magnificent street in the capital, arose in 1847. . . . surely in this instance it must be admitted that speculation has been employed at least as much for the benefit of the public as for that of the projectors, by removing every vestige of a noisome neighbourhood, and substituting in lieu thereof a spacious open street, abounding in all those salubrious and other advantages, never experienced by or contemplated in its gloomy precursor.[9]

Traffic congestion seems to have been at least as annoying to the Victorians as it is today. 'To a freshman from the country there is nothing more amazing throughout the metropolis . . . than its teeming population and vehicular traffic,' wrote the *Building News* in 1866.[10] 'How to get from one part of the town to another without loss of time, temper, and money, is one of the social problems of the day, apparently the most difficult of solution,' the same journal observed in 1858:

City men who live in the distant suburbs of the metropolis are compelled to lose at least an hour each way in going to and from business every day. Inhabitants of the West-end, when called to the east side of Temple-bar, brace up their nerves to run the gauntlet of all sorts of annoyances. . . . If Jones is called over to the Continent on business, ten to one but he is blockaded in Fleet-street until he misses the train. . . .

There is no denying the fact . . . that our system, or rather disorganisation of street traffic is a monster nuisance to everybody . . . Ten years ago we were told it was too bad and could not last. To-day it is a hundredfold worse, with greater chances of enduring another decimal period in a more malignant form. Already the retail trade in the City suffers materially from the periodical congestion of traffic . . . Foot passengers can scarcely venture to cross our more crowded thoroughfares without risk to life or limb.[11]

The still essentially mediaeval street pattern of the City, combined with its vastly increased

90 '"For some years past
a very large section of the
City has been in possession
of surveyors and masons,
undergoing processes of
demolition and recon-
struction . . ."' Works
for Holborn Viaduct,
1860's.

commercial importance and daytime population, made street improvements there especially pressing. The barriers to east-west traffic were particularly frustrating.

Certainly the most conspicuous and aesthetically the most satisfactory of the street improvements of the Metropolitan Board of Works was the Thames Embankment. The *Times* in 1868, shortly before it opened, predicted that it would significantly ease London's traffic problem by enabling vehicles to avoid the congested Strand and Fleet Street route to the City:

> The two chief centres of life in London are now the City and Westminster, and the transaction of business – which means the maintenance of the activity of the Empire – depends on the communication between those two centres. At present they are united by an indirect, a tortuous, an obstructed, and a narrow lane, which it is a mockery to call a thoroughfare. If the streets of a city may be compared to the veins of a complex animal, the Strand constitutes a kind of aneurism in the most vital part of the body.[12]

Yet in the event traffic perversely refused to desert its accustomed streams for the Embankment route. 'Practically speaking, the Embankment is a desert, scarcely recognised among Metropolitan highways . . .' exclaimed the *Building News* in 1874:

> The metropolis acquired a splendid thoroughfare, reared on foundations of Roman solidity, a hundred feet wide, protected by a handsome parapet, with two side-walks and an ample carriage-way, admirably paved . . . While Fleet-street is gorged, crowded from end to end, with the pole of one omnibus threatening the door of another, ponderous waggons turning at every hundred yards out of court, inn, or alley, a dislocated line of vehicles wriggling its way along, light carts and railway-vans making a Hellespont of the Middle Passage, and no safety or expedition from point to point of the encumbered gorge . . . a few foreigners or country people, or Hansoms with uncommonly knowing drivers, have the Embankment almost entirely to themselves . . . what proportion of the traffic has turned itself aside from the Strand or Fleet-street to rattle lightly over its . . . pavement? Scarcely any. It is as though a police prohibition closed the passage.[13]

The *Builder* in 1882 remarked on 'the loneliness and desertion that reign after dark' along the Embankment, 'except to a few stray foot-passengers, a few rattling hansom-cabs, and a few heavy wagons and drays . . .'. Anticipating Jane Jacobs, it observed that 'the gaiety of the shops [in the Strand] . . . attract[s] more than the silence of the electrically lighted Embankment – the brilliant light only serving to enhance the darkness'.[14]

There was no question as to the success in easing traffic flow of the other great improvement of the sixties: the Holborn Viaduct, spanning the ancient valley of the Fleet. '. . . The Holborn Valley Viaduct ranks second to no work which the Metropolis can boast as the production of the present century,' exulted the *Architect* in 1869.[15] The *Daily News* was equally enthusiastic:

> . . . A magnificent level roadway stretches across the valley, along which the great stream of traffic will run unhindered. The saving of wear and tear to man, horse, and vehicle, the

91 *top* '"*New Oxford-street*, a splendid pile of buildings similar in character to the erections in Regent-street, is of recent date . . ."' New Oxford Street, 1847.

92 *above* '"Already the retail trade in the City suffers materially from the periodical congestion of traffic . . ."' The Royal Exchange, 1897.

saving of time, and we may even add, the saving of life, will altogether make this improve-ment the greatest ever made in the metropolis. . . . We go now in a straight line where before there was a curve, glide easily along the arc of a bow instead of going down one dip of the curve and up the other. With this Viaduct open, the great line of thoroughfares from the Marble Arch to the Post-Office will be the finest line of street in London.[16]

It might have been expected that building new streets through both the City and the West End would have been profitable investments, and that the initial expense, though high, would have been compensated for by the greatly increased value of the new building sites created. This had proved to be so in Regent Street, and would be in Northumberland Avenue, and it was in at least the earlier new streets Haussmann had built in Paris; but it was for the most part not true in London: most of the Victorian street improvements, whatever their social benefits, proved economic failures. G. Herbert West explained why it was more hazardous to create new streets in London than in Paris to the Royal Institute of Architects in 1871:

> The difference in the nature of the traffic of the two cities is such that in London you cannot drive streets at haphazard through old quarters of the town and be sure of their bringing in a profit upon the outlay. In Paris, if they form a new street in which the ground-floors of the houses are shops, as is almost invariably the case, they are sure to meet with occupiers, and the upper floors will let in flats. So there is sure to be a good return on the money spent. But if you were to drive a new street through Drury-lane, you may be quite certain no one would live there; shop-keepers would not take the shops, and the houses would not let in flats, or as respectable lodgings, but the street would re-main as poor as before. In Paris . . . you are sure to have a traffic through the street, for Paris is a round city, while London is a long city. Our great avenues of traffic are by Oxford-street and the Strand; that in the other streets goes in no particular direction, but in Paris wherever you drive a new street you are sure to have traffic through it, since it forms one of the radii of a circle. This is clearly seen in comparing the omnibus maps of Paris with those of London. . . . In London you may have passage streets, but nothing more, however good the houses may be. In Paris you are certain to have a street more or less of palaces . . .[17]

Even Holborn Viaduct, occupying a strategic position along a well-established through route, took some years to attract investors. The *Architect* described it as still a 'vast extent of waste howling wilderness' in 1872.[18]

The economic failure of New Oxford Street was notorious. 'It is only within recent years that the property has been at all a success,' Robert Vigers told a select committee of the House of Lords in 1894. 'When the houses (in New Oxford Street) were built they were occupied for short times. People went bankrupt in the street. . . . it was a great failure.'[19] It had been expected that it would share in the prosperity of Holborn and Oxford Street. 'That has never yet been the case,' Edward Tewson reminded the same committee. 'The buildings in New Oxford Street have never yet realised the rents even now . . . which were

93 'Certainly the most conspicuous . . . of the
street improvements of the Metropolitan Board
of Works was the Thames Embankment.'
Making the Victoria Embankment, 1864.

realised and are realised by the premises in Oxford Street and in Holborn.' Victoria Street similarly failed to live up to its promise:

> . . . Victoria Street, Westminster . . . also remains to this day unfinished. I have offered myself, only a few months ago, one of the largest sites in Victoria Street for sale, and failed to find a buyer. . . . there is scarcely a building in that street that has been a success and that has paid the owner a reasonable interest on his outlay.

Queen Victoria Street had also disappointed investors: 'Enormous sums of money were spent on the buildings all through that street, and . . . many very heavy losses have been sustained . . .'.[20] The *Architect* declared, in 1898, that of all the major new streets, only Northumberland Avenue, with its enormous hotels, had made a profit.[21]

With all the new streets, and even with the building of the Metropolitan and District underground systems, London's traffic congestion continued to worsen. New thoroughfares were demanded to alleviate the congestion that earlier improvements had failed to relieve. 'Notoriously, it is more difficult and tedious to get from Bayswater to Whitechapel, from St. John's Wood to Mile End, from Hampstead to Camberwell, than from the Borough to Brighton,' complained the *Building News* in 1874:

> The improvement of London Bridge and its approaches has not to the slightest extent alleviated the daily deadlock from forenoon to evening; the widening of Cannon-street has not lessened the pressure in Cheapside, which is often scarcely better than impassable; and nothing has come . . . of the several schemes propounded; tunneled streets; streets carried on iron frames; continuous balconies; house-to-house tramways, far above the common level; a central railway terminus, and so forth . . . As to the relations between . . . Middlesex and Surrey, similar remarks apply. Some of the bridges are overthronged, and . . . overweighted, while others appear hardly to serve any general purpose at all. In effect, this metropolis, in the height of the commercial and fashionable season, is choked by its own attractions and its own prosperity, and thoroughfares like Fleet-street or Holborn, Bond-street or Regent-street, are scarcely less passable than Chancery-lane or Fetter-lane.[22]

However inadequate they seemed to critics, street improvements continued, and the road-pattern of central London gradually acquired its present configuration. '. . . A visitor to the Metropolis twenty years ago . . . would now, if he paid a visit, find considerable alterations,' the *Building News* observed in 1889:

> Northwards of Charing-cross he would . . . find a wide and newly-built road stretching from the back of the National Gallery all the way to Oxford-street, instead of the tortuous route through Seven Dials, through purlieus which were always unsavoury . . . A little further to the west he would discover that Piccadilly-circus . . . had disappeared in all but its name. The circus, indeed, only exists in part, while the rest is a wide 'oasis' of paving stones and roadways of no particular form, but very chaotic and bewildering . . .

94 'Even Holborn Viaduct . . . took some years
to attract investors. The *Architect* described it as
still a "vast extent of waste howling wilderness"
in 1872.' Holborn Viaduct, 1869.

the thoroughfares which lead out of Holborn Circus, notably Holborn-viaduct, Farring-don-road, Theobald's-road, and Clerkenwell have made one continuous thoroughfare to the east end. In the neighbourhood of St. Paul's the streets are being widened, and Ludgate-hill – a little while ago a narrow street – is nearly wholly rebuilt on the south side, while Queen Victoria-street carries the southern line of the Embankment to the heart of the City . . . Within the bounds of the City the changes have been chiefly confined to straightening, here and there widening, and in rebuilding old premises. . . . the neighbourhood of London Bridge has put on quite a new aspect with the completion of the line of street from Cannon-street to the Tower.[23]

Most of the old houses on the south side of Ludgate Hill were 'swept away, and in their place stately blocks of business premises have been erected'. In connection the roadway was widened.[24]

The end of the century, despite complaints about the slowness with which street improve-ments were being carried out, saw much rebuilding of metropolitan thoroughfares, and seemed to promise an equally active twentieth century. The *Building News* in 1898 reported the rebuilding of the north side of Leicester Square, the widening of Cranbourn Street, demolition and rebuilding at the Elephant and Castle, the widening of the Oxford Street end of Tottenham Court Road, the widening of the Strand between St Mary-le-Strand and St Clement Danes, and the widening of Southampton Row between High Holborn and Theobald's Road.[25] In the same year Sir J. Wolfe Barry, chairman of the London County Council, told the Society of Arts of ambitious plans for the new century:

To meet the traffic of London it was not so much additional railways, underground or overground . . . that were wanted as wide arterial improvements of the streets themselves. Strictly urban railways only tended to add to the congestion from the point of view of both urban movement and suburban influx. . . . A scheme of new main thoroughfares of adequate width for present and future traffic should be laid down, and realised as time and finance permitted. . . . the provision of means for allowing the north-and-south traffic to cross the east-and-west traffic with the least possible confusion. . . . at places like Hyde-park-corner, Piccadilly-circus, Ludgate-hill, and Wellington-street . . . In the case of the Strand, Fleet-street, and Piccadilly the only course was a systematic widening of all three thoroughfares, with a broad, diagonal street from Piccadilly circus, *via* Coventry-street, to join the widened Strand near Wellington-street. Another want that was beginning to be pressing was a route for bicycle traffic. They wanted one new and spacious thoroughfare east and west, about 120ft. wide. It might leave the Bayswater-road near Westbourne-terrace, follow the line of Wigmore-street to Russell-square . . . and thence run to near Broad-street Station. In addition, there should be two or three thoroughfares north and south, slightly less in width, which should be carried over the east and west route by bridges at the points of intersection, and all these new routes should have a raised or sunken road for bicycles.[26]

Fortunately nothing of the sort took place, although one hears the voice of the modern

95 '"... Victoria Street, Westminster ...
remains to this day unfinished ... there is scarcely
a building in that street that has been a
success ..."' Victoria Street, 1854.

traffic engineer, and visions of motorways and spaghetti junctions pass before our eyes: the fact that they are to be filled with Hansom cabs and bicycles rather than motor cars and lorries gives the vision a certain anachronistic appeal, to be sure. But in our inevitable sorrow at the successful destruction of both Georgian and Victorian London by the twentieth century, we can at least be grateful that most of the grandiose schemes for cutting new roads through central London have remained stillborn.

RAILWAYS

'We, who are constantly in presence of the wondrous results produced by the locomotive and the rail, are apt to pass them by unnoticed, or at least without comment,' remarked the *Building News* in 1862:

> The invasion of the metropolis by the 'Steam Horse' has, during the last quarter of a century, produced changes, not only in the physical features of the metropolis, but also in the manners, customs, mode of living, and even in the thoughts of its inhabitants, which are almost incredible. For a century previous to the year 1834, stagnation was the order of the day; but then came the locomotive into London, and all was changed.[27]

It has become customary to play down the quantitative impact of the railway on Victorian London, pointing out how small a proportion of the population of supposedly railway suburbs actually travelled to and from work by train; and to show how railways, by their demolitions in built-up areas, contributed to rather than alleviated urban crowding.[28] By their salutary challenges to earlier, oversimplified explanations of suburban growth as resulting directly and solely from the building of railways, Dyos and Kellett may have unwittingly contributed to an equally false popular impression that the significance of the railways was – at the outset at least – the wholly malign one of displacing the poor from their homes, congesting the streets, polluting the air, blighting districts through which they passed, and distorting the value and uses of land near their stations and termini. It is only just to remember that they also gave employment – a great deal of it – both in their construction and their operation, that they stimulated and made more efficient the operation of the London economy as a whole, and that they did encourage more people to live farther from the centre than they would have had the omnibus, the short stage coach, and the river boat offered the only alternatives to the horse, the private carriage, and the feet of the suburban-dweller.

That the poor displaced from Agar Town by the St Pancras extension or from Southwark by that to Charing Cross not only failed to benefit but positively suffered in their housing conditions is undeniable. But while it is inaccurate to picture them moving happily into houses vacated by the artisans and middle-class families who did take advantage of the new railway suburbs, it is legitimate to speculate on the congestion of central London and the older, inner suburbs like Islington and Paddington had London's railway network not been built.

Had the outlying suburbs been populated only by the kind of people who did so in the eighteenth century – by those who had retired from active life, by the leisured equivalents

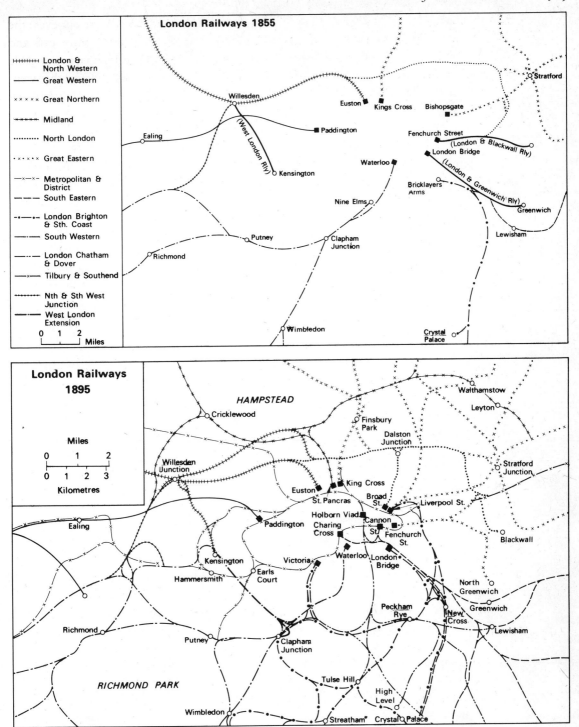

Map VI   London railways in 1855. Seaman,
Life in Victorian London.

Map VII   London railways in 1895. Seaman.

of Mr Robert Ferrars, and by those who could afford private carriages or could crowd into one or another of the horse-drawn public conveyances that served the surrounding villages – it is hard not to imagine central London proving even more congested that it became, with land values and rents even higher than they were. The middle classes, like the railways, both took up a great deal of room and gave a great deal of employment. That room and that employment tended increasingly to be in places like Ealing and Denmark Hill rather than in places like Bloomsbury and Pimlico.

While Kellett is right to remind us that 'only one person in twelve in the southern suburbs used public transport of any sort, railway, tram or omnibus, to get to his work in 1890 . . .' he would be the last to suggest that if that person had not done so, the other eleven would have remained living where they did.[29] Eight of the 12 were non-employed members of the wage-earner's family, and of the three employed locally, it is reasonable to assume that at least one was engaged in providing services for the resident commuter. The proportion of non-commuting residents in middle-class suburbs was far higher than in working-class ones, for the middle-class family demanded more people – both as household servants and in the local service industries – to provide for their needs and comforts:

> . . . The relatively exclusive first class daily travellers . . . though relatively small in numbers, were able to release great potentialities for expansion in the undeveloped rural districts around London . . .
>
> . . . Most of the products required by the family and servants in the mid-Victorian outer suburb were produced locally . . . The money spent with local tradesmen . . . in turn stimulated the growth of local service industry, and drew in further labour from the surrounding countryside.[30]

If middle-class suburbs required a large proportion of resident non-commuters, working-class suburbs provided the largest proportion of daily commuters. Sixty-one per cent of the tenants on the l.c.c. Becontree estate in 1937 worked in central London.[31]

That most Victorians of sensibility themselves either condemned or ignored the railway in their writings may mislead the modern scholar. So may the future reader of journals of opinion of the late twentieth century conclude that everyone today loathes motor cars, and that our system of motorways has been forced on an unwilling public. Just as no one really likes our motorized civilization except the vast majority of the population, so enthusiasm for the steam engine and the iron rail was confined in early Victorian England to those who did not write poetry or periodical essays.

'. . . Cast your eye for a moment on yonder train about to start,' demanded an article in the *New Quarterly* for 1854, 'and answer conscientiously whether it is possible to conceive anything much more clumsy or more thoroughly frightful than the boxes into which some 200 passengers are being stowed, unless it be the snorting and shrieking machine they are about to pursue.'[32] Such was the fashionable contemporary response to what would today attract admiring pilgrims were it on display at York. But assuming that most people find noise more exhilarating than silence, and that speed is inherently appealing, one suspects that the love affair of the British with their trains became very early as intense as those with their horses and their dogs. The *Builder*, many of whose readers were themselves involved in railway construction, did not feel it necessary to muffle its shouts of triumph at each new extension of the iron road. In an article in 1851 celebrating the impact on national life of the cheap excursion train, then still a novelty, it quoted *The Times* with approval: 'Englishmen are beginning to live on railways like Chinese on rivers, or Dutchmen on canals. The rail has an architecture, a *cuisine*, and a literature of its own.'[33]

The railway made possible the existence of a larger London, greater even than Greater London, by facilitating not only residence, but employment, business, and play at distant parts of the kingdom. 'What would London do now without a railway?' asked the *Builder* in 1870. 'What would become of the immense holiday crowds who are regularly whirled over the country, fifty miles and back, in a single day, with "eight hours at the sea-side included", if the railways were suddenly to "shut up shop"?'[34] Brighton and Southend became seaside extensions of the metropolis, while Birmingham and Bradford could appropriately be regarded as outposts of the City. Physical contiguity or even proximity ceased to be necessary prerequisites to the kinds of activities, whether involving business or pleasure, associated with cities. The network of interdependency linking the farthest corners of England with the metropolis that Defoe had celebrated in his *Tour* reached its logical culmination with the creation of the Victorian railway and telegraph systems. It could be said that all England was a suburb of London,[35] and each part of that real Greater London proceeded to specialize not only in its material but in its aesthetic, intellectual, and emotional production; knowing that whatever it did not provide could be had a short railway journey away.

Whatever their impact on the physical and economic structure of the realm and on both the cultivated and the popular imagination, the railways in their early years were not a part of the daily experience of the ordinary Londoner. For the most part they were intended for neither urban nor suburban traffic. Although the London and Greenwich and the London and Blackwall necessarily confined themselves to short-distance travel, the London and Birmingham – together with most other railways running north and west out of London – was built with long-distance traffic only in mind. When it opened in 1837 its first station was as far out as Harrow, 11½ miles from Euston.* Not until the twentieth century did suburban traffic south of Watford achieve any significant level, although the company did open stations at Willesden in 1841, the present Wembley Central in 1842, Kilburn in 1852, and South Hampstead and Queen's Park in 1879.[36] As early as 1850 it was 'contemplating laying out a large plot of surplus land at Pinner (13½ miles from London) as a park, in which villas of a respectable character will be erected'. Each purchaser would receive a free season ticket for several years 'in order to afford parties from London facilities in the erection and habitation of substantial dwellings . . .'. The L&NWR (successor to the London and Birmingham)

---

* At the openings, respectively, of the Great Western and the Great Northern, their first stations were Ealing (5¾ miles) and Hornsey (4 miles).

then had 'less suburban travelling than most of the other metropolitan railways', and hoped that the scheme would 'assist in developing this important source of revenue'.[37] Three years later it was offering free first-class season tickets 'for a series of years to persons who will build houses worth not less than 50l. per ann. at Harrow, Pinner, Bushey, Watford, King's Langley, Boxmoor, Berkhampstead, or Tring'.[38] Of course in the 1850's these localities were country rather than suburban, and would not involve the railway in the intensive short-distance services that the North London and some of the southern lines were beginning to provide. In any event, few took advantage of the free seasons, and the L&NWR's suburban services remained infrequent.[39]

The Great Eastern Railway, which was to become pre-eminently the line of the working-class commuter, also carried many middle-class residents to and from its outer-suburban stations. In 1854 its predecessor, the Eastern Counties Railway, was offering a free first-class season ticket for 14 years to each builder of a £50 house in Enfield, with a second-class ticket for each £30 house.[40]

The London and South Western, which enjoyed from its early years significant suburban business, also made use of season tickets to encourage building. In 1852 the *Builder* reported that the railway, 'in order to encourage the erection of cheap suburban dwellings', was planning 'to contract with persons building such houses in the vicinity of the line for the issue of residential tickets for any given number of years, the same to be transferred with the key of the house to the occupier, for the conveyance of himself and family'.[41] Building along the L&SWR lines tended to be of a substantial sort, and some distance out: the company never operated the sort of intensive inner-suburban services that the other railways south of the Thames did.[42]

The numbers taking advantage of such services as were offered were still comparatively small. No more than about 6,000 persons commuted into central London by rail in 1854.[43] Yet the prospects for expansion were evident. 'We can scarcely, even at present, form an idea of the changes which will be effected in the metropolis when the London and suburban railways are more completely carried out, although already the effect is considerable', commented the *Builder* in 1859:

> During the summer months large numbers of the middle classes run off by rail in search of healthy villages, or farm-houses, at a moderate distance from the metropolis, where their families can be lodged, and which can be reached after business in the evening, and allow of the return by sufficient time in the morning.
>
>   . . . There are indications that the metropolis will, in a very brief space of time, extend in an extraordinary manner: from villages which are near railways, rows of dwellings are spreading towards town, and London is branching towards the villages . . .[44]

The great suburban railway of the fifties, and for many decades thereafter, was the North London. Today Broad Street is probably the most melancholy of the London termini – Marylebone, after all, was always a place for withdrawal and repose – and a trip over the line to Richmond via the Northern Heights, through deserted or demolished stations and past countless back gardens, is to experience the transitory nature of all human things. For

96 '"What would London do now without a railway?"' London and Croydon Railway at New Cross. London and Greenwich Railway in background.

today, with newer tube lines providing, in most cases, more direct access to central London, it is one of the backwaters of London transport. In the latter half of the nineteenth century it was the busiest of all suburban lines.

Opened in 1850 and 1851, the line had originally looped eastward through Hackney to terminate at Fenchurch Street. The construction of a line from Dalston to Broad Street, which opened in 1865, shortened the journey and further encouraged building development in the Northern Heights. By 1866 trains ran at fifteen-minute intervals as far as the new Willesden Junction Station, from where they proceeded alternately to Richmond and the present Kensington Olympia, the latter by way of the West London Railway.[45] The line carried 14 million passengers in 1866 and more than 32 million in 1880.[46] On Sundays and bank holidays it carried immense loads of excursionists to and from Hampstead Heath. By the early nineties it was selling seven million workmen's tickets annually. It sold about 21,000 season tickets in a six-month period in 1883, and 34,000 in a similar period in 1895.[47]

The first properly urban railway in London, and the first underground railway in the world, came in the early sixties with the construction of the Metropolitan from Paddington to Farringdon and Moorgate Street. Long before it opened, the excavations for it – combined as they were with the massive works for the new main sewers being carried out by the Metropolitan Board – served as visible evidence of the radical transformation London was undergoing. 'Never . . . were the streets and thoroughfares of the metropolis so much disturbed as they have been recently,' reported the *Builder* in 1860:

> In all directions bands of workmen are busy as moles burrowing the earth, each in his way, advancing the great drainage works; and now operations have been commenced for making the underground of London available for railway purposes, and soon below the crowded streets the locomotive whistle will sound and trains roll rapidly along. The squares north of Hyde-park are blockaded, and poor ladies look out of their windows aghast, and postpone intended 'parties'.[48]

The sixties saw mainline railways as well extending their termini further into central London, and their trains, often using the Metropolitan for a portion of the journey, carried a greatly increased number of suburban residents. The *Building News* contemplated the new railway invasion in 1861:

> . . . At length, the notion of extending the termini into the very heart of the metropolis has assumed a practical form. The London, Chatham, and Dover will be pushed forward into Farringdon-street, the South Eastern into Charing-cross, and the Great Western and Great Northern will be linked together by the Metropolitan . . . Whether for good or whether for ill, these lines will be completed. One effect of them will be to give greater facilities to city-men to dwell in suburban homes, and to furnish the same accommodation on other lines as the London-bridge railways now almost exclusively afford. Now a man may reach his place of business as quickly from Reigate by rail as he can from Bayswater by omnibus. There is no reason why with the Metropolitan Railway he may not, without loss of time, dwell in one or other of the beautiful villages adjacent to stations on the Great Western or Great Northern lines.[49]

One of the railways physically linked with the new underground was the Great Northern, which opened the present Finsbury Park Station at Seven Sisters in 1861, and in the following decade began developing a substantial suburban traffic. From Finsbury Park it built branches to Edgware and High Barnet (portions of which today form part of the Northern Line) in 1867 and 1872 respectively. The opening of the Alexandra Palace brought a branch from Highgate to Muswell Hill in 1873, while another, opened in 1871, already connected Wood Green with Enfield.[50] Before the railway came to the parish of Finchley in the sixties it was served by no more than five or six omnibuses a day bound for Charing Cross or the Bank. From Whetstone, in the northern portion, the journey took an hour and three quarters, and the return fare was 2s. By 1870 there were 20 trains daily from Church End taking about a half-hour for the trip to Moorgate; with a yearly second-class season, one could make the return journey six times weekly at the rate of 8d. per day. There were two and a half times as many commuters using the Great Northern in 1874 as in 1867, but the really substantial growth would come in the last quarter of the century.[51] In 1873 the Great Northern built a connecting link between Finsbury Park and the North London at Highbury, thereby giving their trains direct access to the City at Broad Street. The *Architect* predicted that 'the new branch will . . . have the effect of giving a considerable impetus to building along the district intersected . . . large numbers of the population residing between Finsbury and Highbury daily travel to and from the City'.[52]

'So continuous are the lines of streets and roads between London and Highgate that the latter may now be reckoned quite as much a part of the great metropolis as Kensington or Chelsea,' wrote Edward Walford in the nineties. He attributed much of the growth to the railway:

> Perhaps no line has felt more rapidly the increase of the suburban traffic than the Great Northern. 'There was a time, indeed,' said the *North Londoner* some years ago, 'when, in common with all the leading railway companies, it rather threw cold water upon it. It has now at least 4,000 season-ticket holders, and trains call at Holloway and Finsbury Park continuously during the working hours of the day, and every train is crowded with passengers. Speculative builders have been very busy in the north of London, which was till lately regarded by them as a *terra incognita*. . . . A fatal blow was dealt to this state of things by the connection of the Great Northern with the Underground Railway. All at once London discovered that there were no more salubrious breezes, no greener fields, no more picturesque landscapes, no more stately trees than could be shown in the district of country bounded by Highgate Hill on one side and Barnet on the other. The green lanes of Hornsey and Southgate ceased to be such. . . . Ancient mansions . . . were pulled down; broad parks were cut up into building lots; and instead we have semi-detached villas – much better, as a rule, to look at than to live in – advertised as being in the most healthy of all neighbourhoods, and within half an hour's ride of the City.'[53]

The railway, together with other new forms of mass transit, enabled neighbourhoods to specialize in function more than they would otherwise have done. The most extreme example was, of course, the City. 'In the architectural and social transformation of the central

97 'The first properly urban railway in London,
and the first underground railway in the world,
came in the early sixties with the construction of
the Metropolitan from Paddington to Farringdon
and Moorgate Street.' Broad-gauge trains at
King's Cross, Metropolitan Railway, 1863.

part of London the railways have had no small share,' explained the *Builder* in 1868:

> . . . No traffic pays like a metropolitan traffic. The powerful engines and well-managed trains of the underground railway conduct a constant stream of human life to and fro (without any apparent diminution of the crowds that fill the streets), that resemble only the march of an enormous army. While the interior traffic of the metropolis assumes such commanding dimensions, the suburban traffic is hardly less important. For the constant circulation of the former is substituted the steady tidal flow of the other part of the same great system. To reach the business centre from eight to eleven, to leave it from four to eight or even later, is the daily habit of a large mass of persons . . .

The profitability of an intensive suburban business was far from universal. Although the North London paid tidy dividends, the ruinous rivalry, involving much duplication of lines and termini, among the railways of the southeast cut into all their profits, and kept one – the London, Chatham and Dover – from paying dividends at all except at the rarest of intervals. 'To catch and convey this steady and increasing stream [of London commuters] has been, for many years, the great object of railway rivalry,' the article continued:

> A third line [the LC&D] was created to snatch a portion of the wealth for which the Brighton and the South-Eastern Companies were flying at each other's throats. Nothing was too much to attract the public. Lofty and costly stations, so far in advance of the requirements of the traffic that they must be regarded rather as advertisements in brick, and glass, and iron, than as the provision made by public carriers for the accommodation of their customers, form the most prominent objects to be seen from London and from Westminster Bridges. Duplicate bridges of gigantic proportions span the Thames. Acre after acre of London has been denuded of its ancient roofing.[54]

With the flurry of competitive construction in the sixties, the London suburban network was very nearly completed. Except for the tubes, practically all of the rail lines that provide suburban service today were in existence by the mid-1870's, with in many instances trains over routes and to stations that have long since ceased to offer passenger service.[55] The seventies most notably saw the extensive construction of new track and facilities by the Great Eastern Railway which allowed it in subsequent years to offer inner-suburban service of unparalleled density and efficiency. By building a new line directly north from Bethnal Green through Stoke Newington and Tottenham to Edmonton it cut through what became a populous working-class district. By moving its terminus from Shoreditch to Liverpool Street it provided more convenient access to the City. From 1876 it ran trains from Liverpool Street to the East London Railway, which used Sir Marc Brunel's Thames Tunnel from Wapping to Rotherhithe on its way to junctions at New Cross with the Brighton and South Eastern Railways.[56]

Legislation authorizing the Great Eastern to build its branches to Edmonton and Chingford in 1864 required it to run workmen's trains on those lines at a return fare of 2d. One could travel into Liverpool Street from Enfield and back, a 21½-mile trip, for that fare. The Great Eastern ran more workmen's trains, at cheaper fares, than any other line, and came to be regarded as the working man's railway. Such a policy inevitably lowered the social tone of the suburbs so served. The general manager, in his evidence before the Royal Commission on the Housing of the Working Classes in 1884, described the impact of workmen's fares on Stamford Hill, Tottenham, and Edmonton:

> That used to be a very nice district indeed, occupied by good families, with houses of from £150 to £250 a year, with coach houses and stables, a garden and a few acres of land. But very soon after this obligation was put upon the Great Eastern to run workmen's trains . . . speculative builders went down into the neighbourhood and, as a consequence, each good house was one after another pulled down, and the district is given up entirely, I may say, now to the working man. I lived down there myself and I waited until most of my neighbours had gone; and then, at last, I was obliged to go.

By the end of the century 19,000 people arrived early every morning in Liverpool Street by workmen's trains, followed by another 35,000 on trains on which reduced, but not workmen's fares were charged; followed after 9:00 by the regular season-ticket holders. There was thus a threefold segregation of commuters by fare and time of arrival, in addition to their universal segregation into first, second, and third-class carriages.[57] The successor to the GER, the London and North Eastern, was the last railway in Britain to operate three-class suburban trains, which it did until 1938.

Improved and cheaper rail service of all sorts could lower as well as raise the value of property in a community. While a certain minimal level of transport was necessary for a suburb to be developed at all, unduly fast or frequent service and low fares encouraged dense building development and consequent social deterioration. It was this that led the residents of Tunbridge Wells to petition against a proposal to lower railway fares to the town in 1874.[58] Banister Fletcher explained in the *Builder* in 1875 how the coming of a railway could depreciate property values:

> . . . It might be that a locality had become dotted over with gentlemen's residences, occupied by persons of good means, all able to keep their carriages and saddle-horses, and that the comparative remoteness of the neighbourhood from a station was an element of value, as tending to promote selectness and privacy. The establishment of a new railway station in the immediate vicinity of this select locality would obviously much lessen the value of the existing house property. Vacant sites would no doubt improve in value, because they would be suitable for the erection of smaller dwellings, to be occupied by clerks and business people . . . but their selectness being disturbed, the old residents would leave the neighbourhood . . .[59]

The quality and quantity of transport contributed to the increasing degree of social segregation characteristic of Victorian London.[60] '. . . Nothing would so much depreciate the value of property in the Thames Valley as railways which enabled masses of people to be poured into it for day excursions,' wrote the *Builder* of the proposal, later withdrawn, to extend the Marlow branch of the Great Western to Henley-on-Thames in 1898. 'It is not . . . a holiday resort, like a seaside place; what property owners desire is that it should be essentially a residential neighbourhood.'[61]

OMNIBUSES AND TRAMS

One puzzling feature of London's transport history is the failure of the tram – with its inherent technical and economic advantages – to triumph over the bus at any stage, horse-drawn or electric. Only in the twentieth century did the tram come closer than the fringes of central London, and then it did so underground, in the Kingsway tunnel. The tramway network of London, while extensive, remained overwhelmingly suburban, and working-class suburban, to the end. Even more unusual has been the development in London of what are perhaps the only really *loved* buses in the world.

It is less surprising that buses and trams were from the start assimilated to the English social structure. 'There was a time,' recalled the *Builder* in 1881, when it was considered to be hardly respectable to be seen on an omnibus, and even yet there is a certain *mauvaise honte* visible in a man whose richer or more luxurious friend meets him as he emerges from the interior of a public omnibus.'[62] But if one might fear to be seen getting off an omnibus by one's social superior, one would at least be free from the company of one's inferiors while on board. For the omnibus was an overwhelmingly middle-class conveyance. It did not start operating before eight in the morning, by which time the working classes were at work; it had a cushioned interior and an obsequious conductor; its fares approximated those of second-class travel by rail, and were too high for the working man or his family. '. . . The working man is rarely seen on the upholstered cushions,' an article in the *Cornhill Magazine* for March 1890 pointed out; 'he feels himself uncomfortable and *de trop*. The tramcar is *his* familiar vehicle and he can ensconce himself there in his mortar-splashed clothes without restraint.'[63]

The existence of omnibus connections with the City and the West End was an essential prerequisite to the success of any suburban development. An advertisement for building ground, laid out 'for the Erection of single or double detached Villas of a superior class', at Tufnell Park in 1844, was careful to point out that, 'From the Holloway Road, the Brecknock Arms, and Kentish Town, Omnibuses are constantly running to all parts of London'.[64] The omnibus not only made it possible for those who could not afford to keep their own carriage to live a distance from the City, but made it unnecessary even for those who could afford it. '. . . With accommodation such as is now provided, many respectable women and children are led to use the omnibuses, and it is a very prudent thing to foster such habit,' wrote the *Building News* in 1857. 'There are many districts where, in an omnibus line being introduced, most of the private conveyances of the district, even to broughams, are given up . . .'.[65] Alfred Cox noted the infrequency with which carriages were kept in St John's Wood in the fifties:

That there should be maintained here and in other suburbs so large a number of houses whose unfurnished rent is from 100*l.* to 200*l.* a-year, and a few *at more* still, demonstrates that the occupiers are a 'money-spending' as well as a 'money-earning' class. They seldom,

98   '"It is needless to comment upon their
miserable proportions, the inadequacy and
poverty of their accommodation upon deck . . ."'
River steamers, 1860.

however, keep carriages; the pervading practice here among an essentially-practical people is to hire, which is, no doubt, the least trouble, as well as the most economical method, the large supply of well-appointed omnibuses affording abundant facilities for locomotion to all those who will condescend to use these public conveyances.[66]

Three decades later W.S. Clarke commented on the excellence of local transportation to St John's Wood, which by then had the Metropolitan Railway extension from Baker Street to supplement the abundant omnibuses: 'The railway and omnibus accommodation is of the best as to quantity, and the omnibus especially as to quality. No better-appointed conveyances enter London.'[67]

However genteel the omnibus, the Victorian passion for segregation and classification was not wholly satisfied. 'It is probable . . . that we shall ultimately have a first and second class omnibus,' predicted the *Builder* in 1851; 'for we understand that the working classes, unless when in holiday attire, dislike to enter omnibuses occupied by people better dressed at the moment than themselves, and it is but fair that they should have a workday-class carriage of their own.'[68] It returned to the suggestion thirty years later:

> There is no substantial reason why there should not be first and second class omnibuses, the former for ladies and those who preferred economical and yet fairly comfortable travelling, the latter for those who preferred cheap and somewhat rough locomotion.[69]

Actually in 1866 a three-class omnibus, 'the body being divided into two, having each its own entrance, and the roof', operated from Victoria Station via Regent Street and Portland Place to the Portland Road (now Great Portland Street) Station on the Metropolitan Railway.[70] The Metropolitan Railway operated the buses in connection with its trains, selling through tickets from stations on its line. First-class accommodation came to an end in 1882.[71] With that exception the omnibus remained a one-class vehicle.

STEAMBOATS

So were the Thames steamboats, whose low fares enabled them to wage a prolonged if losing battle with the railways for local traffic.[72] But the *Building News* in 1866 suggested that they, too, ought to pursue a policy more in accordance with the structure of society:

> There is no doubt that the very small fares are the chief reason of the popularity of our steamboat traffic. From London Bridge to Lambeth Bridge for a penny is what might be called the minimum of tariffs. It is worth while considering . . . why the river is not more universally used as a means of locomotion. . . . So far as the vessels themselves are concerned, the only circumstance that can be mentioned in their favour is that they are kept scrupulously clean. It is needless to comment upon their miserable proportions, the inadequacy and poverty of their accommodation upon deck only equalled by the bare and destitute appearance of the den below, dignified with the name of cabin. . . . The herding together all classes of the community at one price has universally proved a failure, whether tried on land or water. There is not the slightest reason why there should not be a second and first class on board our metropolitan steamers . . . as well as on board any other vessel.[73]

The advice was heeded, for *Dickens's Dictionary of London, 1879*, shows separate 'Fore Deck' and 'Aft Deck' fares between all steamboat piers from Chelsea to Woolwich, and states that 'passengers using the after or saloon deck and after cabin must pay chief cabin fare . . .'. The fare between Chelsea and London Bridge was 2d. and 4d. in the two classes respectively.[74]

Although it no doubt failed to achieve ultimate refinements in adapting itself to the fine gradations of the Victorian social structure, London's system of public transport – with its three-class underground and overground networks, its competing omnibuses and trams, its Thames steamers, its Hansoms and four-wheel cabs, each with its own special tariff and clientele – was, on the whole, one worthy of the metropolis of the world. Offering variety, segregation, a choice among differing degrees of privacy and publicity, it both served the needs and mirrored the attributes of the greater London. Most of what makes movement about London even today moderately efficient and pleasurable – from the platform-level pub at Sloane Square to the No. 9 bus – are Victorian survivals.

CHAPTER EIGHT

London in 1901: the Victorian Legacy

What sort of London did the Victorians bequeath to the Edwardians? How did that London differ from the one they had inherited from their Georgian predecessors? How representative was the new London of that abstraction, the modern industrial city, or the twentieth-century metropolis? How much was it specifically and uniquely itself?

To a great extent what happened to London happened to all big cities, but happened sooner and more intensely here than anywhere else. London had the problems of size, complexity, poverty, and disorder long before the Industrial Revolution. London had massive suburbanization and the whole commuting pattern before any other city. Some novelties it imported, often from Paris, and then developed in its own idiosyncratic way: the omnibus, the grand hotel, the department store.

MOVEMENT IN SPACE AND TIME

One characteristic of urban life is an orderly succession of sharply differentiated experiences, involving movement in space from one contrasting environment to another. The commuting experience permitting the daily exchange of the leafy seclusion of the suburb for the organized chaos of the City, the sudden transition from the ordered respectability of Regent Street to the raffish squalor of Piccadilly Circus, the burst from darkness into blinding light as the tube train emerges from the tunnel – to experience London is to find the magical transformation of the pantomime continually being translated into life. But the assaults on the senses and emotions are not haphazard: they are intentional and reassuringly predictable. The mind approves what the body enjoys.

All great cities have something of this quality, but London has more of it. It is far more comprehensive in the experiences it can offer than, for instance, the single-purpose cities of the North: Blackpool is a more *necessary* extension of Manchester than Brighton is of London.

Paul Hazard has suggested that the transition from seventeenth to eighteenth-century civilization consisted of the abandonment of an earlier passion for stability for a new one for movement.* By the nineteenth century movement had triumphed, yet was in turn

---

* Demeurer: éviter tout changement, qui risquerait de détruire un équilibre miraculeux: c'est le souhait de l'âge classique. . . . Pascal a découvert que tout le malheur des hommes vient d'une seule chose, qui est de ne pas savoir demeurer en repos dans une chambre.' Paul Hazard, *La crise de la conscience européenne, 1680–1715*, Paris, Boivin & Cie., 1935, p. 3.

subjected to a governing order as ritualized as anything the Court of Louis XIV could have imposed.

Life for the well-to-do Victorian was a pattern of orderly movements: from room to room, from suburb to City, from town to country, from London to Brighton, from England to the Riviera. Such movement through space was accompanied by equally lengthy movements through time, from Pall Mall club in the shape of a cinquecento palazzo to Palladian office block to Elizabethan suburban villa to thirteenth-century church. Architectural eclecticism gave the cultivated Victorian visual experiences that alternately shocked and soothed: and since each architectural style came from a particular period, with historical, literary, and moral associations on which to reflect, as well.

Unlike his American contemporary he did not have to rely on architectural revivals, for much of the real thing was readily available: as yet unrestored mediaeval churches, Tudor high streets, and seventeenth-century town houses long since swept away in the name of progress or sanitation or the demands of traffic. Most of the environment of the Victorians was pre-Victorian; and the coming of Romanticism, the beginnings of academic art history, and the development and diffusion of a sense of history enabled the educated Victorian to enjoy the physical remains of the past more than the man of any preceding age. Attempts were made to replace dogmatic neoclassicism by dogmatic gothicism or claims of other historical styles to an absolute primacy transcending the period that produced them; but the result of the battle of the styles for most people was to give a degree of aesthetic legitimacy to all styles of architecture. Georgian and Regency art and architecture were excluded from such catholic and benevolent acceptance; since Victorian London was and remained overwhelmingly Georgian and Regency in its physical structure and appearance, the exception was an important one.

VARIETY

The variety of London that Dr Johnson celebrated was multiplied and intensified by the Victorians. We have tried but not succeeded in submerging that variety in the sober and egalitarian dress of our own age. Victorian London, like Georgian London, is too solid and obtrusive to be easily smothered by a later generation's notion of good taste or modernity. Architecture spoke louder in the nineteenth than in the eighteenth century, partly to make itself heard. It had to be more vivid to be seen through the fog and smoke. And it was speaking to a larger and less educated audience than Georgian architecture had deigned to address.

London shares many of the qualities of English weather. Its moments of delight give more intense stabs of pleasure than they would in a more uniform and predictable city: like periods of sunshine in an English summer they are particularly precious because they are at once so unexpected and so precarious. When Victorian exponents of the picturesque applied their aesthetic to the streets of London, they usually spoke of their pleasure in discovering Tudor and Stuart survivals – some half-timbering here, a leaded-glass window there – but the contrasts and juxtapositions of the contemporary rebuilding of central London were doing even more to make it truly picturesque. It may require a twentieth-century sensibility – after

Dada, the surrealists, and the theatre of the absurd – wholly to appreciate Victorian London, but even at the time the spectacle of an LC&D tank engine moving across the west front of St Paul's must have produced many an agreeable *frisson*.

The startling discontinuities were not the result of mere chance, any more than the sudden appearance of a grotto or a ruined temple in an eighteenth-century garden, but resulted from the pervasive sorting-out and classification that characterized the growth and reconstruction of Victorian London. A model lodging house was an attempt to segregate the virtuous poor, but as placed in a central London street it could only serve as an architectural shock. And while the exponents of each successive architectural fashion might have wished to rebuild London entirely in their new image, they rarely got farther than imposing their ideas on a few streets before the money ran out or a new fashion came to supersede theirs. Even the residential suburb was dull and uniform only in contrast to the exuberant variety of the West End and City, and was usually perfectly distinguishable from neighbouring districts, topographically, architecturally, and socially. The ease and necessity of movement in Victorian London ensured that the ordinary middle-class householder would experience several contrasting aspects of the metropolis in any given day, and certainly over the week or year. His children, if they went away to boarding school, would experience a comparable rhythm of ritualized life styles. His wife, more totally confined to house and suburb, was in greater danger of succumbing to boredom: the possibilities offered by the department store being perhaps her greatest solace. For all, the annual seaside holiday would both extend and contrast with the possibilities inherent in London itself.

Like the discipline of the Benedictine Rule, the 'New Discipline' which the Hammonds discerned in the nineteenth-century industrial town contained within it the pleasures of variety and the comfort of predictability as well as the constraints of regularity.

PLEASURE

Modern cities in general and London in particular have too often been seen as mindless responses to dramatically changed economic and demographic conditions. While such an approach may work reasonably well with Manchester or Leeds, towns devoted to the manufacture or distribution of necessities, it is wholly inadequate when dealing with London, so much of whose energy was involved with the provision of pleasure. The providers, needless to say, far outnumbered the enjoyers; but the imbalance grew less extreme as the nineteenth century progressed, so much so that the age can be seen as characterized by the democratization of aristocratic pleasures.

Victorian London as a manufacturing centre concentrated as it had for centuries more on the provision of luxuries than of necessities, on consumer rather than capital goods: silks rather than woollens; watches, pianos, jewellery, fine furniture, beer, spirits, sugar, tobacco rather than steel rails. Even more important to its economy were the service industries: hairdressing, education, tailoring, music, drama, domestic service, prostitution. Whenever possible the production of such pleasures was kept discreetly out of sight, in the sweatshops and manufacturing establishments of the East End that provided the luxury goods, and the counting houses of the City that provided the money to spend on them.

But London existed not merely as a place that made toys for the rich (and not so rich) to play with: it was itself a gigantic and complicated toy that provided increasing pleasure for resident and visitor alike. 'Toy' may be an unfortunate metaphor: 'work of art', which it certainly was, might suggest something static and unchanging, which it was not, as well as something pompous and pretentious, which it rarely was; 'machine', while suggesting moving parts, has utilitarian connotations: machines ordinarily exist to produce something; toys and works of art exist and function for their own sake. London's existence is its own justification; it is a luxury, and as such has always earned the condemnation of moralists. It is a vast baroque opera or masque with hidden stage machinery and a cast of millions who also constitute the audience. It excels in the production of useless things, like the Crystal Palace: things that nobody needs but that many are prepared to enjoy. (It also produced things like the Alexandra Palace and the Wembley Tower that nobody wanted either, of course.) London not only makes and contains things that give pleasure, it gives pleasure in itself by simply being or, more accurately, by functioning: for a city must be in motion in order to exist.

Motion is itself one of the important pleasures of London. The pleasures of movement were once the preserve of royalty, in its progresses; and of the aristocracy, taking the once-in-a-lifetime Grand Tour, and then annually moving from country to town and back again, and periodically moving from country house to country house. The daily progress from Tulse Hill to London Bridge on the Brighton Line and the annual move to a seaside boarding house may have been less splendid, but differed in degree rather than in kind.

The environments one entered at the different ends of the journey were satisfyingly different. London never overwhelms by its vastness: its neighbourhoods retain intimacy and individuality. It has within it a bewildering variety of environments to choose from and to move between. Turn the corner from Oxford Street into Park Lane, move out of a side door of Liberty's into Carnaby Street, leave the Criterion Theatre by the exit into Piccadilly Circus or into Jermyn Street, take the Northern Line from Cornhill to Hampstead Heath: the shocks and discontinuities are what London is all about.

The examples are not all Victorian: Liberty's and Carnaby Street suggest that the 1920's and 1960's retained some of the Victorian's skill at using the pleasurable shock as a merchandizing device. But most of the recent additions and alterations to London show all of the monotony of Gower Street with none of its underlying good taste and good manners. For most of our pleasures we still rely on Victorian London.

THE VICTORIAN LEGACY

If the darker aspects of Victorian London predominate in literature and historical scholarship, the physical survivals are more benign. In 1901 the failures loomed larger than the successes; from the standpoint of 1975 the opposite is true. In 1901 the dirt, the ugliness, the poverty, the disease, the injustice that pervaded the London scene obscured its more positive qualities. London was viewed as the cause of many evils of which it was in fact the innocent victim.

The evils proved more transitory than the blessings. It is the happy side of Victorian

London that, by and large, has persisted to form what is perhaps the most precious part of the present-day Londoner's inheritance. Its slums have gone, either absolutely or, sometimes, transformed into expensive neighbourhoods for the professional classes, but its drains and sewers remain, still admirably performing their duties. The cholera, the severe overcrowding, the mud, and the smoke have gone; but the Holborn Viaduct, the Embankment, Fitzjohn's Avenue, the theatres that line Shaftesbury Avenue, the villas on Sydenham Hill survive for our convenience and delight. Most of what is best in today's London we owe to the nineteenth century. If London shows signs of breaking down today we must blame the twentieth century: its speculators and developers, its architects, and – in part at least – its well-meaning but usually inept attempts at social engineering and economic planning: whether they take the form of a system of taxation that at once encourages the fragmentation of responsibly managed estates and rewards property speculation, or the destruction of the segment of the private building industry that produced, however inadequately, rental housing for the working classes; the favouring of private, at the expense of public transport; the encouragement, by both private and public bodies, of programmes of massive demolition that would have horrified a Haussmann. Even the best legislation has produced undesirable side-effects: the creation of the Green Belt and the imposition of planning restrictions inevitably made the remaining building land in the London area more costly, and raised house-prices and rents to a level higher than they would otherwise have been.

The Victorians left to the twentieth century a healthy, liveable, and even, in many respects, a beautiful city. We have taken away the smoke, washed the façades, cleaned the streets, given the working classes decent housing and – far more important – incomes that permit them to exercise some choice as to their life-styles. But the basically Victorian fabric and structure of London insofar as they remain put to shame our more recent attempts at town-building. Even the much-maligned speculative housing of the Victorians, when painted, cleaned, fitted with bathrooms and central heating and manageably compact kitchens, provides as satisfactory a domestic environment as anything our architects and builders and town planners can construct for us afresh.

CITIES AND CIVILIZATION

The very word 'civilization' assumes that cities are a necessary prerequisite for the higher types of human creativity. The assumption may be a false one, particularly now that revolutions in transport and communication have ensured that life away from urban concentrations need be neither rustic nor boorish. Whatever the ultimate fate of the city, the achievement of Victorian London ought not to be obscured by its shortcomings.

The Victorian makers and re-makers of London succeeded in reconciling what might have seemed the irreconcilable: density at the centre with openness at the periphery, uniformity with variety, the demands of society with the needs of the individual, the eighteenth century with the nineteenth, the private house and garden with unprecedented population growth, the village with the city, the past with the present.

Just as the late Victorians' rediscovery and re-evaluation of the eighteenth century profoundly affected their attitude toward themselves, so our own age is taking a new look at the nineteenth century as a means of self-discovery. No more impressive example of what the Victorians could do exists than Greater London. We may ultimately decide that our efforts to save and revitalize London and other cities are as hopeless and quixotic as were Victorian efforts to revive primitive Italian painting or mediaeval stone-carving. Victorian London may, like Venice, prove to be no more than an interesting historical survival, giving more pleasure than instruction. But in an age of instant nostalgia, already treasuring the artifacts of the 1960's, it would be a pity to ignore the solid achievements of the builders and architects, landowners and speculators who made Victorian London.

THE INDIVIDUAL AND THE ENVIRONMENT

London reveals more about the aspirations and pretensions of the Victorians than about the concrete realities of their age. The never-resolved conflict between architect and engineer – symbolized by the uneasy juxtaposition of hotel and trainshed at St Pancras – suggests an inner conflict in a society equally fascinated with the technology of the present and the styles of the past. Its desire to reconcile the economic benefits of mass production with the aesthetic and moral values associated with individual craftsmanship produced a townscape that displayed astonishing richness of shape, colour, texture, and style. Some parts of London – most notably those devoted to working-class housing – were more remarkable for extent and grim uniformity, with public house and railway providing the only interruptions in the long rows of grimy terraces. But if working-class streets had all the uniformity but nothing of the beauty of an eighteenth-century street, middle-class neighbourhoods grew increasingly individualized. Any building – private or public – that had been designed by an architect would be to some extent a personal statement. If the multiplicity and irreconcilability of such statements suggest want of agreement as to ends, the universal encouragement of invention and originality suggests the high regard in which individual creativity was held.

The Victorians were individualistic without being egalitarian, yet went far beyond the glorification of the exceptional – the poet, the seer, the hero – of Romantic ideology. Everyone, whatever his station or abilities, was to be encouraged to realize his potentialities. The family, far from the enemy of the individual, was seen as the best support for individual effort and development.

The conviction that the environment, both natural and artificial, profoundly affected human behaviour accounts in part for the passionate disputes over what would otherwise seem trivial issues. The efficiency of ventilation, the size and number of rooms, the height of ceilings, the appropriateness of decoration, the location of doors, were seen as significantly influencing the quality of the lives lived within a house. The larger environment of the town as a whole was equally crucial in determining the moral and physical welfare of its inhabitants.

The Victorians were forced by inexorable logic to build bigger and bigger cities while convinced that cities as such worked to weaken the values they most cherished. They responded by making their cities as little city-like as they could. The suburb, with its separate villas hidden behind walls and hedges, worked to reinforce domestic as opposed to communal values. Striving, with whatever limited success, to maintain the qualities of the villages that it overran, expanding suburbia sought to provide rural seclusion for a metropolitan population. Even the illusion of rurality was impossible for inner London: the best that could be done for it was to break it up into its component segments, to stress the parts at the expense of the whole, to mitigate any sense of overpowering size or grandeur.

Victorian London was a statement against absolutism, a proud expression of the energies and values of a free people, unwilling to subordinate their lives to the ambitions of a monarchy or the pretensions of an aristocracy. The re-introduction of royal patronage as an element in urban planning by the Prince Regent was seen as an unfortunate aberration. The better-established tradition of aristocratic guidance of metropolitan growth through the operation of the leasehold system proved harder to undermine. But the decreasing ability of even the richest and most determined ground landlords to maintain the integrity of their estate plans shows how strong were the forces of fragmentation.

Yet the ultimate result of concerted attempts to deprive London of urban qualities was to create an eminently satisfactory city: if not 'urban' in the sense that Paris or New York or Vienna is urban, it is a uniquely successful amalgam of urban, suburban, and rural characteristics, a good place to live.

THE CITY AS A LIBERATING FORCE

'The cities have always been the cradles of liberty, just as they are to-day the centres of radicalism,' wrote Adna Weber in 1899.[1] *Stadtluft macht frei.* The liberating function of the city in mediaeval Europe is an historical commonplace. Offering both personal freedom and widened opportunities for its exercise, the town, more than any other institution, made possible the great upsurge of creative energy that brought about the economic and cultural explosion of the eleventh and twelfth centuries. But the even more remarkable expansion of urban society of the nineteenth century has been regarded with less enthusiasm. The modern 'industrial' city has been seen as an agent of oppression. The emphasis placed by much recent scholarship on the condition of the suppressed minority of the very poor has encouraged the view of the modern city as a machine designed to crush individuality, impose conformity, and extinguish the creative spark.

Victorian London was too vast and multiform for its influence ever to have been simple or uniform, but on the whole its impact was liberating rather than oppressive, and more liberating as it became more Victorian. Offering a wider choice of jobs for the worker, a wider choice of goods and services for the consumer, a wider choice of environments for the householder, wider educational opportunities for the young, a wider and more critical audience for the artist, and a wider range of sensual experiences for everyone, Victorian London both encouraged and embodied the expanded opportunities of modern industrial society. That the freedom its residents enjoyed remained in absolute terms highly circumscribed – by poverty, custom, habit, prejudice, ignorance, and the built-in constraints of the English social structure – goes without saying. But the forces inhibiting individual freedom were for the most part pre-Victorian or non-urban – certainly non-metropolitan – in origin. Victorian London – as a city, as a particular city, and as a specifically Victorian phenomenon

– worked to loosen traditional bonds and to break newly-wrought chains.

It did so in spite of the increasingly rigorous social segregation that informed its development. Why England, for centuries one of the freest and most open of European societies, should have become by the twentieth century the one most obsessed by class is a question to which no satisfactory answer has yet been given. Whether or not the social geography of Victorian London helped to further that obsession, it certainly reflected it.

Victorian England worried continually about class, and about the outward manifestations of social distinctions, and that preoccupation formed a part of a larger passion for order and hierarchy, subordination and classification. London showed the results of such preoccupation and passion. Yet despite such efforts society was more fluid, opportunities were more widespread, and social restraints less confining in 1901 than they had been in 1837. Whatever the intention behind the policies of segregation, its manifestation had, if anything, worked to weaken the older structure of society.

The liberating effect of Victorian London is most startlingly displayed in its architecture. No period before or since has seen such exuberant, even anarchic proliferation of styles, materials, constructional techniques, colours, outlines, ethical and intellectual statements. None offered the architect greater freedom to pursue his particular vision of the beautiful. If the variety and invention were greater in some districts than in others – in the City and Fitzjohn's Avenue than in Chalcots or the Cromwell Road – the total impact of Victorianism on London was one of vastly-increased diversity.

Whether people led more varied lives in the new, individualized buildings and functionally differentiated neighbourhoods is a more open question. Insofar as the isolation of the suburban villa reinforced the authority of the head of the household, it may have encouraged parental tyranny, or at the very least strengthened the authority of the nuclear family at the expense of its individual members. The family, on the other hand, stood between the individual and the rest of society. Can it more usefully be seen as strengthening or as repressing its individual members, as reinforcing or breaking down the cohesion of the larger hierarchy? Ought greater stress to be placed on the reunion for family prayers in the dining room or on the withdrawal to separate bedrooms? Whatever its ultimate effect on English social evolution, the family was clearly strengthened by the layout and structure of Victorian London.

Even assuming a repressive role for the family, London at least contained more refuges for the rebellious individual than any other English community: whether in neighbourhoods like Bedford Park or St John's Wood for the eccentric or immoral, in railway termini offering temporary escapes to the seaside, or in clubs and public houses that provided an evening's alternative to stifling domesticity. Women, children, and the poor had the fewest routes of escape, but certainly more in London than in a village community, a market town, or a northern industrial city.

Individual rebellion and social protest have, in England, ordinarily been nurtured within a closely differentiated social structure. Liberation is more often the result of the efforts of groups than of isolated individuals. Some specialized neighbourhoods contributed to a more general emancipation by bringing together like-minded individuals or facilitating concerted action by those with shared grievances. The early development of trade unions in London – the fact that it was the London Dock Strike that marked the turning point for the organization of unskilled workers in England – suggests that Victorian London was at least as successful in fostering radicalism as Tudor and Stuart London had been. Charles Booth found a healthier sort of working-class life in the single-class districts of the East End than in the more mixed communities to the west. Working-class culture may thrive best in comparative isolation, as much as that produced by more self-conscious communities of artists and intellectuals.

If Victorian London contributed significantly to the total stock of human freedom, there is less certainty that it added to the quantity of either happiness or beauty. The emotional satisfactions to be gained from membership in an isolated, traditional community are not to be lightly abandoned. The aesthetic satisfactions to be derived from a true vernacular style, rooted in the place and in the past, based on individual craftsmanship within accepted limits of performance; or, on the other hand, of an assured classicism, based on the patronage of a cultivated aristocracy and the union of scholarship and taste, are not to be given up without regret.

Victorian London was a better place for the strong than the weak, for the alert than the apathetic, for the adventuresome than the timid, for the gluttonous than the squeamish, for the man hungry after experience than the fastidious. For those who could find happiness in struggle, beauty in variety, novelty, and contrast, Victorian London offered rewards such as no other city ever had: excitement, promise, and an indication of the infinite possibilities of human endeavour. It was a worthy reflection of the civilization that produced it.

THE REMAINS OF VICTORIAN LONDON

Whatever pleasure we derive from the surviving Victorian features of London, they can at best alleviate the pain we must feel at its overall deterioration. Simon Jenkins concludes his thoughtful analysis of the postwar rape of London by condemning equally private developers and public authorities: 'The streets of London teach us that under present commercial and architectural conditions, the free market can no longer provide us with an environment which is acceptable . . . Yet they also teach us that the public sector is equally inadequate.'[2] The speculative builders and developers of the 1970's really deserve the vituperation their predecessors unjustly received in the 1870's. While 'public architecture has often been the worst offender of all. (A few developers' office blocks may be listed for preservation before I am dead: I very much doubt if the same will be true of any creation of the Department of the Environment.)'[3]

It is tempting to search for villains, but there is little reason to believe that any combination of political or administrative decisions could have done more than mitigate the progressive degradation of twentieth-century London. London, after all, is not the only city that is facing a financial crisis, escalating rates and contracting services, a middle-class flight to increasingly unsatisfactory suburbs, blighted neighbourhoods, growing crime, a shortage of decent housing, and a centre composed of lethal office blocks and very little else. It has probably not been deteriorating faster than any other of the world's great cities. Why the twentieth century, and especially the third quarter of the twentieth century, should have been so universally unfavourable to cities is a question outside the scope of this book. Perhaps inexorable historical forces are destroying it, and all our best efforts can do will be to prolong its death agonies.

Whether an understanding of the nature of past successes at city-building – and Victorian London had more than its share – can help us to stop the rot is doubtful. Our best architects and planners blight whatever they touch. But if we shall probably not be able to emulate the creativity and exuberance of the builders of Victorian London, any more than we can the taste and judgment of the makers of Georgian London, we can at least try to preserve the products of both. As we wait for whatever the local equivalent of sinking into the Adriatic will be, the historical sense that is one Victorian blessing that has persisted into our day ought to intensify our pleasure as we contemplate and make use of what remains of an earlier and better London.

Stanford's Library Map of London and its Suburbs (c. 1863)

A1   Cricklewood, Golder's Green, and Hampstead.
A2   Highgate, Kentish Town, and Upper Holloway.
A3   Stoke Newington and Upper Clapton.
A4   Walthamstow and Leyton.

B1   Willesden, Kensal Green, Kilburn, and St John's Wood.
B2   Regent's Park, Camden Town, and Somers Town.
B3   Islington, Hoxton, Bethnal Green, and Hackney.
B4   Bow and Stratford.

C1   Bayswater, Notting Hill, and Kensington.
C2   Marylebone, Mayfair, Belgravia, Soho, and Bloomsbury.
C3   The City, Whitechapel, and Southwark.
C4   Limehouse, Poplar, and Rotherhithe.

D1   Hammersmith, Fulham, and West Brompton.
D2   Chelsea, Pimlico, Kennington, and Stockwell.
D3   Walworth, Camberwell, and Peckham.
D4   New Cross, Greenwich, and Blackheath.

E1   Putney and Wandsworth.
E2   Clapham, Balham, and Brixton.
E3   Herne Hill and Dulwich.
E4   Lewisham and Lee.

F1   Wimbledon and Merton.
F2   Tooting, Mitcham, and Streatham.
F3   Norwood, Upper Sydenham, and Penge.
F4   Lower Sydenham and Beckenham.

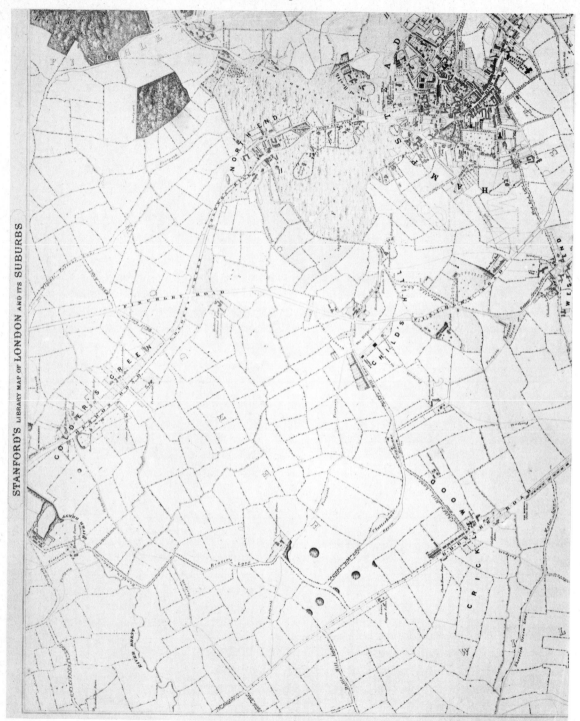

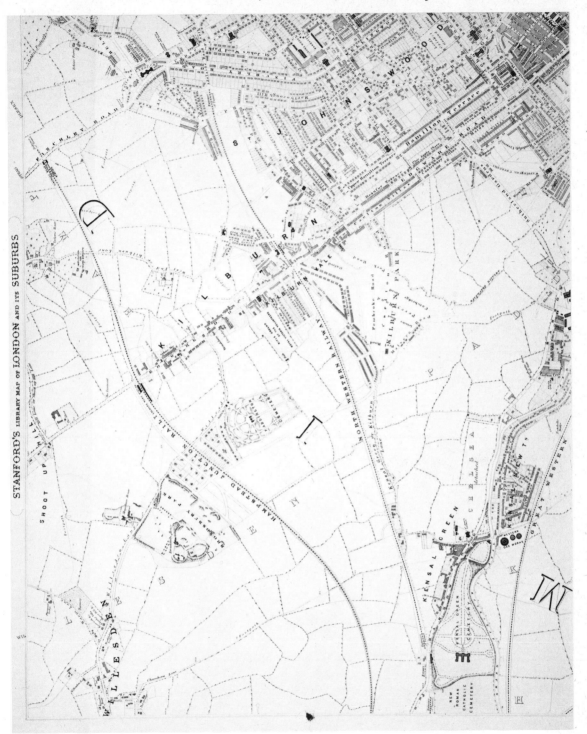

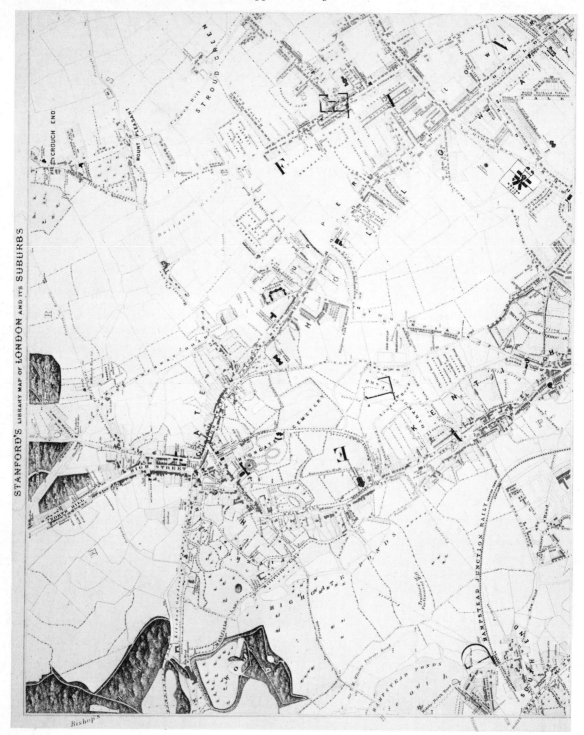

STANFORD'S LIBRARY MAP OF LONDON AND ITS SUBURBS

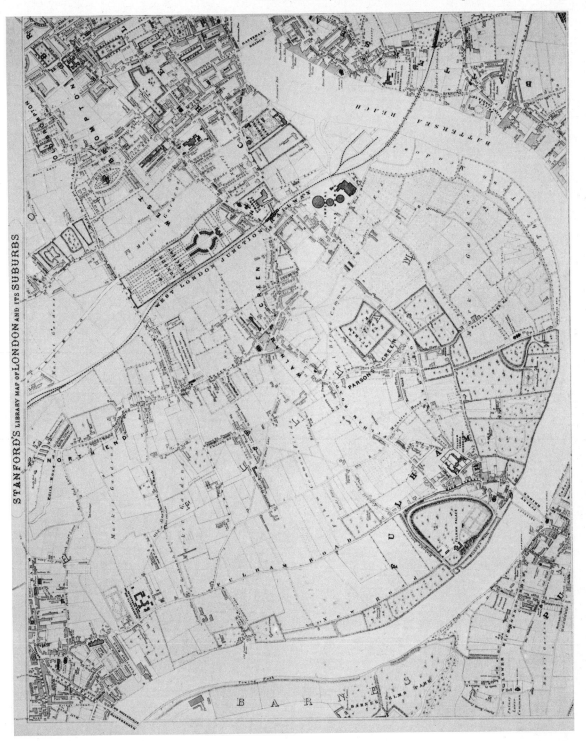

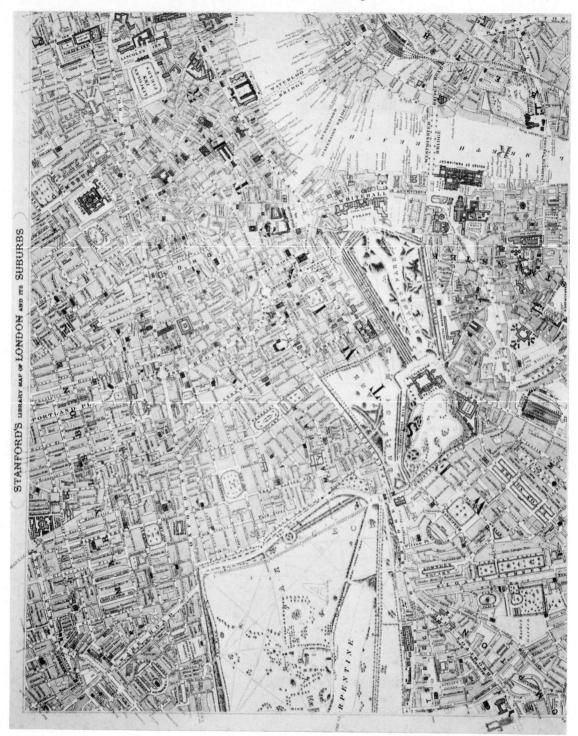

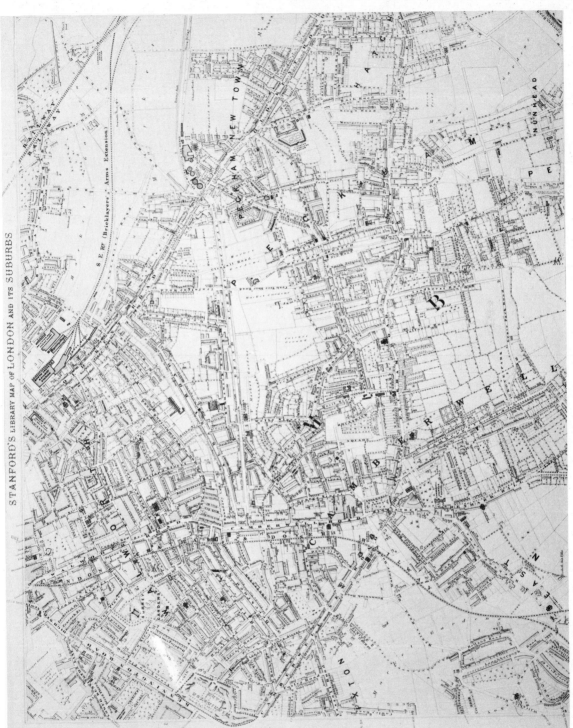

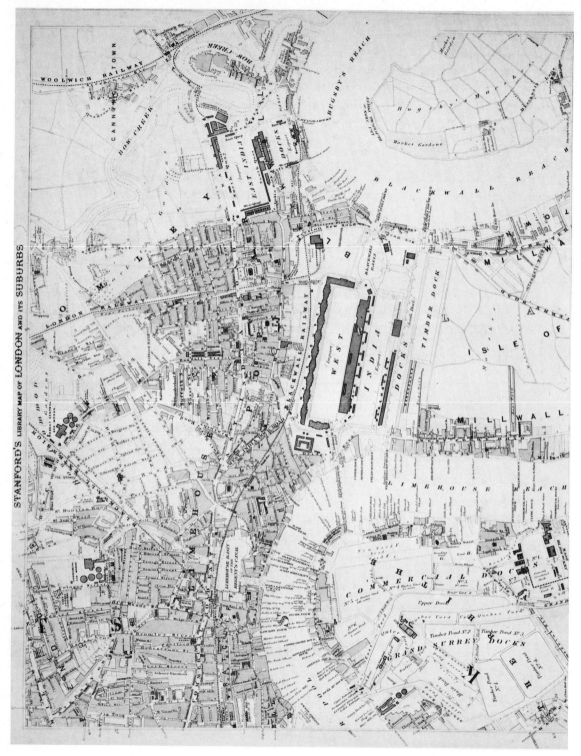

STANFORD'S LIBRARY MAP OF LONDON AND ITS SUBURBS

STANFORD'S LIBRARY MAP OF LONDON AND ITS SUBURBS

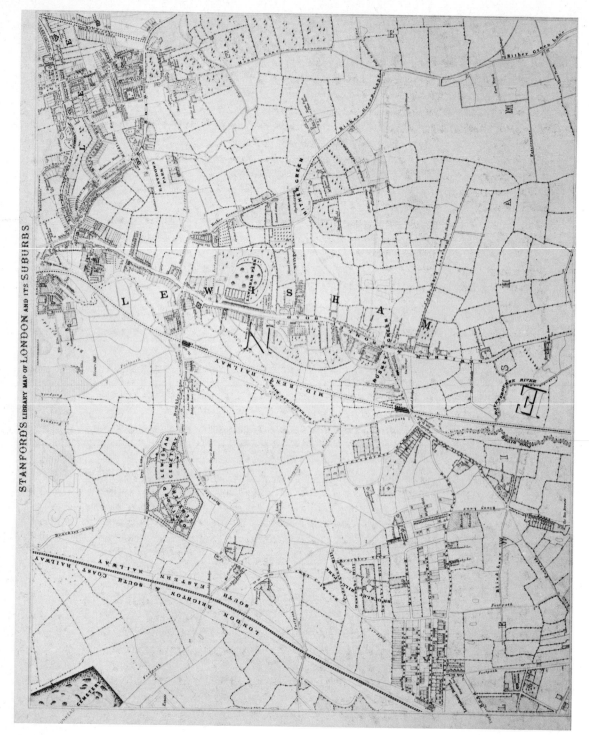

Notes

Preface (pp. 13–14)

1   'Private Town Planning: The Bedford and Foundling Estates in London during the Eighteenth and Nineteenth Centuries' (Ph.D. diss., Yale, 1954) held up the two estates as models of what careful and intelligent planning can achieve in shaping a city like London

2   Donald J. Olsen, *Town Planning in London*, Yale University Press, 1964, 215

3   *ibid.*, 200

4   Donald J. Olsen, 'House upon House', in H.J. Dyos and Michael Wolff, eds., *The Victorian City*, Routledge & Kegan Paul, 1973, I, 345

5   *ibid.*, 353

Chapter One: A Topography of Values (pp. 17–30)

1   An earlier version of the first part of this chapter appeared under the title, 'Victorian London: Specialization, Segregation, and Privacy,' in *Victorian Studies*, XVII (1974), 265–78

2   H. Jephson, *The Sanitary Evolution of London*, T. Fisher Unwin, 1907, 78

3   Sir John Summerson, *Georgian London*, Pleiades Books, 1948, 272–6. For a recent, more sympathetic appraisal, see his 'London, the Artifact', in Dyos and Wolff, I, 311–32

4   Adna Ferrin Weber, *The Growth of Cities in the Nineteenth Century*, New York, 1899, 442

5   *Builder*, IV (1846), 445. Hereafter cited as *B*.

6   Weber, 439

7   *ibid.*, 419

8   *ibid.*, 432

9   George Augustus Sala, *Gaslight and Daylight*, 1859, 218–19

10   Steen Eiler Rasmussen, *London: the Unique City*, Jonathan Cape, 1937, 292

11   *ibid.*, 294

12   Sir Osbert Lancaster, *All Done from Memory*, John Murray, 1963, 36

13   Charles B.P. Bosanquet, *London: Some Account of its Growth, Charitable Agencies, and Wants*, 1868, 13

14   W.M. Ackworth, *The Railways of England*, 5th ed., John Murray, 1900, 195–6

15   [W.S. Clarke], *The Suburban Homes of London*, 1881, 390

16   *B*, XIV (1856), 145

17   W.M. Thackeray, 'The Book of Snobs', *Works*, 1882, IX, 148–56

18   Gertrude Himmelfarb, 'The Culture of Poverty', in Dyos and Wolff, II, 707–31

19   Charles Booth, *Life and Labour of the People in London*, 1892, II, 21.

20   Review of Enid Gauldie, *Cruel Habitations*, Allen and Unwin, 1974; and John Nelson Tarn, *Five Per Cent Philanthropy*, Cambridge University Press, 1974, in the *Times Literary Supplement*, 2 August 1974, 823

21   William Morris, 'The Revival of Architecture', *Fortnightly Review*, May 1888, reprinted in Sir Nikolaus Pevsner, *Some Architectural Writers of the Nineteenth Century*, Oxford: Clarendon Press, 1972, 318

Chapter Two: London in 1837: the Georgian Legacy (pp. 31–48)

1   Sir John Summerson, 'London, the Artifact', in Dyos and Wolff, I, 312

2   *Building News*, XXXIV (1878), 206–7. Hereafter cited as *BN*

3   *BN*, XXIX (1875), 358

4   Sir George Laurence Gomme, *London in the Reign of Victoria (1837–1897)*, Chicago, 1898, 138

5   *BN*, LXXVII (1899), 684

6   Sir John Soane, *Lectures on Architecture*,

Publication of Sir John Soane's Museum, No. 14, 1929, 156, 178

7   *Civil Engineer and Architect's Journal*, I (1838), 336–7. Hereafter cited as *CE*.

8   *B*, XXII (1864), 93

9   *BN*, III (1857), I

10 Charles Dickens, *Little Dorrit*, Chapman & Hall, 1903, 201–2

11 *ibid.*, 267

12 Henry Kett, essay dated 29 December 1787, in *Essays by Bishop Horne, etc.*, 1820, II, 121–2

13 Summerson, *Georgian London*, 160

14 Anon., *Letter to Sir Charles Long*, 1825, 6

15 [J.C. Robertson and T. Byerley], *London*, 1823, III, 353–5

16 'Marquis de Vermont,' *pseud.*, in Marquis de Vermont and Sir Charles Darnley, Bart., *pseud., London and Paris, or Comparative Sketches*, 1823, 221–3

17 Quoted in Edward Walford, *Old and New London*, 1897, V, 267

18 Quoted in W.H. Leeds, ed., *Illustrations of the Public Buildings of London . . . by Pugin and Britton*, 1838, II, 369

19 Summerson, *Georgian London*, 181

20 James Elmes, *Metropolitan Improvements; or London in the Nineteenth Century*, 1827–31; reprinted New York: Benjamin Blom, 1968, 1–3

21 *ibid.*, 114

22 *ibid.*, 67

23 *ibid.*, 102

24 *ibid.*, 115

25 *ibid.*, 4

26 Hermione Hobhouse, *Thomas Cubitt, Master Builder*, Macmillan, 1971, 81, 147–9

27 *Blackwood's Magazine*, XL (1836), 237

28 *B*, LXV (1893), 24.

29 Summerson, *Georgian London*, 184

30 *CE*, I (1838), 219

31 Leeds, II, 374

32 Reprinted in *CE*, III (1840), 310

33 *B*, II (1844), 392–3

34 Francis Cross, *Hints to all about to Rent, Buy, or Build, House Property*, Third ed., quoted in *CE*, XIV (1851), 201–2

35 Charles d'Arlincourt, *The Three Kingdoms*, 1844, I, 24–5, quoted in Ann Saunders, *Regent's Park*, Newton Abbot: David & Charles, 1969, 138

36 Thackeray, IX, 21

37 *B*, VII (1849), 140

38 *BN*, XVIII (1870), 42

39 *Dickens's Dictionary of London*, 1880, 230

40 Saunders, 165–77

41 For its building and subsequent history, see Hermione Hobhouse, *A History of Regent Street*, Macdonald and Jane's, 1975

42 Henry-Russell Hitchcock, *Early Victorian Architecture in Britain*, New Haven: Yale University Press, 1954, I, 395

43 For the appearance of the west side of the street in mid-century, see the *Grand Architectural Panorama of London, Regent Street to Westminster Abbey. From Original Drawings . . . by R. Sandeman . . .*, 1949, reproduced 1966 by Edward Stanford Ltd. for the London Topographical Society, No. 105

44 *B*, VI (1848), 530

45 *Architect*, X (1873), 87. Hereafter cited as *A*

46 *BN*, XLI (1881), 350

47 *B*, LXXII (1897), 287

48 *BN*, LXVI (1894), 145

Chapter Three: The Rejection and Destruction of Georgian London (pp. 49–126)

1   *Parliamentary Papers*, 1840, XII (410), First Report from the Select Committee on Metropolis Improvement, v–vi

2   For an extended comparison between Paris and London in the nineteenth century, see Lynn Lees, 'Metropolitan Types', in Dyos and Wolff, I, 413–28

3   Reprinted in *CE*, III (1840), 311

4   'Report to the . . . Committee upon Improvements of the Commissioners of Sewers of the City of London . . .' in *BN*, VII (1861), 131

5   *BN*, VII (1861), 86

6   *B*, XXVI (1868), 582

7   *BN*, XVIII (1870), 1

8   *BN*, XXV (1873), 557

9   *B*, XL (1881), 419

10 *BN*, IV (1858), 260

11 *B*, XXII (1864), 95

12 *B*, II (1844), 370

13 *B*, VII (1849), 220

14 Anon., *London as it is Today*, 1851, 5–7

15 Ernest Maltravers, quoted in *B*, XIII (1855), 73

16 *B*, XL (1881), 419

17 *BN*, LIV (1888), 727

18 *B*, XV (1857), 471

19 *B*, XXIX (1871), 820

20 *B*, XXXIV (1876), 454

21 *B*, XL (1881), 789

22 *BN*, LVI (1889), 821

23 *BN*, LXXI (1896), 689

24 *BN*, LVII (1889), 101

25 *Architectural Magazine*, I (1834), 113–16

26 *B*, III (1845), 28

27 'Marquis de Vermont', 222–3

28 *BN*, LXIX (1895), 361

29 Morris, 317

30 *BN*, IV (1858), 34

31 *A*, I (1869), 98

32 *BN*, XXXII (1877), 112

33 *BN*, LXXVII (1899), 684

34 Gomme, 140

35 *A*, XXXIII (1885), 295–6

36 Summerson, 'London, the Artifact', 312

37 *BN*, XLIV (1883), 179

38 *ibid.*, 735

39 *A*, XIII (1875), 169–70

40 *BN*, XXXI (1876), 357

41 *A*, XXXII (1884), 47

42 *BN*, XXV (1873), 557

43 *BN*, LXI (1891), 491. See also *BN*, LXIII (1892), 98; *A*, L (1893), 132

44 *BN*, XXIX (1875), 166

45 *BN*, LXXVIII (1900), 851

46 *BN*, XLI (1881), 1

47 Nicholas Taylor, 'The Awful Sublimity of the Victorian City', in Dyos and Wolff, II, 444–5

48 Hitchcock, I, 359

49 Taylor, 432

50 Hitchcock, I, 397

51 *B*, IV (1846), 422

52 *BN*, III (1857), 1

53 *B*, XX (1862), 273

54 *BN*, XV (1868), 647

55 See, for example, chapters XV and XVI, 'Early Railway Stations and Other Iron Construction', and 'The Crystal Palace: Ferrovitreous Triumph and Ensuing Reaction', in Hitchcock, 492–571

56 Henry James, 'English Hours', *Century Magazine*, December 1888, in Henry Steele Commager, ed., *Britain through American Eyes*, Bodley Head, 1974, 525, 527

57 *BN*, XL (1881), 253

58 *BN*, XXXV (1878), 207

59 *BN*, XLI (1881), 349–50

60 *BN*, XXIX (1875), 166

61 *BN*, XLIV (1883), 1

62 *A*, XL (1888), 167

63 *BN*, LVII (1889), 101

64 *BN*, LXI (1891), 497

65 *A*, L (1893), 147

66 *BN*, LXVIII (1895), 682

67 *BN*, LXVII (1894), 240–1

68 *BN*, LXXVIII (1900), 851

69 *B*, LXX (1896), 202

70 *B*, LXXII (1897), 287

71 *BN*, LXXV (1898), 811

72 *BN*, LXIV (1893), 361

73 Charles Eyre Pascoe, *London of To-day*, 1888, 24

74 *B*, XXVI (1868), 501

75 *A*, XVII (1877), 77

76 *A*, IX (1873), 229

77 T. Roger Smith and W.H. White, 'Model Dwellings for the Rich', paper read to the Society of Arts, in *A*, XV (1876), 209

78 *BN*, LXXVI (1899), 701

79 *CE*, I (1837), 9

80 *B*, II (1844), 503

81 Sir Walter Besant, *London in the Nineteenth Century*, Adam & Charles Black, 1909, 260

82 A. Hayward, *The Art of Dining*, 2nd ed., 1883, 122–3

83 Carroll L.V. Meeks, *The Railway Station*, New Haven: Yale University Press, 1957

84 *A*, X (1873), 54

85 *BN*, XXIX (1875), 133. Quoted in Meeks, 90

86 *A*, X (1873), 54

87 *BN*, XXIX (1875), 133

88 *BN*, XIII (1866), 705

89 *BN*, XV (1868), 714

90 See Jack Simmons, 'The Power of the Railway', in Dyos and Wolff, I, 303. For the anxiety as to the 'social costs' of railways penetrating built-up areas, see John R. Kellett, *The Impact of Railways on Victorian Cities*, Routledge & Kegan Paul, 1969, 25–59

91 *BN*, XXIX (1875), 133

92 See Hitchcock, I, 415; Hermione Hobhouse, *Lost London*, Macmillan, 1971, 198–206; Summerson, 'London, the Artifact', I, 324–5

93 *BN*, IX (1862), 255

94 John Timbs, *Curiosities of London*, n.d. 441

95 *CE*, XIV (1851), 355

96 *BN*, IX (1862), 255

97 Summerson, 'London, the Artifact', 318

98 Timbs, 442

99 Hobhouse, *Lost London*, 199

100 *BN*, IV (1858), 230

101 *Dickens's Dictionary of London*, 134

102 *BN*, XL (1881), 1

103 *BN*, XLVIII (1885), 877–8

104 Karl Baedeker, *London and its Environs*, Leipzig, 1905, 8

105 Pascoe, 27–9

106 *BN*, III (1857), 1012

107 *A*, XXI (1879), 31

108 *BN*, III (1857), 947

109 *ibid.*, 979–80

110 *BN*, XVII (1869), 374

111 *BN*, XXXV (1878), 207

112 *ibid.*, 502

113 See Guy Deghy and Keith Waterhouse, *Café Royal*, Hutchinson, 1955, 25–39

114 *BN*, XXIV (1873), 632

115 *B*, XXXI (1873), 521–2

116 *A*, X (1873), 141

117 *BN*, XXX (1876), 439.

118 *BN*, XXVIII (1875), 1. See also Summerson, 'London, the Artifact', 325

119 *A*, XXI (1879), 31

120 *Dickens's Dictionary of London*, 230–1

121 Hobhouse, *Lost London*, 212–16. For the Holborn Restaurant, see *BN*, LXVII (1894), 59

122 *A*, L (1893), 131–2

123 *BN*, LXVII (1894), 59

124 Besant, *London in the Nineteenth Century*, 263–4

125 *BN*, LXXVII (1899), 365

126 *BN*, LXXIX (1900), 421

127 *A*, LXIII (1900), 409

128 *Architectural Magazine*, IV (1837), 553

129 Brian Harrison, 'Pubs', in Dyos and Wolff, I, 170

130 *BN*, III (1857), 480–1

131 Harrison, 171

132 Michael R. Booth, 'The Metropolis on Stage', in Dyos and Wolff, I, 212

133 *BN*, IX (1862), 308

134 *BN*, III (1857), 481

135 For an account of the suspicion with which the flat was viewed by the Victorian middle classes, see J.N. Tarn, 'French Flats for the English in Nineteenth-century London', in Anthony Sutcliffe, ed., *Multi-Storey Living*, Croom Helm, 1974, 19–39

136 Hitchcock, I, 475–9. See also Summerson, 'London, the Artifact', 317

137 *BN*, XV (1868), 323

138 *B*, XXX (1872), 23

139 *BN*, III (1857), 181

140 *BN*, III (1857), 1050

141 *A*, X (1873), 141

142 *A*, X (1873), 168

143 *B*, XXXIV (1876), 26

144 *B*, XXXIV (1876), 291. For White see Pevsner, *Some Architectural Writers*, 231–2, and P. Thompson, 'The Writings of William White', in Summerson, ed., *Concerning Architecture*, Penguin, 1968, 226–37

145 Report on paper, 'Middle Class Houses in Paris and Central London', in *BN*, XXXIII (1877), 522

146 *A*, V (1871), 157

147 *BN*, XV (1868), 323

148 *Dickens's Dictionary of London*, 111–12. See also *BN*, XLI (1881), 615–16; *A*, XXVI (1881), 78

149 *BN*, LXIII (1892), 302

150 *BN*, LXXVIII (1900), 533

151 Summerson, 'London, the Artifact', 315

152 *BN*, III (1857), 1

153 *A*, V (1871), 167

154 *B*, XXXI (1873), 6

155 *B*, XXXIV (1876), 305. See also Hitchcock, I, 375; Nicholas Taylor, 'The Awful Sublimity of the Victorian City', 441–2

156 Hitchcock, I, 345–6

157 See *ibid.*, 359

158 *ibid.*, 347, 396–7; Summerson, 'London, the Artifact', 315–16

159 Hitchcock, I, 371–2, 375

160 *A*, V (1871), 167

161 *Modern London*, *c.* 1887, quoted in Alison Adburgham, *Shops and Shopping 1800–1914*, George Allen and Unwin, 1964, 156

162 James B. Jefferys, *Retail Trading in Britain 1850–1950*, Cambridge University Press, 1954, 326

163 *ibid.*, 328

164 *ibid.*, 33

165 Lancaster, *All Done from Memory*, 35

166 Richard S. Lambert, *The Universal Provider*, George G. Harrap & Co., 1938, 69, 73–4

167 *ibid.*, 76–7, 85

168 *ibid.*, 72

169 *ibid.*, 76, 94

170 *ibid.*, 115

171 *ibid.*, 219

172 *ibid.*, 242

173 See Dorothy Davis, *A History of Shopping*, Routledge & Kegan Paul, 1966, 288–93

174 Besant, *London in the Nineteenth Century*, 30

175 Charles Booth, *Life and Labour of the People in London*, Second Series: *Industry*, III (1903), 68–9

176 For the expanding and varied retail establishments that contrived to fit themselves into Regent Street, see Hobhouse, *A History of Regent Street*, 95–107

177 *BN*, XL (1881), 731

178 *BN*, XLI (1881), 384

179 Baedeker, *London*, 16–19

180 *ibid.*, 70

Chapter Four: The Preservation and Extension of Georgian London (pp. 127–186)

1 For an extended description of the policies of the great London estates, see Olsen, *Town Planning in London*

2 *ibid.*, 110–11

3 *B*, II (1844), 386

4 William Gaspey, *Tallis's Illustrated London*, [1852], II, 24–5

5 Alfred Cox, *The Landlord's and Tenant's Guide*, [1853], 213

6 *BN*, VII (1861), 18

7 *BN*, XVI (1869), 247

8 *A*, VIII (1872), 143

9 *B*, XXXI (1873), 857–8

10 Pascoe, 42

11 Edward Walford, *Old and New London*, [1873–8], IV, 483–4

12 *BN* XXXII (1877), 484

13 *B*, LXXII (1897), 314

14 *BN*, III (1857), 158

15 *BN*, IV (1858), 912

16 For the frustrations suffered by the Bedford Office in its attempts to raise the social standing of Gower Street, see Olsen, *Town Planning in London*, 174–7

17 *B*, LII (1887), 143

18 *BN*, XXXII (1877), 609, commenting on an article in the *Liverpool Mercury*

19 *BN*, XXXIX (1880), 143

20 *B*, XL (1881), 154

21 *B*, LII (1887), 144

22 *B*, LXXII (1897), 314

23 *BN*, LVII (1889), 101

24 *BN*, LXVII (1894), 184

25 *B*, LXXII (1897), 314

26 Pevsner, *London, Except the Cities of London and Westminster*, Penguin Books, 1952, 217

27 G.L.C., *Survey of London*, XXXVI, *The Parish of St. Paul Covent Garden*, Athlone Press, 1970, 42

28 See Olsen, *Town Planning in London*, 184–8

29 G.L.C., *Survey of London*, XXXVI, 12–13

30 *ibid.*, XXXVI, 43–4

31 *BN*, XXIX (1875), 246

32 *A*, XVII (1877), 342

33 Olsen, *Town Planning in London*, 188

34 *BN*, XXXII (1877), 209

35 *BN*, XXXII (1877), 611

36 G.L.C., *Survey of London*, XXXVI, 48

37 I base this generalization on the impressions gathered by Francis Sheppard in his work in the two offices in gathering information for the G.L.C. *Survey of London*

38 For the management of the Grosvenor Office before 1845, see Hobhouse, *Thomas Cubitt*, 103–15

39 *CE*, VI (1843), 228

40 Hitchcock, I, 484–5

41 *BN*, IV (1858), 1272

42 *B*, XXIII (1865), 152

43 *B*, XXIII (1865), 475

44 *B*, XXV (1867), 121–3. See also *A*, I (1869), 89–90

45 *A*, I (1869), 201

46 *BN*, XVI (1869), 106

47 *BN*, XLVI (1884), 283

48 'London Street Architecture as it is, and

as it might be,' paper read to the Architectural Association, in *A*, XLI (1889), 21

49 *BN*, LXIII (1892), 805. For an attack on what he describes as the tyrannical behaviour of the Duke of Westminster in carrying out the Mount Street improvements, see Frank Banfield, *The Great Landlords of London*, 1888, 57–9

50 'The Advantages of adopting a General Scheme in making Improvements to the London Streets,' in *A*, XLIX (1893), 97. See also Percy Fitzgerald, *London City Suburbs*, 1893, 43

51 Gomme, *London in the Reign of Victoria*, 143–4

52 *B*, LXXI (1896), 226; LXXIV (1898), 137

53 *BN*, LXXVI (1899), 51

54 Booth, *Life and Labour of the People in London*, Third Series: Religious Influences, 1902, III, 98. Date of inquiry: 1899

55 *ibid.*, II, 196. Date of inquiry: 1898

56 *BN*, LXIII (1892), 805

57 *B*, LXXII (1897), 313

58 Hitchcock, I, 420, 439

59 *BN*, XXX (1876), 311

60 *BN*, XLII (1882), 407

61 *BN*, XXXIII (1877), 356

62 *BN*, XXXIII (1877), 401

63 *B*, XL (1881), 789

64 *BN*, LI (1886), 477

65 Booth, *Life and Labour of the People in London*, Third Series: Religious Influences, III, 111. Date of inquiry: 1899

66 *Parliamentary Papers*, 1887 (260) xiii, Select Committee on Town Holdings, Minutes of Evidence, 259

67 *BN*, LVII (1889), 101

68 'London Street Architecture, as it is, and as it might be,' in *A*, XLI (1889), 20

69 Fitzgerald, 48–9

70 'The Advantages of adopting a General Scheme in making Improvements to the London Streets', in *A*, XLIX (1893), 96

71 Walford, *Old and New London*, 1897, V, 100

72 *BN*, LXII (1892), 460

73 *A*, XXXIII (1885), 296

74 *B*, XV (1857), 220. See also H.J. Dyos, 'The Speculative Builders and Developers of Victorian London', *Victorian Studies*, XI (1968), 663; *Parliamentary Papers*, 1889, XV (251), Select Committee on Town

Holdings: Report, 109

75 Alfred Emden, *The Law Relating to Building, Building Leases, and Building Contracts*, 2nd ed., 1885, 160. See also Dyos, 'Speculative Builders', 660–1

76 E.W. Cooney, 'The Origins of the Victorian Master Builders', *Economic History Review*, VIII (1955), argues that Cubitt's techniques were widely imitated, but his biographer, Hermione Hobhouse, is convinced that his methods remained exceptional during his own lifetime. See her *Thomas Cubitt*, 524. See also Dyos, 'Speculative Builders', and Cooney's comments on the article in *Victorian Studies*, XIII (1970), 355

77 Dyos, 'Speculative Builders', 659–60

78 See A.K. Cairncross, *Home and Foreign Investment, 1870–1913*, Cambridge University Press, 1953, 84

79 Dyos, 'Speculative Builders', 663. See also Kellett, 412–13

80 *Parliamentary Papers*, 1884–5, XXX (4402–I), Royal Commission on the Housing of the Working Classes: Minutes of Evidence, 379

81 *Parliamentary Papers*, 1888, XXII (313), Select Committee on Town Holdings: Minutes of Evidence, 641–4; 1889, XV (251), Select Committee on Town Holdings, 109. Dyos, *Victorian Suburb*, Leicester University Press, 1961, 127–32

82 *Parliamentary Papers*, 1887, XIII (260), Select Committee on Town Holdings: Minutes of Evidence, 83

83 John W. Papworth in *B*, XV (1857), 220. See also Dyos, 'Speculative Builders', 651–2. For a description of its operations in the eighteenth century, see Summerson, *Georgian London*, 60–2

84 *B*, XVI (1858), 176–7; *Parliamentary Papers*, 1888, XXII (313), Select Committee on Town Holdings: Minutes of Evidence, 640–3; Dyos, 'Speculative Builders', 660–1, 669

85 Olsen, *Town Planning in London*, 79

86 Hobhouse, *Thomas Cubitt*, 212, 343

87 James Noble, *The Professional Practice of Architects*, 1836, 97. See also 'Report of Messrs. Leverton & Chawner . . .' (1811) in J[ohn] White, *Some Account of the*

Proposed Improvements in the Western Part of London, 2nd ed., 1815, Appendix, xii; John Shaw in *Parliamentary Papers*, 1829, III (343), Select Committee on Crown Leases: Report, 47–8; *BN*, VI (1860), 871

88 Emden, 157; Dyos, 'Speculative Builders', 664–5

89 John Holliday, *A Further Appeal to the Governors of the Foundling Hospital*, 1788, 17

90 *B*, XV (1857), 220

91 *Parliamentary Papers*, 1887, XIII (260), Select Committee on Town Holdings: Minutes of Evidence, 617–24

92 Dyos, 'Speculative Builders', 665–8

93 Took Hallowes and Price, Accounts with respect to Mortgage of Chalcots, 1864–5; Hallowes Price & Hallowes, Chalcots Rental, November 1872. Registrar's Correspondence. All MS. references to material on Chalcots in the Eton College Records (ECR) are by the kind permission of the Provost and Fellows of Eton College

94 Dyos, 'Speculative Builders', 668–9

95 John Nash in White, *Some Account of the Proposed Improvements*, Appendix, xxvii–xxviii. For the role of credit from builders' merchants, see Dyos, 'Speculative Builders', 661, and *B*, XV (1857), 220

96 'Ground Rents have of late years become worth more, owing to the difficulty of getting good investments to pay a fair rate of interest, and if they are well secured will now fetch about twenty-five years' purchase . . .'. Frederick Fowler, *The Valuation of Property and the Various Interests Therein*, Sheffield, 1890, 10

97 Such were the rates Cubitt and his subordinate builders were accustomed to. Hobhouse, *Thomas Cubitt*, 320–1

98 Richard Nation to Thomas Batcheldor, 21 January 1864, Registrar's Correspondence. See also Robert Yeo to Thomas Batcheldor, 15 January 1864, Registrar's Correspondence; Samuel Cuming to George Bethell, 1 August 1850, ECR. 49/133; Samuel Cuming to Thomas Batcheldor, 14 February 1844, ECR.

99 *B*, XXII (1864), 742

100 Gomme, 136

101 *B*, XVI (1858), 630

102 *A*, X (1873), 15

103 *BN*, XXXII (1877), 357

104 Hitchcock, I, 418–19

105 *BN*, IV (1858), 1181

106 *B*, XXII (1864), 94

107 *B*, XXII (1864), 94

108 *A*, XIV (1875), 335

109 *A*, XVI (1876), 86

110 *BN*, XXV (1873), 274

111 'Surveyor', in *B*, XXXVII (1879), 1217

112 *A*, X (1873), 15

113 'The Building of the London House,' in *A*, XXXI (1884), 119

114 See Gordon Toplis, 'The History of Tyburnia', *Country Life* (15, 22, 29 November 1973), 1526–8, 1708–10, 1841–2

115 *B*, II (1844), 389

116 Hitchcock, I, 487–8

117 *London Exhibited in 1851*, 1851, 770

118 William Gaspey, *Tallis's Illustrated London*, II, 42–3

119 Hitchcock, I, 485–6

120 Cox, 212

121 *ibid.*, 215–16

122 *BN*, III (1857), 635

123 *BN*, III (1857), 1007

124 *BN*, III (1857), 277; *BN*, IV (1858), 852; *BN*, V (1859), 818

125 *BN*, IV (1858), 2

126 *BN*, XV (1868), 697

127 *BN*, IV (1858), 470

128 *BN*, V (1859), 36

129 *ibid.*, 1082

130 D.A. Reeder, 'A Theatre of Suburbs: Some Patterns of Development in West London, 1801–1911', in H.J. Dyos, ed., *The Study of Urban History*, Edward Arnold, 1968, 263–4

131 *BN*, VI (1860), 593

132 *B*, XXI (1863), 766–7

133 Quoted in Lambert, 106

134 *B*, XXVII (1869), 670

135 *B*, XXX (1872), 14

136 *Dickens's Dictionary of London*, 273

137 [W.S. Clarke], *The Suburban Homes of London*, 1881, 398

138 G.L.C., *Survey of London*, XXXVII, *Northern Kensington*, Athlone Press, 1973, 195–7

139 *ibid.*, XXXVII, 276

140 *ibid.*, XXXVII, 207–26

141 *ibid.*, XXXVII, 5–7, 232–3

142 *BN*, III (1857), 400

143 *BN*, VI (1860), 593

144 George Rose Emerson, *London: How the Great City Grew*, 1862, 244–5

145 Hitchcock, I, 442–5. See also Pevsner, *London, Except the Cities of London and Westminster*, 310–11

146 G.L.C., *Survey of London*, XXXVII (1973), 229

147 [Clarke], 401–2

148 Fitzgerald, 9–10, 12

149 Booth, *Life and Labour of the People in London*, Third Series: Religious Influences, III, 107–8. Date of inquiry: 1899

150 Lancaster, *All Done from Memory*, 5

151 Elmes, 154

152 Quoted in W.H. Leeds, II, 371–3

153 Hitchcock, I, 419

154 John H. Brady, *New Pocket Guide to London and its Environs*, 1838, 470–1

155 W. Weir, 'The Squares of London', in Charles Knight, ed., *London*, 1841–44, VI, 205

156 *BN*, III (1857), 1218

157 *BN*, IV (1858), 962

158 Cox, 211–12

159 Gaspey, I, 195

160 Hitchcock, I, 431

161 Gaspey, I, 195

162 Quoted in Hobhouse, *Thomas Cubitt*, 185

163 Quoted in *ibid.*, 234

164 Booth, *Life and Labour of the People in London*, Third Series: Religious Influences, III, 87–8. Date of inquiry: 1899

165 For the early development of the north side of Kensington High Street, see G.L.C., *Survey of London*, XXXVII, 58–62

166 Hitchcock, I, 421

167 *ibid.*, I, 440–1

168 *ibid.*, I, 446; G.L.C., *Survey of London*, XXXVII (1973), 151–93

169 Cox, 216

170 *ibid.*, 212

171 Gaspey, I, 198

172 Edgar A. Bowring, 'South Kensington', *Nineteenth Century*, I (1877), 563–4

173 Hitchcock, I, 480–3

174 *BN*, III (1857), 328

175 *BN*, IV (1858), 1096

176 *BN*, III (1857), 383

177 *BN*, IV (1858), 418

178 *BN*, III (1857), 380–3

179 *BN*, IV (1858), 572. See also *BN*, VI (1860), 285

180 *B*, XVI (1858), 260

181 For the strike, or lock-out, of 1859, see R.W. Postgate, *The Builders' History*, National Federation of Building Trade Operatives, 1923, 167–79

182 *BN*, V (30 September 1859), 879–80

183 *B*, XIX (1861), 315

184 *B*, XXI (1863), 85

185 *B*, XXIV (1866), 951

186 *B*, XXVI (1868), 201

187 *BN*, XV (1868), 697

188 *A*, VII (1872), 204

189 *BN*, XXXI (1876), 306

190 *BN*, XXXI (1876), 357

191 W.J. Loftie, *Kensington, Picturesque and Historical*, 1888, 222. See also *BN*, LXXII (1897), 370, on the brick, stone, and terracotta houses of George and Peto between the Cromwell and Fulham Roads.

192 Adburgham, 161–5

193 *A*, IV (1870), 180

194 [Clarke], 282

195 *BN*, XLIII (1882), 285

196 Loftie, 18–19

197 Reeder, 257

198 *B*, LXIII (1892), 199

199 Fitzgerald, 43

200 *ibid.*, 10

201 Booth, *Life and Labour of the People in London*, Third Series: Religious Influences, III, 130–1. Date of inquiry: 1899

Chapter Five: The Villa and the New Suburb (pp. 187–264)

1 *A*, XLV (1891), 330

2 *A*, LIII (1895), 177

3 *BN*, LXIV (1893), 732

4 Besant, *South London*, 1899, 301–2

5 *B*, II (1844), 392

6 Brady, 307

7 *ibid.*, 445–6

8 For an analysis of the different types of suburban settlement and the various causes affecting their nature and location, see Michael Robbins, *Middlesex*, Collins, 1953, 194–7

9 *B*, II (1844), 486

10 Quoted in *B*, VI (1848), 500–1

11 Gaspey, II, 79

12 *ibid.*, II, 82

13 *ibid.*, II, 84

14 L.C.C., *Survey of London*, vol. XXVI, *The Parish of St. Mary Lambeth*, Part Two, *Southern Area*, Athlone Press, 1956, p. 11

15 Emerson, 254–5

16 *ibid.*, 266

17 *ibid.*, 281

18 *ibid.*, 272–3

19 *ibid.*, 251

20 B, XXI (1863), 767

21 B, XLIX (1885), 5

22 B, XXVI (1868), 502

23 B, XXVIII (1870), 324–5

24 James Thorne, *Handbook to the Environs of London*, 1876, I, 128. For the impact of the new London commuters on the old market town, see R.C.W. Cox, 'The Old Centre of Croydon: Victorian Decay and Redevelopment', in Alan Everitt, ed., *Perspectives in English Urban History*, Macmillan, 1973, 186–7

25 Thorne, II, 467

26 *ibid.*, II, 598

27 *ibid.*, I, 220

28 *ibid.*, I, 273

29 B, XLI (1881), 830

30 B, XLIII (1882), 172. See also BN, XLV (1883), 399

31 BN, XLVI (1884), 153. See also BN, XLVIII (1885), 158

32 BN, LI (1886), 371

33 BN, LII (1887), 955. See also BN, LIII (1887), 47

34 B, LVI (1889), 441. See also B, LIX (1890), 304, for the effect on the building industry of the crisis in the money market

35 Pascoe, 22–3

36 BN, LXXIX (1900), 97

37 A, XVI (1876), 33

38 Nicholas Taylor, *The Village in the City*, Temple Smith, 1973, 203

39 Besant, *South London*, 302–3

40 *ibid.*, 307–8

41 E.T. Cook and A. Wedderburn, eds., *The Works of John Ruskin*, 1908, XXXV, 47, quoted in L.C.C., *Survey of London*, XXVI, 10–11

42 Brady, 445–6

43 Emerson, 251

44 B, XXI (1863), 767

45 BN, XXVII (1874), 425

46 BN, LXXI (1896), 290

47 Fitzgerald, 196–9

48 Walford, *Old and New London*, VI, 292–3

49 Henri Bellenger, *Londres pittoresque*, Paris, n.d., 5–7

50 B, XXXVIII (1880), 424

51 BN, XLVI (1884), 74

52 BN, XLIV (1883), 117

53 B, XXIV (1866), 381

54 A, XXX (1883), 169

55 A, XXX (1883), 209

56 BN, XLV (1883), 399

57 BN, XXXIII (1877), 531

58 J.M. Richards, *The Castles on the Ground*, 2nd ed., John Murray, 1973, 60

59 A, XLV (1891), 330

60 Quoted in Leeds, II, 350

61 Robbins, 202

62 Besant, *London in the Nineteenth Century*, 262

63 *ibid.*, 17

64 Robbins, 208

65 Richards, 35–6

66 *ibid.*, 88

67 Taylor, *The Village in the City*, 98

68 Alan A. Jackson, *Semi-Detached London*, George Allen & Unwin, 1973, 21–2

69 *ibid.*, 167–8

70 *ibid.*, 173

71 John Nash in White, Appendix, xxxiv–xxxv

72 Summerson, *Georgian London*, 157–9; Hitchcock, I, 441–2

73 John Shaw to George Bethell, 22 July 1845, ECR. 49/116

74 Cox, 231–2

75 *ibid.*, 232

76 Thomas Smith, *A Topographical and Historical Account of the Parish of St. Mary-le-bone*, 1833, 222

77 [Clarke], 432

78 Fitzgerald, 84

79 Quoted in Francis Sheppard, *London 1808–1870: the Infernal Wen*, Secker & Warburg, 1971, 136

80 BN, IV (1858), 606

81 BN, XXVII (1874), 425–6

82 BN, XLIX (1885), 75

83 [Clarke], 128

84 *ibid.*, 424
85 *ibid.*, 460
86 Fitzgerald, 200–3
87 *BN*, VII (1861), 470
88 *A*, I (1869), 149
89 Report in *BN*, XXXVI (1879), 713
90 *A*, XIV (1875), 335
91 *BN*, XXXIII (1877), 522
92 *A*, L (1893), 35
93 Rasmussen, *London: the Unique City*, 294
94 *A*, XLV (1891), 330
95 *B*, LXVI (1891), 89
96 *BN*, LXXVIII (1900), 391
97 *A*, VII (1872), 207
98 Taylor, *The Village in the City*, 28
99 *ibid.*, 138
100 H. J. Dyos and D.A. Reeder, 'Slums and Suburbs', in Dyos and Wolff, I, 370
101 Taylor, 'The Awful Sublimity of the Victorian City', in Dyos and Wolff, II, 433
102 *B*, XIX (1861), 314. Hope, an amateur architect and patron, became president of the RIBA in 1865, and was the author of *The English Cathedral of the Nineteenth Century*, 1861. As Conservative M.P. he bitterly opposed the Second Reform Bill. Pevsner, *Some Architectural Writers of the Nineteenth Century*, 229–30
103 *BN*, X (1863), 175
104 'Old Houses', *Cornhill Magazine*, XIII (1866), 611
105 *BN*, III (1857), 304
106 Cox, 232
107 Sir John Summerson, 'The London Suburban Villa', *Architectural Review*, CIV (1948), 66
108 *BN*, XIII (1866), 747
109 *BN*, XXIX (1875), 190
110 *BN*, XLI (1881), 159
111 *BN*, XLVII (1884), 159. See also *BN*, XLV (1883), 399
112 *B*, XLVIII (1885), 896
113 *BN*, LXIV (1893), 759–60
114 Robbins, 202
115 *BN*, XXVII (1874), 364
116 *BN*, LXXI (1896), 290
117 The aesthetic governing the layout of any late Victorian suburb is what A. Trystan Edwards wittily attacks in *Good and Bad Manners in Architecture*, Philip Allan & Co., 1924, 123–75. The whole volume, though an attack on Victorian principles of architecture and urban design, by identifying and defining what it sets out to oppose, serves as a lucid introduction to the assumptions underlying what the Victorians did to urban and suburban London
118 Robbins, 206
119 *B*, XXXVII (1879), 1044–5
120 Walford, *Greater London*, [1883–4], II, 100
121 *ibid.*, II, 124
122 [Clarke], 74–5
123 *ibid.*, 128
124 Robbins, 206
125 Fitzgerald, 204–7
126 *BN*, LXIV (1893), 732
127 J. H. Westergaard, 'The Structure of Greater London', in Centre for Urban Studies, ed., *London: Aspects of Change*, MacGibbon & Kee, 1964, 100
128 Gaspey, I, 319
129 Emerson, 264
130 *BN*, XXXI (1876), 409
131 Taylor, *The Village in the City*, 60
132 *BN*, XXXI (1876), 621. See also *BN*, XXXII (1877), 253
133 Walford, *Greater London*, I, 14
134 *ibid.*, I, 123
135 *BN*, XLIII (1882), 470
136 *B*, XLIV (1883), 631
137 *BN*, LIV (1888), 488
138 *A*, XLV (1891), 330
139 Duncan Timms, *The Urban Mosaic*, Cambridge University Press, 1971, 98
140 *ibid.*, 2
141 Taylor, *The Village in the City*, 39
142 Dyos and Reeder, I, 369
143 Elmes, 21. 'Larger houses, about twenty-five years old, border the Regent's Park, and are frequently occupied by merchants.' Cox, 213
144 Smith, 222
145 *B*, II (1844), 393
146 See T.C. Barker and Michael Robbins, *History of London Transport*, 1963, I, 54
147 *BN*, IV (1858), 1191
148 Cox, 231
149 See Olsen, *Town Planning in London*, 115, 130, for the tendency of mews property to deteriorate on the Bedford and Foundling Hospital estates. For their virtual absence

from the Eton College estate, see Thompson, 239–40

150 Cox, 232

151 *Golden Guide to London*, 1879, 43

152 [Clarke], 432

153 *ibid.*, 424

154 Booth, *Life and Labour of the People in London*, Third Series: Religious Influences, I, 1902, 206–7. Date of inquiry: 1897–8

155 *ibid.*, I, 213

156 Elizabeth Bowen, quoted in Pevsner, *London, Except the Cities of London and Westminster*, 354

157 *B*, VII (1849), 459

158 *B*, VII (1849), 572

159 J.R. McCulloch, *London in 1850–1851*, 1851, 108

160 *B*, XXIII (1865), 195

161 *BN*, XVII (1869), 466

162 *A*, X (1873), 170.

163 L.C.C., *Survey of London*, XXVI, 152

164 G.F. Pardon, *Routledge's Shilling Guidebook to London*, quoted in *B*, XX (1862), 666

165 *A*, VIII (1872), 356

166 Besant, *London in the Nineteenth Century*, 29

167 Thompson, 241

168 Edward Hill to W. Carter, 9 October 1871. Registrar's Correspondence, ECR.

169 George Pownall to William Carter, 11 October 1871. Registrar's Correspondence, ECR.

170 Thomas W. Peile to [the Provost of Eton], 28 October 1871. Registrar's Correspondence, ECR.

171 Pencilled notes on the printed stationery of George Pownall. Registrar's Correspondence, ECR.

172 Cope Rose and Pearson to [G. and G.H. Pownall], 29 November 1871. Registrar's Correspondence. G. and G.H. Pownall to the Rev. William Carter, 1 December 1871. Registrar's Correspondence. 'The Provost & College of Eton and The Revd. Thos. Wm. Peile D.D. and others, Agreement for a Lease of a Site for a School,' 19 December 1872. 'Eton College, Chalcots Estate, Schedule of Counterpart Leases handed over to Messrs. Hallowes & Carter November 1894 by Mr. Richard Cope.' ECR.

173 *A*, X (1873), 181

174 *A*, XIII (1875), 99. See also *B*, XXXIII (1875), 420–1

175 *A*, X (1873), 193

176 *BN*, XL (1881), 144–5

177 [Clarke], 56

178 *ibid.*, 13–14

179 *ibid.*, 381

180 *BN*, LVIII (1890), 611

181 Booth, *Life and Labour of the People in London*, Third Series, IV, 166, quoted in L.C.C., *Survey of London*, XXVI, 12

182 *B*, XLI (1881), 59

183 W. Ashworth, 'Types of Social and Economic Development in Suburban Essex', in Centre for Urban Studies, ed., *London: Aspects of Change*, 72–4

184 *ibid.*, 74–6

185 *ibid.*, 76

186 *ibid.*, 78

187 *ibid.*, 81–2

188 Much of the remainder of this chapter first appeared as part of 'House upon House: Estate Development in London and Sheffield', in Dyos and Wolff, I, 333–57. For a more detailed history of the building development of the Eton College estate, see Thompson, 216–44, 346–50

189 Summerson, 'Urban Forms', in Oscar Handlin and John Burchard, eds., *The Historian and the City*, Cambridge, Mass.: M.I.T. Press, 1963, 174

190 Hugh C. Prince in J.T. Coppock and Hugh C. Prince, eds., *Greater London*, Faber and Faber, 1964, 105

191 Kate Simon, *London: Places and Pleasures*, New York: G.P. Putnam, 1968, 293

192 Summerson, 'Urban Forms', 175; and 'The Beginnings of an Early Victorian London Suburb', II, a lecture delivered at the London School of Economics, 27 February 1958, which Sir John kindly allowed me to read

193 Reginald J. Fletcher, *St. Saviour's Church South Hampstead, A Retrospect*, 1918, 6–7

194 Thompson, 225–6

195 *B*, XXXIII (1875), 274

196 Olsen, *Town Planning in London*, 20, 33–4, 81–3, 224–7

197 See, in this connection, Thompson, 370

198 'Report of Messrs. Leverton & Chawner',

in White, Appendix, xv

199 Nash, in *ibid.*, xxxiv–xxxv

200 Summerson, *Georgian London*, 164

201 'Proposed plan to divide the Land belonging to Eton College situate at Primrose Hill . . . into plots of ground to be let for Building', ECR. 51/12

202 'Plan of an Estate . . . with plots of Ground divided thereon proposed to be let for Building,' 20 December 1824, ECR. 51/13. See also George Bethell, 'Observations heard at the meeting relative to the waste', 1825, ECR. 49/22

203 *An Act for effecting an Exchange between Her Majesty and the Provost and College of Eton*, 5 & 6 Vict. cap. lxxviii

204 'Plan of a part of the Estate of Eton College . . . showing a design for building thereon', March 1827, ECR. 51/17

205 'Plan of the Chalcots Farm . . . Shewing a Design for Building thereon,' 1829, ECR. 51/19

206 Chalcots, Hampstead. Proposals for Building, 1 May 1829, ECR. 49/27

207 Summerson, 'Urban Forms', 174

208 'Chalcots estate plan' [January 1840], ECR. 51/25; John Shaw to George Bethell, 14 January 1840, ECR. 49/84

209 William Wynn to Thomas Batcheldor, 12 December 1842, ECR.

210 John Shaw to George Bethell, 8 January 1846, ECR. 49/119

211 John Shaw to George Bethell, 14 January 1840, ECR. 49/84

212 Henry Bird to George Bethell, 7 September 1846, ECR. 49/128; *Proposed District Church, Chalcott's Estate, Haverstock Hill, Hampstead Road*, 5 September 1846, ECR. 49/128; Two plans 'of part of Fourteen Acres Field inserted in a conveyance from the Provost and College of Eton as a site for a Church . . .' 17 December 1846, ECR. 51/34; Tooke Son and Hallowes to the Provost of Eton, 10 July 1847, ECR. 49/130; John Shaw to George Bethell, 21 November 1850, ECR. 49/137

213 *B*, XIV (1856), 390; Stephen Buckland, 'The Origin and Building of S. Saviour's Church', *S. Saviour, Eton Road, Hampstead, Parish Paper*, October 1956

214 'The Provost and College of Eton and The Revd. Chas. James Fuller and others, Agreement for Conveyance of Land . . . for a Site for a Church', 20 July 1870, ECR.

215 William Kingdom to John Shaw, 22 March 1839, ECR. 49/81; John Shaw to George Bethell, 28 March 1839, ECR. 49/82. Kingdom, who seems to have been 'active in the development of Westbourne Terrace and Hyde Park Gardens, Paddington', had in 1838 been negotiating for the purchase of the Norland estate in Notting Hill. G.L.C., *Survey of London*, XXXVII, 278

216 John Shaw to George Bethell, 14 January 1840, ECR. 49/84

217 John Shaw to George Bethell, 14 July 1845, ECR. 49/114

218 John Shaw to George Bethell, 8 January 1846, ECR. 49/119

219 John Shaw to George Bethell, 5 March 1846, ECR. 49/123

220 'Particulars of a proposed letting of part of the Chalcott's Estate to Mr. Saml. Cuming . . . Builder', 5 August 1844, ECR. 49/111

221 'Particulars of a proposed letting . . . to Mr. Saml. Cuming . . . Builder,' 1 January 1845, ECR. 49/112

222 John Shaw to George Bethell, 22 July 1845, ECR. 49/116

223 John Shaw to George Bethell, 16 November 1850, ECR. 49/136

224 'The Provost and College of Eton and Mr. George Frasi, Agreement,' 29 September 1853, ECR.

225 'The Provost and College of Eton and Messrs. Fotheringham and Renton, Agreement,' 29 September 1853. ECR.

226 'Mr. George Frasi Mr. F. Clemow and Miss M.A. Angell to The Provost and College of Eton, Assignment,' 17 November 1858. ECR.

227 'Mr. Thos. Renton to Mr. Robert Yeo, Agreement for assignment of Contract from Eton College for Building Leases,' 3 March 1856. ECR.

228 *BN*, III (1857), 606–7

229 *BN*, II (1856), 251

230 *BN*, III (1857), 607

231 Thomas Batcheldor to John Shaw, 30 December 1857 (press copy), ECR.

232 'Mr. George Frasi Mr. F. Clemow and Miss M.A. Angell to the Provost and College of Eton, Assignment,' 17 November 1858. ECR.

233 John Shaw to Thomas Batcheldor, 29 May 1861, Registrar's Correspondence, ECR.

234 John Shaw to Thomas Batcheldor, 19 February 1862, Registrar's Correspondence, ECR.

235 *B*, xx (1862), 103

236 Tooke Hallowes & Price to Thomas Batcheldor, 18 April 1862; 'Chalcots – Copy of Pownalls paper. Copy made 26 November 1864', Registrar's Correspondence; Tooke Hallowes and Price, Accounts with respect to Mortgage of Chalcots, 1864–5, ECR.

237 'The Provost and College of Eton with Mr. Robert Yeo, Duplicate Agreement for Building Leases,' 19 May 1863, ECR.

238 'The Provost and College of Eton with Messrs. Yeo & Warner, Agreement for Building Leases,' 9 June 1863, ECR.

239 Tooke, Hallowes & Price, Chalcots Accounts, 1864–5, Registrar's Correspondence, ECR.

240 C.U. Price to Thomas Batcheldor, 28 September 1863, Registrar's Correspondence, ECR.

241 Tooke, Hallowes & Price, Chalcots Accounts, 1866, Registrar's Correspondence, ECR.

242 'The Provost and College of Eton with Mr. Jacob Hibberd, Agreement for Building Leases,' 16 March 1866, ECR.

243 'The Provost and College of Eton and Mr. John George Bettinson, Agreement for Building Leases,' 16 March 1866, ECR.

244 Tooke, Hallowes & Price, Chalcots Accounts, 1866, Registrar's Correspondence, ECR.

245 'The Provost & College of Eton and Mr. Saml. Cuming, Agreement for Building Leases,' 24 April 1866, ECR.

246 'Messrs. John Cuming Samuel Cuming & Wm. Ellis, Executors of the late Samuel Cuming Esq. decd. to The Provost & College of Eton, Assignment of Agreement of 24th April 1866,' 18 July 1870, ECR.

247 Clement Uvedale Price to W.A. Carter, 25 May 1870, Registrar's Correspondence, ECR.

248 For his ambitious and equally disastrous operations at Belsize Park, see Thompson, 275–81

249 *BN*, IV (1858), 1190

250 I am indebted to Sir John Summerson for this information

251 'The Provost and College of Eton with Mr. Daniel Tidey, Agreement for Building Leases,' 21 June 1866, ECR.

252 'The Provost & College of Eton with Mr. Jacob Hibberd, Agreement for Building Leases', 14 December 1866, ECR.

253 'The Provost and College of Eton to Mr. J.G. Bettinson, Third Agreement for Building Leases,' 14 March 1867, ECR.

254 Clement Uvedale Price to Richard Cope, 28 November 1867, Registrar's Correspondence, ECR.

255 'The Provost and College of Eton to Charles Gordon Esq., Counterpart Lease of The Eton and Middlesex Cricket Ground,' 19 March 1868, ECR.

256 'The Provost & College of Eton and Mr. Thos. Welbourn & Mr. F.B. Welbourn, Agreement for Building Leases,' 5 May 1868, ECR.

257 Clement Uvedale Price to W.A. Carter, 14 December 1869, Registrar's Correspondence, ECR.

258 Tooke Hallowes & Price, Accounts, 1869–70, Registrar's Correspondence, ECR.

259 Tooke Hallowes & Price, Accounts, 1869–70, Registrar's Correspondence, ECR.

260 C.U. Price to W.A. Carter, 3 November 1870, Registrar's Correspondence, ECR.

261 Hallowes Price & Hallowes to Messrs. Cope Rose & Pearson, 26 January 1871. See also C.U. Price to W.A. Carter, 11 February 1871, Registrar's Correspondence. 'Mr. John Roche and his Mortgagee to The Provost & College of Eton, Surrender and Release,' 20 March 1871, ECR.

262 'The Provost & College of Eton to Messrs. John Roche and Arthur Lucas, Agreement for Building Leases,' 23 March 1871, ECR.

263 'The Provost of Eton College to Mr. John Roche, License to hold Building Agreement of the 16th March 1866,' 23 March 1871, ECR.

264 C.U. Price to W.A. Carter, 3 May 1871, Registrar's Correspondence. He had as recently as 25 March 1870 extended his obligations on the estate, covenanting to build 15 additional houses on an irregular plot extending southward from England's Lane. Hallowes Price & Hallowes, Chalcots Rental, November 1872, Registrar's Correspondence; 'The Provost and College of Eton and Mr. Jacob Hibberd, Agreement,' 7 April 1870, ECR.

265 Hallowes Price & Hallowes, Chalcots Rental, November 1872, Registrar's Correspondence, ECR.

266 'The Provost and College of Eton to Springall Thompson Esquire and others, Agreement,' 18 December 1873, ECR.

267 *B*, XXXIII (1875), 274

268 *B*, XXXIV (1876), 166

269 'Henry Rose Esqre to The Provost and College of Eton, Surrender and Release,' 29 March 1876, ECR.

270 'The Provost and College of Eton to Henry Rose Esquire, Duplicate Agreement for Building Leases,' 30 March 1876, ECR.

271 'The Provost and College of Eton and Messrs. Thomas Welbourn and Frederick Burkwood Welbourn, *Counterpart* Agreement as to Building Leases and extension of time for Building,' 30 March 1876, ECR.

272 G. & G.H. Pownall's Account for 1881, ECR.

273 Thompson, 344

274 'The Provost and College of Eton and Mr. Willm Willett, Agreement for Building Leases,' 27 July 1881, ECR.

275 'The Provost and College of Eton and Mr. William Willett, Agreement for Building Leases,' 31 December 1885, ECR.

276 Hallowes, Price & Hallowes, Chalcots Accounts, 1885–6, Registrar's Correspondence, ECR.

277 'The Provost and College of Eton and Mr. Wm. Willett, Agreement for Building Leases,' 18 December 1890, ECR.

278 Endorsement, dated 14 December 1895, on *ibid*.

279 Entry for William Willett, the younger (1856–1915) in *Dictionary of National Biography: Twentieth Century, 1912–1921*, quoted in Thompson, 346–7

280 Thompson, 347

281 H.G. Wells, *Ann Veronica*, Penguin Books, 1969, 108

Chapter Six: Salubrious Dwellings for the Industrious Classes (pp. 265–293)

1 Pevsner, *London, Except the Cities of London and Westminster*, 30

2 Quoted in Taylor, *The Village in the City*, 221–2

3 Thomas Babington, Lord Macaulay, *History of England*, 1849, I, 425.

4 Hitchcock, I, 413.

5 *A*, LXIV (1900), 301

6 C.W. Chalklin points out that the overwhelming predominance of new housing in Georgian provincial towns was intended for working-class occupation from the start. Chalklin, 61–2

7 Pevsner, *London, Except the Cities of London and Westminster*, 30

8 *Architectural Magazine*, I (1834), 38–9

9 Olsen, *Town Planning in London*, 129–37

10 *ibid*., 103

11 'Report of Messrs. Leverton & Chawner,' in White, Appendix, xii–xiii

12 Smith, 222

13 Booth, *Life and Labour of the People in London*, Third Series: Religious Influences, I, 204

14 Noble, 92. See also Olsen, *Town Planning in London*, 20–1

15 Thompson, 368

16 *ibid*., 366–7

17 Nash in White, Appendix, xii–xiii

18 *B*, II (1844), 386

19 John Hollingshead, *Ragged London in 1861*, 1861, 143

20 *B*, IV (1846), 166

21 Quoted in Barker and Robbins, I, 55

22 *B*, XIX (1861), 169

23 *B*, XIV (1856), 511

24 *B*, XVII (1859), 572

25 Thorne, II, 471–2

26 *ibid*., II, 578. For another description of Stratford, see Walford, *Old and New*

London, V, 572–3

27 [Clarke], 51

28 *B*, LI (1886), 656

29 [Clarke], 197

30 Fitzgerald, 148

31 Booth, *Life and Labour of the People in London*, Third Series: Religious Influences, I, 73–4. Date of inquiry: 1897–8

32 *ibid.*, I, 74–9

33 *B*, XXXVI (1878), 935

34 Booth, *Life and Labour of the People in London*, Third Series: Religious Influences, I, 151. Date of inquiry: 1897–8

35 Brady, 361

36 *ibid.*, 374

37 Fitzgerald, 157–8

38 *ibid.*, 200

39 Booth, *Life and Labour of the People in London*, Third Series: Religious Influences, I, 151–3. Date of inquiry: 1897–8

40 *ibid.*, I, 182–3

41 *ibid.*, I, 172

42 *BN*, XLIV (1883), 385

43 *BN*, III (1857), 946

44 *A*, X (1873), 15

45 *A*, X (1873), 41

46 *A*, X (1873), 171

47 *BN*, LXXI (1896), 290

48 See, for instance, *BN*, XXVII (1874), 449

49 *BN*, XLIV (1883), 149

50 *BN*, VII (1861), 223

51 *BN*, VII (1861), 470

52 *A*, XXVI (1881), 142

53 *BN*, LXII (1892), 618

54 *A*, XII (1874), 43

55 *BN*, LXIII (1892), 168. See also *BN*, XLIV (1883), 211

56 L.C.C., *Survey of London*, XXVI, 13

57 Quoted in *ibid.*, XXVI, 138

58 *BN*, XIII (1866), 193. See also *BN*, XV (1868), 727, 867

59 *B*, XXVII (1869), 284; L.C.C., *Survey of London*, XXVI, 138

60 *A*, I (1869), 184

61 *B*, XXIX (1871), 1036. See also John Nelson Tarn, *Five Per Cent Philanthropy*, Cambridge University Press, 1974, 58

62 *A*, X (1873), 95

63 [Clarke], 58

64 *Artizans Centenary*, privately printed, n.d., 8–9

65 *B*, XXXI (1873), 853

66 *Artizans Centenary*, 11

67 *B*, XXXII (1874), 232. See also *B*, XXXII (1874), 636, and *A*, XII (1874), 42

68 *BN*, XXVII (1874), 482–3. See also *BN*, XXVII (1874), 533–4

69 *Artizans Centenary*, 16

70 [Clarke], 320

71 *Artizans Centenary*, 15

72 *A*, XII (1874), 150

73 *B*, XXXIII (1875), 933

74 *BN*, XLIV (1883), 145. For the reply from the deputy chairman of the company see *BN*, XLIV (1883), 204

75 *BN*, XLVI (1884), 969

76 Booth, *Life and Labour of the People in London*, Third Series: Religious Influences, III, 159

77 *ibid.*, III, 142–3

78 *B*, XLV (1883), 195. For Shaftesbury Park, Queen's Park, and Noel Park, see Tarn, *Five Per Cent Philanthropy*, 57–9

79 Evidence before the Royal Commission on the Housing of the Working Classes, 1884–5, XXX, quoted in Kellett, 437–8

80 *Artizans Centenary*, 17

81 *B*, LIX (1890), 314

82 *BN*, LXII (1892), 392. See also *BN*, LXXI (1896), 290

83 *Artizans Centenary*, 21–3

84 *BN*, LXXVI (1899), 1

85 *BN*, LXXVII (1899), 714

86 *A*, LXIV (1900), 67

Chapter Seven: Grand Lines of Communication (pp. 294–322)

1 For the pedestrian, see G.A. Sekon, *Locomotion in Victorian London*, Oxford University Press, 1938, 1–25

2 *BN*, VI (1860), 567

3 'A Country Architect', in *A*, X (1873), 14

4 Quoted in *BN*, XVII (1869), 311

5 *B*, II (1844), 185

6 *B*, II (1844), 239

7 Quoted in Olsen, *Town Planning in London*, 209

8 *BN*, XLIV (1883), 385

9 Gaspey, II, 34–5

10 *BN*, XIII (1866), 605

11 *BN*, IV (1858), 1019

12 Quoted in *BN*, XV (1868), 209

13 *BN*, XXVII (1874), 481

14 *B*, XLII (1882), 306–7

15 *A*, I (1869), 176

16 Quoted in *BN*, XVII (1869), 311–12

17 *B*, XXX (1872), 23

18 *A*, VIII (1872), 260

19 Evidence of Robert Vigers before the select committee of the House of Lords on 'Town Improvements (Betterment)', quoted in *A*, LII (1894), 178

20 Evidence of Edward Tewson in *A*, LII (1894), 178

21 *A*, LIX (1898), 381

22 *BN*, XXVII (1874), 481–2

23 *BN*, LVII (1889), 311

24 *BN*, LIX (1890), 385

25 *BN*, LXXIV (1898), 151

26 *BN*, LXXV (1898), 712

27 *BN*, VIII (1862), 389

28 Jack Simmons, I, 297–300; Kellett, 365–82; H.J. Dyos, 'Some Social Costs of Railway Building in London', *Journal of Transport History*, III (1957), 23–30

29 Kellett, 369

30 *ibid.*, 370–1

31 Jackson, 297

32 Quoted in *B*, XII (1854), 407

33 *B*, IX (1851), 530

34 *B*, XXVIII (1870), 325

35 See Simmons, I, 277–8

36 Peter Hall, 'The Development of Communications', in Coppock and Prince, 63–4. See also Simmons, I, 299

37 *B*, VIII (1850), 562

38 *B*, XI (1853), 647

39 *A Regional History of the Railways of Great Britain*, III, H.P. White, *Greater London*, Newton Abbot: David & Charles, 1971, 121–2

40 *B*, XII (1854), 68

41 *B*, X (1852), 253

42 H.P. White, 58–9

43 Barker and Robbins, I, 57–8

44 *B*, XVII (1859), 572

45 Barker and Robbins, I, 131–2

46 H.P. White, 75–9

47 Barker and Robbins, I, 220

48 *B*, XVIII (1860), 139

49 *BN*, VII (1861), 773

50 Barker and Robbins, I, 129

51 *ibid.*, I, 170–1

52 *A*, X (1873), 190

53 Walford, *Old and New London*, 1897, V, 392

54 *B*, XXVI (1868), 501. See also Kellett, 262–6

55 Barker and Robbins, I, 163–4

56 *ibid.*, I, 132–3

57 *ibid.*, I, 216–18

58 J.T. Coppock, 'Dormitory Settlements around London', in Coppock and Prince, 274–5

59 *B*, XXXIII (1875), 467

60 See, for instance, Kellett, 383–8; Harold Pollins, 'Transport Lines and Social Divisions', in *London: Aspects of Change*, 29–56

61 *B*, LXXIV (1898), 294

62 *B*, XL (1881), 725

63 Quoted in Barker and Robbins, I, 263

64 *B*, II (1844), facing p. 150.

65 *BN*, III (1857), 1243

66 Cox, 232

67 [Clarke], 432

68 *B*, IX (1851), 706

69 *B*, XL (1881), 725

70 *BN*, XIII (1866), 775

71 Sekon, 41–3

72 See *ibid.*, 53–75

73 *BN*, XIII (1866), 491

74 *Dickens's Dictionary of London, 1879*, Reprinted Howard Baker, 1972, 241–2

Chapter Eight: London in 1901: the Victorian Legacy (pp. 323–332)

1 Weber, 432

2 Simon Jenkins, *Landlords to London*, Constable, 1975, 280

3 *ibid.*, 278

Index